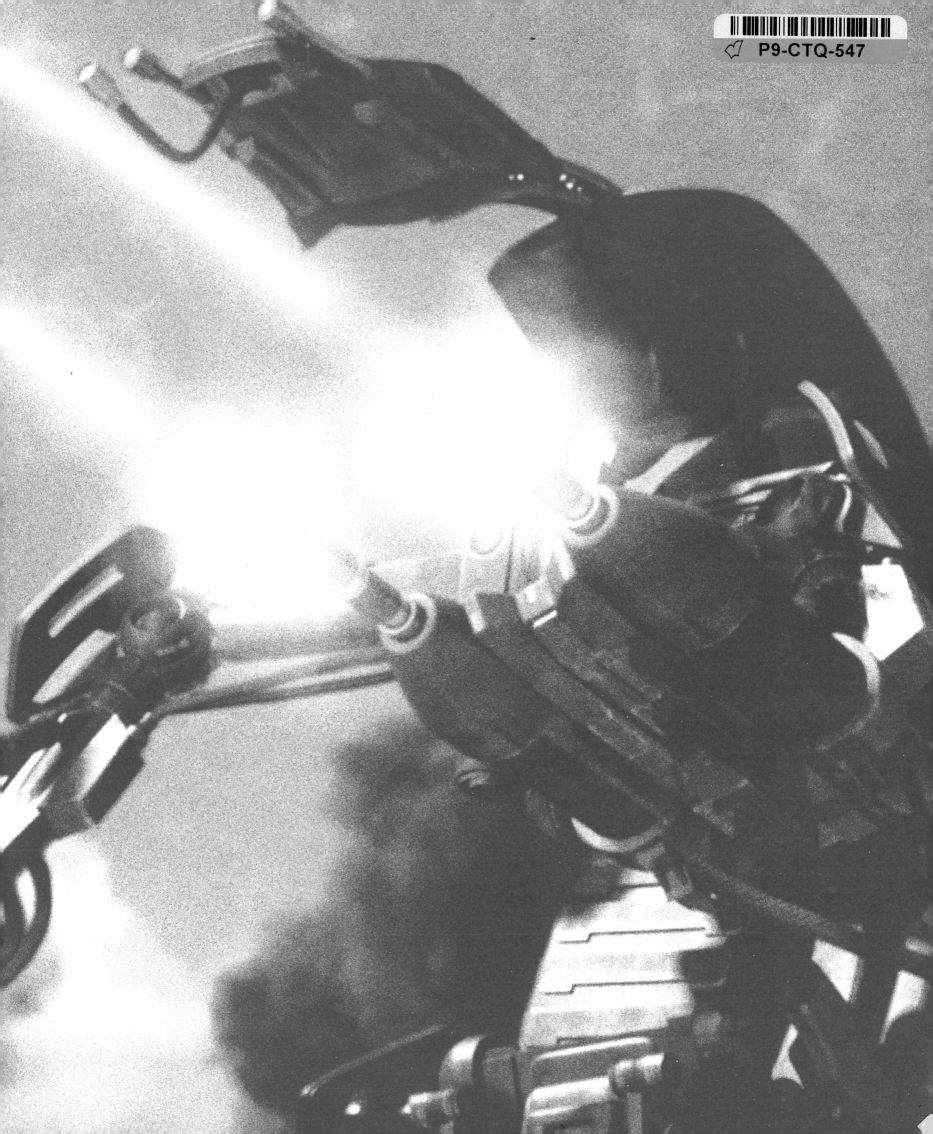

ULTIMATE
STAR
WARS

ULTIMATE STAR WARS®

Written by

Patricia Barr   Adam Bray   Daniel Wallace   Ryder Windham

CONTENTS

"Hello, I am See-Threepio, human-cyborg relations. How might I serve you?"

EPISODE I: *THE PHANTOM MENACE*

"I never wanted to be in *Star Wars*. My agent made me take the meeting. So there I was, sitting in front of George Lucas and a concept painting. Ralph McQuarrie's portrait of a quirky metal figure staring bleakly at me from an inhospitable landscape instantly grabbed my imagination. My fate was sealed. I was doomed to wander strange worlds like Tatooine. I would chill on the planet Hoth and party on the Forest Moon of Endor. I would walk the halls of Cloud City and fear for my very survival in the Death Star's labyrinths. All experienced through the tunnel vision peepholes in the middle of Threepio's eyes. So you can imagine that seeing the finished films came as quite a surprise. Another surprise: I'm now the only actor to work on all six, soon to be seven, Episodes of the saga.

And it's not over yet. Along with the movies, I've had the luck and the joy of being See-Threepio in many spin-offs too, such as the animated series *Star Wars: The Clone Wars, Star Wars Rebels* and the ever-hilarious LEGO *Yoda Chronicles*. Then there's my involvement in so many exhibitions and events and radio serials and concerts and Disney rides and… well, you'd think I'd know every fact about the *Star Wars* galaxy. I must admit, I don't.

As the years and Episodes go by, the saga's become stuffed with so many exciting details that I couldn't really keep up. But now I have this book to remind me of things I've forgotten, didn't know, or never understood and was too embarrassed to ask. It's a hugely significant and entertaining resource—an essential guide for anyone who wants to explore that galaxy far, far away, particularly for younger fans, eager to explain it all to their parents and grandparents. Or the other way round. Because there are now *three* generations who love to share the enthralling worlds of *Star Wars*, at the movies and beyond.

The saga is unlike any other story in popular culture. From the moment audiences ducked down as that Star Destroyer roared overhead it has enchanted fans around the planet. Children and parents have been absorbed into the larger international family for whom the saga has become part of their own history and tradition. *Star Wars* has developed into an international language and in these pages there's something for everyone. And everyone who reads them is keeping the story alive. It's a story that came from the inspired and inspiring mind of George Lucas. A story that came alive through the work of exceptionally talented artists and craftsmen for whom these pages are a terrific testament."

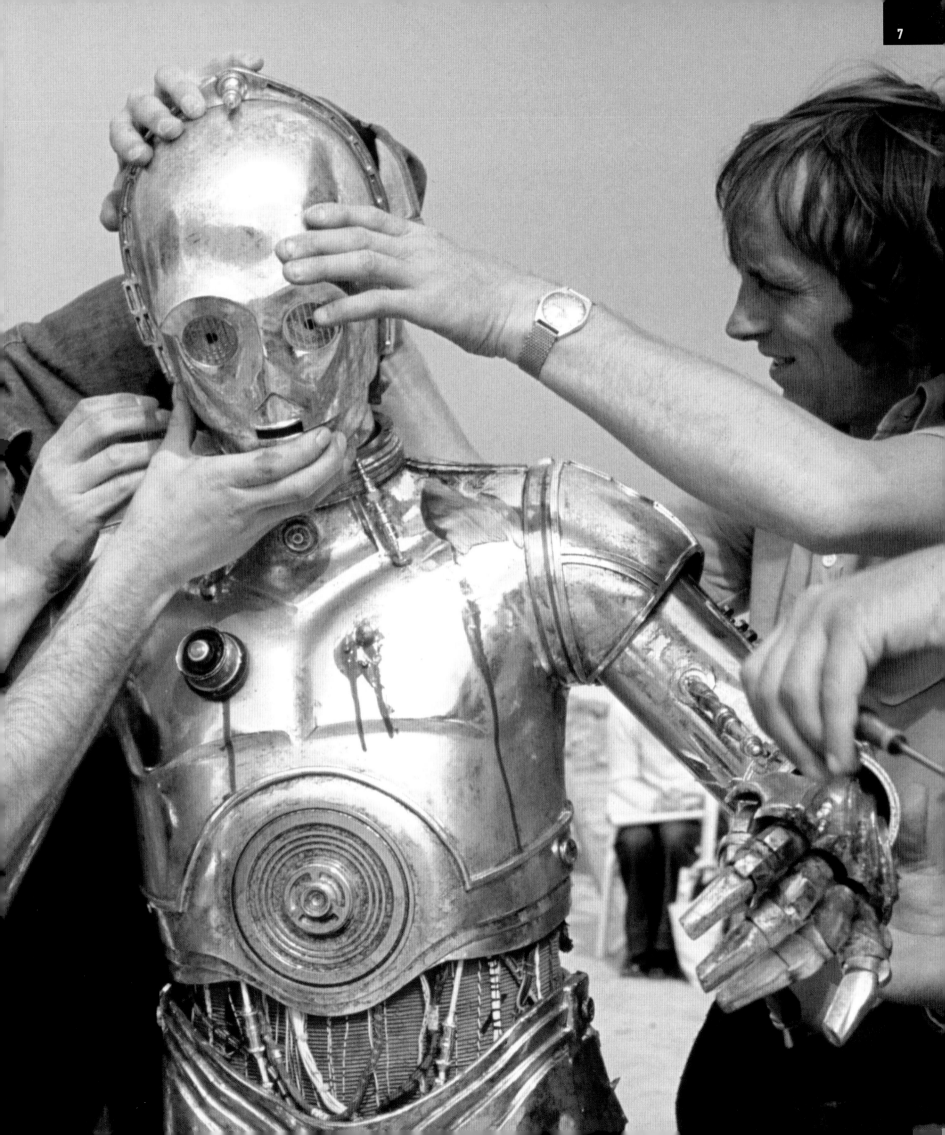

INTRODUCTION

If you're familiar with Ric Olié, the sando aqua monster, *Slave I*, Varykino, IG-88, Lobot, and Ewoks, you must be a fan of *Star Wars*. But if you recognize any of those names, that's remarkable because none are mentioned in the *Star Wars* movies themselves, so you must have gained that knowledge elsewhere, possibly from toy packages, comics, books, or pure osmosis.

Because numerous aliens, droids, starships, weapons, and locations are never identified on screen, it can be quite a challenge for fans to learn more about specific subjects. How does one go about looking up a subject in an encyclopedia if one doesn't know the name of the subject? That's almost as difficult as trying to pinpoint the origin of an unusual lethal dart for which no records exist in the Jedi Archives.

Fortunately, the editors, designers, and authors of *Ultimate Star Wars* are here to help. Unlike any previously published *Star Wars* reference books, this unique compendium features a wealth of images and information about many characters, creatures, vehicles, devices, and locations, each one presented in chronological order according to its first appearance in the *Star Wars* movies, *Star Wars: The Clone Wars*, and *Star Wars Rebels*.

So if you're familiar with the *Star Wars* saga, you should have little difficulty finding what you're looking for. And if you're new to the *Star Wars* galaxy, I encourage you to keep *Ultimate Star Wars* handy as you watch the movies and TV episodes. Soon, you'll be a *Star Wars* expert, too!

RYDER WINDHAM

CHARACTERS AND CREATURES

Remarkable individuals, incredible life forms, and sentient droids coexist throughout the galaxy. Space travel brings them together in fascinating, and at times combustible, combinations.

From the smallest scavengers and largest monsters on the desert planet Tatooine to the impoverished denizens, cultured aristocrats, and droid servants on the metropolitan city-planet Coruscant, the galaxy is populated by innumerable beings. Although not every civilization has achieved or acquired the appropriate technology, and some remain isolationists, space travel has led to commercial trade and cultural exchanges between thousands of worlds and cultures. It is not unusual to find literally dozens of alien species in any given spaceport.

For millennia, many planets have been protected by the Jedi, an ancient order of peacekeepers with seemingly supernatural powers. The Jedi maintain that every life form in the galaxy, as well as the universe itself, is bound together and connected by an energy field called the Force. The Jedi's battles with their evil, power-hungry Sith enemies leave a significant impact on many worlds, affecting lives and the course of galactic history.

CHARACTERS TIMELINE

It is often the humblest individuals who are the greatest forces for change. A slave boy grows up to destroy a republic and create an evil empire. Years later, his long-lost son, a farm boy, sets the galaxy free.

CRISIS IN THE REPUBLIC:
Spans Episodes I and II

THE CLONE WARS:
Spans Episode II, CW, and Episode III

THE EMPIRE ERA:
Spans Episode III, R, and Episodes IV to VI

Invasion of Naboo
Dressed in lavish royal attire, Queen Amidala of the Naboo sends a transmission to the Trade Federation, which has imposed a trade blockade against her world and plans a secret invasion.

Battle of Naboo
The Gungan army meets the Trade Federation's droid army on the battlefield. The Gungans serve as a diversion so Queen Amidala and her loyal forces can infiltrate the palace in Theed City.

The Jedi and the Gungans
Qui-Gon Jinn and Obi-Wan Kenobi ask the Gungan leader, Boss Nass, for a submarine so that they may travel through the planet's undersea core to Theed Palace, along with their new friend Jar Jar Binks.

Anakin's podrace
Anakin Skywalker enters the Boonta Eve podrace, hosted by Jabba the Hutt. The best racers from around the galaxy participate. By winning, Anakin helps his new friends acquire vital starship parts, and also gains his own freedom from Watto. Anakin leaves his home on Tatooine to become a Jedi.

Padmé meets Anakin
Disguised as one of the Queen's handmaidens, Padmé Amidala meets the young slave, Anakin Skywalker at Watto's Junkyard on Tatooine. The friendly boy is most helpful to Padmé and Qui-Gon Jinn. Qui-Gon senses that there is something special about the boy.

The droid foundry

Anakin and Padmé arrive on Geonosis to rescue Obi-Wan, who has been taken captive by Count Dooku. In the process they discover the Geonosian droid foundries, which are manufacturing an army for the Separatist Alliance.

Gladiator arena

As Count Dooku watches from a balcony, Anakin, Padmé, and Obi-Wan are sentenced to death in the Geonosian arena, where they are confronted with three deadly creatures: an acklay, a reek, and a nexu.

The Battle of Geonosis

Yoda arrives on Geonosis with the Jedi and their new clone army, to rescue Anakin, Padmé, and Obi-Wan, and fight against the Geonosians' battle droids. This event marks the beginning of the Clone Wars.

The cloning facility

Obi-Wan Kenobi discovers previously unknown Republic cloning facilities on Kamino, ordered by a mysterious Jedi named Sifo-Dyas. The clones are derived from a notorious bounty hunter named Jango Fett.

Victory celebration on Naboo

With the battle won, the Gungans and the people of Naboo are joined by Senate dignitaries and the Jedi Council for celebrations in Theed City. A decade of peace follows.

Yoda and Dooku Duel

After he bests Obi-Wan and Anakin (who loses his hand in the fight), Count Dooku, alias Darth Tyranus, is confronted by his former Jedi Master, Yoda. Dooku manages to escape, fleeing to Coruscant.

Darth Maul duels the Jedi

Qui-Gon Jinn and Obi-Wan Kenobi are confronted by the Sith Lord Darth Maul. Qui-Gon is killed by Maul but Obi-Wan avenges his master's death by cutting the Sith in half.

Anakin and Padmé marry

Padmé and Anakin are secretly married on Naboo, witnessed only by C-3PO and R2-D2. Their union defies basic tenets of the Jedi Order and forces them to live a lie.

Second Battle of Geonosis

Anakin Skywalker and Luminara Unduli send their Padawans Ahsoka Tano and Barriss Offee into the catacombs beneath a droid factory. They destroy the facility's reactor, but nearly lose their lives.

Alderaan Refugee Conference

Experiencing troubling visions about Padmé Amidala's murder, Ahsoka Tano accompanies the senator to a diplomatic conference on Alderaan. The Jedi foils Aurra Sing's assassination attempt with help from Padmé and Bail Organa.

Slaughter on Dathomir

Angered by Mother Talzin's machinations against him, Count Dooku dispatches General Grievous to wipe out her clan of Nightsisters. After Talzin disappears into thin air, Asajj Ventress is the sole survivor.

Hunt for Maul

Mother Talzin sends Savage Opress on a quest to find his brother Maul, left for dead by Obi-Wan Kenobi during the Battle of Naboo. Savage finds Maul, weakened and crazed, on Lotho Minor.

Liberating Ryloth

On the planet Ryloth, Jedi Master Mace Windu and Republic forces help revolutionary leader Cham Syndulla repel a Separatist invasion of the Twi'lek homeworld.

Anakin's apprentice

During the Battle of Christophsis, Anakin Skywalker is presented with a new apprentice: Ahsoka Tano. The Council hopes this new Padawan will aid in Anakin's growth as a Jedi.

Seeds of rebellion

When Anakin Skywalker and Obi-Wan Kenobi witness Ahsoka Tano's capable guidance of the Onderon rebels, they depart the planet. She remains the sole Jedi advisor until the Separatist regime is overthrown.

Death of Grievous

Riding a varactyl, Obi-Wan chases General Grievous through a sinkhole city on Utapau. After an epic lightsaber duel, Obi-Wan uses Grievous's own blaster, firing at the cyborg's one vulnerability: his exposed vital organs.

Anakin's fall

Anakin is tortured by nightmares in which his wife Padmé dies in childbirth, nightmares he's convinced may come true. In a desperate bid to find a way to save her life, Anakin comes to the aid of Palpatine (alias Darth Sidious) by helping him kill Jedi Mace Windu, and vows to serve the evil Sith Lord.

Anakin kills Dooku

During the Battle of Coruscant, Anakin and Obi-Wan duel Count Dooku to save the kidnapped Chancellor Palpatine. Anakin defeats Dooku, and ruthlessly executes him. In so doing, he moves closer to the dark side.

Ahsoka betrayed

Disillusioned by the war, Barriss Offee frames Ahsoka for murder and treason. The Council initially refuses to back her innocence, and Ahsoka leaves the Jedi Order after her subsequent exoneration.

Order 66

Darth Sidious enacts the final stages of his grand scheme to create and rule an empire, by invoking Order 66, a secret command that programs the clone army to immediately eliminate all Jedi. On planets across the galaxy, soldiers turn against their Jedi commanders.

Maul's revenge

After Maul's successful coup on Mandalore, he murders its former leader, Duchess Satine Kryze, in front of Obi-Wan Kenobi in revenge for the Jedi's victory over him years earlier.

Duel on Stygeon Prime

Kanan and Ezra fall into the Inquisitor's trap when they try to rescue the Jedi Luminara Unduli from the Imperial prison on Stygeon Prime. There, Kanan must fight off the Inquisitor for the first time.

The Galactic Empire

Having survived Jedi attempts to arrest him, and masterminded the destruction of the Order, Darth Sidious goes before the Senate and declares the formation of a new Galactic Empire, with himself elevated to Emperor.

Ezra meets the rebels

Ezra Bridger, a Force-adept on Lothal, meets an important rebel cell and joins their crew aboard the *Ghost*. He becomes the Padawan of Kanan Jarrus and trains to be one of the last Jedi.

Rise of Darth Vader

Having severed all ties to his former life as a Jedi, and having been severely injured by Obi-Wan Kenobi on the volcanic planet of Mustafar, Darth Vader is rescued, reconstructed, and transformed by Darth Sidious into a cyborg Sith Lord.

Vader's message to the Inquisitor

With the Jedi Order almost completely destroyed, Darth Vader sets the Inquisitor on a new task: to hunt down the "children of the Force" and either turn them to serve the Emperor, or kill them.

Birth of Luke and Leia

Just before her death, Padmé gives birth to twins. Leia is given to Bail Organa and his wife to raise on Alderaan, while Luke is sent to live with Owen and Beru Lars on Tatooine.

Ezra's lightsaber

After enduring trials at an ancient Jedi temple in the mountains of Lothal, Ezra obtains a kyber crystal and constructs his first lightsaber, marking a major milestone on his way to becoming a Jedi.

The Battle of Yavin

The Rebel Alliance's ragtag team of X-wing and Y-wing fighter pilots launches a desperate assault on the Death Star. Nearly all are destroyed, but Luke Skywalker makes the decisive shot, destroys the Death Star, and wins the battle.

Leia is captured

On her way to deliver stolen plans of the Empire's Death Star battle station to the Rebel Alliance, Princess Leia's ship is captured by Darth Vader. However, R2-D2 and C-3PO, manage to escape with the plans in R2-D2's memory banks.

Darth Vader and Kenobi duel

For the first time since Obi-Wan left him for dead on Mustafar 19 years earlier, Vader confronts Obi-Wan and the two duel with lightsabers. Vader strikes down Obi-Wan, who then becomes a Force spirit.

Luke encounters the droids

Luke Skywalker and his uncle Owen Lars purchase R2-D2 and C-3PO from a group of Jawas on Tatooine. The droids then spark Luke's own journey to meet Obi-Wan Kenobi and become a Jedi.

Meeting at the Cantina

Luke, Obi-Wan, and the droids travel to Mos Eisley, where they meet Han Solo and Chewbacca at the cantina. The two smugglers agree to take Luke and his friends to Alderaan in their ship, *Millennium Falcon*. for a hefty fee.

Rescue of Princess Leia

The *Millennium Falcon* is captured and drawn aboard the Death Star, where Luke, Han, and Chewbacca attempt to rescue Princess Leia Organa. Luke and Han must pose as stormtroopers to reach her prison cell.

Luke and the wampa

While patrolling on Hoth, the location of the Rebel Alliance's new HQ, Echo Base, Luke is attacked by a wampa and dragged back to its cave. When he comes around, he finds himself hanging from his feet but draws his lightsaber just in time to kill the beast.

Death of Yoda

Luke returns to Dagobah and visits Yoda one last time. Yoda confirms that Darth Vader is indeed Luke's father, just before he passes away. The spirit of Obi-Wan then tells Luke that Leia is his sister.

An audience with Jabba

After Leia fails to rescue Han, Luke comes before Jabba in a futile attempt to persuade the Hutt to release his friends. Jabba is unmoved, however, and drops Luke into his rancor den. However, the rebels, plus C-3PO and R2-D2, eventually escape, and Leia kills Jabba.

The Battle of Hoth

The Empire discovers the secret rebel base and sets down on Hoth. Launching an assault, the Imperials destroy Echo Base's shield generators and capture the rebel facility. However, the rebel leaders escape and Luke travels to Dagobah to train as a Jedi.

Luke meets Yoda

Sent by Obi-Wan Kenobi, Luke arrives on swampy Dagobah in search of a powerful Jedi Master. He meets an unlikely little creature called Yoda who turns out to be the very teacher he is looking for.

Vader confronts Luke

Using Luke's friends as bait, Darth Vader lures the young Jedi to Cloud City where the two clash. Luke loses his hand to Vader before the Sith Lord reveals he is Luke's father.

Frozen in carbonite

At Cloud City, Han Solo's friend, Lando Calrissian, makes a secret deal with the Empire and betrays the rebels. Han Solo is captured by Darth Vader and encased in carbonite, before being handed over to the bounty hunter Boba Fett. Boba Fett delivers him to the crime lord Jabba the Hutt, who has placed a bounty on Han's head.

Rebel briefing on *Home One*

The Rebel Alliance gathers for a briefing about the most important battle of the rebellion. Mon Mothma, leader of the Rebel Alliance, has learned that the Emperor himself is overseeing the final construction of a new Death Star above the forest moon of Endor, and believes that now is the time to attack.

Victory celebrations

The war against the Empire is won. Joyful festivities are held on worlds all over the galaxy. The Rebel Alliance joins the Ewoks to celebrate the victory, and Luke sees the spirits of Obi-Wan, Yoda, and Anakin at peace.

Leia meets Wicket

The rebel strike team arrives on Endor. Leia is separated from the group during a speeder bike chase, but meets a friendly Ewok who takes her back to his village.

Battle of Endor

After violent clashes with Imperial troops, General Solo and his team, helped by the Ewoks, manage to destroy the Death Star's shield power generator on the forest moon. This enables General Calrissian and the rebel pilots to attack the Death Star.

Anakin saves Luke

Darth Vader delivers Luke to the Emperor aboard the Death Star. Palpatine pits the two against each other, but Luke refuses to fight his father. Vader sacrifices himself to save Luke and destroys the Emperor. Shortly afterward, the rebel fighter group successfully detonates the Death Star's main reactor. Luke escapes in an Imperial shuttle just before the battle station explodes.

"The Force will be with you... always!" OBI-WAN KENOBI

OBI-WAN KENOBI

A Jedi and veteran of the Clone Wars, Obi-Wan Kenobi's achievements include surviving duels with three Sith Lords and training two generations of Skywalkers before he became one with the Force.

APPEARANCES I, II, CW, III, R, IV, V, VI **SPECIES** Human **HOMEWORLD** Stewjon **AFFILIATION** Jedi Order

GALACTIC PEACEKEEPERS

As members of the Jedi Order, Jedi Master Qui-Gon Jinn and his Padawan Obi-Wan Kenobi use their Force powers and training in service to the Galactic Republic. Their duties include settling diplomatic disputes and apprehending interplanetary criminals across the galaxy. Like most Jedi, Obi-Wan is identified within six months of his birth and begins his Jedi training immediately so that he can learn to control emotions of fear and anger at an early age.

Although Obi-Wan is often frustrated by Qui-Gon's decisions and baffled by his Master's tendency to take apparently hapless life forms under his wing, he respects Qui-Gon's leadership and knowledge. Together, Qui-Gon and Obi-Wan make a formidable team.

Jedi Master and apprentice
Attacked on a Trade Federation Battleship, Qui-Gon and Obi-Wan defend themselves.

Clone Wars heroes
Commander Cody and General Kenobi watch for enemies during the Clone Wars.

REPUBLIC ARMY GENERAL

After the Republic's government is fragmented by the Separatist movement and subsequent Confederacy of Independent Systems, a sprawling civil war begins. The Galactic Senate conscripts many Jedi Knights as commanding officers of the rapidly formed Grand Army of the Republic. As Jedi generals, Obi-Wan and his apprentice Anakin Skywalker fly their starfighters into numerous battles against the Confederacy and confront droid armies on many worlds. While Anakin is the better star pilot, Obi-Wan's diplomatic skills, specifically his reputation for preventing and stopping battles without using a single weapon, earn him the appellation "The Negotiator."

FRIENDS BECOME ENEMIES

Obi-Wan does his best to train Anakin as a Jedi and loves him like a brother. However, after he learns that Anakin has become the Sith Lord Darth Vader and is responsible for destroying the Jedi Order, he attempts to bring his former friend to justice. Vader is unwilling to surrender, and they duel with lightsabers on the volcano planet Mustafar. Obi-Wan cuts down Vader and takes his lightsaber before leaving him seriously wounded on the shore of a lava river *(see also p. 189)*.

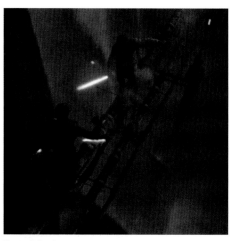

Heated duel
Anakin and Obi-Wan trade blows as the mining facility collapses around them on Mustafar.

SECRET GUARDIAN

After the Clone Wars, Obi-Wan delivers the infant Luke Skywalker to Anakin's relatives Owen and Beru Lars on Tatooine. Obi-Wan assumes the name "Ben" Kenobi and lives as a hermit in an abandoned hut while discreetly watching over Luke, protecting him from harm. Unknown to Darth Vader, Luke is his son. Obi-Wan knows that if Vader or the Emperor ever learn of Luke's existence, they will try to capture him and make him join the dark side. He also knows that if they fail, Luke could be killed.

Anakin's lightsaber
When Obi-Wan gives Anakin's lightsaber to Luke, he believes that Luke may be the galaxy's only hope for defeating Darth Vader and the Emperor.

From hero to exile
Throughout his entire life, Obi-Wan honors the ways of the Jedi Order by using his powers to help those in need. After the fall of the Republic, he assumes the persona of a hermit on Tatooine while secretly safeguarding Luke Skywalker and his family.

Jedi training
Raised at the Jedi Temple on Coruscant, Obi-Wan becomes Qui-Gon's Padawan.

▲ **Mission to Coruscant**
While escorting Queen Amidala to Coruscant with Qui-Gon, Obi-Wan meets R2-D2 and Anakin.

▲ **Battle of Naboo**
Obi-Wan defeats the Sith Lord who killed Qui-Gon and promises to train Anakin to become a Jedi.

▲ **Battle of Geonosis**
Obi-Wan duels Count Dooku, a renegade Jedi who helps lead the galaxy into civil war.

Order 66
Obi-Wan survives Order 66, but learns that Anakin has become a Sith Lord.

Duel on Mustafar
Obi-Wan defeats Anakin and takes Luke to the desert planet Tatooine.

▲ **Secret transmission**
Obi-Wan's message warns surviving Jedi not to return to the Jedi Temple.

Years in hiding
"Ben" Kenobi protects Luke from harm, including an attack by Tusken Raiders.

▲ **Death Star rescue**
Obi-Wan duels Darth Vader for the last time and becomes one with the Force.

Battle of Hoth
On the ice planet, Obi-Wan's spirit sends Luke to Jedi Master Yoda on Dagobah.

▲ **Battle of Endor**
Obi-Wan's and Yoda's spirits smile as Anakin's spirit returns to the Jedi fold.

timeline

Jedi training
Raised in the Jedi Temple, Qui-Gon becomes the Padawan of Jedi Master Count Dooku.

▼Jedi peacekeeper
After becoming a Jedi Knight, Qui-Gon eventually accepts Obi-Wan Kenobi as his apprentice.

▼Mission to Naboo
Investigating the Neimoidian Trade Federation's blockade of Naboo, Qui-Gon discovers that the Federation is determined to invade the planet.

▼Mission to Coruscant
While escorting Queen Amidala to Coruscant, an emergency detour to Tatooine leads Qui-Gon to discover Anakin Skywalker.

▼Battle of Naboo
Mortally wounded by Darth Maul, Qui-Gon Jinn instructs Obi-Wan to train Anakin to become a Jedi.

▼Communion with Yoda
By the will of the Force, Qui-Gon's spirit survives, and Yoda eventually hears Qui-Gon's disembodied voice.

Communion with Obi-Wan
After Order 66, Yoda informs Obi-Wan that Qui-Gon's spirit lives, and that he will resume communication with Obi-Wan, teaching him to become one with the Force.

"Anakin will become a Jedi... I promise you."
QUI-GON JINN

QUI-GON JINN

Unlike Jedi Masters who lose themselves in contemplation of the unifying Force, the Jedi Knight Qui-Gon Jinn lives for the moment and espouses this philosophy: "Feel, don't think. Use your instincts."

APPEARANCES I, II, CW **SPECIES** Human **HOMEWORLD** Coruscant **AFFILIATION** Jedi Order

EMPATHETIC NATURE

Soon after arriving on the swamplands of Naboo, Qui-Gon rescues the Gungan outcast Jar Jar Binks from a stampede of creatures fleeing from the Trade Federation's invading warships. Jar Jar swears a life-debt to Qui-Gon, whose compassionate nature is such that he takes the hapless Gungan under his protection, much to the consternation of his Jedi apprentice, Obi-Wan Kenobi. With Jar Jar's help, the Jedi journey to the city of Otoh Gunga and obtain a submersible that allows them to proceed through Naboo's core to Theed. Noble, patient, wise, and closely attuned to the Force, Qui-Gon is also a cunning warrior whose greatest strength is perhaps his empathy for other life forms, including the most unfortunate.

Deep trouble
Inside a Gungan submersible, Jar Jar, Qui-Gon, and Obi-Wan travel through Naboo's hazardous underwater passages.

THE CHOSEN ONE?

While escorting Queen Amidala to Coruscant, Qui-Gon and his allies make an unscheduled stop on the Outer Rim world of Tatooine, where he discovers a young slave boy named Anakin Skywalker. Qui-Gon senses that Anakin is strong in the Force and soon has reason to believe that Anakin is the "Chosen One" of an ancient prophecy, and is destined to become a Jedi, destroy the Sith, and bring balance to the Force. Qui-Gon helps liberate Anakin from slavery and resolves that Anakin will be trained as a Jedi on Coruscant (see also p. 28).

Escape plan
Stranded on Tatooine, Anakin and Shmi welcome Qui-Gon, Jar Jar, and Padmé Naberrie to their home, where they plot to repair the latter's damaged ship.

THE DARK WARRIOR

On Tatooine, a black-cloaked warrior wielding a lightsaber attacks Qui-Gon. Qui-Gon escapes with his allies and tells the Jedi Council that he believes his opponent is a Sith Lord, strong in the Jedi arts. At the Battle of Naboo, the dark warrior attacks again, mortally wounding Qui-Gon. With his dying breath, Qui-Gon makes Obi-Wan promise to train Anakin to become a Jedi.

Duel in the desert
Qui-Gon's clash with Darth Maul is perhaps the first battle between a Jedi and a Sith in a thousand years.

FROM THE NETHERWORLD OF THE FORCE

More than a decade after Qui-Gon's death, Obi-Wan and Anakin travel to the mysterious planet Mortis, where they are astonished to encounter a ghostly apparition of the slain Jedi. Qui-Gon's spirit tells Obi-Wan that the planet is a conduit through which the Force flows and that it presents great dangers for the Chosen One. He tells Anakin to remember his training and trust his instincts.

Jedi spirit
On Mortis, Qui-Gon's spirit maintains his belief that Anakin is fated to bring balance to the Force.

Jedi maverick
A highly trained Jedi Master, Qui-gon Jinn is nonetheless an instinctive, restless soul who steadfastly follows his own path in bringing balance to the Force.

NUTE GUNRAY

APPEARANCES I, II, CW, III **SPECIES** Neimoidian
HOMEWORLD Neimoidia **AFFILIATION** Trade Federation, Separatists, Confederacy of Independent Systems

Neimoidians are well known for their exceptional organizational and business skills, but Nute Gunray, Viceroy of the Trade Federation, is more unscrupulous and cutthroat than most. The assurances of his shadowy Sith benefactor, Darth Sidious, prompt Gunray to take the ambitious and blatantly illegal path to power as he oversees the blockade and subsequent invasion of Naboo. But Gunray's true, cowardly nature is revealed when Queen Amidala and her Naboo freedom fighters blast his droid protectors, reclaim their planet, and declare the Trade Federation's occupation is over. During the Clone Wars, Nute Gunray continues to obey the Sith Lords. While hiding on the planet Mustafar, he is unprepared when Darth Vader arrives to kill him.

Separatist ally
When Count Dooku invites the Trade Federation to join the Separatists, Gunray insists that Dooku first disposes of a bothersome senator from Naboo, Padmé Amidala.

"Your feeble skills are no match for the power of the dark side."

EMPEROR PALPATINE

SHEEV PALPATINE

A seemingly unassuming representative of the peaceful planet Naboo, Palpatine is in fact the Sith Lord Darth Sidious, who schemes to destroy the Jedi Order and rule the galaxy as Emperor.

APPEARANCES: I, II, CW, III, V, VI   **SPECIES:** Human   **HOMEWORLD:** Naboo   **AFFILIATION:** Galactic Republic, Order of the Sith, Galactic Empire

SENATOR OF NABOO

When the Trade Federation invades Naboo, Queen Amidala seeks advice from Palpatine, who serves as Naboo's representative in the Galactic Senate. Palpatine confides that the Republic's leader, Supreme Chancellor Valorum, has little power in the Senate and that bureaucrats are in charge. Palpatine adds that if Amidala wants the Trade Federation brought to justice, her best course of action is to call for a vote of no confidence in Valorum and then push for the election of a stronger leader. At Palpatine's urging, Amidala follows his advice, and Valorum is forced to leave office. To Amidala's surprise, the Senate elects Palpatine as Supreme Chancellor (see also p. 40).

Meeting Anakin
After the Battle of Naboo, Palpatine meets the young pilot who helped defeat the Trade Federation's invasion force.

POLITICAL MANEUVERING

After the Senate learns that the Separatists are using Geonosian foundries to manufacture a massive droid army, the Senators vote to grant emergency powers to Supreme Chancellor Palpatine. This vote enables Palpatine to immediately conscript an army of clones to fight the Separatists, even though the Jedi Order is baffled by the clones' dubious origins. Palpatine professes his regret that the civil war requires him to take emergency powers, and claims that he looks forward to relinquishing those powers when the war is over. During the ensuing Clone Wars, Palpatine assumes even more responsibilities; his many duties include working with the Senate to pass laws to fund the war and to prevent bureaucracy from interfering with programs that the Jedi Council considers vital to the war effort.

Supreme leader
Palpatine addresses the Senate at the height of the Clone Wars, convincing it to grant him full autonomy to successfully prosecute the war.

SITH LORD REVEALED!

In the last days of the Clone Wars, Palpatine tells Anakin a story about the Sith Lord Darth Plagueis, who used the Force to create life and prevent death. According to Palpatine, only the dark side of the Force offers a route to Plagueis's secrets. Palpatine later reveals that he himself is a Sith—Darth Sidious—and promises to teach Anakin his dark side knowledge if Anakin allies with him. As a Jedi, Anakin knows it is his duty to stop Palpatine. However, nightmarish visions of his beloved Padmé dying in childbirth convince him that only Palpatine's Sith powers can save her. Anakin agrees to become Sidious's apprentice, Darth Vader, and to crush the Jedi Order.

Sith secrets
In his chambers, Palpatine draws Anakin into his confidence by revealing his true identity and suspicions about the Jedi's seditious activities.

THE EMPEROR'S DOWNFALL

As the Republic is reorganized into the Galactic Empire, the self-appointed Emperor Palpatine makes good on his vows to end corruption in the Senate, and many citizens of the Republic believe he is indeed restoring stability to the galaxy. Even as Palpatine's remaining opponents continue to vanish and rumors circulate about his dark-armored lieutenant, Darth Vader, few comprehend that the galaxy is now under the command of a Sith Lord and that the Emperor's new order is based on tyranny and brutality. Palpatine meets his fate at the hands of his former apprentice, when Vader, in a bid to protect his son, Luke Skywalker, hurls his Master down the Death Star's core to a fiery death.

Before the fall
Having lured Luke to the Death Star, Palpatine manipulates the young Jedi into a fight with his father, Darth Vader.

The phantom menace
Palpatine's true goals are known only to himself, but to achieve them he uses a terrifying combination of political intrigue, deception, ruthlessness, and raw dark side power.

timeline

Path to the dark side
A native of Naboo, Palpatine secretly becomes Darth Sidious, apprentice to the Sith Lord Darth Plagueis. He eventually kills Plagueis and assumes the mantle of Sith Master.

Mission to Dathomir
Darth Sidious takes a male Zabrak infant named Maul from Dathomir and raises him as his apprentice.

▲ Galactic Senate
Keeping his Sith Lord identity secret, Palpatine becomes a senator of Naboo.

▲ Battle of Naboo
Palpatine manipulates events to become Supreme Chancellor. Darth Sidious instructs Darth Maul to kill Queen Amidala, but Maul fails. Palpatine then meets Anakin Skywalker.

Battle of Geonosis
After Darth Sidious takes Count Dooku as his new apprentice, they conspire to conquer the galaxy.

The Clone Wars
Having survived the Battle of Naboo, Darth Maul tries to take revenge on Darth Sidious.

Battle of Coruscant
Captured by General Grievous, Palpatine manipulates Anakin Skywalker to kill Count Dooku and lures him to the dark side. Anakin becomes the Sith apprentice, Darth Vader.

▲ Order 66
A Jedi task force learns that Palpatine is a Sith Lord and tries to capture him. Palpatine kills them, but his own Force lightning leaves him disfigured.

Galactic Empire
After destroying the Jedi Order, Palpatine seizes power and declares himself Emperor. He recovers the wounded Darth Vader from Mustafar and transforms him into a cybernetic nightmare.

▼ The Death Star
The Emperor directs Vader to oversee the construction of the enormous Imperial battle station.

Battle of Endor
On the second Death Star, the Emperor fails to lure Luke Skywalker to the dark side and also does not anticipate Darth Vader's fatal attack.

"I will not condone a course of action that will lead us to war." QUEEN AMIDALA

PADMÉ AMIDALA

A representative of her idyllic homeworld Naboo, and an idealist during a time of corruption and war, Padmé Amidala is determined to do what she can to right wrongs in the ailing Republic.

APPEARANCES I, II, CW, III **SPECIES** Human **HOMEWORLD** Naboo **AFFILIATION** Royal House of Naboo, Galactic Senate

THE QUEEN AND THE SLAVE

Born to humble parents on Naboo, Padmé Amidala serves as supervisor of the city of Theed for two years before being elected Queen of Naboo at the age of 14. She adopts the formal name Queen Amidala, and her loyal staff includes five handmaidens. When in danger, she disguises herself as a handmaiden, introducing herself simply as "Padmé," while one of her actual handmaidens, Sabé, impersonates her as queen. When the Trade Federation invades Naboo, Amidala and Sabé duly switch roles, and it is in her handmaiden guise that Padmé, en route to Coruscant, makes an emergency detour to Tatooine. Accompanying the Jedi Qui-Gon Jinn to a Mos Espa scrap yard, she meets a young slave, Anakin Skywalker. Little does she know that young Anakin will become a Jedi Knight and one day her husband.

"Are you an angel?"
Meeting Anakin in a junk shop, Padmé is touched when he likens her to one of "the most beautiful creatures in the universe."

LOVE AND WAR

During the Clone Wars, the galaxy becomes a dangerous place for a loyalist senator, but Padmé journeys to many trouble spots in her efforts to use diplomacy to resolve problems. She is increasingly distracted by the prolonged absences of her secret husband, Anakin, whose effectiveness in the war means that he is assigned to the most intense battlefronts. Padmé is deeply worried for his safety, and because the war is concentrated in the Outer Rim, far from Coruscant, she sees very little of him. While the few moments they can snatch together are all too brief, by the time the Outer Rim Sieges end, Padmé has some stunning news for Anakin: He is to be a father.

Precious respite
Meeting on Coruscant, Padmé and Anakin sometimes struggle to remain close while their responsibilities to the Republic frequently keep them apart.

THE SENATOR AND THE JEDI

When, years later, Padmé meets Anakin again, he has become a Jedi and she is committed to her work as a senator of Naboo. Taken aback when Anakin confesses his love for her, Padmé responds that she has more important things to do than fall in love. However, during a desperate mission to Geonosis, when death seems imminent, Padmé admits that she loves Anakin, too. They survive Geonosis and marry in secret, with only R2-D2 and C-3PO as witnesses.

Fateful retreat
After surviving two assassination attempts on Coruscant, Padmé grows close to Anakin when he serves as her bodyguard on Naboo.

Assisted delivery
On Polis Massa, Obi-Wan watches a midwife droid deliver Padmé's twins.

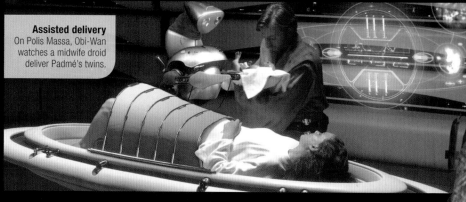

A TRAGIC END

Padmé, like the rest of the Republic, is unaware that Chancellor Palpatine is actually a Sith Lord who is using his powers to lure Anakin to the dark side. After Obi-Wan tells Padmé that Anakin has turned to evil and become Palpatine's Sith apprentice, she travels to the planet Mustafar to confront Anakin, but he becomes enraged and nearly kills her. Obi-Wan defeats Anakin in a terrible duel, leaving him for dead on the shores of a lava river, before rushing Padmé to a medical facility, where she gives birth to twins. Ignorant of Anakin's fate, and having lost the will to live, Padmé tries to convince Obi-Wan with her dying breath that there is still some good in Anakin.

Regal persona
Queen Amidala's makeup and gown are covered with historic symbols that express the majesty of the free people of Naboo. Her elaborate costume also serves to hide her feelings and help her stay courageous and aloof.

timeline

Early life
At age 8, Padmé Naberrie joins the Apprentice Legislators on Naboo and later becomes a Senatorial adviser.

Democratic Queen
At age 14, Padmé is elected Queen of Naboo and adopts Amidala as her name of office.

Invasion of Naboo
Failing to prevent the Trade Federation's invasion, Padmé leaves Naboo with her new allies: Qui-Gon Jinn, Obi-Wan Kenobi, Jar Jar Binks, and R2-D2.

▲ **Tatooine detour**
Briefly stranded on Tatooine during an emergency mission to Coruscant, Padmé meets Anakin, C-3PO, and Anakin's mother, Shmi.

Battle of Naboo
With help from the Jedi and an alliance with the Gungans, Queen Amidala helps defeat the Federation's droid troops. After her term as Queen ends, Amidala becomes a senator of Naboo.

Reunion with Anakin
Ten years after the Battle of Naboo, Anakin and Obi-Wan are assigned to protect Senator Amidala from an assassin on Coruscant. A second assassination attempt prompts Padmé to discreetly return to Naboo with Anakin as her bodyguard.

Battle of Geonosis
Padmé attempts to prevent civil war, but the Senate conscripts an army of clones to fight the Separatists' droids.

▲ **Secret wedding**
After declaring their love for each other, Padmé and Anakin are married on Naboo. Because Jedi are forbidden to marry, they choose to keep their union a secret.

▲ **The Clone Wars**
Padmé fights a losing battle to maintain democracy among the worlds that have yet to defect to the Confederacy of Independent Systems.

Order 66
After the destruction of the Jedi Temple, a fugitive Obi-Wan informs Padmé that Anakin has turned to the dark side and is responsible for the deaths of many Jedi. Padmé leaves for Mustafar to help Anakin, but her husband attempts to kill her and Obi-Wan.

▲ **Funeral on Naboo**
After Padmé dies during childbirth, her body is brought back to Naboo. Jar Jar Binks and Boss Nass are among the many dignitaries who attend her funeral.

DEPARTURE FROM TATOOINE

"I will come back and free you, Mom. I promise." ANAKIN SKYWALKER

On the remote desert world of Tatooine, Jedi Master Qui-Gon Jinn discovers a young slave boy with prodigious strength in the Force: Anakin Skywalker.

Within the Galactic Republic, the Jedi are able to identify infants with strength in the Force and train them to use their powers throughout childhood. In the desolate Outer Rim, however, things are quite different. On sandy Tatooine, Anakin Skywalker and his mother Shmi live as slaves to the Toydarian junk dealer Watto. In addition to Anakin's uncanny knack for repairing technology—including building his mother a protocol droid assistant named C-3PO from spare parts—he is the only human capable of competing in the dangerous, ultra-fast sport of podracing. No one realizes his supernaturally quick reflexes are a Jedi trait, flowing from his strength in the Force—until one day, when a mysterious visitor arrives.

TRUST THE FORCE
Mere chance brings Jedi Master Qui-Gon Jinn to Tatooine when, while protecting Naboo's Queen Amidala on her journey to the capital planet Coruscant, their starship lands for repairs. When Qui-Gon recognizes Anakin's gifts, however, he immediately realizes the boy's significance. With sharp insight and a savvy wager, Qui-Gon guides Anakin to win not only the Boonta Eve Classic race, but his freedom from Watto. Eager to train as a Jedi, Anakin bids a somber farewell to his mother Shmi before leaving Tatooine and the grim life of slavery far behind.

Fateful meeting
After leaving his mother, Anakin follows Qui-Gon back to the Naboo starship. The first person he meets is Qui-Gon's Padawan apprentice, Obi-Wan Kenobi. Their relationship will shape the next three decades of galactic history.

Destiny calling
Shmi insists her son must leave Tatooine and fulfill his destiny to become a Jedi Knight. She assures Anakin that they will see one another again someday, then sends him on his way with the parting words, "Don't look back."

SIO BIBBLE

APPEARANCES I, II, CW, III
SPECIES Human **HOMEWORLD** Naboo
AFFILIATION Royal House of Naboo

A noble philosopher and member of the Naboo Royal Advisory Council, the outspoken Governor Sio Bibble aids Queen Amidala in her regal duties and deals directly with regional representatives and town governing officials. Unflinching in his refusal to increase Naboo's armament, he remains on Naboo during the Trade Federation's occupation of the planet.

CAPTAIN PANAKA

APPEARANCES I **SPECIES** Human
HOMEWORLD Naboo
AFFILIATION Royal Naboo Security Forces

The brave and resourceful Captain Panaka is the head of Queen Amidala's Security Forces, and personally oversees her safety. Although he trained his forces to the best of their abilities, he knows that his world is vulnerable to a planetary assault. Prior to the Trade Federation's invasion, Panaka argued for stronger security measures to protect Naboo, but the Queen's Advisory Council convinced her to maintain their government's pacifist policies. After the invasion begins, Panaka agrees to accompany the Queen to Coruscant so that she can submit an appeal to the Galactic Senate to bolster Naboo's defenses.

Royal security
The highly capable Captain Panaka (left) leads the Naboo Royal Security Forces, the closest thing to a regular infantry on Naboo. Intensely loyal, Panaka fights alongside Padmé during the Battle of Naboo, as they face heavy fire in the halls of Theed Palace (above).

OOM-9

APPEARANCES I **MODEL** OOM command battle droid **MANUFACTURER** Baktoid Combat Automata **AFFILIATION** Trade Federation

Like all B1 battle droids, OOM-9 is incapable of independent thinking, and receives instructions from a central source aboard a Trade Federation Droid Control Ship. However, OOM-9 was specially programmed to serve as a command droid for the Federation's invasion of Naboo, and to act as the primary contact for the Federation's leaders, the Neimoidians Nute Gunray and Rune Haako. On Naboo, OOM-9 directs droid ground troops and pilots to occupy settlements and destroy communication transmitters, preventing the planet's citizens from reporting the invasion or summoning help. OOM-9 leads the battle droids against Gungan warriors in the Battle of Naboo.

Receiving orders
Communicating via holographic transmissions, the Trade Federation leaders direct OOM-9 during the invasion of Naboo.

Leader in the field
OOM-9 signals Trade Federation multi-troop transports and armored assault tanks to move into position as the Battle of Naboo commences.

KAADU

APPEARANCES I, CW **HOMEWORLD** Naboo
SIZE 2 m (7 ft) tall **HABITAT** Swamps

Kaadu are two-legged reptavians indigenous to Naboo. They are swift, agile creatures with sharp hearing and a keen sense of smell, and although primarily land-dwellers, they can also breathe underwater for extended periods. For generations, Gungans have used domesticated kaadu as steeds to travel through Naboo's swamps and forests, so much so that the Gungan Grand Army comes to rely on them as mounts for their patrols.

Battle steed
Decorated with giant feathers, kaadu carry Gungan warriors into battle. In return, Gungans respect kaadu for their strength, endurance, and loyalty.

Reluctant guide
Jar Jar is hesitant to bring Obi-Wan and Qui-Gon to Otoh Gunga because he fears Boss Nass may still be angry with him for destroying Nass's property.

JAR JAR BINKS

APPEARANCES I, II, CW, III
SPECIES Gungan **HOMEWORLD** Naboo
AFFILIATION Gungan Grand Army, Galactic Senate

Banished from the underwater city Otoh Gunga after accidentally destroying Gungan leader Boss Nass's prized submersible, Jar Jar Binks is foraging for raw shellfish in the murky Naboo swampland when the Trade Federation's invasion force nearly crushes him. Fortunately, the Jedi Knight Qui-Gon Jinn rescues Jar Jar, who immediately declares himself the Jedi's humble servant. The hapless Gungan guides Qui-Gon and his apprentice, Obi-Wan Kenobi, to Otoh Gunga, where they obtain a bongo submarine that allows them to proceed to the Jedi's destination, the city of Theed, so they can aid Queen Amidala against the Trade Federation.

After the Galactic Senate fails to help Amidala's people, she asks Jar Jar to contact his fellow Gungans. With Jar Jar's help, the Naboo and the Gungans forge an alliance to liberate their besieged world. Immediately prior to the ground battle against the Trade Federation's droid armies, Boss Nass makes Jar Jar

a general in the Gungan Grand Army. After the battle, Jar Jar continues to ascend in Gungan society, putting his awkward past as an outcast behind him.

Eventually elected as a senior representative for Naboo, Jar Jar serves alongside Padmé Amidala in the Galactic Senate. While his compassion speaks volumes for the quality of his character, his inherent gullibility and trusting nature are easily exploited by the less scrupulous in the field of politics. Although Jar Jar is opposed to the Military Creation Act, he unwittingly enables Supreme Chancellor Palpatine to conscript an army of clones to fight Separatist forces. Still, in the corrupt inner confines of Senate, he stands as a rare example of a virtuous politician, interested only in the greater good of the Republic and his people.

Bold proposal
During a Senate meeting, Jar Jar takes the initiative and proposes the motion granting emergency powers to Supreme Chancellor Palpatine, a move that has profound impact on the Galactic Republic.

"Yousa guys bombad!"

JAR JAR BINKS

Affable companion
Although his bungling, erratic ways constantly land him in trouble, Jar Jar's innately good nature and loyalty somehow help him triumph in the end.

Gungan culture

The native inhabitants of the planet Naboo, Gungans are an amphibious species with hardy lungs, who are capable of holding their breath for extended periods. As such, they are as comfortable in water as they are on land. Gungans are represented by at least two distinct races. The Otolla Gungan, typified by Jar Jar Binks, is characterized by a tall and lanky build, long ears, inquisitive eyes atop short stalks, and a pronounced bill. The Ankura Gungan, exemplified by Boss Nass (below, right), is an older race, with a stockier build, shorter bill and haillu (ear lobes), and hooded eyes. While they have great reverence for nature and balance, making every effort not to overburden their native ecosystem, the Gungans are suspicious of outsiders and maintain a large standing militia, the Gungan Grand Army.

CAPTAIN TARPALS

APPEARANCES I, CW
SPECIES Gungan **HOMEWORLD** Naboo
AFFILIATION Gungan Grand Army

A kaadu patrol chief in Otoh Gunga, Captain Tarpals watches out for thieves and dangerous creatures that threaten the underwater city. He blames the accident-prone Jar Jar Binks for numerous altercations before Jar Jar becomes a hero, whom Tarpal fights alongside in the Battle of Naboo. During the Clone Wars, the courageous Tarpals subdues and helps capture General Grievous on Naboo, but at the cost of his own life.

BOSS NASS

APPEARANCES I, III
SPECIES Gungan **HOMEWORLD** Naboo
AFFILIATION Gungan Rep Council,
Gungan Grand Army

As the ruler of Otoh Gunga, Boss Nass chairs the Rep Council, which is responsible for governing Naboo's Gungan inhabitants. He dislikes Naboo's human population because he believes they view the Gungans as a primitive species. However, after the Trade Federation invades Naboo, and Queen Amidala asks Nass for help, he realizes that the Gungans and the Naboo must join forces to defend their world.

SANDO AQUA MONSTER

APPEARANCES I **LENGTH** 200 m (656 ft)
HOMEWORLD Naboo

A muscular monster with webbed hands and immense snapping jaws, the sando aqua monster is the largest predator in Naboo's oceans, and the only one able to bite through an opee sea killer's armored shell. The sando must constantly eat to maintain its enormous form, and easily devours entire schools of fish. Rarely seen by Gungan explorers and navigators, the sando is also somehow capable of hiding in deep environments.

Killer instinct
The mysterious, gigantic, and always voracious sando aqua monster closes in for the kill *(above)*. Using its razor-sharp teeth, the sando easily dismembers a hapless opee sea killer that has strayed within its reach *(right)*.

OPEE SEA KILLER

APPEARANCES | **AVERAGE LENGTH** 20 m (65.5 ft) **HOMEWORLD** Naboo

A vicious crustacean, the opee sea killer lurks inside caves in Naboo's ocean depths. Using a long lure to attract potential prey, the opee employs a combination of swimming and jet propulsion to pursue its target. Snagging victims with its adhesive tongue, the creature then draws its captured meal into its deadly maw. As aggressive as they are persistent, opees are unafraid of larger predators. Even the most experienced Gungan navigators avoid routes inhabited by these creatures, as they know opees regard the bongo's passengers as irresistible treats.

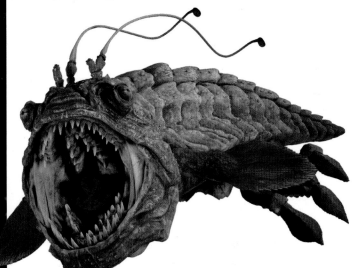

Tongue lashing
An opee sea killer's long, sticky tongue snares the Gungan bongo that carries Qui-Gon Jinn, Obi-Wan Kenobi, and Jar Jar Binks through the core of Naboo. Fortunately, a larger fish unwittingly intervenes, and they escape intact.

"Big gooberfish! Huge-a teeth!"
JAR JAR BINKS

COLO CLAW FISH

APPEARANCES |
AVERAGE LENGTH 40 m (131 ft)
HOMEWORLD Naboo

Hidden in tunnels along Naboo's oceanic floor, the serpentine, spine-studded colo claw fish can lie still for hours waiting to capture its prey within the huge pectoral claws for which it is named. Before attacking, the colo emits a hydrosonic shriek to disorient its victim, which it stuns with its venomous fangs, distending its jaw so wide that it can swallow prey much larger than its own head. If the colo does not render its victim unconscious prior to swallowing, there is a big risk that the consumed creatures will attempt to chew their way out of its stomach.

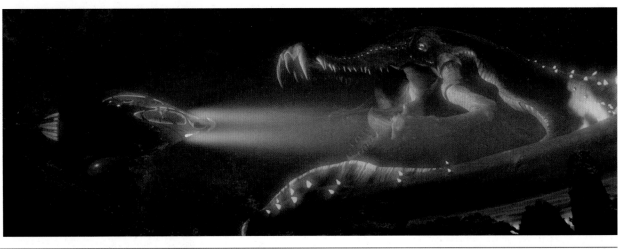

SABÉ

APPEARANCES |
SPECIES Human **HOMEWORLD** Naboo
AFFILIATION Royal House of Naboo

A Royal Handmaiden, Sabé serves Queen Padmé Amidala, and is one of her most trusted confidantes. Under the supervision of the Royal Security Forces, she occasionally impersonates the Queen to deceive Amidala's enemies. Amidala personally coached her in regal bearing and speech, and during the Trade Federation's invasion of Naboo, Sabé and Amidala switch roles, successfully fooling the Neimodians into believing that Sabé is the Queen.

RIC OLIÉ

APPEARANCES |
SPECIES Human **HOMEWORLD** Naboo
AFFILIATION Royal Naboo Security Forces, Royal Naboo Space Fighter Corps

A veteran flier and the top pilot in the Space Fighter Corps, Ric Olié is qualified to fly any craft in the Corps' fleet, and answers directly to Captain Panaka. It is his honor to captain the Queen's Royal Starship, and soon after meeting 9-year-old Anakin Skywalker, he shows the boy how to operate the starship's controls. During the Battle of Naboo, Olié pilots an N-1 starfighter, leading Bravo Squadron's assault on the Federation battleship.

"Excuse me, sir, but that Artoo unit is in prime condition. A real bargain." C-3PO

R2-D2

Never reluctant to risk his own destruction to help his allies, R2-D2 has a close association with the protocol droid C-3PO, with whom he has participated in numerous historic battles.

APPEARANCES I, II, CW, III, R, IV, V, VI, VII **MANUFACTURER** Industrial Automaton **TYPE** R2 series astromech droid
AFFILIATION Galactic Republic, Rebel Alliance

BRAVE ASTROMECH

A versatile utility robot generally used for the maintenance and repair of starships and related technology, the astromech droid R2-D2 is equipped with a variety of tool-tipped appendages that are stowed in recessed compartments. As property of the Royal Security Forces of Naboo, R2-D2 is one of several droids who serve aboard Queen Padmé Amidala's Royal Starship. After the Trade Federation forces Padmé to flee Naboo and droid starfighters attack her ship, R2-D2 is instrumental in helping Amidala and her Jedi allies escape across space. R2-D2 subsequently meets a young pilot, Anakin Skywalker, and inadvertently serves as Anakin's co-pilot during the Battle of Naboo.

Fearless mechanic
Ignoring enemy laserfire, R2-D2 quickly repairs Queen Amidala's starship to save the Queen and her allies.

Secret plans
Princess Leia entrusts R2-D2 with the stolen plans for an Imperial superweapon, the Death Star battle station.

DETERMINED MESSENGER

Nearly two decades after the rise of the Empire, R2-D2 and C-3PO serve Princess Leia Organa of Alderaan, who is also an agent of the rebellion. While attempting to deliver data about the Death Star to her allies, Leia's blockade runner is captured by Darth Vader. She hastily records a message and instructs R2-D2 to deliver it and its accompanying data to Obi-Wan Kenobi. Despite C-3PO's protests, the faithful astromech doggedly follows his orders and ultimately helps the rebels destroy the Death Star.

Reunion on Tatooine
Ten years after first meeting C-3PO, R2-D2 travels with Anakin and Padmé to the sand planet and reunites with the protocol droid.

SECRET AGENT

Because astromech units are among the most ubiquitous droids, they attract relatively little attention or suspicion at Imperial spaceports and criminal outposts. R2-D2 becomes extremely skilled at covertly insinuating himself into enemy territory in order to help his friends.

Droid bartender
Apparently reduced to menial labor on Jabba the Hutt's sail barge, R2-D2 is actually concealing Luke's lightsaber and is part of a daring plan to rescue Han Solo.

SERVICE TO THE REPUBLIC

After Padmé's reign as queen ends, R2-D2 continues to serve her during her travels as a Republic senator. When an assassin attempts to kill Padmé on Coruscant, the Jedi Order assigns Anakin to be her bodyguard, and R2-D2 provides backup for Anakin. Along with C-3PO, R2-D2 is present for the secret wedding of Padmé and Anakin. During the Clone Wars, he serves as Anakin's astromech support in Jedi starfighters. He also witnesses Anakin's fall to the dark side of the Force and the birth of Padmé and Anakin's twins, Luke and Leia. Unlike C-3PO, R2-D2 is not subjected to a memory wipe. He remembers everything.

Durable droid
Having survived countless battles
and desperate situations, R2-D2
has developed a remarkably resilient
attitude for a droid. He remains an
endlessly reliable astromech and
is never reluctant to put himself in
danger to help his allies.

timeline

Invasion of Naboo
When Federation droid starfighters attack
Queen Amidala's starship, R2-D2 makes an
emergency repair that allows Padmé and her
allies to escape.

▲ **Detour to Tatooine**
R2-D2 ventures into Mos Espa and meets
Anakin, who introduces the droid to C-3PO and
his mother, Shmi. Anakin leaves Tatooine with
R2-D2 on Queen Amidala's starship, but Shmi
and C-3PO remain on the sand planet.

Battle of Naboo
After taking protective cover in a Naboo
starfighter, Anakin and R2-D2 race into space to
attack the Trade Federation Droid Control Ship.

Return to Tatooine
Following Shmi Skywalker's funeral on
Tatooine, Anakin, Padmé, and R2-D2 leave the
Lars family homestead with C-3PO.

▲ **Battle of Geonosis**
R2-D2 and C-3PO infiltrate a Geonosian
droid factory and help the Jedi fight the
Separatist Droid Army.

The Clone Wars
Frequently serving as Anakin's co-pilot on
dangerous assignments, R2-D2 also proves
resourceful when confronted with deadly
predators, including a gundark on Vanqor.

Order 66
After Anakin turns to the dark side and
destroys the Jedi Order, R2-D2 helps
Obi-Wan bring the injured Padmé to a
medical center on Polis Massa.

Secret mission to Tatooine
After the end of the Clone Wars, Padmé's
daughter, Princess Leia, entrusts R2-D2 to
deliver the stolen plans for the Death Star battle
station to Obi-Wan on Tatooine.

▲ **Battle of Yavin**
R2-D2 serves as Luke's droid co-pilot during
the rebel assault on the Death Star. R2-D2 is
damaged during the battle, but the rebels
destroy the Death Star and repair the
astromech in time for their victory celebration.

Mission to Dagobah
Following the Battle of Hoth, R2-D2 travels
with Luke to find the Jedi Master Yoda on
the planet Dagobah. Neither Yoda nor R2-D2
acknowledge that they have met previously.

Escape from Cloud City
After Imperial forces surround the rebels on
Cloud City, R2-D2 hastily repairs the
Millennium Falcon's hyperdrive.

Battle of the Great Pit of Carkoon
Infiltrating Jabba the Hutt's palace, R2-D2 helps
the rebels rescue Han from Jabba the Hutt.

Battle of Endor
R2-D2 befriends the Ewoks and helps them
defeat Imperial ground troops.

CRISIS IN THE REPUBLIC

timeline

Witch's son
Mother Talzin of the Nightsister coven of witches on Dathomir, gives birth to a son, Maul.

Sith Apprentice
The Sith Lord Darth Sidious takes Maul from Dathomir, trains him to become a warrior and assassin, and eventually proclaims Darth Maul as his apprentice.

▲**Duel on Tatooine**
Darth Maul fights Qui-Gon Jinn on Tatooine, the first duel between a Sith and a Jedi in a thousand years.

Battle of Naboo
Darth Maul slays Qui-Gon on Naboo, but is cut in half by Qui-Gon's Padawan, Obi-Wan Kenobi. However, Maul survives and escapes capture.

▼**The lost years**
In hiding on Lotho Minor, Maul loses most of his memories, but remains consumed by desire for vengeance against Obi-Wan.

The Clone Wars
Savage Opress recovers an amnesiac Maul on Lotho Minor and delivers him to Mother Talzin, who restores his memories and strength, and gives him cybernetic legs.

Second duel with Obi-Wan
Teamed with Savage Opress, Maul seeks vengeance with Obi-Wan. He duels the Jedi on the planet Raydonia, but Kenobi escapes.

Shadow Collective
Maul organizes the Shadow Collective, an alliance of criminals and renegade bounty hunters, which briefly takes control of the planet Mandalore.

Splinter of the Sith Order
Although the Sith Order traditionally consists of only two members, and although Darth Sidious remains alive, Darth Maul proclaims that he and Savage Opress are respectively the new Sith Master and Sith apprentice.

▲**Showdown with Darth Sidious**
On Mandalore, Darth Sidious kills Savage Opress and captures Maul, but Maul escapes.

Duel on Zanbar
On the planet Dathomir, Maul joins forces with Mother Talzin to fight Count Dooku and General Grievous, but Talzin sacrifices herself so Maul can escape.

THE CLONE WARS

"At last we will reveal ourselves to the Jedi. At last we will have revenge."

DARTH MAUL

DARTH MAUL

Forged by Darth Sidious into a hate-fueled killing machine, Maul is the first Sith to slay a Jedi in combat in over a thousand years, but is ultimately betrayed by his own Master.

APPEARANCES: I, CW **SPECIES:** Zabrak **HOMEWORLD:** Dathomir **AFFILIATION:** Sith, Nightbrothers

THE PATH TO EVIL
Born a Nightbrother on Dathomir, Maul is taken by Darth Sidious as his Sith apprentice, and learns the power of the dark side. Sidious trains Maul to wield a double-bladed lightsaber, with which Maul intends to exact vengeance upon the Jedi for the decimation of the Sith ranks. Dispatched by Sidious to kill the troublesome Queen Amidala, Maul tracks her to Tatooine, where he duels briefly with one of her two Jedi protectors, Qui-Gon Jinn, who escapes with Amidala. But when the two Jedi escort Amidala back to Naboo, Maul goes to finish them all. He confronts the Jedi, drawing them into Theed's generator complex. Although he manages to kill Qui-Gon Jinn, Qui-Gon's apprentice, Obi-Wan Kenobi, strikes Maul down *(see also p. 158)*.

Generator duel
Maul slays a Jedi Knight on Naboo, but underestimates the lightsaber skills of the Knight's apprentice, who cuts the murderous Sith in half.

SHATTERED CREATURE
For over a decade, the Jedi Order believes Darth Maul is dead. But during the Clone Wars, after Asajj Ventress betrays Savage Opress, Mother Talzin informs Savage that he has an exiled brother in the Outer Rim who can teach him to become more powerful. Opress goes to the planet Lotho Minor, where he finds Maul in a wretched state, his damaged torso grafted to spider-like droid legs. Opress helps Maul recover, and together they seek revenge against those who turned them into monsters.

SHADOW COLLECTIVE
After Mother Talzin restores Maul's mind, and gives him new cybernetic legs, Maul and Savage Opress lure Obi-Wan into a trap so Maul may at last take his revenge. They fail to kill him, but proceed to cause death and destruction on several worlds as Maul draws support from the ranks of space pirates and the Mandalorian Death Watch to build his own army, the Shadow Collective. Ultimately, Darth Sidious dashes Maul's schemes, but by the end of the Clone Wars, Maul's whereabouts remain unknown.

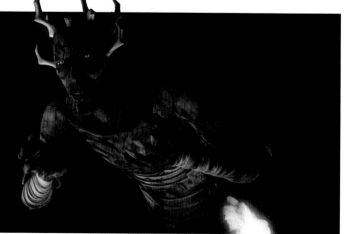

New Sith Order?
With his Sith memories restored, and Savage Opress on his side, Darth Maul believes they can take on Darth Sidious.

Craving vengeance
The burning desire to kill the Jedi who crippled him is the only thing that keeps Maul alive.

Vengeful warrior
One of the deadliest, most efficiently trained Sith in the Order's history, Darth Maul's tattooed face is as symbolic of his utter devotion to the dark side, as it is marking his hatred of the Jedi.

BANTHA
APPEARANCES I, II, CW, IV, VI
HOMEWORLD Tatooine **AVERAGE SIZE** 2 m (8 ft) tall **HABITAT** Desert

Large, shaggy-furred quadrupeds with bright, inquisitive eyes, banthas are easily domesticated, and are bred on many worlds throughout the galaxy. Male banthas are distinguished by a pair of long, spiraling horns. Bantha meat and milk are common food items, and bantha-hide boots, jackets and other wares are quite popular. On Tatooine, banthas are used as beasts of burden by moisture farmers, and as loyal pack animals by the savage Tusken Raiders. Tuskens are known to ride their banthas in single file, thus leaving few tracks in the desert, and effectively concealing their numbers.

DEWBACK
APPEARANCES I, CW, IV
HOMEWORLD Tatooine **AVERAGE SIZE** 9 m (6 ft) tall **HABITAT** Desert

Dewbacks are large lizards used as mounts and beasts of burden on their native Tatooine, where they can be found hauling goods for merchants or moisture farmers, pulling podracer

parts to starting grids, or serving stormtrooper patrols assigned to the planet's Imperial garrison. A dewback is able to withstand the heat and dust that often leads to mechanical breakdowns in high-tech conveyances. When the suns set and the temperatures plunge, dewbacks become lethargic and very rarely move about.

JAWA
APPEARANCES I, II, CW, IV, VI
SPECIES Jawa **HOMEWORLD** Tatooine
AFFILIATION Desert scavengers

Combing the deserts in search of discarded scrap and wayward mechanicals, Jawas are meter-tall humanoids with small bodies completely hidden behind rough, hand-woven robes. Using cobbled-together weaponry, they incapacitate stray droids and haul them into their immense mobile fortress-homes, known as sandcrawlers. Because Tatooine moisture farmers live far from droid dealers and scrap yards, they routinely trade with Jawas, even though Jawas are notorious hucksters of hastily-refurbished junk.

WATTO
APPEARANCES I, II **SPECIES** Toydarian
HOMEWORLD Toydaria
AFFILIATION Watto's Shop, Mos Espa

Watto moves by flapping his wings to guide his lightweight body through the air. The proprietor of a junk shop and scrap yard, the Toydarian is an inveterate gambler and an avid fan of podracing. In a wager over a podrace with another gambler, Gardulla the Hutt, Watto wins two of Gardulla's slaves, Shmi Skywalker and her son Anakin, who happens to be a gifted mechanic. Some years later, after a tall, bearded stranger (Qui-Gon Jinn) tries to buy a used hyperdrive motivator from Watto, the latter is simultaneously intrigued and perturbed when the stranger proposes a wager that may result in Watto either losing Anakin or winning a starship. Watto loses the bet, and Anakin leaves Tatooine to become a Jedi.

"Someday I will be the most powerful Jedi ever." ANAKIN SKYWALKER

ANAKIN SKYWALKER

A child born of prophecy, possibly conceived by the will of the Force itself, Anakin Skywalker leaves an indelible mark on the history of the galaxy, leading it through periods of light and darkness.

APPEARANCES I, II, CW, III, R, IV, V, VI **SPECIES** Human **HOMEWORLD** Tatooine **AFFILIATION** Podracing, Jedi Order, Sith Order

PODRACE TO FREEDOM

When the Jedi Qui-Gon Jinn and his allies become stranded on Tatooine and require replacement parts for their starship, Anakin Skywalker, a young slave, endeavors to help them. He enters a podrace, hoping to win prize money to buy the necessary starship parts, but unknown to the boy, Qui-Gon makes a wager with Anakin's owner, Watto. When Anakin wins, he not only defeats the reigning podracer champion, Sebulba, and gains the prize money, but also gains his freedom. Anakin later becomes Obi-Wan Kenobi's Jedi apprentice.

Daring pilot
Anakin's heightened perception and quick reflexes make him a podracing legend and the only human ever to win the Boonta Eve Classic

VENGEFUL SON

As a Jedi apprentice, Anakin knows that revenge is not the way of the Jedi. However, after he locates his dying mother in a Tusken Raider camp on Tatooine, he slaughters the Tuskens without mercy. Shattered by his mother's death, he promises that he will become the most powerful Jedi ever—and learn how to stop people from dying.

Solemn vow
Although Anakin does all he can to rescue his mother from her captors, he blames himself for her death. At her graveside, he regrets not being strong enough to save her and vows he will not fail again.

SECRET LOVE

Although Anakin is aware that the Jedi Order prohibits Jedi from falling in love because such strong emotions can lead to the dark side, he is unable to conceal his affection for Padmé Amidala. Padmé tries to resist because of her own political career, but ultimately admits her love for Anakin.

Wedding on Naboo
Anakin and Padmé marry in secret at a lake retreat on Naboo; their marriage remains a secret throughout the Clone Wars.

DRAWN TO THE DARK SIDE

Supreme Chancellor Palpatine takes a strong interest in Anakin's career as a Jedi, and Anakin comes to regard Palpatine as a valued friend. Anakin even trusts him with his dark secret about how he killed the Tuskens on Tatooine. However, during the Clone Wars, Anakin learns that Palpatine and the Jedi Council don't trust each other and is torn between loyalty to Palpatine and his obligations to the Council. After Anakin learns Palpatine is a Sith Lord, he notifies the Council but then allies with Palpatine, who promises to give him life-prolonging powers *(see also p. 84)*.

Sith tales
During a performance at Galaxies Opera House, Anakin listens to Palpatine's tale of a powerful Sith Lord who used the Force to defeat death.

BECOMING DARTH VADER

Anakin becomes Palpatine's Sith apprentice, Darth Vader, and helps destroy the Sith's enemies, enabling Palpatine to declare himself Emperor. However, after a duel with Obi-Wan Kenobi leaves Vader dismembered and near death, Palpatine recovers his remains, transforming him into a cyborg. As his damaged lungs are beyond repair, Vader must wear a pressurized helmet and suit of armor with built-in life-support systems, including mechanically assisted breathing, a voice synthesizer, and powerful prosthetic limbs, at all times. In the years that follow, the Emperor rarely leaves his palace on Coruscant, and Vader becomes the face of the Empire.

Armored warrior
After his near-fatal duel with Obi-Wan Kenobi, Anakin Skywalker is reborn as Darth Vader, a cyborg encased in life-sustaining armor.

DEATH STAR DUELS

On the first Death Star, Vader confronts Obi-Wan after nearly two decades. Subsequently, Vader learns of the existence of his own son, Luke Skywalker, and attempts to lure Luke to the dark side when they meet on Cloud City. Failing to gain Luke's allegiance, he later helps the Emperor draw Luke and his rebel allies into a trap at the second Death Star in orbit around Endor. But when the Emperor unleashes a barrage of Force lightning on Luke, Vader realizes he must destroy the Sith Lord *(see also p. 147)*.

Father vs. son
The Emperor manipulates Vader into fighting Luke, but Luke's faith in his father's innate goodness ultimately restores Anakin Skywalker.

Darth Vader
Widely feared as Emperor
Palpatine's deadliest enforcer,
Darth Vader is, in reality, a
tormented soul imprisoned inside
life-supporting armor that both
sustains his horrifically damaged
body and enhances it, with
advanced prostheses, and
augmented sensory, skeletal and
nervous systems.

timeline

Tatooine slave
Anakin Skywalker and his mother, Shmi,
are slaves owned by Gardulla the Hutt before
she loses them in a podracing bet to Watto,
a junk dealer on Tatooine.

Battle of Naboo
After winning his freedom, Anakin leaves
Tatooine, destroys the Federation Droid
Control Ship orbiting Naboo, and becomes
Obi-Wan's Jedi apprentice.

Reunion on Coruscant
Ten years after the Battle of Naboo, Anakin and
Obi-Wan serve as bodyguards for Padmé Amidala.
Anakin and Padmé fall in love.

Return to Tatooine
Hunting the Tusken Raiders who abducted his
mother, Anakin finds their camp but is too late to
save her. He kills every Tusken in the camp.

Battle of Geonosis
Anakin and Obi-Wan duel with Count Dooku
on Geonosis. Later, Anakin weds Padmé in a
secret ceremony on Naboo.

▲The Clone Wars
Anakin serves the Republic as a Jedi general
and takes an apprentice, Ahsoka Tano.
At Palpatine's command, Anakin kills a
defenseless Count Dooku.

Order 66
Seduced to the dark side by Palpatine's alter
ego, Darth Sidious, Anakin becomes Darth
Vader and helps destroy the Jedi Order.

Duel on Mustafar
Left crippled by Obi-Wan, Vader is rescued
by Palpatine, who transforms him into an
armored cyborg and convinces him that he
is responsible for Padmé's death.

▲Death Star duel
On the Death Star battle station, Darth
Vader duels Obi-Wan for the last time.

Battle at Yavin
Vader senses that the rebel pilot (Luke)
who destroys the Death Star is
extremely strong with the Force.

▲Duel on Cloud City
Vader identifies himself as Luke's
father, but fails to persuade Luke to
join the dark side and help him
defeat the Emperor.

▲Battle of Endor
Vader duels Luke and learns that
Princess Leia is his own daughter.
Vader kills the Emperor and
becomes one with the Force.

CRISIS IN THE REPUBLIC

THE CLONE WARS

THE EMPIRE ERA

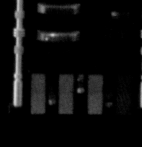

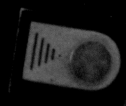

A VOTE OF NO CONFIDENCE

"If this body is not capable of action... new leadership is needed."

QUEEN PADMÉ AMIDALA

Queen Amidala of Naboo advocates Chancellor Valorum's removal from office, inadvertently causing a political upheaval that leads to the creation of the Empire.

The Trade Federation maintains a stranglehold on commerce throughout the Outer Rim. Nute Gunray, viceroy of the Trade Federation, initiates a blockade of the planet Naboo as a protest against the Republic's taxation of trade routes. The blockade is a disaster for the people of Naboo, but Supreme Chancellor Valorum seems incapable of action. When the Trade Federation's blockade turns into a full-scale invasion, Naboo's Queen Padmé Amidala escapes the planet with help from Jedi Master Qui-Gon Jinn and his Padawan Obi-Wan Kenobi.

A BUREAUCRATIC NIGHTMARE

Queen Amidala arrives on Coruscant, hoping to win governmental approval for the liberation of her homeworld. Instead, she becomes frustrated by the do-nothing bureaucracy that has apparently paralyzed the Senate. The Queen agrees with the suggestion of Naboo's Senator Palpatine that only a change of leadership will bring results. During the next session of the Senate, Queen Amidala calls for a vote of no confidence in Valorum as Supreme Chancellor. This leads to Valorum's expulsion from office and the election of Palpatine as his replacement. Palpatine, now wielding considerable power, is free to initiate his secret long-term plan of turning the Republic into a new Galactic Empire.

Cunning counsel
Senator Palpatine offers advice to Queen Padmé Amidala of Naboo, who never suspects that Palpatine aims to install himself as the new Supreme Chancellor.

Fateful speech
Queen Amidala speaks powerfully before the assembled Galactic Senate, airing her grave concerns about Chancellor Valorum's weak leadership. Seated behind her, Senator Palpatine looks on approvingly.

RONTO

APPEARANCES I, IV **HOMEWORLD** Tatooine
AVERAGE SIZE 5 m (16 ft) high
HABITAT Desert

Indigenous to Tatooine, the saurian ronto is a huge, four-legged herbivore. Jawas use these easily domesticated beasts as mounts and to haul cargo to and from trading posts. Despite their imposing size and appearance, rontos are skittish and easily startled, but also loyal to their masters. They require a great deal of water, but are well suited to the desert. Their skin sheds heat, as do the flaplike folds framing their faces, which can extend to cover their small eyes during sandstorms.

Dastardly Dug
Sebulba uses very shady tactics to win podraces.

SEBULBA

APPEARANCES I **SPECIES** Dug
HOMEWORLD Malastare
AFFILIATION None

The reigning champion of the Outer Rim podrace circuit is Sebulba, an arboreal Dug, who pilots a souped-up, overpowered orange racer. Although no one disputes that his expensive racer is fast, the shifty Dug's winning streak has less to do with his piloting skills and more to do with his refusal to let rules and regulations get in the way of victory. He is not above sabotaging a competitor's vehicle before a race and frequently uses illegal weaponry hidden aboard his own racer to distract or even bring down other pilots. Despite his utterly unsportsmanlike conduct, Sebulba is popular with many race fans because he is an excellent showman, as podrace organizers and promoters are well aware. Whenever Sebulba competes, he guarantees large crowds and thus high profits. At the Boonta Eve Classic, Sebulba wears a custom-made leather racing outfit that is decorated with coins, his victory prizes from previous races. Although Sebulba is the favorite to win the Boonta, a local slave boy, Anakin Skywalker, evades the Dug's vicious tactics and is first to cross the finish line. As if losing the race isn't bad enough, Sebulba also loses control of his podracer in the final stretch and crashes into the desert sands. Fortunately for him, he survives the crash and lives to race in many more competitions.

QUINLAN VOS

APPEARANCES I, CW **SPECIES** Kiffar **HOMEWORLD** Kiffu
AFFILIATION Jedi, Galactic Republic

A Jedi Knight with a sarcastic sense of humor and a reputation for not playing by the rules, Quinlan Vos is an expert tracker, renowned for his psychometric ability to perceive the memories of others by touching objects that they handled. He often takes missions that bring him into contact with members of the galactic underworld, which is how he met Aayla Secura, the Force-sensitive Twi'lek who became his Jedi apprentice. He happens to be on a covert assignment on Tatooine when Qui-Gon Jinn and Obi-Wan Kenobi arrive in Mos Espa just before the Boonta Eve Classic.

During the Clone Wars, Vos is partnered with Obi-Wan Kenobi to track the fugitive crime lord Ziro the Hutt. Thanks to his underworld connections, Vos has reason to believe that the Hutt Council hired bounty hunter Cad Bane to break Ziro out of prison. Vos and Obi-Wan travel to the swampy Hutt homeworld of Nal Hutta and meet with the Hutt Council. The Hutts deny all knowledge of Ziro's or Cad Bane's whereabouts, but Vos touches a drinking cup that helps him detect Ziro's presence on Nal Hutta. The Jedi eventually learn that Ziro has escaped to the planet Teth and that Cad Bane is also stalking Ziro. They proceed to Teth, where they find Cad Bane lurking near Ziro's corpse. Although Bane claims he isn't responsible for killing Ziro, the Jedi attempt to apprehend him for previous crimes, but he escapes into space.

Hunt for Ziro
Seeking Ziro the Hutt, Quinlan and Obi-Wan confront members of the Hutt Council in a club on Nal Hutta (left). Although accomplished with a lightsaber, Quinlan is not afraid to use his bare knuckles to face a deadly bounty hunter (above).

SHMI SKYWALKER

APPEARANCES I, II, CW **SPECIES** Human
HOMEWORLD Tatooine
AFFILIATION Slave, moisture farmer

Anakin's mother, Shmi, is a loving, soft-spoken woman. Although they are both slaves of the junk-dealer Watto, Shmi provides a good home for her son and is determined that he will have a better future. She is aware that Anakin has special powers—he can see things before they happen. But it is not until the Jedi Knight Qui-Gon arrives in Mos Espa that Shmi realizes her son has the potential and opportunity to become a Jedi. With Qui-Gon's help, Anakin wins his freedom by competing in a podrace, but Qui-Gon is unable to persuade Watto to release Shmi, too. Before Anakin departs with Qui-Gon, he promises he will return to free her. He also leaves behind C-3PO, the protocol droid that he built to help his mother.

Watto's chronic gambling habit leaves him virtually destitute and he is forced to sell Shmi. Cliegg Lars, a moisture farmer, falls in love with Shmi and purchases her freedom. Shmi and Cliegg wed, and she becomes a loving stepmother to Cliegg's son, Owen. Along with C-3PO, they live a quiet but happy existence on the moisture farm. In the years that follow, Shmi spends many nights gazing up at the stars, feeling an ache in her heart as she worries about her son's whereabouts and well-being.

Ten years after Anakin's departure, Shmi is alone, gathering mushrooms that grow on moisture vaporators, when a band of Tusken Raiders abducts her. Cliegg and a posse of moisture farmers attempt to rescue her, but the Tuskens ambush the farmers, maiming Cliegg and leaving most of his allies dead. A month later, Anakin—plagued by nightmares about Shmi being tortured—returns to Tatooine, determined to find his mother. Although Cliegg insists that Shmi must be dead, Anakin borrows a speeder bike and tracks the Tuskens across the desert. When he arrives at their camp, he finds his mother barely alive. She has just enough strength to tell him that she loves him before she dies. Enraged, Anakin gives in to the dark side and slaughters the Tuskens. He returns to the Lars homestead, where he buries her. This traumatic experience makes Anakin desire the power to prevent his loved ones from dying.

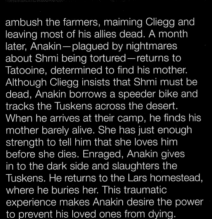

Slave quarters
Inside the hovel she shares with her son, Shmi refurbishes machinery and technology at her workstation.

Anxious spectator
Although Shmi trusts Anakin's skills as a pilot, she fears for his safety during podracer competitions.

"No matter where you are, my love will be with you." SHMI SKYWALKER

Close to death
Anakin finds his captive mother in a Tusken Raider camp, but is too late to save her life.

"Don't call me a mindless philosopher, you overweight glob of grease!" C-3PO

C-3PO

Perpetually fussy, timid, and prone to worry, the human-cyborg relations protocol droid C-3PO is also a loyal friend who survives numerous adventures with his astromech counterpart, R2-D2.

APPEARANCES I, II, CW, III, R, IV, V, VI, VII MODEL Protocol droid HOMEWORLD Tatooine AFFILIATION Galactic Republic, Rebel Alliance

"THANK THE MAKER"

Cobbled together from discarded scrap and salvaged parts from Watto's junkyard on Tatooine, C-3PO is created by 9-year-old Anakin Skywalker, who programs the droid to help his mother, Shmi. Initially lacking an outer shell, C-3PO endures the indignity of being "naked," with his parts and wiring showing. Shortly after activation, he meets R2-D2, Qui-Gon Jinn, Padmé Amidala, and Jar Jar Binks, who are en route to Coruscant. Anakin departs with his new allies, leaving C-3PO with Shmi. Eventually, Shmi and C-3PO move to the Lars moisture farm, and Shmi adds metal coverings to C-3PO's body.

Anxious friend
Though C-3PO is embarrassed when he realizes his unplated body leaves his framework exposed, he still manages to serve with R2-D2 as Anakin's podracer pit crew during the Boonta Eve Classic at Mos Espa Grand Arena.

Mission to Rodia
C-3PO serves Senator Padmé Amidala and Senator Jar Jar Binks during the Clone Wars.

SENATORIAL SERVICE

A decade after Anakin leaves C-3PO on Tatooine, the protocol droid reunites with his maker and is swept into the battle that begins the Clone Wars. Along with R2-D2, he witnesses the secret wedding of Anakin and Padmé and subsequently becomes a translator and personal assistant for senatorial meetings and diplomatic missions. After the Sith seize control of the Republic, C-3PO is present for the birth of Padmé's twins, Luke and Leia. To ensure that no one—especially the Sith—learns about the twins' existence, C-3PO is given a memory wipe, leaving him without any knowledge of his past.

DROID SALE

Almost 20 years after the Clone Wars, C-3PO is the property of Princess Leia Organa when he reluctantly joins R2-D2 on a mission to find Obi-Wan Kenobi on Tatooine. Both droids are captured by Jawas, who bring them to the Lars moisture farm and sell them to Owen Lars and his nephew, Luke Skywalker. Although Owen and C-3PO coexisted on the farm years earlier, Owen does not recognize C-3PO, and C-3PO's memories of Owen are long gone.

Versatile translator
Owen Lars buys C-3PO because the droid understands the binary language of moisture vaporators.

GOLDEN DEITY

Accompanying a rebel strike team to Endor's forest moon, C-3PO encounters the Ewoks, an indigenous species of primitive warriors who are wary of humans, but regard the golden droid as a god. Although C-3PO does not consider himself a good storyteller, his retelling of key events of the Galactic Civil War encourages the Ewoks to ally with the rebels. By gaining their allegiance, C-3PO plays a crucial part in the rebellion's victory at the Battle of Endor.

Elevated status
Discreetly levitated by Luke's Force powers, C-3PO appears to fly before the awed Ewoks.

Expert translator

Like most protocol droids, C-3PO is fluent in over six million forms of communication. However, he is more talkative than typical protocol models, and some friends say he talks too much. Through his exploits, he has accumulated over 30 secondary functions, including landspeeder piloting and programming binary loadlifters.

timeline

Tatooine origins
Built by Anakin, C-3PO remains on Tatooine with Shmi after Anakin leaves to become a Jedi.

Lars family homestead
Shmi gains her freedom and marries Cliegg Lars, a moisture farmer. Shmi and C-3PO move to Cliegg's farm, where his son, Owen, also lives.

▲Reunion with Anakin
A decade after leaving Tatooine, Anakin returns too late to save his mother. C-3PO leaves with Anakin and R2-D2 and participates in the Battle of Geonosis.

The Clone Wars
C-3PO serves as a translator for Senator Amidala and other Senate representatives.

Order 66
After learning of Anakin's role in the destruction of the Jedi Order, Alderaan senator Bail Organa gives C-3PO a memory wipe for security reasons.

▲Secret mission to Tatooine
After Darth Vader captures Princess Leia, C-3PO follows R2-D2 to Tatooine, where they meet Luke on their way to find Obi-Wan.

Escape from Mos Eisley
After stormtroopers kill Luke's aunt and uncle, C-3PO and his allies flee Tatooine aboard the *Millennium Falcon*.

Escape from the Death Star
C-3PO helps rescue Princess Leia from the Death Star and travels to the rebel base on Yavin 4.

▲Cloud City capture
When a captive C-3PO comes in close proximity to Darth Vader on Cloud City, he remains unaware that Vader was once his own maker, Anakin Skywalker.

▲Rescuing Han Solo
Accompanied by R2-D2, C-3PO infiltrates Jabba the Hutt's palace and helps rescue Han Solo.

Battle of Endor
C-3PO helps the Ewoks defeat Imperial ground forces on Endor.

EOPIE

APPEARANCES I, II, CW, III **HOMEWORLD**
Tatooine **AVERAGE SIZE** 2 m (7 ft) high
HABITAT Desert

An herbivore and a stubborn beast of
burden on Tatooine, the eopie is renowned
for its endurance and is often pushed to the
limit by the denizens of the twin-sunned
world. This sure-footed quadruped has pale
skin, a flexible snout, and a grumpy
temperament. Because their young are
extremely vulnerable and often fall prey to
predators, eopies instinctively travel in
herds. Moisture farmers use older eopies
to eat excess desert weeds that would
otherwise sap crops of valuable moisture.

KITSTER BANAI

APPEARANCES I **SPECIES** Human
HOMEWORLD Tatooine

An optimistic boy about the same age as
Anakin, Kitster is one of Anakin's best
childhood friends. When Anakin competes
in the Boonta Eve Classic, Kitster serves
as a member of his trusted pit team.
After winning the Boonta, Anakin gives
a few prize credits to Kitster, who uses
the money to improve his livelihood.

BEN QUADINAROS

APPEARANCES I **SPECIES** Toong
HOMEWORLD Tund
AFFILIATION None

Short by Toong standards, Ben
Quadinaros is the tallest entrant in
the Boonta Eve Classic and also the
least experienced. His hastily put
together podracer malfunctions,
stalling on the starting grid before its
four engines break loose and blast off
in all directions. Quadinaros perseveres
with the sport and is eventually billed
as Sebulba's greatest rival.

CLEGG HOLDFAST

APPEARANCES I **SPECIES** Nosaurian
HOMEWORLD New Plympto
AFFILIATION None

A journalist for *Podracing Quarterly*,
the arrogant Clegg Holdfast enters
competitions to cover stories from
the inside. Although his fellow racers
maintain that he's a better writer than
pilot, he proudly displays a set of
decorative medals on his lapel as
testament to his racing prowess.
In the second lap of the Boonta,
Sebulba opens up his own podracer's
flame-jets while next to Holdfast. The
blaze cooks Holdfast's engines and
forces him to crash into the desert.

GASGANO

APPEARANCES I **SPECIES** Xexto
HOMEWORLD Troiken
AFFILIATION None

A highly competitive pilot
with 6 arms and 24 fingers,
Gasgano is naturally able
to manipulate multiple
controls at the same
time. His predilection for high
speed combines with a nasty
temper that ignites when other
pilots attempt to pass him. He
races on behalf of Gardulla the
Hutt in the Boonta and is the
object of intense betting between
Gardulla and Jabba. Gasgano
finishes the Boonta in second
place, after Anakin Skywalker.

Custom racer
Gasgano pilots
a custom Ord
Pedrovia
podracer with
9-meter (29-foot)
bulbous engines
that boast great
acceleration.

TEEMTO PAGALIES

APPEARANCES I **SPECIES** Veknoid
HOMEWORLD Moonus Mandel
AFFILIATION None

An outcast from his homeworld, the
flamboyant Teemto Pagalies pilots an
IPG-X1131 LongTail podracer with
10.67-meter (35-foot) engines. During the
second lap of the Boonta, Tusken Raiders
snipe his podracer, causing him to crash.
Fortunately, Pagalies survives to race again.

Long engines
Seated in the
cockpit of his
IPG-X1131
LongTail *(above)*,
Pagalies boasts
the longest pair
of engines in the
Boonta *(left)*.

ODY MANDRELL

APPEARANCES I **SPECIES** Er'Kit
HOMEWORLD Tatooine
AFFILIATION None

A foolhardy thrill-seeker with an insatiable
appetite for high speeds, Ody Mandrell
pilots his massive Exelbrok podracer with
wild abandon and a blatant disregard for
safety. During a pit stop in the Boonta,
one of his pit droids is sucked into his
pod's engine intakes, crippling his vehicle
and eliminating him from the race.

FODE AND BEED

APPEARANCES I **SPECIES** Troig
HOMEWORLD Pollillus
AFFILIATION None

Exuberant, colorful, and not always too
accurate with facts, Fode and Beed are
the popular announcers of the Boonta
Eve Classic. Like all Troigs, Fode and
Beed share a body with two heads,
each with its own distinctive personality
and speech patterns. Fode's red-mottled
head provides commentary in Basic,
while Beed's green-mottled head
provides counterpoint in Huttese.

JABBA THE HUTT

APPEARANCES I, CW, IV, VI **SPECIES** Hutt
HOMEWORLD Tatooine **AFFILIATION** Grand
Hutt Council, Crymorah Syndicate

A loathsome slug and a vile gangster, Jabba the Hutt is the preeminent kingpin of crime in the Outer Rim Territories. Basing his operations out of Tatooine, Jabba's lucrative and unsavory rackets include slavery, gunrunning, spice smuggling, gambling, and extortion. Protected by shiftless henchmen and hired guns, he lives in an opulent palace that is the most prominent feature of Tatooine's Northern Dune Sea. Jabba also has properties in the spaceports Mos Eisley and Mos Espa. He also financed the construction of the grandstands at Mos Espa Arena, where he controls all gambling and concessions. Although many assume Jabba is a fan of podracing, his depraved senses are not stimulated by screaming, high-speed vehicles. Except for the gambling aspects, the races bore Jabba.

To spread his influence and business across the Outer Rim, Jabba employs a number of smugglers to traffic his illicit goods. The best smuggler on his payroll is Han Solo, captain of the *Millennium Falcon*. But while running a shipment of Kessel spice, Han's ship is boarded by an Imperial patrol, prompting him to jettison Jabba's cargo into space to escape arrest. Jabba later demands compensation for the lost contraband and sends bounty hunters after Han. One bounty hunter, Greedo, attempts to gun down Han in the Mos Eisley Cantina, but fails. Afterwards, Han confronts Jabba, who agrees to give the smuggler an extension on his repayment, but with the addition of a hefty percentage.

Jabba is still waiting for Han to pay up when informants claim that Han has become involved with the rebellion against the Empire. Uninterested in political ideals or civil wars, Jabba places a large bounty on Han's head. Eventually, the bounty hunter Boba Fett delivers a carbonite-frozen Han to Jabba's palace. Jabba displays Han's frozen form as a decoration that serves to remind others of the Hutt's intolerance for those who do not pay their debts on time. Jabba anticipates that Han's friends will attempt to rescue him from the palace, but is confident that they will fail.

Bad business
Han assures Jabba inside Docking Bay 94 at Mos Eisley spaceport that he'll repay the Hutt for a lost shipment of valuable spice. Jabba reminds Han that failure to do so could cost the smuggler his life.

Death of a Hutt

After Princess Leia and her rebel allies infiltrate Jabba's palace to rescue Han, Jabba captures them, chains Leia, and attempts to kill her friends at the Pit of Carkoon. Although Jabba is physically strong and has many bodyguards, he is unprepared when the rebels attack. Leia uses the chain that binds her to Jabba's dais to strangle him.

Podracing
Jabba presides over the Boonta Eve Classic from the royal box at Mos Espa Arena.

Holding court
Jabba puffs regularly on a hookah filled with Marcan herbs. On his left is his jester, Kowakian monkey lizard Salacious B. Crumb; on his right is Oola, a Twi'lek slave who dances for him. She later refuses his advances—and suffers the ultimate penalty.

"There will be no bargain, young Jedi. I shall enjoy watching you die."

JABBA *(translated from Huttese)*

GARDULLA THE HUTT

APPEARANCES I, CW **SPECIES** Hutt **HOMEWORLD** Nal Hutta
AFFILIATION Hutt crime syndicates

The Hutts control the smuggling trade in the Outer Rim, earning their crooked profits far outside the watchful eyes of law and order. In the years leading up to the Battle of Naboo, Gardulla the Hutt is one of the most powerful Hutt crime lords on Tatooine, and alongside Jabba the Hutt, wields control over the criminal underworld. Both Anakin Skywalker and his mother Shmi are Gardulla's slaves, but she loses them to Watto in a bet. During the Clone Wars, Gardulla imprisons the traitorous Ziro the Hutt in her palace on Nal Hutta, which brings the unwanted attention of Jedi investigators Obi-Wan Kenobi and Quinlan Vos.

BIB FORTUNA

APPEARANCES I, VI **SPECIES** Twi'lek
HOMEWORLD Ryloth
AFFILIATION Jabba's court

This sharp-toothed Twi'lek works for Jabba the Hutt as his chief aide and majordomo for over three decades. Fortuna demonstrates tremendous patience in dealing with his master's bad habits, including waking Jabba every time the Hutt dozes off during podraces. Originally from Ryloth, Fortuna controls most operations inside Jabba's Tatooine palace, including welcoming visitors who call at the remote stronghold. After Jabba displays a carbonized Han Solo on the wall of his throne room, Fortuna is the first of the Hutt's administrators to intercept Luke Skywalker when he arrives to rescue Han. Fortuna's weak will, makes him particularly susceptible to Jedi mind tricks, which allows Luke to get to Jabba with little trouble.

RATTS TYERELL

APPEARANCES I **SPECIES** Aleena
HOMEWORLD Aleena
AFFILIATION Podracing

Short in stature, but with lightning-fast reflexes, Ratts Tyerell rises through the ranks of the galaxy's best podracers, to earn a starting place in Tatooine's Boonta Eve Classic, just prior to the Battle of Naboo. Tyerell's podracer is capable of tremendous thrust, but a jammed accelerator in the second lap of the race, causes him to lose control as he roars through a cave, and smashes into a rocky stalactite, perishing in a fiery explosion.

AURRA SING

APPEARANCES I, CW **SPECIES** Unknown **HOMEWORLD** Nar Shaddaa
AFFILIATION None

One of the galaxy's most lethal killers, Aurra Sing earns her keep as a freelance assassin. The tell-tale antenna of a biocomputer protruding from her skull means that Sing receives extrasensory data, enabling her to track multiple threats simultaneously and line up distant shots with her long-barreled sniper rifle. Though Sing prefers to work solo, she finds a kindred spirit in space pirate Hondo Ohnaka, with whom she even shares a brief romance. Other associates occasionally recruited by Sing include the cowardly Klatooinian Castas and Bossk, the brutal Trandoshan bounty hunter. During the Clone Wars, Aurra Sing finds an unlikely partner in Boba Fett, a boy who inherits the ship *Slave I* from his bounty-hunting father Jango Fett. Sing entices Boba with the promise of taking revenge on the Jedi who had executed his father, and then exploits the boy's resemblance to younger Republic clones to sabotage and destroy the Republic attack cruiser *Endurance*. Abducting survivors from the wreckage of the *Endurance*, Sing retreats to Hondo Ohnaka's outpost on Florrum, with Jedi investigators in hot pursuit. Sing tries to escape in the *Slave I*, but Ahsoka Tano severely damages the ship, leaving Sing for dead. Unbeknownst to her pursuers, Sing survives and is freed from the crashed ship by Hondo. Disappearing offworld to lick her wounds, Sing later attempts to assassinate Senator Amidala at a refugee conference on Alderaan. Thwarted again by Ahsoka, Sing is taken prisoner, but escapes to find work with Cad Bane, where she serves as team sniper during Bane's bold mission to rescue Ziro the Hutt from a Coruscant prison.

Lethal weapon
Aurra Sing's legendary skills as an assassin keeps her employed for decades *(right)*. During the Boonta Eve Classic podrace, a high-flying Sing watches in astonishment as the young Anakin Skywalker wins the race fairly *(above)*.

TUSKEN RAIDERS

APPEARANCES I, II, IV **SPECIES** Tusken
HOMEWORLD Tatooine **AFFILIATION** None

Tusken Raiders, commonly called Sand People, are fierce desert nomads native to Tatooine. Unlike the Jawas, Tatooine's other intelligent species, Tusken Raiders are aggressive and easily drawn into conflict with moisture farmers and other settlers. Few have seen a Tusken's true face, as they cover their bodies with multiple layers of tight wrappings and wear masks with

Nomadic warriors
Tusken tribesmen stand guard outside a robust, yet easily dismantled and transported, shelter, built to withstand the devastating sandstorms that plague their desert home.

breathing filters to survive Tatooine's harsh desert environment. Tusken Raiders live in small clans within the rocky Jundland Wastes, moving around on the backs of shaggy banthas, and disguising their numbers by marching in single file. Tusken warriors carry stolen rifles and gaderffiis—metal weapons that function as both clubs and axes. A typical Tusken encampment consists of a small cluster of tents guarded by snarling massifs. .

Just before the Battle of Geonosis, Anakin Skywalker's mother, Shmi, is kidnapped by a Tusken raiding party. By the time Anakin arrives at their camp, the injured Shmi has been held captive for weeks, and dies before her son can rescue her. In retaliation, an enraged Anakin slaughters the entire Tusken tribe.

Desert ambush
The Tusken leader URoRRuR'R'R prepares to attack Luke Skywalker, seconds before Obi-Wan Kenobi comes to his rescue.

"I never ask for permission to do anything." **AURRA SING**

SUPREME CHANCELLOR VALORUM

APPEARANCES I, CW **SPECIES** Human
HOMEWORLD Coruscant
AFFILIATION Republic

Finis Valorum rules the Republic as Supreme Chancellor in the years leading up to the Battle of Naboo. Though he is well-intentioned, he has few friends in the political sphere and is unable to prevent the Trade Federation from enforcing a blockade of the planet Naboo. Valorum arranges for two Jedi ambassadors, Qui-Gon Jinn and Obi-Wan Kenobi, to negotiate an end to the blockade, but instead the Trade Federation invades Naboo. Ultimately, Naboo's Queen Amidala calls for a vote of no confidence in Valorum, forcing him out of office and installing Palpatine in his place.

Surrounded
The Jedi and their lightsabers—and Padmé Amidala with a drawn blaster—form a defensive circle in the arena as Separatist battle droids close in from every side.

THE BATTLE OF GEONOSIS

> ## "I truly, deeply love you, and before we die I want you to know." PADMÉ TO ANAKIN

A sentence of execution, a declaration of love, and the start of the Clone Wars. The Battle of Geonosis forever alters the fate of the galaxy.

When Obi-Wan Kenobi uncovers a massive Separatist military buildup on Geonosis, he is able to alert the Republic before the Geonosians seize him as a spy. Anakin Skywalker and Padmé Amidala try to rescue Obi-Wan, but become prisoners themselves. All three are sentenced to die in the execution arena. As Anakin and Padmé are wheeled onto the arena floor to face their doom, they finally confess their love for one another.

ENTER THE JEDI

Mace Windu interrupts the gruesome spectacle, revealing the presence of hundreds of Jedi Knights in the viewing stands. The Jedi Master hopes to force Count Dooku's surrender, but instead the arena explodes into conflict. Geonosian warriors are joined by battle droids, putting the outnumbered Jedi on the defensive. In a one-on-one showdown, Mace Windu strikes down bounty hunter Jango Fett, but the tide turns in favor of the Separatists. Just then, gunships descend from above, carrying a legion of white-armored clone troopers. Master Yoda commands the new arrivals, and soon a massive ground battle consumes the Geonosian wastelands. Count Dooku flees to a starship hangar, defeating Obi-Wan Kenobi and Anakin Skywalker when they try to stop him. Yoda fares better in his lightsaber duel with Dooku, but the count escapes offworld to ensure the continuation of the Clone Wars.

Unafraid to die
Padmé and Anakin believe they are facing their final fates, and are unwilling to hide their true feelings for one another any longer. Their love sets in motion a chain of events that eventually results in Anakin's obsession and corruption.

"Choose what is right, not what is easy." **YODA**

YODA

The highest-ranking Jedi who escaped Order 66, Yoda is 900 years old when he passes into the Force. By training Luke Skywalker, Yoda helps bring the Jedi back to the galaxy.

APPEARANCES I, II, CW, III, R, V, VI **SPECIES** Unknown **HOMEWORLD** Unknown **AFFILIATION** Jedi Order

ON THE COUNCIL

Though little is known of Yoda's early life, his influence within the Jedi Order is tremendous. He serves on the elite Jedi Council with other high-ranking Masters and teaches lightsaber combat to young students in the Jedi Temple. When Qui-Gon Jinn brings Anakin Skywalker before the Council, Yoda argues that the boy is too dangerous to be trained. He later changes his mind after Qui-Gon is killed by a Sith on Naboo, but he never entirely conquers his feelings of unease. Over the next few years, Master Yoda keeps watch over Padawan Skywalker and his Master, Obi-Wan Kenobi.

Discussion among equals
Master Yoda shares his wisdom with Council members. When duty calls the Jedi to other parts of the galaxy, they report to Yoda in the form of a long-distance hologram.

INTO EXILE

Returning to Coruscant, Yoda fights Emperor Palpatine in a spectacular test of Force powers. Their showdown begins inside Palpatine's office and spills into the Galactic Senate Chamber. Though Yoda is a tough combatant,

Duel of Masters
The full power of the light side and the dark side of the Force are on display during Yoda's clash with Emperor Palpatine. Outmatched, Yoda retreats and waits to train a new champion to lead the fight against evil.

the Emperor uses his Sith powers to release lightning bolts and hurl floating platforms at his foe. Ultimately the battle proves too much for Yoda, who barely escapes and is whisked away to safety by Senator Bail Organa. After leaving Anakin and Padmé's twin children in the care of Obi-Wan and Bail Organa, Yoda travels to the swamps of Dagobah to begin a new life away from the Empire's hunters. The remote world gives Yoda the chance to meditate on the Force, and a dark-side cave serves as a place of spiritual trial.

Duel with the dark side
Yoda fights Count Dooku on Geonosis, forcing his former student to flee.

THE RISING DARKNESS

Count Dooku, one of Yoda's former students, emerges as the leader of a Separatist movement. When Dooku becomes a threat to galactic peace, Yoda leads an army of clone troopers against Separatist forces on Geonosis and defeats Dooku in lightsaber combat. During the Clone Wars, Yoda strives to treat each clone soldier as an individual worthy of respect. Yet as the war drags on, Yoda and Mace Windu sense a gathering darkness that diminishes their ability to use the Force. Finally, Yoda is ambushed by his clone troopers on Kashyyyk and flees off-world with help from the Wookiee Chewbacca.

A NEW HOPE

Luke comes to Dagobah after the Battle of Hoth to learn the ways of the Jedi (see p. 200). Throughout Luke's training, Yoda keeps the truth of his relationship to Vader a secret for fear it might trigger Luke's fall to the dark side. Luke loses his first fight with Vader on Cloud City, but Yoda declares him a true Jedi when he returns to Dagobah. Yoda then passes into the light of the Force.

Luminous being
Yoda gains strength from the living things in Dagobah's swamps and tries to teach Luke that the Force is everywhere.

timeline

Jedi Master
Yoda is centuries old and becomes a leading member of the Jedi Council long before the Battle of Naboo.

Evaluating Anakin
Yoda senses fear and attachment in young Anakin's heart, but eventually allows him to be trained as a Jedi.

Return of the Sith
Qui-Gon dies on Naboo at the hands of Darth Maul, a Sith. Yoda becomes gravely worried.

Separatist Crisis
Count Dooku, Yoda's former Jedi student, leaves the Order and forms a Separatist movement that threatens the Republic.

▲Dueling Dooku
On Geonosis, war breaks out with the Separatists. Yoda and Dooku fight one-on-one.

▲Clone Wars
As a Jedi general, Yoda leads the Republic's clone troopers into battles across the galaxy.

Order 66
Yoda's clone troopers turn against him on Kashyyyk. He slips away and meets up with other surviving Jedi.

Facing the Emperor
Yoda tries to stop Palpatine, the new Emperor, from taking control. He loses and barely escapes with his life.

Dagobah
On a distant swamp planet, Yoda goes into exile and awaits the rise of one who can overthrow the Empire.

▲Training a Jedi
Luke, Anakin's son, becomes Yoda's final student.

One with the Force
After instructing Luke, the great Jedi Master passes on and is reborn as a Force spirit.

CRISIS IN THE REPUBLIC

THE CLONE WARS

THE EMPIRE ERA

More than he seems
Both Count Dooku and Luke Skywalker seem to underestimate Yoda, thinking his small size and advanced age make him less formidable. But Yoda's true strength comes from within.

> "I'm going to put an end to this, once and for all!" MACE WINDU

MACE WINDU

Second only to Master Yoda in reputation, Master Mace Windu leads the Jedi Council during the waning years of the Republic. Betrayal costs him his life, but he never relents in his fight against the dark side.

APPEARANCES I, II, CW, III SPECIES Human HOMEWORLD Haruun Kal AFFILIATION Jedi

SITH THREAT

A high-ranking member of the Jedi Council at the start of the Battle of Naboo, Mace Windu is troubled by signs indicating the return of the Sith. He investigates the growing influence of the dark side as Count Dooku's Separatist movement takes shape, and when Obi-Wan Kenobi discovers evidence that the Separatists are preparing to go to war against the Republic, Mace leads a task force of 200 Jedi to Geonosis to do battle. He faces off against Dooku's agent Jango Fett in the Geonosian execution arena and beheads the bounty hunter with one swipe of his lightsaber (see also p. 51).

High standards
Mace Windu isn't impressed by young Anakin Skywalker and initially refuses his admittance to the Jedi Order.

Jedi authority
As a Jedi general during the Clone Wars, Mace is an elite military figure.

THE CLONE WARS

Mace Windu accepts the rank of general in the Grand Army of the Republic during the Clone Wars and serves as both a strategist and a frontline combatant in numerous conflicts with the Separatists. On Ryloth, Mace leads the AT-RT drivers of Lightning Squadron to assist freedom fighter Cham Syndulla in the liberation of his world.

Against the Separatists
Mace gives counsel to Anakin as the Clone Wars rage across the galaxy.

He discovers the slumbering Zillo Beast on Malastare and escapes several attempts on his life from Boba Fett, the orphaned son of Jango Fett, who is out for revenge. Late in the war, Mace becomes alarmed by the rising threat of the dark side and steps up his efforts to unmask the suspected Sith manipulator behind it all.

Final battle
The dark-side power wielded by Palpatine is a shocking surprise for Mace.

CONFRONTING EVIL

Following the Battle of Coruscant, Mace receives news that Supreme Chancellor Palpatine is actually the Sith Lord behind the recent turmoil across the galaxy. Mace selects a small squad of Jedi—Agen Kolar, Kit Fisto, and Saesee Tiin—to arrest the Chancellor, but they die when Palpatine fights back. Mace seems to be winning until Anakin suddenly intervenes and cuts off the Jedi Master's hand. Palpatine seals Mace's fate with a blast of Force lightning, sending him through the window to his death.

timeline

Jedi recognition
For his skill and wisdom, Mace Windu earns a place on the Jedi Council next to Master Yoda.

▲ The Chosen One
Mace believes that young Anakin should not be trained to become a member of the Jedi Order.

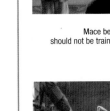

▲ Geonosis
When Count Dooku captures Obi-Wan Kenobi on Geonosis, Mace leads the team to rescue him.

▲ War leader
On Ryloth, Mace helps liberate the capital from the Separatists during the Clone Wars.

▲ Zillo beast
Mace's efforts during the Battle of Malastare lead to uncovering the gigantic, terrifying creature.

Revenge target
Aboard a Republic fleet carrier, Mace escapes an assassination attempt by Boba Fett.

War's end
As the Clone Wars wind down, Mace realizes that Chancellor Palpatine might be a Sith Lord.

Arresting the Chancellor
Forced into revealing his true nature, Palpatine cuts down Mace's three Jedi escorts.

▲ Fatal battle
Desperate to preserve Palpatine's life, Anakin cuts off Mace's arm. A blast of lightning sends the Jedi Master through the window to his death.

CRISIS IN THE REPUBLIC

THE CLONE WARS

Defender of the Force
Mace Windu is a formidable warrior and a stern judge of character. He believes in action, not words, and is the first Jedi to move against Count Dooku on Geonosis, assembling a squad to arrest Chancellor Palpatine when he learns of Palpatine's Sith secret.

KI-ADI-MUNDI

APPEARANCES I, II, CW, III **SPECIES** Cerean
HOMEWORLD Cerea **AFFILIATION** Jedi

Ki-Adi-Mundi is a Cerean Jedi Master whose white beard and wise features attest to his years spent in service to the Jedi Order. He joins the Jedi Council prior to the Battle of Naboo and helps evaluate Anakin Skywalker's Force potential when Qui-Gon Jinn brings the young boy to Coruscant. Qui-Gon's concerns that the Sith may have returned aren't enough to trouble Ki-Adi-Mundi, who reminds the Council that the Sith haven't been sighted for a millennium. When Count Dooku later abandons the Jedi Order and emerges as the head of a Separatist movement, Ki-Adi-Mundi refuses to believe Dooku could be capable of orchestrating bombings, emphasizing to his colleagues that Dooku is a political idealist who seems incapable of murder.

Nevertheless, war soon breaks out between the Republic and Dooku's Separatists. Ki-Adi-Mundi is one of the Jedi who travels to Geonosis, where he infiltrates the execution arena to ignite his lightsaber at Mace Windu's signal. He survives the subsequent battle and receives the rank of general in the Grand Army of the Republic. Ki-Adi-Mundi leads the Galactic Marines, a group of clone troopers led by Commander Bacara, in engagements against the Separatist droid armies. As the war continues, Ki-Adi-Mundi sees how much Anakin has grown as a Jedi and a warrior, and during the

Second Battle of Geonosis, he engages Anakin in a friendly wager over which of them can destroy the most battle droids.

With the Galactic Marines, Ki-Adi-Mundi scores a number of Republic victories and forms a close professional bond with Commander Bacara. During the late-stage Outer Rim Sieges, Ki-Adi-Mundi leads his clones to capture Mygeeto from the Separatists, which is where they are stationed when Darth Sidious issues Order 66. Commander Bacara orders his troopers to open fire on their Jedi general as he leads the charge across a bridge, and Ki-Adi-Mundi falls under the surprise onslaught.

Evaluating Anakin
With his fellow Council members, Ki-Adi-Mundi decides the fate of young Anakin.

Unprepared
Ki-Adi-Mundi's clone troopers betray him on Mygeeto.

PLO KOON

APPEARANCES I, II, CW, III **SPECIES** Kel Dor
HOMEWORLD Dorin **AFFILIATION** Jedi

Plo Koon is a Kel Dor who needs a mask to protect his eyes and lungs from oxygen-rich environments. Early in his Jedi career, Plo Koon discovers a young, Force-sensitive Togruta girl named Ahsoka Tano and brings her to Coruscant to become a Jedi. Plo Koon sits on the Jedi Council, where his guidance is always respected, but the outbreak of the Clone Wars

allows him to demonstrate his battle skills as well. One early engagement pits Plo Koon's armada against the Separatist cruiser *Malevolence*, which ends in near-total defeat for the Republic. Plo Koon and a small number of clone troopers survive in an escape pod and evade battle droid clean-up squads until they are rescued.

Koon quickly jumps back into the fight, helping Ahsoka navigate the Coruscant underworld to uncover the whereabouts of Aurra Sing. Plo Koon and Ahsoka travel to the headquarters of space pirate Hondo Ohnaka on Florrum

and arrest a young Boba Fett. On a later mission, Koon leads the Republic fleet to the prison planet of Lola Sayu to rescue Jedi Master Even Piell from the Citadel, and personally pilots the gunship that extracts the groundside rescue team.

At the end of the Clone Wars, Plo Koon flies his Jedi starfighter during the Republic's capture of Cato Neimoidia. During a post-battle patrol flight, his clone pilot escorts receive Order 66 and fire shots that cripple Koon's ship. He dies when his starfighter crashes into one of Cato Neimoidia's bridge cities.

Meeting Ahsoka
Plo Koon senses the Force in a Togruta girl while visiting her planet. Impressed by her potential, he brings young Ahsoka Tano to the Jedi Temple for training.

SAESEE TIIN

APPEARANCES I, II, CW, III **SPECIES** Iktotchi
HOMEWORLD Iktotch **AFFILIATION** Jedi

Saesee Tiin is a Jedi Master and a member of the Jedi Council who belongs to the horned species known as the Iktotchi. One of the quieter members of the Council, Tiin is known more for his starfighter piloting skills than his Force teachings. During the Clone Wars, Tiin is among the Council members who receive the distressing news that their colleague Even Piell has been captured by the Separatists and imprisoned in the impenetrable Citadel on the planet Lola Sayu. While Obi-Wan Kenobi and Anakin lead the rescue mission, Tiin flies cover for Plo Koon's gunship during the dangerous extraction process and commands fellow pilots Adi Gallia and Kit Fisto in the

War veteran
A war weary General Saesee Tiin *(left)* has seen more than his fair share of combat during the Clone Wars, including the audacious rescue of Obi-Wan, Anakin, and Padmé during the Battle of Geonosis *(above)*.

fight against Lola Sayu's droid forces. The Battle of Umbara offers another opportunity for Tiin to provide air cover for Republic troops when he helps Obi-Wan, Anakin, and Jedi Master Pong Krell capture the shadowy world for the Republic.

At the end of the Clone Wars, Mace Windu entrusts Tiin with the news that Supreme Chancellor Palpatine is actually a powerful Sith Lord. Tiin follows Master Windu into the Chancellor's office, backed up by fellow Jedi Agen Kolar and Kit Fisto. None of the Jedi expect resistance, but when Mace announces he is placing Palpatine under arrest, the Chancellor suddenly springs into action. Agen Kolar is the first to fall. Tiin moves to strike, but Palpatine is faster and cuts down the Iktotchi Jedi Master.

Under fire
Adi Gallia uses her lightsaber to deflect an incoming blast. Over the course of the Clone Wars, Master Gallia grows into her role as a military commander and Jedi warrior.

ADI GALLIA

APPEARANCES I, II, CW **SPECIES** Tholothian
HOMEWORLD Tholoth **AFFILIATION** Jedi

Both Adi Gallia and her cousin Stass Allie serve in the Jedi Order, but Gallia wins a post on the Jedi Council prior to the Battle of Naboo. She serves in this elite role for years, observing with concern the rise of Count Dooku's Separatists. When armed conflict finally breaks out on Geonosis, she is on the frontlines and becomes a battlefield commander as the Clone Wars take hold of the galaxy. With Anakin, Gallia leads the effort to rescue Jedi Master Eeth Koth from the flagship of General Grievous, and in a later engagement, she pilots a starfighter during a daring prison break from the Citadel of Lola Sayu. Gallia becomes a prisoner of the Separatists when General Grievous destroys her fleet and takes her captive. Plo Koon pursues Grievous, boarding his vessel with a contingent of clone troopers, and brings Gallia safely back to the Republic.

Gallia meets her end when she decides to team up with Obi-Wan on a hunt for the dangerous team of Darth Maul and Savage Opress, the vengeful dark-side Nightbrothers determined to destroy the Jedi. At the Cybloc transfer station, Gallia picks up their trail and follows the duo to Florrum. They arrive to find a battle raging between pirate leader Hondo Ohnaka and the two Nightbrothers, with many of Ohnaka's former crew members now working for the Sith. Obi-Wan and Gallia try to even the odds, but the power of their foes proves to be too great. Savage Opress gravely injures Gallia by ramming her with his horns and then delivers a killing blow with his red-bladed lightsaber.

EETH KOTH

APPEARANCES I, II, CW **SPECIES** Zabrak
HOMEWORLD Nar Shaddaa
AFFILIATION Jedi

An esteemed Zabrak Jedi Master who sits on the Jedi Council at the time of the Battle of Naboo, Eeth Koth is among the Masters that evaluate Anakin Skywalker's fitness for Jedi training. Koth remains on the Council throughout the Separatist crisis and serves on the strike force that invades Geonosis at the beginning of the Clone Wars. He is believed to have been killed in battle when his gunship takes a direct hit, but Koth later returns to active duty, and is placed in command of the Republic Star Destroyer *Steadfast*. General Grievous attacks the ship and captures Koth, but the latter shrewdly reveals his location using a secret tap-code during a hologram transmission from Grievous. This enables the High Council to track Koth and dispatch Anakin Skywalker and Adi Gallia to lead the mission to free him.

OPPO RANCISIS

APPEARANCES I, II, CW **SPECIES** Thisspiasian **HOMEWORLD** Thisspias
AFFILIATION Jedi

The long-lived Oppo Rancisis is a curious sight in the Jedi Council. A Thisspiasian, he has the lower body of a snake and often sits coiled in quiet contemplation. Master Rancisis has long, claw-like fingernails and a thick beard that masks his face. A skillful tactician, he gains a position on the Council prior to the Battle of Naboo, and is among the first Jedi to learn that the Sith have returned after the appearance of Darth Maul. Rancisis remains a high-ranking Jedi and a key military adviser throughout the Clone Wars, during which he becomes a Jedi General coordinating Republic forces across the galaxy.

EVEN PIELL

APPEARANCES I, II, CW **SPECIES** Lannik **HOMEWORLD** Lannik
AFFILIATION Jedi

The battle-scarred Even Piell earns a place on the Jedi Council prior to the Battle of Naboo. Master Piell takes part in the Republic assault on Geonosis at the start of the Clone Wars, and later becomes a prisoner of war when Separatist forces capture him and Republic Navy captain Wilhuff Tarkin. Incarcerated in the impregnable Citadel prison on Lola Sayu, Piell withstands torture to preserve the top-secret coordinates of the hyperlane known as the Nexus Route. Despite a rescue effort led by Anakin Skywalker and Ahsoka Tano, Piell is mortally wounded by a wild anooba hound as he escapes from the Citadel.

> "To walk the path of the Jedi, one's spirit must be strong. That requires discipline."
>
> **OPPO RANCISIS**

DEPA BILLABA

APPEARANCES I, II **SPECIES** Chalactan
HOMEWORLD Chalacta
AFFILIATION Jedi

Belying her youthful appearance, Depa Billaba is highly regarded for her wisdom, becoming a valued member of the Jedi Council during the events leading up to the Battle of Naboo. Depa Billaba's sister, Sar Labooda, also serves as a Jedi, but is killed in the Battle of Geonosis at the start of the Clone Wars. During the wars, Master Billaba trains a human boy named Caleb Dume as her Jedi Padawan, and when the Republic's clone troopers attack the Jedi during Order 66, she dies protecting her student from an ambush. Caleb Dume takes the name Kanan Jarrus, and later honors his Master's memory by operating a rebel cell on Lothal.

Elite company
Backed by Mace Windu, Saesee Tiin, and Ki-Adi-Mundi, Depa Billaba attends the ceremony marking the defeat of the Trade Federation in the Battle of Naboo.

YADDLE

APPEARANCES I **SPECIES** Unknown
HOMEWORLD Unknown **AFFILIATION** Jedi

Very little is known about Yaddle's species. Her short build, long ears, and extended lifespan mark her as a member of the same species as Jedi Master Yoda, and Yaddle also shares Yoda's remarkable affinity for the Force. After rising through the ranks of the Jedi Order, Yaddle achieves the highest possible reward for her contribution—a seat on the Jedi Council. She helps judge Anakin Skywalker's fitness for Jedi training and contributes to the Jedi efforts to resolve the Naboo blockade crisis and uncover clues about the return of the Sith. Following the Battle of Naboo, Yaddle takes a less active role in Jedi affairs.

YARAEL POOF

APPEARANCES I **SPECIES** Quermian **HOMEWORLD** Quermia
AFFILIATION Jedi Order

This famed Jedi hails from the planet Quermia, homeworld of a species known for their willowy appearance and craning necks. After being promoted to Jedi Master, Yarael Poof wins a place on the Jedi Council, where he serves alongside Yoda and Mace Windu. Blessed with two brains, Master Poof is an expert practitioner of Jedi mind control. He stands out among his fellow Council members thanks to his towering stature and possesses a second pair of arms that he hides beneath his robes. By the time of the Battle of Geonosis, Yarael Poof's spot on the Jedi Council has been filled by Jedi Master Coleman Trebor.

LOTT DOD

APPEARANCES I, CW **SPECIES** Neimoidian
HOMEWORLD Neimoidia
AFFILIATION Trade Federation, Galactic Senate, Separatists

The Trade Federation controls most interstellar shipping in the Outer Rim, making it one of the most powerful entities in the galaxy. Its influence is evident when Lott Dod is appointed to the Galactic Senate, a post normally reserved for representatives of systems and sectors. As a senator, Dod thwarts the taxation of the Free Trade Zones and secretly helps organize the Trade Federation's invasion of Naboo. When Naboo's queen, Padmé Amidala, comes to Coruscant to plead for the liberation of her world, Dod claims that she has no proof of her accusations. Throughout the Clone Wars, Dod continues to advance the interests of the Separatists while claiming neutrality.

MAS AMEDDA

APPEARANCES I, II, CW, III **SPECIES** Chagrian **HOMEWORLD** Champala **AFFILIATION** Republic, Galactic Senate, Empire

This politically-savvy Chagrian is given an elite post in the Republic's government when he becomes Vice Chancellor during the tenure of Supreme Chancellor Valorum. The events surrounding the Battle of Naboo result in a vote of no confidence against Valorum and his removal from office, yet Amedda retains his position under Valorum's successor, Chancellor Palpatine. Power-hungry and pragmatic, Amedda advises Palpatine during the Separatist Crisis, and before the Clone Wars arranges the sudden Senate vote that grants the Chancellor emergency war powers, allowing the Republic to seize control of the clone army discovered at Kamino. His longstanding loyalty to Palpatine later earns him the position of Grand Vizier in the Galactic Empire.

"This is a crisis. The Senate must vote to give the chancellor emergency powers."
MAS AMEDDA

SENATOR TIKKES

APPEARANCES I, II, III **SPECIES** Quarren
HOMEWORLD Mon Calamari **AFFILIATION** Republic, Galactic Senate, Separatists

Tikkes represents Mon Calamari in the Galactic Senate. Sympathizing with Count Dooku's Separatist movement, he resigns from the Senate to support the Confederacy of Independent Systems, and is rewarded with a seat on the Separatist Council. At the end of the Clone Wars, Tikkes, along with the rest of the Council, is killed by Darth Vader on Mustafar.

SLY MOORE

APPEARANCES II, III **SPECIES** Umbaran
HOMEWORLD Umbara **AFFILIATION** Republic

A pale-skinned Umbaran, Sly Moore serves as the senior administrative aide to Supreme Chancellor Palpatine following his election to that office. Always at Palpatine's side—even when he addresses the galaxy from atop the Chancellor's podium in the center of the Senate Chamber—Moore keeps silent in most situations and zealously guards her Master's secrets.

ORN FREE TAA

APPEARANCES I, II, CW, III **SPECIES** Twi'lek
HOMEWORLD Ryloth **AFFILIATION** Galactic Senate

A larger-than-life senator who represents Ryloth in the Galactic Senate, Orn Free Taa is a symbol of greed and corruption. Senator Taa serves as the leader of Chancellor Palpatine's Loyalist Committee and pushes for the Military Creation Act, which results in the creation of the Republic's clone army. When the Separatists occupy Ryloth during the Clone Wars, Taa agrees to an alliance with his rival Cham Syndulla to help Mace Windu retake the planet. Taa later becomes a hostage during Cad Bane's strike on the Senate building.

Enormous appetites
Orn Free Taa is known for his enjoyment of the good things in life.

Security duty
Captain Typho confers with Senator Padmé, disguised as a Naboo starfighter pilot, after landing on Coruscant.

CAPTAIN TYPHO

APPEARANCES II, CW, III **SPECIES** Human
HOMEWORLD Naboo
AFFILIATION Royal House of Naboo

Captain Typho serves as Padmé Amidala's unswervingly loyal bodyguard and security adviser following the Battle of Naboo, succeeding Captain Panaka in that post. Initially Typho works for Padmé in her position as Queen, but when she steps down to become Naboo's representative to the Galactic Senate, Typho follows her to Coruscant. During the rise of the Separatist movement, Senator Amidala experiences an increased number of threats to her safety, including the bombing of her starship and the release of venomous kouhuns in her apartment. Captain Typho endorses a plan to send Padmé back to Naboo in disguise under the protection of Anakin Skywalker. Meanwhile, Padmé's handmaiden Dormé stays on Coruscant as a decoy, Captain Typho by her side.

Battle scarred
Though Captain Typho lost his left eye, it does not shake his devotion to the Royal House of Naboo.

KIT FISTO

APPEARANCES II, CW, III **SPECIES** Nautolan
HOMEWORLD Glee Anselm **AFFILIATION** Jedi

As the Jedi Council's only amphibious member, Kit Fisto leads the Republic's armies to victory on strategic waterworlds across the galaxy. His Nautolan physiology makes him ideally suited to battle above and below the waves. During the Clone Wars, Master Fisto first sees action on Geonosis, serving as one of the Jedi who infiltrate the execution arena to battle Count Dooku's droid soldiers. Later in the war, he trails General Grievous to the third moon of Vassek, only to find his team trapped inside Grievous's fortress, where he witnesses his former Padawan Nahdar Vebb lose his life to Grievous's pet roggwart. Fisto dives under the waves again to save Prince Lee-Char of Mon Cala from a Separatist insurrection led by Karkarodon commander Riff Tamson and backed by the revolutionary forces of the Quarren Isolation League.

As the Clone Wars begin to wind down, Mace Windu learns that Supreme Chancellor Palpatine has been successfully living a double life as a Sith Lord. Kit Fisto, as well as Masters Agen Kolar and Saesee Tiin, accompany Mace to the Chancellor's office to confront him and make an arrest. Instead, Palpatine reveals a hidden lightsaber and explodes into lethal motion, cutting down Fisto before the shocked Nautolan can raise his own blade in defense and block the attack.

Battle tactics
Consulting with a medical officer clone, Fisto is trying to determine what to do with a medical frigate that is approaching a Republic outpost and is believed to be infected with contagion.

Leading the charge
Fisto commands a unit of clone troopers during the fierce fighting on Geonosis. Throughout the war, Master Fisto keeps his famously good humor intact.

LUMINARA UNDULI

APPEARANCES II, CW, III
SPECIES Mirialan **HOMEWORLD** Mirial
AFFILIATION Jedi

With their matching robes and facial tattoos, Jedi Master Luminara Unduli and her Padawan Barriss Offee are an unmistakable duo during the Clone Wars. Honoring the cultural traditions of the near-humans of Mirial, Unduli selected fellow Mirialan Barriss Offee as her apprentice.

By the time the Clone Wars break out, Offee's skills have grown enough for Unduli to trust Offee in combat,

and both Jedi serve as members of the vanguard force that participates in the Battle of Geonosis. As the war takes shape, Master Unduli accepts a command rank and takes control of the 41st Elite Corps, working closely with Clone Commander Gree. She later helps escort high-ranking Trade Federation captive Nute Gunray, only to be surprised when Separatist commander Asajj Ventress boards the vessel to free its prisoner. Luminara rejects Padawan Ahsoka Tano's offer of help and loses the fight against Ventress, allowing Nute Gunray to escape Republic custody.

During the Second Battle of Geonosis, Master Unduli pursues Separatist leader

Poggle the Lesser into a remote network of catacombs where insectoid matron Queen Karina keeps her nest. Overwhelmed by Queen Karina's drones, Luminara nearly becomes an unwilling host for mind-controlling brain worms, until Anakin and Obi-Wan free her.

As the Clone Wars draw to a close, Luminara participates in the series of battles known as the Outer Rim Sieges. She leads Commander Gree and the 41st Elite Corps to the contested planet of Kashyyyk, the Wookiee homeworld where Master Yoda is also stationed. Though the Republic forces win the day against the Separatist invaders, the Jedi generals cannot foresee the shocking betrayal of their clone troops. When Darth Sidious transmits the top-secret Order 66 to all clone commanders, Gree and his clone troopers turn their weapons on the Jedi. Unlike Master Yoda, Luminara does not escape their ambush.

In hot pursuit
On Geonosis, Luminara pilots a speeder bike to chase down the fleeing Poggle the Lesser.

BARRISS OFFEE

APPEARANCES II, CW **SPECIES** Mirialan
HOMEWORLD Mirial **AFFILIATION** Jedi

Barriss Offee, the Padawan of revered Jedi Master Luminara Unduli, serves with distinction during the Clone Wars until she turns on the Republic in a shocking act of betrayal. Both Offee and Luminara share the heritage of the Mirialan people, though they share a much stronger bond as Jedi. When the Clone Wars break out, Master Unduli feels her student has earned the right to fight her own battles. Offee fights at Geonosis and later returns to the planet to target an advanced droid factory. Teaming

up with Padawan Ahsoka Tano, Offee damages the facility and helps bring about a Republic victory. On the way back from Geonosis, Offee and Ahsoka struggle to contain an outbreak of mind-controlling brain worms aboard their starship. Offee falls under the influence of the worms, but Ahsoka breaks their spell by exposing them to freezing temperatures.

Later in the war, following Offee's participation in the Battle of Umbara, a mysterious explosion at the Jedi Temple causes multiple deaths and prompts an investigation that names Ahsoka as the chief suspect. Placed on trial and forced to defend her loyalties, Ahsoka is exonerated only after Anakin's own investigation reveals Barriss Offee as

the culprit. Offee makes a full confession, claiming that the Jedi had become the aggressors in the war and that her actions were a justifiable blow against a corrupt, misguided Order.

Clone Wars combatant
Barriss Offee struggles with her role as a warrior, eventually falling to the dark side and concluding that the Jedi have lost their way.

Jedi no more
After refusing the Jedi Council's offer of
reinstatement, Ahsoka exits the Temple with
Anakin in pursuit. Despite her former Master's
pleas, Ahsoka remains steadfast in her decision,
trusting in the Force to reveal her new path.

AHSOKA WALKS AWAY

"I'm sorry, Master, but I'm not coming back."
AHSOKA TANO

Her faith in the Jedi badly shaken after she is framed for treason, Ahsoka Tano refuses to return to the Order.

Darkness clouds the Force, hiding the sinister plot to rip asunder the Jedi Order. When a Jedi Temple hangar is bombed, Anakin Skywalker and his Padawan, Ahsoka Tano, are recalled to Coruscant to investigate. After a series of events falsely suggests Ahsoka may be part of the treasonous scheme, the Council refuses to support her. She flees, only to be captured by Anakin's forces when the true traitor leads her into a trap. Ahsoka is expelled from the Order to stand trial before a military tribunal. Certain of her innocence, Anakin continues his hunt for the truth. Clues provided by an unlikely ally, former Sith acolyte Asajj Ventress, help him clear Ahsoka in the nick of time.

ONE LESS JEDI
Ahsoka's expulsion and trial shake her beliefs to their core, giving her a clearer understanding of the ways the Jedi Order has compromised its duty to the Force by serving the political needs of the Galactic Republic. When the Jedi Council admits its mistake and proposes reinstatement with a promotion to Jedi Knight, Ahsoka refuses the offer. Taught that attachment can bring ruin to a Jedi, Ahsoka leaves the only home she has ever known, thus fulfilling the prediction of her older self on Mortis that she faced a bleak future remaining at Anakin's side. Anakin is left reeling from the loss, more alone than ever in bearing the expectations of his status as the prophesied Chosen One.

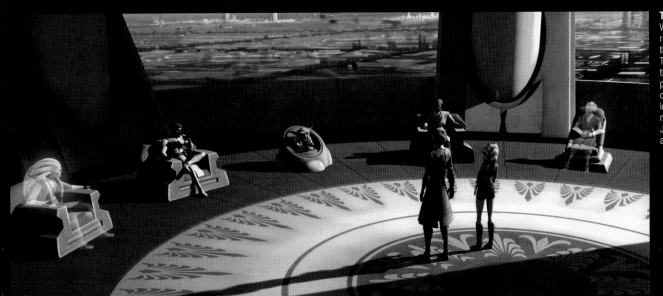

Temple bombing
When Anakin and Ahsoka report the progress of their investigation into the Temple hangar bombing, the Council urges the pair to come to a swift conclusion. Whisperings in the Senate suggest military intervention in Jedi affairs if the terrorists are not found quickly.

Quick pickup
Piloting an airspeeder, Bail Organa is on his way to pick up Yoda after his battle with Emperor Palpatine.

ZAM WESELL

APPEARANCES II **SPECIES** Clawdite
HOMEWORLD Zolan **AFFILIATION** Bounty hunter

A Clawdite shape-shifter, this bounty hunter can assume the appearance of anyone she chooses. Zam Wesell prefers to hit her targets from afar, either with her long-range sniper rifle or her remote-operated probe droids. A frequent accomplice of Jango Fett's, she accepts a job from him to assassinate Senator Padmé Amidala of Naboo. But when her quarry's Jedi guardians corner Wesell and cut off her arm, Wesell becomes a liability, whom Fett silences forever with a poisoned Kamino saberdart.

BAIL ORGANA

APPEARANCES II, CW, III, R **SPECIES** Human
HOMEWORLD Alderaan **AFFILIATION** Galactic Senate, Rebel Alliance

Though he never lives to see the end of the Empire, Bail Organa spends decades fighting its tyranny. A viceroy of the House Organa on Alderaan, Organa is elected to the Galactic Senate, where he befriends

A new hope
Organa and his wife, Queen Breha Organa, raise Anakin Skywalker's daughter Leia as their own.

like-minded politicians such as Mon Mothma of Chandrila and Padmé Amidala of Naboo. The Separatist Crisis sees Organa take up an advisory position to Supreme Chancellor Palpatine and serve on his Loyalist Committee. Given Alderaan's pacifist history, Organa strives to halt the escalation of the Clone Wars and leads relief efforts on Christophsis. With the crisis deepening, he realizes that Palpatine's war

powers threaten to give the Chancellor the authority of a dictator. Speaking out against funding additional troops, Organa finds his suspicions of foul play growing as his colleagues, such as Rodia's Onaconda Farr, die under strange circumstances.

As the Clone Wars draw to a close, Organa watches the remaining Jedi being massacred at the Jedi Temple by Republic clone soldiers. He quickly moves to safeguard two of his closest allies: Obi-Wan Kenobi and Master Yoda. After Padmé's death, Organa and his wife adopt her infant daughter, Leia. Continuing to serve on the Senate, Organa and Mon Mothma secretly plot armed resistance against Palpatine's new Empire as the Rebel Alliance starts to take shape, but the Death Star spells his doom. A single blast from the enormous battle station shatters Alderaan into fragments, killing Organa and millions more.

JANGO FETT

APPEARANCES II **SPECIES** Human
HOMEWORLD Concord Dawn **AFFILIATION** Bounty hunters, Separatists (under contract)

Jango Fett is the prime clone in the creation of the Republic's clone army, becoming the template for millions of soldiers during the Clone Wars. He earns this role after years at the top of the bounty-hunting trade, where he has expertly used his twin blaster pistols and advanced Mandalorian armor to track down fugitives. Count Dooku—calling himself Tyranus—approaches Fett with the lucrative prime clone offer shortly after the Battle of Naboo.

Though it means relocating to the distant, rain-soaked world of Kamino, Fett agrees, as long as the Kaminoan geneticists give him an unaltered clone to raise as his child. Over the next decade, Jango Fett cares for his son, Boba, as the clone army is created around him. Several design elements from Fett's equipment also feature in clone trooper armor, such as the T-shaped visor of Fett's Mandalorian battle helmet.

Alongside his sometime partner, Zam Wesell, Fett also

Flying lessons
Jango teaches his son, Boba, how to fly his prized starship, *Slave I*.

moonlights as an assassin for hire and takes on a contract from the Trade Federation's Nute Gunray to kill Senator Padmé Amidala of Naboo. When Wesell bungles the job, Fett is forced to eliminate her before she can spill her secrets to Jedi investigators. But the dart he leaves behind provides the clue that leads Obi-Wan to Kamino. Jango and Boba Fett escape the planet in their ship, *Slave I*. Later, on the planet Geonosis, the conflict between the Republic's Jedi and Count Dooku's Separatists explodes into war. Fett squares off against Jedi Master Mace Windu, but loses his head to a swipe of his enemy's lightsaber. Boba Fett, who inherits the *Slave I*, continues his father's bounty-hunting legacy.

Equipped to hunt
Fett carries a matching pair of blaster pistols. He locates his quarry using his helmet's built-in computer and wears energized armor designed with a durasteel alloy.

Evasive measures
Jango Fett uses his Z-6 compact jetpack to allow him to rocket out of the reach of his enemies.

KOUHUN

APPEARANCES II **HOMEWORLD** Indoumodo
AVERAGE SIZE 30 cm (12 in) long
HABITAT Throughout the galaxy

The kouhun is a highly venomous, multilegged arthropod with a segmented carapace and stingers on the front and rear of its body. Most victims injected with kouhun venom die within minutes. Because kouhuns easily evade security, bounty hunter Wesell employs two of them in an attempt to kill Padmé in her Coruscant apartment. Anakin and Obi-Wan exterminate the creatures.

COLEMAN TREBOR

APPEARANCES II **SPECIES** Vurk
HOMEWORLD Sembla **AFFILIATION** Jedi

Coleman Trebor earns his place on the Jedi Council during the Separatist Crisis. When he and the other Council members learn of a Separatist force on Geonosis, Master Trebor joins the vanguard to stop Count Dooku before the situation explodes into all-out war. While ambushing Dooku in his viewing box at the execution arena, Trebor is shot and killed by Jango Fett.

"Adversity in war is a constant. The enemy won't play fair." SHAAK TI

SHAAK TI

APPEARANCES II, CW, III **SPECIES** Togruta
HOMEWORLD Shili **AFFILIATION** Jedi

Jedi Master Shaak Ti advances to the Jedi Council in the years leading up to the Clone Wars. Surviving the Battle of Geonosis, she assumes a leadership role among the Republic's newly activated clone troopers. During her deployment on Kamino, Shaak Ti leads a counterattack on the combined forces of General Grievous and Asajj Ventress. Joined by Obi-Wan and Anakin, she rallies the clones, ordering them to take on Separatist aqua droids and other robotic soldiers. Her heroic actions prevent Kamino's vital clone laboratories from falling into enemy hands. At the end of the Clone Wars, Shaak Ti fails to prevent General Grievous from slipping onto Coruscant and kidnapping Supreme Chancellor Palpatine.

High-ranking Jedi
Jedi Master Shaak Ti is stationed on Kamino to keep an eye on the vital cloning operations during the war.

Warm welcome
Dexter Jettster is always glad to see his old friend Obi-Wan Kenobi.

DEXTER JETTSTER

APPEARANCES II **SPECIES** Besalisk
HOMEWORLD Ojom **AFFILIATION** None

The four-armed proprietor and chef of Dex's Diner in Coruscant, Jettster is a brawny Besalisk with a colorful past who is an old friend of Obi-Wan's. Before the outbreak of the Clone Wars, Obi-Wan shows Dex a strange object, which he identifies as a deadly Kamino saberdart, something he had encountered in his former life as a prospector on the planet Subterrel. Dex urges his old friend to continue his investigations on Kamino, which leads Obi-Wan to uncover a mysterious clone army that has been secretly constructed by the Republic. Meanwhile, Dex looks after his loyal customers, ignoring the galaxy-shaking events taking place beyond his humble diner.

JOCASTA NU

APPEARANCES II, CW **SPECIES** Human **HOMEWORLD** Coruscant **AFFILIATION** Jedi

As Chief Librarian of the Jedi Archives, Jocasta Nu has complete confidence in her records, claiming that if an item isn't there, it doesn't exist. Obi-Wan disproves this statement when he learns that the planet Kamino's coordinates have been inexplicably deleted from the library's star maps. During the Clone Wars, Nu is knocked out by Cato Parasitti, a shape-shifter who takes her place until she is unmasked by Ahsoka Tano.

Betrayed
Aayla Secura loses her life on Felucia when the clone troopers she commands turn their weapons on her.

First warrior
At Geonosis, Aayla Secura fought in the earliest battle of the Clone Wars.

AAYLA SECURA

APPEARANCES II, CW, III **SPECIES** Twi'lek
HOMEWORLD Ryloth **AFFILIATION** Jedi

Jedi Knight Aayla Secura is among the first rescuers sent to Geonosis to retrieve Obi-Wan Kenobi, Anakin Skywalker, and Padmé Amidala from the execution arena. She distinguishes herself in combat against the Separatist droid armies, and as the Clone Wars begin, she is in charge of a Republic fleet. An early engagement with a Separatist armada ends badly, with Secura's ship badly damaged by rocket droids. Anakin and Ahsoka Tano come to Secura's aid, but only escape the battle alive by making a highly dangerous, blind hyperspace jump. Their vessel crash-lands on Maridun, where Secura seeks medical assistance from the native Lurmen tribe for the injured Anakin. Secura explains to the leader of the Lurmen that the Republic does not support violence, but despite her words, the actions of Separatist General Lok Durd soon bring the war to Maridun. Thankfully, Secura's heroism brings an end to Durd's deadly defoliator weapon.

Later in the war, Secura accepts a post on Coruscant alongside such high-ranking Jedi as Yoda and Mace Windu. When a strange Zillo beast, brought to the capital for scientific study, escapes and rampages through the city, Secura and Yoda distract the titanic creature in order to give Supreme Chancellor Palpatine enough time to avert its attacks.

By the end of the Clone Wars, Secura achieves the rank of Jedi Master and takes command of the 327th Star Corps, working closely with Commander Bly. The Outer Rim Sieges look as if they will be the final stage in the war. Secura, confident of the Republic's imminent triumph, accepts an assignment to Felucia. But as she leads the 327th Star Corps through the planet's jungles, Commander Bly receives the command to initiate Order 66. Bly's clone troopers open fire, shooting the unsuspecting Secura in the back.

Jedi command
Hologram communication allows Aayla Secura to consult with other Jedi commanders at any given time.

Battle ready
Anakin, Ahsoka, and other Jedi shared Secura's role as battlefield commanders.

QUEEN JAMILLIA

APPEARANCES II **SPECIES** Human
HOMEWORLD Naboo **AFFILIATION** Royal
House of Naboo

As Queen of Naboo, Jamillia
succeeds Padmé in that role and
is in turn succeeded by Queen
Neeyutnee. In light of Padmé's
popularity following the Battle
of Naboo, Jamillia urges her
predecessor to continue
public service by
becoming Naboo's
representative to the
Galactic Senate.

End of a droid
After Arfour is attacked by buzz droids during the Battle
of Coruscant, she is dismantled and there isn't enough
time during the chaotic dogfight to repair her.

Fully loaded
As an astromech unit,
R4-P17 is packed with
tools and gadgets,
including an arc welder
and a fire extinguisher.

R4-P17

APPEARANCES II, CW, III **MANUFACTURER** Industrial
Automaton **TYPE** Astromech droid **AFFILIATION** Republic

R4-P17, known familiarly as Arfour, is the astromech
droid assigned to Obi-Wan's Jedi starfighter. Arfour
has a female personality and shows great bravery in
the face of Separatist aggression. As a product of
Industrial Automaton, Arfour is designed to serve as a
hyperspace navigator for calculating lightspeed jumps
and also as a general-purpose repair and maintenance
droid. Prior to the Clone Wars, R4-P17 joins up with
Obi-Wan as the plug-in counterpart for his Delta-7
starfighter. When Obi-Wan's investigation into
suspicious dealings on Coruscant leads him from
Kamino to Geonosis, Arfour accompanies her
Master through a hazardous asteroid field in
pursuit of Jango Fett. She continues in this role
throughout the Clone Wars, transferring from the
Delta-7 to the new Eta-2 interceptor as Obi-Wan
runs missions to Teth, Rodia, Mandalore, and other
trouble spots across the galaxy. At the end of the
Clone Wars, Arfour and Obi-Wan team-up one last
time during the Battle of Coruscant. As Obi-Wan
pilots his interceptor through a cloud of enemies,
a swarm of buzz droids attaches to his ship, bent
on sabotage. The droids pull Arfour's dome loose
from her head, ending her operational life. Obi-Wan
replaces Arfour with another droid, R4-G9, for his
mission to Utapau.

TAUN WE

APPEARANCES II **SPECIES** Kaminoan
HOMEWORLD Kamino **AFFILIATION** Cloners

This graceful Kaminoan is the project
coordinator of the Republic's clone army
and serves Lama Su as the administrative
aide to the prime minister. When Obi-Wan
arrives on Kamino, Taun We arranges
for a meeting between the visitor and
Prime Minister Lama Su to discuss
the progress of the cloning project.
She later brings Obi-Wan to visit the
prime clone, Jango Fett, where she
introduces the Jedi Master to Jango
and his clone son, Boba.

PRIME MINISTER
LAMA SU

APPEARANCES II, CW **SPECIES** Kaminoan
HOMEWORLD Kamino **AFFILIATION** Cloners

The prime minister of Kamino during
the years leading up to the Battle of
Geonosis, Lama Su filled the order for
the vast clone trooper army on behalf
of a buyer he knew only as Sifo-Dyas.
It is likely that Lama Su isn't concerned
that Darth Sidious and Count Dooku
have secretly arranged for the army's
creation, and concentrates instead on the
performance of his ready-made soldiers.
During the Clone Wars, Lama Su continues
to oversee new batches of troopers as they
move from Kamino to the frontlines.

> "We're just clones, sir.
> We're meant to be expendable." **CLONE SERGEANT**

CLONE TROOPER

Lacking an army to fight Count Dooku's Separatists, the Republic took delivery of thousands of clone troopers. But the clones existed only to make Palpatine into the Emperor by eliminating the Jedi Knights.

APPEARANCES II, CW, III **SPECIES** Human **HOMEWORLD** Kamino **AFFILIATION** Republic

SECRET CREATION

Supreme Chancellor Palpatine and Count Dooku join forces to create a clone army in the genetics laboratories of Kamino. Each clone, an altered copy of bounty hunter Jango Fett, grows at an accelerated rate and receives extensive training in battlefield tactics. Some fill elite roles as Advanced Recon Commandos, while others study tactics to become officers. Yet none of the clones know the details of Palpatine's scheme, and when the order comes to go into action as the soldiers of the Grand Army of the Republic, the clones do their duty and fight with honor.

Programmed learning
Young clones receive educational instruction *(above)*. Obi-Wan Kenobi reviews the inner workings of the cloning facility on Kamino *(right)*.

General Yoda
The wise Jedi Master leads a squad of new clone troopers during the Battle of Geonosis.

FIRST GENERATION

After Master Yoda takes delivery of the first batch of clones, they quickly see action at the Battle of Geonosis. The earliest clone troopers wear all-white armor with fins on the top of their helmets. On Geonosis, they deploy their heavy equipment, including AT-TE walkers and LAAT/i gunships, and achieve a hard-fought victory against the Separatists.

Preparing a counterstrike
Three first-generation clones take the initiative against a wave of Separatist battle droids.

THE CLONE WARS

The Republic's clone troopers give the conflict between the Republic and the Separatists its name: the Clone Wars. Shipping out to every part of the galaxy on vast warships, the clones fight on Christophsis, the Kaliida Nebula, Maridun, Ryloth, and elsewhere. With the Jedi as generals, clone troopers such as Captain Rex and Commander Cody work closely with Anakin Skywalker, Obi-Wan Kenobi, and others. The original armor is retired in favor of more advanced Phase 2 armor, more easily customized with patterns and colors.

Treachery
Jedi Master Aayla Secura is shot in the back by the clone troopers she once commanded.

ORDER 66

Palpatine arranges for the Kaminoans to give each clone trooper an inhibitor chip implant. This ensures the clones will be unable to resist certain commands, in particular one designed to wipe out the Jedi, code-named Order 66. The conspiracy nearly comes to light when one clone's inhibitor chip malfunctions, but the evidence is suppressed by the Kaminoans. When the Clone Wars come to a close, Darth Sidious issues Order 66, causing the clone troopers to turn on the Jedi.

Perfect soldier
Clone troopers are bred to never question orders and are identical so that they can easily share all armor and equipment.

timeline

Placing an order
Manipulated by Count Dooku, Jedi Master Sifo-Dyas commissions the Kaminoan cloners to grow an army for the Republic.

▲ Growing clones
Bounty hunter Jango Fett becomes the template for the clones, who receive advanced military training.

Ready for action
Soon after Obi-Wan discovers the clone army, it sees action against the Separatists in the Battle of Geonosis.

▲ Shipping out
With the Clone Wars in full swing, the Republic sends clone troopers into battlefields across the galaxy.

Further training
More clones continue to roll out from Kamino, leading to a Separatist attack on the cloning facility.

Serving with Jedi
With Jedi Knights as their commanders, clone troopers fight at Orto Plutonia, Ryloth, Lola Sayu, and elsewhere.

▲ Umbara
Clones show heroism on Umbara, where a duplicitous Jedi general tries to sabotage their efforts.

Coruscant and Utapau
Late in the war, clone troopers defend the capital and pursue General Grievous in the Outer Rim.

Order 66
After receiving orders from Palpatine, the clones turn on their Jedi commanders.

▲ Jedi Temple
Anakin leads clone troopers into the temple to kill any Jedi who remain.

"He's no good to me dead." BOBA FETT

BOBA FETT

A clone of Jango Fett who is raised as Jango's son, Boba Fett survives the Clone Wars to become a relentless and highly paid bounty hunter.

APPEARANCES II, CW, IV, V, VI SPECIES Human HOMEWORLD Kamino AFFILIATION Bounty hunter

CLONE ORIGINS
When Jango Fett agrees to become the genetic template for a clone army being grown on Kamino, he requests an unaltered clone to raise as the heir to his legacy. For 10 years, Boba Fett grows up in the sterile environs of Kamino's Tipoca City, occasionally accompanying his father on the ship *Slave I* to track down bounties for money. Obi-Wan Kenobi eventually uncovers the Kamino cloning operation, prompting Jango and Boba to flee to Geonosis. There, a Jedi strike force raids the execution arena and overwhelms the Separatist defenders. The leader of the Jedi, Mace Windu, uses his lightsaber to behead Jango Fett.

His father's legacy
When Jango dies on Geonosis, Boba continues his father's work. He carries a grudge against the Jedi, and Mace Windu in particular.

TRACKING DOWN HAN
Over the years, Boba uses the *Slave I* and a customized suit of Mandalorian armor to become the galaxy's most notorious bounty hunter. After the Battle of Hoth, Darth Vader assembles a group of top bounty hunters to find Han's *Millennium Falcon*. Boba arranges a trap for Han at Cloud City, which ends with Han being safely encased in a slab of carbonite. Boba delivers Han to Jabba the Hutt and is present at Jabba's palace when Luke Skywalker attempts a rescue. During a fight at the Great Pit of Carkoon, Boba's jetpack malfunctions and he falls into the mouth of the Sarlacc monster.

Rough crowd
The young Boba receives tips on the bounty hunting trade from *(left to right)* Bossk, Castas, and Aurra Sing, among others.

LEARNING THE ROPES
The orphaned Boba finds guidance from assassin Aurra Sing. Joined by bounty hunters Bossk and Castas, Fett poses as a clone cadet and causes the crash of the Republic vessel *Endurance*. Fett is captured by the Republic on Florrum, but later pulls together a new team to execute a hovertrain robbery on Quarzite.

The hunt for Han Solo
The Dark Lord hires only the best bounty hunters to track the *Millennium Falcon* and its passengers *(above)*. With Han trapped in carbonite, Boba completes another successful hunt *(right)*.

Battle hardened

Boba Fett's career as a professional hunter is legendary, and the scrapes and dents of his armor attest to his numerous last-minute escapes and near-death experiences. He is considered by many to be the best bounty hunter in the galaxy.

timeline

▲ Young clone
A cloned copy of his father, Jango, Boba grows up in the laboratories of Kamino.

Death of Jango
Boba's father dies while fighting Mace Windu on Geonosis, after which Boba inherits the starship *Slave I.*

Becoming a hunter
Boba joins Bossk, Aurra Sing, and others to learn the tricks of the bounty hunting trade.

▲ Looking for revenge
During the Clone Wars, Boba tries to kill Mace Windu in retaliation for his father's death.

▲ Working for Jabba
Many jobs bring Boba into the employ of notorious gangster Jabba the Hutt on Tatooine.

▲ Cloud City
Boba works with Vader to set a trap for Han and his friends. He leaves with his bounty, Han frozen in carbonite, aboard the *Slave I.*

Jabba's palace
Boba delivers the carbonite slab containing Han's body to Jabba's palace, where it hangs on the wall.

Sarlacc
During Han's execution, Luke springs a surprise rescue, during which Boba falls into the mouth of the Sarlacc.

YODA'S TRIALS

"Let the Force guide, I will." YODA

Yoda knows more about the nature of the Force than almost any Jedi Knight, but his experiences on a mysterious planet teach him the astonishing secret of immortality.

Guided by the spirit of Qui-Gon Jinn, who speaks of a way to retain one's consciousness after death, Yoda journeys to a strange world near the center of the galaxy. He finds a place rich in the Force, covered with thriving plant life and tendrils of light that extend deep into the planet's core. Five Force Priestesses intercept him, each identical save for the masks they wear. Yoda learns that each priestess represents a specific emotion—joy, anger, confusion, sadness, and serenity—and that he will need to pass their trials to gain the knowledge that Qui-Gon spoke of.

LIFE IN THE FORCE
The first trial sees Yoda face off against a twisted, shadowy version of himself. Only by admitting that the shade is part of his true nature is Yoda able to overcome the challenge. The second trial takes place in the Valley of Extinction, where Yoda sees a vision of an alternate present where the Clone Wars never happened and Count Dooku remained a loyal member of the Jedi Order. Yoda rejects this tempting falsehood, winning the approval of the Force Priestesses. For his third trial, Yoda travels to the Sith homeworld of Moraband. There he confronts a vision of Sith Lord Darth Bane and battles Darth Sidious inside an illusion, eventually emerging victorious. In the years to come, Yoda will perfect the ability he gained from the Force Priestesses by living on in the Force after his physical body passes into death.

Force priestesses
These enigmatic beings can fly and disappear or reappear at will. There is nothing but emptiness behind their masks.

Fateful meeting
Owen and Beru meet Padmé Amidala and Anakin Skywalker, the couple whose son Luke they will later raise as their own (right). By the time Luke becomes a teenager, time and Tatooine's harsh climate have left their marks on Owen's visage (below).

OWEN LARS

APPEARANCES II, III, IV **SPECIES** Human
HOMEWORLD Tatooine **AFFILIATION** None

A pragmatic and serious-minded Tatooine moisture farmer, Owen Lars has learned his strong work ethic from his father, Cliegg Lars. When his father marries Shmi Skywalker, a former slave, Owen is drawn into the complicated life of Shmi's son Anakin. Owen and Anakin meet for the first time following Shmi's kidnapping at the hands of Tusken Raiders. Anakin manages to retrieve Shmi's lifeless body and returns to the Lars's farm, while Cliegg dies not long after from wounds sustained in the search for his wife. Owen and his new wife Beru inherit the moisture farm and agree to Obi-Wan Kenobi's request that they raise Anakin's son Luke as their own. Many years later, and despite Owen's best efforts to keep Luke safe from the Empire, stormtroopers arrive at the Lars homestead, and on orders from Darth Vader execute both Owen and Beru.

> "I guess I'm your stepbrother.
> I had a feeling you might
> show up someday."
> **OWEN LARS TO ANAKIN**

BERU WHITESUN LARS

APPEARANCES II, III, IV **SPECIES** Human **HOMEWORLD** Tatooine
AFFILIATION None

Tatooine native Beru Whitesun falls in love with Owen Lars just prior to the Battle of Geonosis and is present at the Lars moisture farm when Anakin Skywalker arrives in search of his mother Shmi. Beru and Owen later marry, and Obi-Wan Kenobi places Anakin's infant son Luke in their care. Where Owen presents a gruff face to the boy, Beru shows a more caring side and does her best to raise Luke, while keeping his true parentage a secret. When Imperial stormtroopers arrive at the farm searching for the droids R2-D2 and C-3PO, Beru and Owen die under the blasters of a stormtrooper execution squad.

Eyes on the future
Beru Lars plays a vital role in shaping the destiny of the galaxy when she agrees to raise Luke Skywalker (below). Her sensitive and nurturing nature instill in Luke a love of family and a strong moral sense (above).

CLIEGG LARS

APPEARANCES II **SPECIES** Human
HOMEWORLD Tatooine **AFFILIATION** None

The tough and strong-willed Cliegg Lars lives as a moisture farmer on Tatooine with his wife, former slave Shmi Skywalker. He loses his love—and his right leg—to a hunting party of Tusken Raiders. Anakin Skywalker retrieves his mother's body, but Cliegg dies shortly after, leaving the farm to his son Owen and Owen's wife Beru.

POGGLE THE LESSER

APPEARANCES II, CW, III **SPECIES** Geonosian
HOMEWORLD Geonosis **AFFILIATION**
Separatists

Archduke Poggle the Lesser controls the droid factories of Geonosis during the Clone Wars. Backed by Darth Sidious, Poggle manufactures millions of B1 battle droids for the Trade Federation and later produces the new super battle droid on behalf of Count Dooku's Separatists. When Poggle's warriors capture Obi-Wan Kenobi, Anakin Skywalker, and Padmé Amidala on Geonosis, Poggle orders their executions, and remains on the scene to fight the Republic's invading clone troopers. Later in the Clone Wars, Poggle destroys his droid factory to prevent it from falling into the hands of the Republic. He hopes to find refuge with the Geonosian Queen Karina, but instead becomes a prisoner of war. Although he escapes custody, he dies with the rest of the Separatist Council on Mustafar.

Commanding presence
Poggle is in charge of all Geonosians and most of the robotic products produced in their factories, such as this T-series tactical droid.

WAT TAMBOR

APPEARANCES II, CW, III
SPECIES Skakoan **HOMEWORLD**
Skako **AFFILIATION** Separatists,
Techno Union

As a Skakoan, Emir Wat Tambor wears an elaborate pressure suit and speaks through an electronic loudspeaker. As lead engineer of the Techno Union, he controls the most advanced war assets in the galaxy. Tambor serves on the Separatist Council during the Clone Wars and briefly becomes a Republic prisoner following the Battle of Ryloth. He later perishes on Mustafar.

Environmental armor
The atmosphere and pressure of Wat Tambor's home planet Skako is so different from the galactic standard that his suit is the only thing keeping him alive when off-world.

SHU MAI

APPEARANCES II, III **SPECIES** Gossam **HOMEWORLD** Castell
AFFILIATION Commerce Guild, Separatists

As Presidente of the Commerce Guild, Shu Mai controls the pooled financial resources of some of the galaxy's largest corporations. She uses her influence to gain a seat on the Separatist Council, but tells Count Dooku that the Guild will only covertly support his movement. It is a secret allegiance that leads to her death on Mustafar.

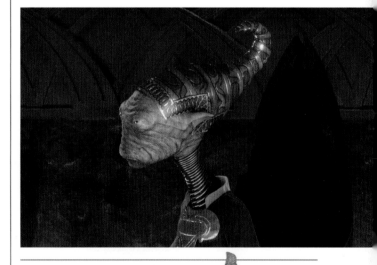

PASSEL ARGENTE

APPEARANCES I, II, III **SPECIES** Koorivar
HOMEWORLD Kooriva **AFFILIATION**
Corporate Alliance, Separatists

After winning the post of Magistrate of the Corporate Alliance, Passel Argente serves in the Galactic Senate and is among the senators who support Chancellor Valorum's removal from office. Argente resigns from office to become a member of the Separatist Council, and is among those killed on Mustafar.

"I have become more powerful than any Jedi. Even you." COUNT DOOKU

COUNT DOOKU

No one suspected that Count Dooku was a Sith. Yet the ex-Jedi worked as Darth Sidious's apprentice, secretly pulling the strings of a false war that tore the galaxy in two.

APPEARANCES II, CW, III **SPECIES** Human **HOMEWORLD** Serenno **AFFILIATION** Separatists

SEPARATIST LEADER

Jedi Master Dooku takes Qui-Gon Jinn as his Padawan, but leaves the Jedi Order after Qui-Gon's death on Naboo. Seduced to the dark side of the Force, Dooku resigns from the Order and learns the ways of the Sith from Supreme Chancellor Palpatine, also known as Darth Sidious. Dooku assumes the Sith name Darth Tyranus and supervises the creation of a massive clone army on Kamino. He also emerges as the leader of a Separatist movement that persuades thousands of star systems to split away from the Republic. On Geonosis, war finally breaks out between the Separatists and the Republic. Dooku slips away safely after a lightsaber duel with Master Yoda.

Geonosis escape
Pursued by a Republic gunship, Dooku flees on a speeder bike to a hangar so that he can abandon the Battle of Geonosis.

Sith Master
While Count Dooku controls the Separatist forces, his Master Darth Sidious rules over the Republic. Between them, they plot to bring the galaxy under Sith control.

CLONE WARS

Count Dooku leads the Separatists' battle droid armies, aided by his dark-side apprentice Asajj Ventress and the cyborg General Grievous. After failing to pit the Hutts against the Republic by kidnapping Jabba's son, Rotta, Dooku briefly becomes a hostage of the pirate king Hondo Ohnaka. Later, when Darth Sidious orders Dooku to eliminate Ventress, he abandons his apprentice to her fate and obtains the Zabrak warrior Savage Opress as a replacement bodyguard from Mother Talzin's Nightsisters. Ventress and the Nightsisters try to assassinate Dooku, but he retaliates by obliterating their Dathomir stronghold. When the Separatists strike at Coruscant, Dooku obeys the orders of his Master Darth Sidious and waits aboard the flagship *Invisible Hand* to set a trap for Anakin Skywalker.

THE ENDGAME

Despite his own machinations, Dooku never suspects that Sidious plans to remove him all along. Dooku defeats Obi-Wan Kenobi and challenges Anakin while Palpatine watches, pretending to be a helpless prisoner. Because Dooku has beaten Anakin before, on Geonosis, he does not expect the Jedi Knight to put up much of a fight. Anakin, however, has gained considerable power over the years and engages Dooku in an intense duel. After disarming his opponent, Anakin picks up Dooku's fallen lightsaber and holds both blades to Dooku's throat. Dooku hopes his Master will intervene, but when Palpatine growls "Kill him," Dooku finally understands the inevitability of Sith betrayal.

Playing his part
Dooku believes that his Master will come to his aid if his duel with Anakin grows dangerous, but he is unprepared for Palpatine's duplicity.

From Jedi to Sith
When Count Dooku grows disillusioned with the Jedi Order, no argument can convince him to remain. He seems devoted to the Separatist movement, but his true allegiance is to the Sith and his secret Sith identity, Darth Tyranus.

Leaving the Order
Dooku resigns from the Jedi ranks following the Battle of Naboo and assumes his hereditary title of Count.

Clone army
As Darth Tyranus, Dooku commissions the creation of millions of clone troopers on Kamino.

Rise of the Separatists
Over the next several years, Count Dooku emerges as a political leader and encourages star systems to withdraw from the Republic.

▲ **Separatist summit**
Dooku holds a meeting on Geonosis to gain the support of the galaxy's most powerful corporations.

▲ **Fighting Yoda**
After the Republic attacks Dooku's operations on Geonosis, Dooku escapes, but only after facing Yoda, his former teacher.

False war
The Clone Wars begin, but the Republic does not know that Dooku has arranged the conflict on orders from Supreme Chancellor Palpatine.

▲ **Hostage**
During the war, Dooku briefly becomes the prisoner of the pirate king Hondo Ohnaka.

▲ **Savage Opress**
Dooku dismisses his apprentice Asajj Ventress and recruits a tattooed Zabrak warrior in her place.

Nightsisters
To get revenge on Mother Talzin for arranging an attempt on his life, Dooku wipes out the Nightsisters in the Battle of Dathomir.

Death
Above Coruscant, Dooku duels Anakin Skywalker but loses his life to the young Jedi.

SAN HILL

APPEARANCES II, III **SPECIES** Muun
HOMEWORLD Scipio **AFFILIATION**
InterGalactic Banking Clan, Separatists

As the Chairman of the InterGalactic Banking Clan, San Hill wields considerable influence. Just prior to the Battle of Geonosis, he meets in secret with Count Dooku and pledges the support of his financial cartel to the Separatists. Along with others in the Separatist Council, he is murdered by Anakin Skywalker on Mustafar.

MASSIFF

APPEARANCES II, CW **HOMEWORLD** Various
AVERAGE SIZE 1 m (3 ft) high **HABITAT** Desert

Massiffs are snarling hunters found on both Tatooine and Geonosis. Though their powerful bites are dangerous, trained massiffs are employed by many, including Tusken Raider tribes, Weequay pirates, and clone troopers, as guard beasts. The spines on a massiff's back provide an extra level of defense, and the creature's large eyes allow it to see well in nighttime conditions.

ONACONDA FARR

APPEARANCES I, II, CW **SPECIES** Rodian
HOMEWORLD Rodia
AFFILIATION Galactic Senate

Republic Senator Onaconda Farr kidnaps Senator Amidala on behalf of the Separatists when she visits his homeworld, Rodia. Farr later delivers Trade Federation Viceroy Nute Gunray into custody and is welcomed back into the Senate. When Farr joins forces with Senator Bail Organa to stop the deregulation of the banks in order to help the Republic finance the war, his aide poisons him for the benefit of the Separatists.

ORRAY

APPEARANCES II **HOMEWORLD** Geonosis
AVERAGE SIZE 2 m (7 ft) high,
3 m (10 ft) long **HABITAT** Desert

Orrays serve as mounts for picadors in the Geonosian execution arena. Due to their strength, Geonosians use orrays to haul heavy loads, including the carts that carry condemned prisoners into the arena. The tamed orrays in the arena have had their tails removed; metal caps cover their tail stumps.

REEK

APPEARANCES II, CW **HOMEWORLD** Ylesia,
Codian Moon **AVERAGE SIZE** 2 m (6 ft) high,
4 m (13 ft) long **HABITAT** Grasslands

Reeks are three-horned herbivores with stubborn attitudes and a dangerous headlong charge. In the execution arena on Geonosis, reeks are used to threaten prisoners, and these specimens have rings through their noses that their Geonosian handlers use to keep them under control. The animals are found on Ylesia and the Codian Moon but have been exported across the galaxy due to their strength and ability to resist injury. When Anakin faces a reek in the arena, he calms the creature by using the Force and then hitches a ride on its back. Sadly, the reek proves no match for a blaster pistol—bounty hunter Jango Fett takes it out with a single shot.

Warning signs
When a reek paws at the ground, it is preparing to charge at its target *(above).* An orray and its handler provoke the reek into a suitable frenzy *(right).*

ACKLAY

APPEARANCES II **HOMEWORLD** Vendaxa
AVERAGE SIZE 3 m (10 ft) high
HABITAT Land and water

The acklay is a gigantic amphibious crustacean originally from Vendaxa. Protected by a hard carapace, it scuttles around on six pointed legs and uses its claws to spear prey. It has a mouth filled with sharp teeth and uses an organ beneath its chin to sense the body electricity of its prey. On Geonosis, acklays are used as killer beasts inside the execution arena. Geonosian picadors keep the larger creatures under control by jabbing at them with long-handled spears. Obi-Wan Kenobi nearly loses his life to an acklay inside the arena, avoiding the beast's claws until he retrieves his lightsaber and finishes off the acklay.

Deadly standoff
Armed with a spear, Obi-Wan faces off against an acklay in the execution arena.

Predator and prey
An angry nexu bares its teeth at the Geonosian wrangler.

NEXU

APPEARANCES II **HOMEWORLD** Cholganna
AVERAGE SIZE 1 m (3 ft) high,
2 m (7 ft) long **HABITAT** Forests

The nexu is a feline-like predator with multiple eyes and a long, hairless tail. Nexus evolved on the forested planet Cholganna and have spread off-world, owing to their value as attack beasts. Once a nexu has pinned its prey beneath its sharp claws, it bites down and savagely shakes its victim to death. Padmé Amidala faces death in the Geonosis execution arena from a fierce nexu, which first kills one of the Geonosian guards before turning its attention to her. Padmé suffers a slash from one of the nexu's claws before the animal dies after being struck by a charging reek.

ADMIRAL WULLF YULAREN

APPEARANCES CW, IV **SPECIES** Human **HOMEWORLD** Coruscant **AFFILIATION** Republic Navy, Empire

Wullf Yularen was one of the Republic's most notable fleet commanders during the Clone Wars. He had a long history of naval conflicts prior to the outbreak of war, including a loss to Admiral Trench at the Battle of Malastare Narrows. The Clone Wars saw Admiral Yularen fight at Christophsis, Ryloth, Devaron, and Geonosis, working with high-ranking Jedi at nearly every engagement. After the war, Yularen becomes a colonel in the Imperial Security Bureau and is assigned to the Death Star.

Taking command
Admiral Yularen issues orders from the bridge of his flagship, never far from the frontlines in the struggle against the Separatists.

STASS ALLIE

APPEARANCES II, III **SPECIES** Tholothian
HOMEWORLD Tholoth **AFFILIATION** Jedi

Stass Allie sits on the Jedi Council during the Clone Wars and fights bravely as a member of the Jedi strike team assigned to the First Battle of Geonosis. Stationed on Saleucami during the Outer Rim Sieges, Master Allie dies during the Jedi betrayal of Order 66. Her clone trooper escorts suddenly fire on her speeder bike, sending her into a fatal crash.

ADMIRAL TRENCH

APPEARANCES CW **SPECIES** Harch
HOMEWORLD Secundus Ando
AFFILIATION Separatists

This spider-faced Harch earned fame as a naval commander prior to the Clone Wars when he defeated Wullf Yularen in the Battle of Malastare Narrows. Named an admiral in the Separatist fleet, Trench blockades Christophsis but loses his cruiser to Anakin's stealth ship. He survives and later assumes command of Separatist operations at Ringo Vinda.

CLONE COMMANDER CODY

APPEARANCES CW, III **SPECIES** Human clone
HOMEWORLD Kamino **AFFILIATION** Republic

Assigned the designation CC-2224, this clone takes the name "Cody" and assumes command of the Republic's Ghost Company, 7th Sky Corps, and 212th Attack Battalion. Cody enjoys camaraderie with Captain Rex and fights alongside General Kenobi at Christophsis, Teth, and the Second Battle of Geonosis. He helps extract Jedi Master Even Piell from the Citadel prison on Lola Sayu and later captures Umbara's capital city, despite Master Pong Krell's treachery. At the end of the Clone Wars, Cody accompanies Obi-Wan to Utapau, where he receives Order 66. At Cody's command, an AT-TE fires at Obi-Wan, knocking him into the water.

Under orders
Cody fights side by side with Obi-Wan (left). Cody receives Order 66 (far left). The clone troopers receive orders remotely from a holographic image of their Jedi (below).

> "You swore an oath to the Republic. You have a duty."
>
> **CAPTAIN REX**

CAPTAIN REX

Assigned the designation CT-7567 on Kamino, this high-ranking clone chooses the name Rex and spends the Clone Wars working side by side with Jedi commanders.

APPEARANCES CW **SPECIES** Human **HOMEWORLD** Kamino **AFFILIATION** Republic

Commanding presence
Though he is bred for the task, Rex is a natural leader and commands other clone troopers *(far left)*. Rex is easily identified by his blue-patterned armor, and over time, the stresses of war give his face a unique character *(left)*.

PARTNER OF THE JEDI

When the Clone Wars begin, Captain Rex is assigned command of Torrent Company in the 501st Legion and immediately ships out to handle Separatist trouble spots across the galaxy. On Christophsis, Rex serves under Anakin Skywalker and Anakin's new Padawan, Ahsoka Tano. This is the beginning of a long partnership between Rex and a tightly knit group of Jedi, including Anakin, Ahsoka, and Obi-Wan Kenobi, through which Rex learns that his opinions are valued.

REPUBLIC VICTORIES

The trust between the Jedi and Captain Rex leads to Rex's participation in high-priority engagements, including the destruction of Skytop Station and the fight against General Lok Durd on Maridun. On the Rishi moon, Captain Rex and Commander Cody play vital roles in uncovering a Separatist takeover of a Republic listening post. Rex pushes for total success in every mission despite the personal risk, even becoming infected with the Blue Shadow Virus in his zeal to destroy a Separatist laboratory on Naboo. When Captain Rex leads a squad into battle, the Republic usually wins the day.

Planning the attack
Rex received advanced tactical training on Kamino, and uses his knowledge to test new battle strategies.

Fighting shadows
Anakin and Captain Rex react to a threat from hidden attackers on the shadowy world of Umbara.

GROWING DOUBTS

Not every mission is clear-cut. On Saleucami, a blaster shot from a commando droid leaves Rex near death. He recovers in the care of a fellow clone who abandoned the Republic army to live the quiet life of a farmer. Initially disgusted with the deserter, Rex learns to take a more nuanced view. In later engagements of the Clone Wars, Rex stands up for himself and his troopers when given foolish or self-sabotaging demands. On Umbara, Rex refuses to obey dangerous orders issued by Jedi Master Pong Krell, leading to Krell's exposure as a Separatist sympathizer. These experiences show Rex a different side of the war. He begins to see that duty is more than just blind obedience.

With the Jedi
Rex is one of the few clone troopers to spend extensive time with high-ranking Jedi commanders such as Anakin and Ahsoka. He has a high opinion of the Jedi, having seen their courage under fire.

Kamino
After completing his training, Rex becomes a captain in Torrent Company of the 501st Battalion.

First action
On Geonosis, Captain Rex fights alongside his fellow clone troopers against the Separatists.

▲ Battle of Christophsis
Rex serves with Anakin and Ahsoka in many engagements, including an early battle to defeat General Loathsom.

Crash landing
Stranded on Maridun, Rex guards a wounded Anakin and frees the planet from invaders.

▲ Blue Shadow Virus
While assaulting a bioweapons lab on Naboo, Rex becomes infected with the virus. Fortunately he receives the antidote in time.

▲ Another side to war
A clone trooper who abandoned the war to live in exile on Saleucami challenges Rex's views of honor and duty.

Battle-hardened
Heroism at Kamino and the Citadel demonstrates Captain Rex's value as an elite soldier.

▲ Umbara
Jedi General Pong Krell makes things difficult for Rex during the campaign to seize Umbara's capital.

▲ War continued
Rex continued to do his duty, even when his orders forced him into difficult situations. When Ahsoka fell under suspicion as a traitor, Rex helped track her down on Coruscant.

CRISIS IN THE REPUBLIC

THE CLONE WARS

▲ Taken
Her mother is forced to trade Ventress to the criminal Hal'Sted to protect their clan.

▲ Jedi training
Jedi Ky Narec observes Ventress's Force sensitivity and trains her until he is murdered.

The bet
Ventress attempts to bring Toydaria into the Separatist fold, but loses both a bet to Yoda and the King's allegiance.

Liberating Nute Gunray
Dooku dispatches Ventress to free Nute Gunray, who is being imprisoned and questioned by the Republic.

Dooku's betrayal
Sensing Ventress's growing strength in the Force, Sidious orders Count Dooku to kill his apprentice.

Making a monster
Ventress recruits Nightbrother Savage Opress, whom the Nightsisters offer to Count Dooku as a new apprentice.

▼ Nightsister massacre
General Grievous invades Dathomir and wipes out the Nightsister clan. Mother Talzin disappears, leaving Ventress alone.

Train heist
Ventress alters the deal when an unexpected twist arises in a bounty hunter team-up with Boba Fett.

▲ Unexpected rescuer
Seeking to collect the bounty for Savage, Ventress instead ends up rescuing Obi-Wan Kenobi from Opress and Maul.

▲ Unlikely ally
Ventress helps Anakin Skywalker clear Ahsoka Tano of treason charges by providing clues to the real traitor's identity.

"Now you fall... as all Jedi must." ASAJJ VENTRESS

ASAJJ VENTRESS

Her life marred by tragedy—from the death of a Jedi mentor to a Sith master who wants her dead—Asajj Ventress is a lethal assassin with her own agenda: to be seen as a true Sith.

APPEARANCES CW **SPECIES** Dathomirian **HOMEWORLD** Dathomir **AFFILIATION** Separatists, Nightsisters

DARK ASSASSIN

As Count Dooku's apprentice, Asajj Ventress is an agent for his machinations. On Tatooine, she kidnaps Jabba the Hutt's son Rotta for Dooku, who intends framing the Republic to bring the Hutts into the Clone Wars on the Separatist side. However, the Jedi attack Ventress on Teth and return Rotta to his father. Later, Dooku sends Ventress to free Nute Gunray from a Republic cruiser and take him to Coruscant. There she duels Jedi Master Luminara Unduli, nearly defeating her until Ahsoka Tano joins the battle. Helped by a traitorous Senate guard, Argyus, Ventress rescues Gunray, but then kills Argyus when he boasts of his role in the mission. On Kamino, Ventress tries to steal the clone DNA, but is foiled by Anakin Skywalker.

Nightsister found
When Ventress arrives on Dathomir, the Nightsisters are prepared to kill her, until Mother Talzin reveals that Ventress is one of them.

Showdown
In the B'omarr Order Monastery on Teth, Ventress prepares for battle with Jedi intent on rescuing Rotta the Huttlet.

NIGHTSISTER

Sensing Ventress growing more powerful in the Force, Sidious orders Dooku to kill his dark acolyte. When her command ship is destroyed at Sullust, Ventress flees to Dathomir, where Mother Talzin reveals the assassin's past as a Nightsister, leading Ventress to swear vengeance on Dooku. While she undergoes a Rebirth Ritual to signify her allegiance to the clan, Dooku sends General Grievous to Dathomir to annihilate the Nightsisters. At the urging of Talzin, Ventress flees the planet, believing she is the only remaining Nightsister.

BOUNTY HUNTER

After killing bounty hunter Oked, Ventress takes his place on a mission led by Boba Fett to protect a chest on a train which, when opened, reveals a young girl held captive inside. Ventress double-crosses Fett and frees the girl. Later, discovering a bounty on Savage Opress, Ventress hunts down the Nightbrother. Her search leads her to Opress and Darth Maul, who are holding Obi-Wan Kenobi prisoner. Ventress and Obi-Wan join forces, barely escaping with their lives. Obi-Wan tries to enlist Ventress, but she refuses.

Catching a Jedi
Now a bounty hunter, Ventress pins down former Jedi Ahsoka Tano, who has a price on her head after escaping an Imperial prison.

GENERAL WHORM LOATHSOM

APPEARANCES CW **SPECIES** Kerkoiden
HOMEWORLD Kerkoidia **AFFILIATION**
Separatists

After General Loathsom captures the planet Christophsis, the Republic invades to liberate it. Loathsom counters the attack, pushing forward his battle droids, which are protected behind a powerful deflector shield. Unable to penetrate the barrier, Obi-Wan Kenobi discusses terms of surrender with Loathsom, allowing Anakin Skywalker and Ahsoka Tano time to destroy the shield generator. Loathsom is captured and taken to Coruscant, where he is imprisoned for treason.

Dark side apprentice
A lethal assassin trained in the Force and ruthlessly tested by Count Dooku, Asajj Ventress burns to be accepted as a true Sith, and wields her unique twin light sabers/saberstaff with deadly force.

ANAKIN'S CHOICE

"Just help me save Padmé's life. I can't live without her." ANAKIN SKYWALKER

Anakin Skywalker faces a tragic choice: allow Mace Windu to execute the evil Darth Sidious and risk losing his beloved Padmé forever, or save the Sith Lord and lose himself.

When Anakin returns to Coruscant and is reunited with Padmé, he learns that she is pregnant. Soon after, he is plagued by nightmare visions of her dying during childbirth. Anakin knows that he is seeing glimpses of the future because he had experienced similar premonitions of his own mother's death. He vows to find a way to save Padmé, but fears that the Jedi will not permit him to attain the necessary knowledge. He believes—not without justification—that the Jedi Council has become secretive, and even deceptive at times. Chancellor Palpatine requests that Anakin become his liaison to the Jedi Council, and the Council grants Anakin a seat, but denies him the title of Jedi Master. Anakin is insulted and bitterly resents the Council's decision. At the same time, the Council, suspicious of Palpatine's motives, asks Anakin to spy on the Chancellor. Anakin suddenly finds himself torn between his loyalty to the Jedi—in particular Obi-Wan Kenobi—and his deep respect for Palpatine.

TEMPTED TO THE DARK SIDE

Palpatine tantalizes Anakin with stories of Darth Plagueis, telling him that the Sith had the power to prevent loved ones from dying. Palpatine then reveals that he is a Sith himself and claims to have the ability to save Padmé. Anakin refuses his offer and dutifully informs the Jedi Council. A team of Jedi, led by Mace Windu, attacks Palpatine. Distraught that Palpatine's death will mean he will lose all hope of saving Padmé, Anakin intervenes at the vital moment, helping Palpatine to kill the remaining Jedi, Mace Windu. Anakin then swears to serve Palpatine, who bestows a new name upon Anakin: Darth Vader.

A self-fulfilling prophecy
Anakin's first instructions from Sidious are to
massacre all the Jedi in their temple and then
travel to Mustafar and assassinate the Separatist
leaders. Little does Anakin know that now his own
choices will bring about Padmé's death.

"I look forward to adding your lightsabers to my collection."

GENERAL GRIEVOUS

GENERAL GRIEVOUS

Commander of the Separatist military, General Grievous is feared throughout the Republic. The cyborg has a vengeful lust for slaying Jedi and keeps their lightsabers as trophies.

APPEARANCES CW, III **SPECIES** Kaleesh (cyborg) **HOMEWORLD** Kalee **AFFILIATION** Separatists

JEDI HUNTER

The leader of the Separatist army, General Grievous frequently clashes with the Republic's Jedi generals. Even members of the Jedi Council struggle to challenge him. Grievous annihilates a fleet commanded by Plo Koon, leaving only a handful of survivors. Soon afterward he almost adds apprentice Ahsoka Tano's lightsaber to his collection during a duel at Skytop Station. He flees when her powerful teacher, Anakin Skywalker, intervenes at the last second. Jedi Master Kit Fisto is then dispatched to track down Grievous's lair, but he barely escapes with his life after his former Padawan Nahdar Vebb is slain by the cyborg. Grievous later kidnaps Master Eeth Koth and taunts the Jedi via holo-recording; the rescue mounted by Anakin, Obi-Wan Kenobi, and Adi Gallia nearly fails.

Mortal combat
Jedi General Obi-Wan Kenobi and Separatist General Grievous face off early in the Clone Wars aboard the *Malevolence*.

SEPARATIST STRIKES

Attacking key targets, General Grievous's army wreaks havoc across the galaxy. At Kamino, his cautious tactics make Obi-Wan suspect a bigger plan, which is confirmed when Obi-Wan discovers aqua droids mounting underwater assaults. The droids are bent on destroying the cloning facility crucial to the Republic war effort, but the Jedi turn the tide and Grievous retreats. Count Dooku also dispatches the cyborg on missions to serve the Sith's vengeful ends: at Naboo, Senator Amidala is forced into a prisoner exchange with Grievous to save Anakin, and on Dathomir, Grievous wipes out an entire clan of Nightsisters witches.

No surrender
Grievous refuses to surrender on Naboo and fights off the Gungans one by one. General Tarpals finally stuns him, but not before receiving a mortal wound.

Standoff
General Grievous assumes an aggressive stance before attacking Obi-Wan on Utapau.

SITH DISTRACTION

General Grievous's flagship, *Invisible Hand*, leads the Separatist assault on Coruscant that captures Supreme Chancellor Palpatine. Obi-Wan and Anakin board the vessel to rescue Palpatine, and Grievous flees, leaving his MagnaGuards to fend off the Jedi. While the Jedi Council focuses its attention on pursuing the cyborg across the galaxy, Palpatine—truly Darth Sidious hiding in plain sight—unfolds his nefarious plot to wipe out the Jedi and declare himself Emperor. He tips off Grievous's location on Utapau, and Obi-Wan is sent in pursuit. After Obi-Wan makes a sudden appearance during the Separatist gathering on Utapau, Grievous and Obi-Wan battle and the Jedi kills him.

Feared by Jedi

Once a feared Kaleesh warrior, General Grievous is now more cybernetic machine than living flesh. He believes his mechanical limbs have made him superior to all foes. Scientists implanted his brain and eyes into a duranium alloy body, and his remaining vital organs are protected by a synthskin gut-sack. Count Dooku trains Grievous in the art of lightsaber combat, for which his cyborg enhancements are well suited. Grievous lacks Force powers, instead relying on agility and strength when in combat with a Jedi. A master of many of the classic forms of Jedi arts, he is able to adapt quickly to an opponent's fighting style.

Stolen weapons
Grievous revels in using the lightsabers of his victims in battle.

Cybernetic limbs
Grievous's LX-44 robotic legs have magnetic, talon-like feet.

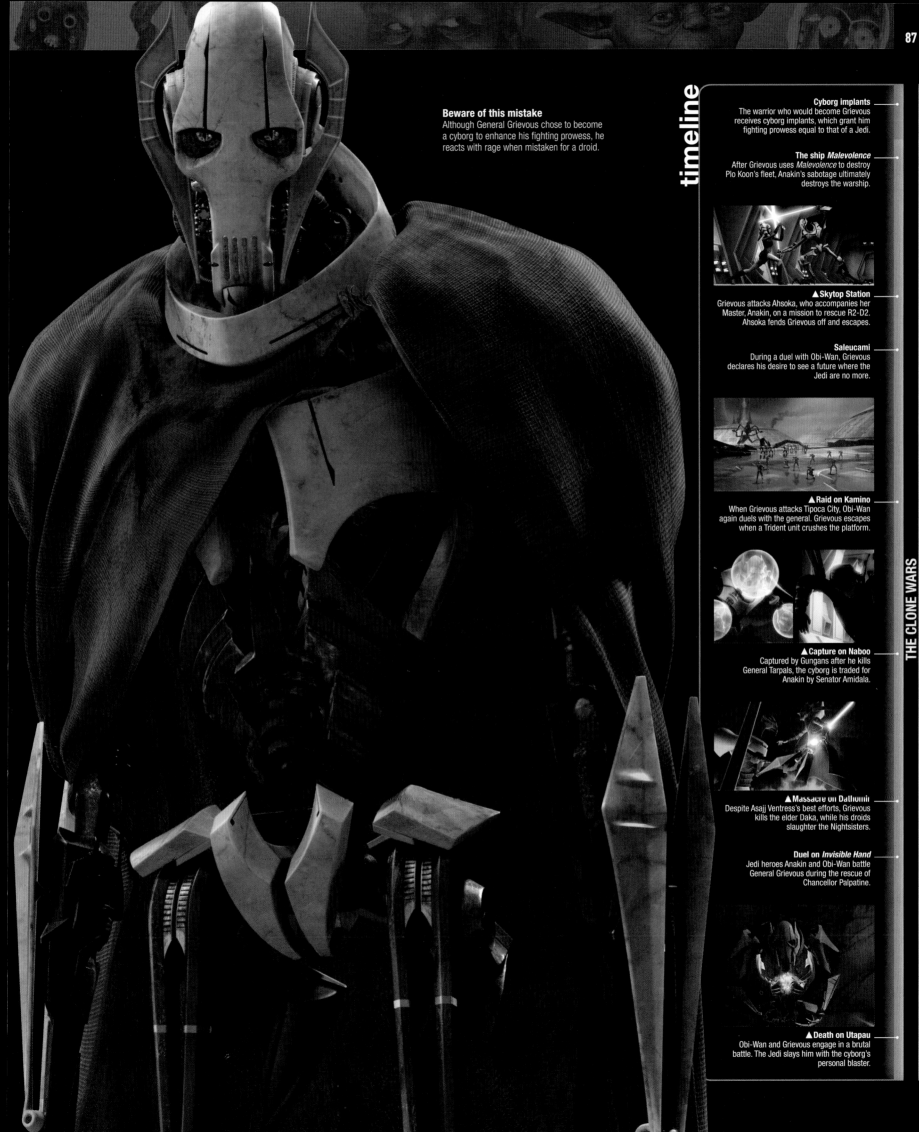

Beware of this mistake
Although General Grievous chose to become a cyborg to enhance his fighting prowess, he reacts with rage when mistaken for a droid.

timeline

Cyborg implants
The warrior who would become Grievous receives cyborg implants, which grant him fighting prowess equal to that of a Jedi.

The ship *Malevolence*
After Grievous uses *Malevolence* to destroy Plo Koon's fleet, Anakin's sabotage ultimately destroys the warship.

▲ Skytop Station
Grievous attacks Ahsoka, who accompanies her Master, Anakin, on a mission to rescue R2-D2. Ahsoka fends Grievous off and escapes.

Saleucami
During a duel with Obi-Wan, Grievous declares his desire to see a future where the Jedi are no more.

▲ Raid on Kamino
When Grievous attacks Tipoca City, Obi-Wan again duels with the general. Grievous escapes when a Trident unit crushes the platform.

▲ Capture on Naboo
Captured by Gungans after he kills General Tarpals, the cyborg is traded for Anakin by Senator Amidala.

▲ Massacre on Dathomir
Despite Asajj Ventress's best efforts, Grievous kills the elder Daka, while his droids slaughter the Nightsisters.

Duel on *Invisible Hand*
Jedi heroes Anakin and Obi-Wan battle General Grievous during the rescue of Chancellor Palpatine.

▲ Death on Utapau
Obi-Wan and Grievous engage in a brutal battle. The Jedi slays him with the cyborg's personal blaster.

THE CLONE WARS

"No one has her kind of determination." ANAKIN SKYWALKER

AHSOKA TANO

The apprentice Anakin Skywalker never expected, Ahsoka Tano is as headstrong as her Master. She earns his respect and friendship, taking his Jedi lessons and passing them on. Ultimately, on her path to becoming a Jedi, she remains true to herself.

APPEARANCES CW **SPECIES** Togruta **HOMEWORLD** Shili **AFFILIATION** Jedi Order

Rebel leader
Ahsoka fights alongside Onderon rebels during a battle against a Separatist droid army supporting King Rash.

ANAKIN SKYWALKER'S PADAWAN

When the Jedi Council assigns Ahsoka to train beside Anakin, they believe that the rule-following, optimistic new Padawan will be a good influence on her high-strung Master. They also hope that mentoring the talented young Jedi will help Anakin learn to let go of his attachments. Her Master's training quickly makes an impression: When she teams with Barriss Offee, apprentice of Luminara Unduli, during the second Battle of Geonosis, Ahsoka's bold style contrasts with the more reserved demeanor of her counterpart. Their partnership falters, however, on the mysterious monolith Mortis, where a Force vision of her older self warns Ahsoka that her future seems bleak if she remains with Anakin.

Reluctant Master
At first Anakin Skywalker is not enthusiastic about his new apprentice, but he accepts his duty as a Jedi, passing along his experience to Ahsoka.

Important lessons
When Ahsoka is kidnapped during a mission, she must use all her Jedi training to escape her Trandoshan captors.

SOLO MISSIONS

Ahsoka's exceptional Jedi skills lead to missions away from her Master early in her apprenticeship. When Pantoran Chairman Papanoida's daughters are kidnapped, she volunteers to help her friend Senator Riyo Chuchi investigate the crime, using Force levitation and her first Jedi mind tricks along the way. Soon after, she assists Duchess Satine Kryze in exposing corruption at the highest levels of Mandalore's government. Plagued by visions of Padmé Amidala's assassination, Ahsoka insists on joining the senator's security detail and thwarts assassin Aurra Sing's attempt. By the time Ahsoka is captured by Trandoshan hunters and taken to Wasskah, she possesses the confidence to lead abducted Jedi younglings to fight back against their captors.

THE TEACHER

While working with Duchess Satine's nephew Korkie and his friends to root out traitors, Ahsoka exhibits a talent for leadership. When the Jedi Council agrees to Anakin's proposal to train Onderon insurgents striving to depose the Separatist-allied king, Ahsoka and Obi-Wan join him for the mission. Impressed by Ahsoka's development, the two senior Jedi have enough confidence to leave her behind as the sole Jedi adviser during the final stages of the successful Onderon uprising. Not long after, Yoda entrusts Ahsoka with safeguarding the travels of Jedi younglings venturing to Ilum, where they undergo rigorous tests of physical and inner strength before they can construct their own lightsabers.

Jedi trial
After she stands trial for treason before a military tribunal on Coruscant *(above)*, Ahsoka walks away from Anakin and the Jedi Order *(right)*.

JEDI NO MORE

Following a bombing of the Jedi Temple, Ahsoka and Anakin are recalled to investigate. While Ahsoka interrogates the bomber, Letta Turmond, about her Jedi accomplice, the prisoner is Force-choked by an unseen person. Despite protesting her innocence to Admiral Tarkin, Ahsoka is arrested for Turmond's murder. Mysterious assistance—a keycard outside her cell, incapacitated guards, and a comlink—aid Ahsoka's escape from prison, but also further incriminate her. Anakin finds her but cannot convince his Padawan to turn herself in. Ultimately, she finds an unlikely ally in Sith outcast Asajj Ventress, who leads Anakin to clues proving Barriss Offee is the true traitor. Her faith in the institution shaken, Ahsoka refuses the Jedi Council's offers of reinstatement *(see also p. 63)*.

Instinctive Jedi

While Ahsoka is gifted with raw Force talent, her tendency to follow her heart challenges her path to knighthood. As a young Jedi, emotions inhibit her ability to make wise decisions. Eventually Ahsoka gains the confidence to make the right choice, even at great cost to her own feelings.

timeline

▼ Discovered
Plo Koon finds the three-year-old Force-sensitive child on the planet Shili and brings her to the Jedi Temple.

Battle of Christophsis
Ahsoka is sent by Yoda to train as Anakin's Padawan.

Battle of Ryloth
Ahsoka is forced to take command after Anakin makes a reckless solo assault on the Droid Control Ship.

▼ Second Battle of Geonosis
Ahsoka and Barriss Offee infiltrate and destroy the Geonosian droid factory.

Death on Mortis
Anakin enlists the Father to use the remaining life force from the Daughter to resurrect Ahsoka.

Citadel rescue
Before his death, Even Piell entrusts Ahsoka with Nexus Route information she must deliver to the Jedi Council.

Trandoshan hunt
Hunted on a moon by Trandoshans, Ahsoka teams with Chewbacca to help a group of captive Jedi younglings escape.

▲ Battle of Kadavo
Ahsoka and Anakin free Obi-Wan, Rex, and Togrutans held captive in a Zygerrian slaver facility.

Liberation of Onderon
Ahsoka, Anakin, and Obi-Wan assist Onderon rebels in liberating their planet from Separatist occupation.

Framed and betrayed
Framed by Barriss Offee for murder and treason, Ahsoka is expelled by the Jedi Order and made to stand trial.

▲ Ahsoka leaves Jedi Order
After she is cleared of wrongdoing, Ahsoka refuses the offer to rejoin the Jedi Order.

THE CLONE WARS

ROTTA THE HUTTLET

APPEARANCES CW **SPECIES** Hutt
HOMEWORLD Tatooine
AFFILIATION Hutts

Rotta is the son of Jabba the Hutt. After the Huttlet is kidnapped by Asajj Ventress, Jabba makes a deal with the Galactic Republic to rescue him. When Anakin Skywalker and Ahsoka Tano free Rotta on Teth, they realize that the Huttlet has fallen ill. Ahsoka finds the medicine that saves him.

COMMANDER FOX

APPEARANCES CW **SPECIES** Human
HOMEWORLD Kamino **AFFILIATION** Galactic Republic

Fox, clone trooper commander CC-1010, leads the famed Coruscant Guard. He assists Padmé Amidala in the capture of Ziro the Hutt. Assigned to a Republic military base, he pursues the fugitive Ahsoka, who is blamed for the murder of Letta Turmond, but she evades capture. Fox later kills rogue trooper Fives before he can reveal a conspiracy within the Republic.

Ziro's capture
The Coruscant Guard, led by Commander Fox, catches up to Ziro in his club on Coruscant *(top)*. However, the Hutt escapes from prison with the aid of Cad Bane *(above)*.

ZIRO THE HUTT

APPEARANCES CW **SPECIES** Hutt
HOMEWORLD Sleheyron
AFFILIATION Hutts

Crime lord Ziro is Jabba the Hutt's uncle. Ziro conspires with Count Dooku to kidnap Jabba's son, Rotta. Senator Padmé Amidala tries to open communications with the Hutts, who believe the Jedi abducted Rotta. After a failed assassination attempt on Padmé, Ziro is arrested. Via holocomm, Ziro confesses to Jabba his part in Rotta's kidnapping and is imprisoned on Coruscant. Cad Bane later frees Ziro and hands him over to the Hutt Council, which fears that Ziro might reveal its many dirty dealings to the Republic. With the help of Sy Snootles, Ziro escapes the Hutts. Snootles follows Ziro to Teth, retrieves a holopad filled with Hutt secrets, and then kills him.

CLONE TROOPER ECHO

APPEARANCES CW **SPECIES** Human
HOMEWORLD Kamino
AFFILIATION Galactic Republic

CT-21-0408 is nicknamed "Echo" for constantly repeating rules. As a cadet, he is part of Domino Squad. Echo and other rookies thwart General Grievous's attempt to capture Rishi Station and are inducted into the 501st Legion. Echo subsequently participates in the rescue of Jedi Master Even Piell from the Citadel, but ends up missing in action.

CLONE TROOPER FIVES

APPEARANCES CW **SPECIES** Human
HOMEWORLD Kamino
AFFILIATION Galactic Republic

Fives's nickname comes from his clone designation, CT-27-5555. As a cadet, he trains with Domino Squad. After defending Rishi Station from General Grievous's attack, he is inducted into the 501st Legion. On Umbara, Fives is the loudest voice against Jedi General Krell, who is revealed to be a traitor. Fives also uncovers the truth about Chancellor Palpatine and Order 66, but is killed by Commander Fox before he can expose the conspiracy.

CHAM SYNDULLA

APPEARANCES CW **SPECIES** Twi'lek
HOMEWORLD Ryloth
AFFILIATION Twi'lek Resistance

Cham Syndulla believes Senator Orn Free Taa and the Galactic Senate do not care about Ryloth's citizens. After the Separatists invade the planet, Syndulla forms the freedom fighters who oppose them. When Mace Windu arrives with clone forces, Syndulla resolves his issues with Senator Taa and allies with the Republic. He then leads the combined army and liberates his homeworld from the Confederacy.

KING KATUUNKO

APPEARANCES CW **SPECIES** Toydarian
HOMEWORLD Toydaria
AFFILIATION Galactic Republic

Due to his planet's reliance on the Trade Federation, King Katuunko could only secretly aid the planet Ryloth during the Clone Wars. When Chancellor Palpatine requests negotiations to use Toydaria as a base, he sends Yoda to Rugosa. Yoda impresses Katuunko with his Jedi character, and the king commits Toydaria to the Republic. Dooku's apprentice Savage Opress eventually kills the king for supporting the Jedi.

COMMANDER WOLFFE

APPEARANCES CW **SPECIES** Human
HOMEWORLD Kamino
AFFILIATION Galactic Republic

Commander Wolffe, also known as clone CC-3636, leads Wolf Pack Battalion, which serves under Jedi General Plo Koon. During a mission to eliminate the *Malevolence*, the entire Wolf Pack is killed, except for Wolffe, Sinker, and Boost. At the Battle of Khorm, Wolffe loses his right eye during a fight with Asajj Ventress. Despite this, Wolffe continues to serve, assisting in liberating Togruta slaves on Kadavo and helping recover Jedi Sifo-Dyas's lightsaber.

HONDO OHNAKA

APPEARANCES CW **SPECIES** Weequay
HOMEWORLD Sriluur
AFFILIATION Ohnaka Gang

Hondo Ohnaka is the leader of the Ohnaka Gang based on the planet Florrum. When his pirates kidnap Count Dooku, Hondo attempts to sell him to the Galactic Republic for a hefty ransom. The hostage situation allows Hondo to also capture Obi-Wan and Anakin. With the assistance of clone troopers brought by Senator Jar Jar Binks, Obi-Wan, Anakin, and Dooku escape. The Jedi later face Hondo's gang on the planet Felucia, where the Jedi help defend farms alongside hired bounty hunters. During the Clone Wars, Anakin pays Ohnaka to deliver missile launchers to the Onderon rebels. Ohnaka teams up with Ahsoka and a group of Jedi younglings to repel General Grievous's attack on Florrum. When Darth Maul and Savage Opress arrive to hire a gang of bounty hunters for the Shadow Collective, Ohnaka allies with Obi-Wan to drive off the two brothers.

Pirate life
Hondo Ohnaka leads his fierce gang of Weequay pirates *(bottom)*, who specialize in extortion and kidnapping, from a base on Florrum *(below)*.

Monkey business
Hondo's pet Kowakian monkey-lizard, Pikk Mukmuk, helps him do the dirty work.

GUNDARK

APPEARANCES CW **HOMEWORLD** Vanqor
AVERAGE SIZE 2 m (7 ft) high
HABITAT Caves

Gundarks are fierce, aggressive creatures known for their overwhelming strength. After crash-landing on Vanqor, Anakin and Obi-Wan disturb a gundark in a cave. Using the Force to pelt the beast with rocks, the Jedi successfully repel it. When the *Endurance* crashes on Vanqor, R2-D2 faces off with a gundark. The droid ties the creature to Anakin's starfighter and sends it blasting off.

RIYO CHUCHI

APPEARANCES CW **SPECIES** Pantoran
HOMEWORLD Pantora
AFFILIATION Galactic Republic

When a Republic base falls silent, Senator Riyo Chuchi joins Chairman Chi Cho, Anakin, and Obi-Wan to investigate. After Cho is killed, Chuchi negotiates peace between the Pantorans and Talz. When the daughters of Baron Papanoida are kidnapped, she enlists Ahsoka Tano's help. Finding one daughter on a Trade Federation vessel, they overhear a conversation that confirms the Federation is working on behalf of the Separatists.

THI-SEN

APPEARANCES CW **SPECIES** Talz **HOMEWORLD** Orto Plutonia
AFFILIATION Talz village

Thi-Sen leads a peaceful tribe caught between the Galactic Republic and Separatist task forces. Protecting their territory, the tribe attacks the Republic outpost and the droid forces. A second Republic task force under the command of Anakin and Obi-Wan negotiates a ceasefire. Believing the Talz to be trespassers, Chairman Cho of the neighboring moon Pantora declares war on them. After the chairman dies, Senator Riyo Chuchi uses C-3PO to make peace with Thi-Sen.

NARGLATCH

APPEARANCES CW **HOMEWORLD** Orto Plutonia **AVERAGE SIZE** 6 m (20 ft) long
HABITAT Adaptable

The narglatch is a stealthy predator that can live in a variety of climates. On the frozen world of Orto Plutonia, narglatch are used as mounts by the Talz. Narglatch hide is vulnerable to blaster fire and valued by some cultures as a trophy. Narglatch cubs are cute and often taken as pets, but become extremely dangerous when they mature. Escaped narglatches are a threat on Coruscant.

DR. NUVO VINDI

APPEARANCES CW **SPECIES** Faust
HOMEWORLD Adana
AFFILIATION Separatists

Nute Gunray sponsors Nuvo Vindi's work to re-create the Blue Shadow Virus in a Trade Federation laboratory built beneath Naboo's swamps. Padmé stumbles upon the lair while investigating the death of a shaak herd. Arriving on Naboo, her Jedi friends help to capture Vindi. He refuses to hand over the antidote to save Padmé and Ahsoka, but Obi-Wan and Anakin travel to Iego to find a cure.

CLONE TROOPER WAXER

APPEARANCES CW **SPECIES** Human
HOMEWORLD Kamino **AFFILIATION** Republic

Waxer serves in the Ghost Company during campaigns to retake Ryloth and defeat Geonosis. The recon team of Waxer and Boil scouts an abandoned Twi'lek village and finds a young girl, Numa, who reveals the underground passages the clone troopers use to free the Twi'leks. Waxer dies when General Krell deceives the clones on Umbara.

TODO 360

APPEARANCES CW **MANUFACTURER**
Vertseth Automata **TYPE** Techno-service droid
AFFILIATION Bounty hunter

Todo-360 is destroyed in a ventilation shaft as a distraction when Cad Bane steals a holocron from the Jedi Temple for Darth Sidious. Todo is rebuilt by Anakin Skywalker and escapes. He assists Bane in capturing C-3PO and R2-D2.

CATO PARASITTI

APPEARANCES CW **SPECIES** Clawdite
HOMEWORLD Zolan
AFFILIATION Bounty hunter

Posing as Ord Enisence and Chief Librarian Jocasta Nu, changeling Cato Parasitti neutralizes the Jedi Temple's security so that Cad Bane can reach the Holocron Vault. Ahsoka Tano later defeats Parasitti in a duel, and while he is in Jedi captivity, Parasitti offers information on Bane's next target: Bolla Ropal, the keeper of the kyber memory crystal.

CAD BANE

APPEARANCES CW **SPECIES** Duros
HOMEWORLD Duro **AFFILIATION** Bounty hunter

In his day, Cad Bane is the best bounty hunter in the galaxy. His reputation earns him jobs for Count Dooku and Darth Sidious. Working for Sidious, Bane steals a holocron from the Jedi Temple that can unlock the kyber memory crystal, a repository of the identities of all Force-sensitive infants. After stealing the crystal from Jedi Bolla Ropal on Devaron and forcing Anakin to unlock it, Bane is sent to kidnap four Force-sensitive infants. Foiled halfway through his job by Anakin and Ahsoka, Bane escapes. Jabba the Hutt hires Bane to break his uncle Ziro out of a Republic prison. Bane captures several prominent members of the Galactic Senate and uses them as hostages to compel Chancellor Palpatine to free Ziro, whom Bane delivers to the Hutt Council. When Ziro escapes from their custody, Bane is hired again to track him down. He fails to secure this bounty and has to evade Obi-Wan Kenobi and Quinlan Vos.

Mastermind Moralo Eval offers Bane a fortune to break him out of the Republic Judiciary Central Detention Center. Bane succeeds and enters Eval's competition, the Box, which is an event that will determine which five mercenaries will be hired in a plot to kidnap Chancellor Palpatine. After passing the tournament test, Bane is personally selected by Dooku to lead the team of Embo, Derrown, Twazzi, and Rako Hardeen, who is really Obi-Wan undercover. They travel to Naboo to abduct Palpatine during the Festival of Light. The team succeeds, but Dooku betrays Bane. Having intended that the bounty hunters' operation should just be a diversion, Dooku misses his rendezvous with the team. Bane is then defeated by Obi-Wan.

Tackling the Box
Cad Bane and his fellow contestants study the next phase of Moralo Eval's bounty hunter skills challenge, the Box.

Always prepared
Cad Bane uses a pair of personalized BlasTech LL-30 blaster pistols and custom-made wrist gauntlets that conceal a cable launcher and contact stunners.

Taking aim
Sugi's weapon of choice is an EE-3 carbine rifle.

SUGI

APPEARANCES CW **SPECIES** Zabrak
HOMEWORLD Iridonia
AFFILIATION Mercenary

Mercenary Sugi owns the starship *Halo*. She is guided by a strong sense of honor and duty. She is hired to defend a Felucian farming village plagued by the Ohnaka Gang. Along with fellow mercenaries Rumi Paramita, Embo, and Seripas, Sugi joins forces with Obi-Wan, Anakin, and Ahsoka to fight off the pirate gang. Paramita dies and Embo is wounded during the battle. With the pirates chased off, Sugi and her remaining allies receive their payment, and she offers the stranded Jedi a ride back to Galactic Republic space aboard her ship.

Honorable mercenary
Seripas teams with Sugi to defend a Felucian farming village harassed by a pirate gang.

EMBO

APPEARANCES CW **SPECIES** Kyuzo
HOMEWORLD Phatrong
AFFILIATION Bounty hunter

Embo is deadly with a shot from his bowcaster or a decisive blow from his pan-shaped hat. He often works with Sugi and is hired as part of her team to defend farmers on Felucia. Embo and Sugi are both present at Jabba's palace when Pantoran Chairman Papanoida searches for Greedo, who kidnapped Papanoida's daughters. He is one of 11 bounty hunters, including Obi-Wan, disguised as Rako Hardeen, and Cad Bane, to fight in the Box competition. Embo is hired to target Rush Clovis, but fails when Anakin interrupts his plans. Later, he defends the Hutt Grand Council from Darth Maul and Savage Opress.

Bounty hunter pet
Embo's anooba Marrok accompanies him to Nal Hutta, where Embo is contracted to protect the Hutt leaders.

SIONVER BOLL

APPEARANCES CW **SPECIES** Bivall
HOMEWORLD Protobranch
AFFILIATION Republic

Sionver Boll designs the electro-proton bomb that is deployed during the Battle of Malastare to deactivate an entire Separatist droid invasion force. The bomb awakens the Zillo beast. Despite Boll's protest, Chancellor Palpatine orders the beast killed. The beast escapes, rampaging on Coruscant before Boll creates enough toxin to kill it.

ZILLO BEAST

APPEARANCES CW **HOMEWORLD** Malastare
AVERAGE SIZE 97 m (318 ft) high
HABITAT Underground

The Zillo beast is a legendary monster unearthed during the Battle of Malastare by an electro-proton bomb. The beast's armor proves nearly invulnerable to Republic weaponry, earning interest from Chancellor Palpatine. The creature is captured and transported to a research facility on Coruscant. The Zillo beast breaks free from its restraints, wreaking havoc through the capital. It is killed by a toxin created by Sionver Boll, but its body is kept for possible cloning.

SERIPAS

APPEARANCES CW **SPECIES** Unknown **HOMEWORLD** Unknown
AFFILIATION Bounty hunter

Diminutive bounty hunter Seripas wears a mechanical bodysuit to make up for his size. As part of Sugi's team of mercenaries, he protects a Felucian farm from a band of Weequay pirates led by Hondo Ohnaka. Alongside Ahsoka, Seripas trains the farmers to fight. Despite Seripas's suit being destroyed, he still manages to defeat a pirate during the farmers' successful defense of their homes. Later, Seripas and Sugi bring Wookiees in to help rescue Chewbacca and Ahsoka, who are being held captive by Trandoshans on Wasskah.

MON MOTHMA

APPEARANCES CW, III, VI **SPECIES** Human
HOMEWORLD Chandrila **AFFILIATION** Republic

Alongside fellow senators Padmé Amidala, Bail Organa, and Onaconda Farr, Mon Mothma promotes a movement to put an end to the fighting and let diplomacy resume during the Clone Wars. When Farr is murdered by his aide Lolo Purs, Mothma carries on the cause in the Senate while Organa and Padmé investigate the crime.

Mothma, Organa, and Padmé oppose Chancellor Palpatine's abuse of wartime powers and worry that the Chancellor will refuse to relinquish them after the war. Mothma seeks diplomatic alternatives to the prolonged fighting, pushing cautionary legislation in the Senate and reaching out to Separatist politicians. Her fears are realized when Palpatine uses the attempt on his life to reorganize the Galactic Republic into the First Galactic Empire. She loses her friend Padmé shortly after Palpatine's power grab.

Mothma and Organa help unite disparate factions into the Rebel Alliance to oppose Palpatine's Empire. Organa is lost when Alderaan is destroyed by the Death Star. Later, prior to the Battle of Endor, Rebel Alliance leader Mothma briefs the soldiers and pilots who have volunteered to destroy the Empire's second Death Star.

Rebel leader
Mon Mothma addresses the members of the Rebel Alliance strike team set to attack the second Death Star in the Endor system.

GWARM

APPEARANCES CW **SPECIES** Weequay
HOMEWORLD Florrum
AFFILIATION Ohnaka Gang

Gwarm serves as second-in-command of the Ohnaka Gang that extorts Felucian farmers. The pirates are challenged by bounty hunters hired by the farmers and three Jedi. When the gang's captain, Hondo Ohnaka, is at the mercy of Anakin, Gwarm calls for retreat to rescue him. The pirates leave Felucia empty-handed.

Senators for peace
Senators Mon Mothma, Bail Organa, and Padmé Amidala discuss methods of countering the Chancellor's increasing war powers.

Temple becomes tomb

Anakin Skywalker, now under the Sith name of Darth Vader, leads the 501st Legion of clone troopers into the Jedi Temple on Coruscant. They march past statues of the temple's original founders and begin their killing spree.

LIBERTY DIES

"So this is how liberty dies—with thunderous applause." PADMÉ AMIDALA

The Sith finally achieve their revenge when Palpatine destroys the Jedi Order and becomes Emperor of the galaxy.

Decades of scheming and maneuvering on a galactic scale by Chancellor Palpatine, in reality the Sith Lord Darth Sidious, culminate in a brutal seizure of power. Palpatine issues Order 66, and thanks to a bioengineered "chip" embedded in the brains of all clones, the soldiers instantly turn on their Jedi commanders and murder them without hesitation. Palpatine orders Darth Vader to go to the Jedi Temple and slaughter all Jedi there, assuring him that the deed will make him strong enough in the dark side of the Force to save Padmé.

DEMOCRACY EMBRACES TYRANNY

Accompanied by the 501st Legion, later known as Vader's Fist, Vader and the troopers massacre the Jedi Order, even killing younglings who hide in the Council Chamber. Senator Bail Organa investigates the disturbance, but is turned away by troopers, before witnessing the murder of a Jedi Padawan and barely escaping himself. Later, Palpatine calls a special session of the Galactic Senate to announce the end of the Clone Wars and the failure of the Jedi attempt to assassinate him. In light of this, Palpatine declares the formation of a new Galactic Empire and installs himself as its Emperor. With growing distrust of the Jedi, now largely blamed for the long war, both the Senate and the public overwhelmingly approve of the new regime.

Decline of the Senate
At the Senate, Bail and Padmé watch as Sidious makes his pronouncement. His genius is that he does not seize power over the Republic directly, rather the Senate willingly bows to him.

RUSH CLOVIS

APPEARANCES CW **SPECIES** Human **HOMEWORLD** Scipio
AFFILIATION InterGalactic Banking Clan

At one time, Senator Rush Clovis is linked romantically with fellow Senator Padmé Amidala. Suspicious of Clovis, the Jedi enlist Padmé to gather information about him. She is poisoned when she discovers his allegiance to the Separatists, but Clovis, who still has feelings for her, forces his co-conspirator, Lott Dod, to provide the antidote. Bitter about Clovis's affection for Padmé, his secret wife, Anakin Skywalker abandons Clovis on Cato Neimoidia. Hoping to atone for his wrongs, Clovis pleads for Padmé's help in exposing corruption in the Banking Clan, but is killed during a battle for control of the planet Scipio when Anakin saves Padmé and Clovis falls to his death.

Intrigue on Scipio
On Cato Neimoidia, Rush Clovis conspires with Separatists to fund a droid factory (above). Clovis and Padmé arrive on Scipio to investigate corruption in the Banking Clan (right).

KARINA THE GREAT

APPEARANCES CW **SPECIES** Geonosian
HOMEWORLD Geonosis **AFFILIATION** Separatists

Residing in the catacombs beneath the Progate Temple, Karina controls an army of Geonosian drones and gives orders to Poggle the Lesser. The Jedi discover Karina after she captures Luminara Unduli, who had followed Poggle to her location. The Geonosian queen is presumably killed when clone troopers destroy the temple while rescuing the Jedi.

TERA SINUBE

APPEARANCES CW **SPECIES** Cosian **HOMEWORLD** Cosia
AFFILIATION Jedi

Jedi Master Tera Sinube is an expert on Coruscant's criminal underworld. When Ahsoka Tano's lightsaber is stolen, the Padawan enlists Sinube's help. They track prime suspect Nack Movers and find him dead in his apartment. With him are the bounty hunters Cassie Cryar and Ione Marcy. Ahsoka chases after the fleeing Cryar, while Sinube interrogates Marcy before she also flees. When the Jedi locate the fugitives on a train platform, Marcy is arrested by nearby police droids and Cryar is cornered on a train by Ahsoka. A desperate Cryar tries to exit the train with two hostages, but is foiled by Sinube, who disarms her before returning the stolen lightsaber to Ahsoka.

DUCHESS SATINE KRYZE

APPEARANCES CW **SPECIES** Human **HOMEWORLD** Mandalore
AFFILIATION New Mandalorians

At the beginning of the Clone Wars, Duchess Satine Kryze advocates for peace. When rumors swirl that she is secretly creating an army for the Separatists, the Jedi High Council sends Obi-Wan Kenobi, whom Satine had befriended during the Mandalorian Civil War, to investigate. Satine and Obi-Wan travel to Mandalore's moon Concordia, where they are attacked by Governor Pre Vizsla and his Death Watch mercenaries. After they narrowly escape, Satine heads to Coruscant to warn the Galactic Senate about the danger the Death Watch presents. Unfortunately, her ship is attacked by Separatist droids, and she is taken hostage by Senator Tal Merrik, a Separatist conspirator. When she is freed with help from Obi-Wan and Anakin, Satine hurries to the Senate and proves that the evidence favoring a military intervention has been faked, resulting in the senators voting down the resolution to invade Mandalore.

As a black-market culture grows on Mandalore, Satine, with the help of the like-minded Senator Padmé Amidala, seeks to prevent the entire population from becoming implicated. She requests aid from the Jedi to expose the smugglers, and Padawan Ahsoka Tano arrives to work with cadets at the Mandalorian Royal Academy to combat them. Satine reveals Prime Minister Almec as the culprit behind the black market. He imprisons her, but she is eventually rescued by Ahsoka and the cadets.

When Darth Maul and Savage Opress arrive on Mandalore, Viszla convinces the planet's people that only the Death Watch is strong enough to stop Maul and Opress's Shadow Collective. Ousted from power, the Duchess sends a distress signal to Obi-Wan, who attempts to rescue her, but they are both captured. Maul mortally wounds Satine before a helpless Obi-Wan, for whom she expresses her eternal love as she dies.

PRIME MINISTER ALMEC

APPEARANCES CW **SPECIES** Human
HOMEWORLD Mandalore **AFFILIATION** New Mandalorians

Almec is a member of the peaceful New Mandalorian faction. He serves in the New Mandalorian government as prime minister, taking up residence in the capital city of Sundari. When Mandalore is cut off from Republic aid, Almec takes it upon himself to establish a black market to bring much-needed supplies to his people. Unfortunately, the smugglers poison the people of Sundari with slabin-tainted tea. Almec's crime is exposed and he is imprisoned for his crimes, though he remains unapologetic for helping his people. After Darth Maul takes over Sundari, he reinstates Almec as a figurehead prime minister.

Duchess's allies
When she travels to Coruscant seeking a peaceful resolution to the conflict on Mandalore, Duchess Satine enlists the help of Senator Padmé Amidala (right). Korkie Kryze and his friends from the Royal Academy free the imprisoned duchess (below).

PRE VIZSLA

APPEARANCES CW **SPECIES** Human
HOMEWORLD Mandalore **AFFILIATION** Death Watch

While governing Mandalore's moon Concordia, Pre Vizsla publicly maintains loyalty to pacifist Duchess Satine Kryze. Secretly he leads the Death Watch, a society of commandos intent on returning the Mandalorians to their ancient roots as warriors. Terrorist attacks on Mandalore bring Obi-Wan and Duchess Kryze to Concordia, where they discover the Death Watch's secret base and Vizsla reveals himself as its leader. After a short duel, Obi-Wan and Satine are forced to flee Concordia.

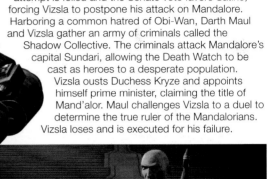

Vizsla dispatches a Death Watch assassin to Coruscant to kill the duchess and silence her opposition to the Senate's upcoming resolution to send Republic troops to occupy Mandalore. However, Vizsla hopes the Republic's occupation would convince Mandalore's people to support the Death Watch. The assassination attempt is foiled and the Senate vote favors Satine, forcing Vizsla to postpone his attack on Mandalore. Harboring a common hatred of Obi-Wan, Darth Maul and Vizsla gather an army of criminals called the Shadow Collective. The criminals attack Mandalore's capital Sundari, allowing the Death Watch to be cast as heroes to a desperate population. Vizsla ousts Duchess Kryze and appoints himself prime minister, claiming the title of Mand'alor. Maul challenges Vizsla to a duel to determine the true ruler of the Mandalorians. Vizsla loses and is executed for his failure.

The toast
Pre Vizsla reveals himself as leader of the Death Watch.

Claiming the title
Pre Vizsla addresses the people after the Death Watch wrests control of the planet from Duchess Kryze.

BOSSK

APPEARANCES CW, V, VI **SPECIES** Trandoshan **HOMEWORLD** Trandosha
AFFILIATION Bounty hunter

Notorious bounty hunter Bossk teams up with Aurra Sing and Castas to mentor young Boba Fett, who has a vendetta against his father's killer, Jedi Mace Windu. Fett destroys the engines of a Republic attack cruiser carrying Windu, causing it to crash. The bounty hunters take hostages recovered from the wreck, but the Jedi eludes them. When the team stops on Florrum to enlist the services of pirate Hondo Ohnaka, Bossk is left in charge of their ship, *Slave I*, and decides to kill the hostages. Ahsoka swoops in on a speeder bike and attacks, freeing the prisoners and capturing the bounty hunters. While imprisoned together on Coruscant for their crime, Bossk acts as Fett's bodyguard.

After they escape, Bossk continues working with Fett. When Oked, a member of Fett's team, is killed in the Mos Eisley Cantina by Asajj Ventress, Bossk and Latts Razzi blackmail her into replacing Oked on their next job—they have been hired by a

Working with Fett
Bossk teams up with young Boba Fett on Quarzite *(left)* and is assigned the same target as Fett years later on the *Executor (above)*.

Belugan, Major Rigosso, to protect a large chest. While on the job, the tram carrying the chest is attacked by Kage warriors. Bossk goes to help Ventress defend the rear, but is blinded by one of the warriors and kicked off the tram. Fortunately, he still receives his payment for the assignment.

During the Galactic Civil War, Bossk is one of six bounty hunters hired by Darth Vader to hunt down the *Millennium Falcon*, but his old partner Boba Fett beats him to the mark. Bossk meets up with Fett at Jabba the Hutt's palace, where the *Falcon*'s captain, Han Solo, is hanging

on a wall, imprisoned in carbonite. Both bounty hunters accompany Jabba's retinue aboard a sail barge to witness the execution of Han and the team of rebels who has tried to rescue him. The barge is destroyed when Han and his friends fight back.

KORKIE KRYZE

APPEARANCES CW **SPECIES** Human **HOMEWORLD** Mandalore
AFFILIATION New Mandalorian

The nephew of Duchess Satine Kryze, Cadet Korkie attends the Royal Academy of Government on Mandalore. With his friends Soniee, Amis, and Lagos, Korkie exposes fabricated food shortages that strengthen the black market supported by Mandalorian Prime Minister Almec. With the help of his friends and Bo-Katan Kryze, the Duchess's sister, Korkie frees Satine from prison after the Death Watch attacks Mandalore.

BARON PAPANOIDA

APPEARANCES CW, III **SPECIES** Pantoran
HOMEWORLD Pantora **AFFILIATION** Republic

During their blockade of Pantora, the Trade Federation kidnaps Chairman Papanoida's two daughters, Chi Eekway and Che Amanwe, as extra leverage to convince the planet's leader to side with the Separatists. Papanoida tracks the kidnapper, the bounty hunter

Greedo, to Jabba the Hutt's palace on Tatooine. When brought before Jabba by Papanoida, Greedo admits Chi Eekway is being held in Mos Eisley. Papanoida and his son Ion rescue Eekway, while Amanwe is recovered by Senator Riyo Chuchi and Ahsoka from a Droid Control Ship. Years later, following the Battle of Coruscant, Papanoida and Eekway visit the Coruscant opera house.

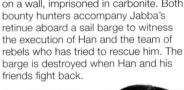

To the rescue
Baron Papanoida may lead a world, but he is not afraid to take matters into his own hands, firing on assailants in a daring rescue of his daughter Chi Eekway.

ROBONINO

APPEARANCES CW **SPECIES** Patrolian
HOMEWORLD Patrolia
AFFILIATION Bounty hunter

Bounty hunter Robonino is regarded for his computer-hacking skills and expertise with explosives. During the Senate hostage crisis led by Cad Bane, Robonino triggers the emergency lockdown in the Republic Executive Building. Later, he grabs and electroshocks Anakin Skywalker when the Jedi battles his partners Shahan Alama and Aurra Sing. Under the employ of Count Dooku, he roughs up Senators Onaconda Farr and Padmé Amidala, who oppose increased funding for the Republic's militarization.

SY SNOOTLES

APPEARANCES CW, VI **SPECIES** Pa'lowick
HOMEWORLD Lowick **AFFILIATION** Hutts

A successful singer and part-time bounty hunter, Sy Snootles dates Ziro the Hutt. Ziro's nephew Jabba hires Sy to steal Ziro's holopad, which contains damaging information about the Hutt crime families. She rescues Ziro from Nal Hutta, then accompanies him to Teth to obtain the holopad. Once she has it, Sy turns on Ziro and shoots him. In the years that follow, she turns her attention to her singing career and helps form the Max Rebo Band.

Entertainer
Sy Snootles *(far right)* sings for Jabba, her performances accompanied by the Max Rebo Band and the Hutt's dancing trio *(right)*.

GREEDO

APPEARANCES CW, IV **SPECIES** Rodian
HOMEWORLD Rodia
AFFILIATION Bounty hunter

During the Clone Wars, Greedo is a criminal who gains notoriety when Pantoran Chairman Papanoida's daughters Chi Eekway and Che Amanwe are kidnapped after his planet lobbies the Galactic Senate for assistance with a Trade Federation blockade. A statue that Che defends herself with is discovered, and the blood on it identifies Greedo, a known criminal, as the kidnapper. Papanoida and his son, Ion, track the Rodian to Tatooine, where they take him to Jabba along with proof of his involvement in the kidnapping. Greedo admits to working for the Separatists. During the rescue of Che, Greedo escapes and continues his work as a bounty hunter. Two decades later, Greedo pursues Jabba's contract for the smuggler Han Solo, who shoots and kills him in the Mos Eisley Cantina on Tatooine.

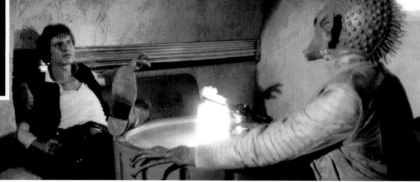

Solo bounty
When Rodian bounty hunter Greedo *(above)* corners Han Solo in the Mos Eisley Cantina *(right)*, Han takes aim.

NIX CARD

APPEARANCES CW **SPECIES** Muun
HOMEWORLD Scipio
AFFILIATION InterGalactic Banking Clan

Nix Card represents the InterGalactic Banking Clan. He plots with Count Dooku to bomb power generators on Coruscant to prevent peace talks. When power is cut to the Senate District, many senators call for the deregulation of the banks to secure the money necessary to finance troop production.

LUX BONTERI

APPEARANCES CW **SPECIES** Human **HOMEWORLD** Onderon
AFFILIATION Onderon rebels

Lux Bonteri's family sides with the Separatists when Onderon secedes at the beginning of the Clone Wars. Count Dooku orders the death of his mother, Mina Bonteri, to stop a peace proposal that she has introduced. Seeking justice after her assassination, Lux allies with the Death Watch. His friend Ahsoka Tano helps him recognize the Mandalorian warriors' dishonorable goals. Returning to Onderon, he joins the rebel movement.

Onderon rebel
Lux Bonteri is appointed the Onderon rebels' representative to the Galactic Senate.

MINA BONTERI

APPEARANCES CW **SPECIES** Human
HOMEWORLD Onderon
AFFILIATION Separatists

Mina Bonteri mentors the young Senator Padmé Amidala from Naboo. She admires Count Dooku for taking a stand against the Republic. Even though clone forces kill her husband, she advocates a peaceful resolution to the war. Padmé and Mina's work to broker peace ends when Mina is killed by Dooku's agents.

Peace talks
In the Separatist Senate, Mina Bonteri moves to open peace negotiations with the Republic.

Duplicitous apprentice
Talzin presents Savage Opress to Count Dooku as his new apprentice. Opress's loyalties have been bound to Talzin by spells that provide his strength and power.

MOTHER TALZIN

APPEARANCES CW **SPECIES** Dathomirian
HOMEWORLD Dathomir
AFFILIATION Nightsisters

Both a clan mother and a shaman on Dathomir, Mother Talzin uses any means to protect her people, including trading the infant Asajj Ventress to the criminal Hal'Sted. Ventress later trains with Dooku, but flees to Dathomir when he tries to kill her. Talzin reveals Ventress's true identity as a Nightsister and sends her and two other Nightsisters to assassinate Dooku, but they fail. Talzin offers Dooku a new apprentice, Savage Opress. Before

sending Opress, she casts a spell on him to make him stronger and ensure his ultimate loyalty to her. After Opress fails to defeat Dooku, Talzin sends him on a quest to find his brother Darth Maul, long believed dead. Dooku orders Grievous to attack Dathomir in retaliation for Talzin's strikes. Talzin uses her witchcraft to destroy numerous battle droids, then retreats to conjure dark magic to torture the Count. When Grievous reaches her, she vanishes into thin air. After finding Maul, Opress brings him to Talzin, and she uses magic to restore Maul's memories and create a pair of cybernetic legs. The disorder strewn by Maul's machinations after his resurrection ultimately draws the attention of Darth Sidious himself, allowing Talzin and her son to seek revenge for Maul's earlier untimely demise.

Nightsister returned
After Asajj Ventress's mentor Count Dooku tries to kill her, Mother Talzin welcomes her back into the Nightsister fold.

SAVAGE OPRESS

APPEARANCES CW **SPECIES** Dathomirian
HOMEWORLD Dathomir
AFFILIATION Nightbrothers

After Savage Opress is handpicked by Asajj Ventress to become her apprentice, Mother Talzin uses dark magic to grant him fearsome abilities and to ensure his loyalty. He kills his brother Feral to prove his allegiance. Mother Talzin offers him to Count Dooku as a dark acolyte. Dispatched alone to the Devaron system, Opress slaughters Jedi Master Halsey and his apprentice Knox. Impressed, Dooku accepts Opress as his Sith apprentice, intending to use him to overthrow his own Sith Master, Darth Sidious. However, Ventress subjects Opress to brutal training in order to pit him against Dooku. When Ventress and Opress battle Dooku on Toydaria, she cannot control his rage-filled impulses. Opress escapes to Dathomir, where he learns from Talzin about the fate that has befallen his brother Darth Maul, who has been cut in half by Jedi Obi-Wan Kenobi. Opress rescues Maul from Lotho Minor and brings him to Talzin, who heals him.

Deadly foe
After winning a competition among his Nightbrothers, Savage Opress is transformed by Nightsister magic into a terrifying opponent for the Jedi.

Opress joins his brother in seeking vengeance on Kenobi, who pursues Opress and Maul across the galaxy. Ultimately the brothers ally with the Death Watch and Shadow Collective to seize control of Mandalore. This attracts unwanted attention from Darth Sidious, who confronts the powerful brothers and strikes down Opress.

Duel to the death
Noting the growing power of the brothers, Sidious confronts Savage Opress and Darth Maul on Mandalore (left). As he dies, Opress expresses regret that he was never Maul's equal.

BROTHER VISCUS

APPEARANCES CW **SPECIES** Zabrak
HOMEWORLD Dathomir **AFFILIATION**
Nightbrothers

A leader of a Nightbrothers village on
Dathomir, Viscus oversees the tournament
used by Asajj Ventress to select Savage
Opress as a worthy apprentice. Mother
Talzin dispatches Viscus and a squad of
Nightbrothers to aid Darth Maul and the
Shadow Collective in capturing Count
Dooku and General Grievous in a clash
at Ord Mantell.

Arrival on Mortis
The landscape shifts seasons as the Jedi travel across Mortis, depending
on whether the Daughter or the Son is influencing the area.

THE DAUGHTER

APPEARANCES CW **SPECIES** Force wielder **HOMEWORLD** Mortis
AFFILIATION The Force

The Daughter is a Force wielder aligned with the light side
of the Force. A visit by Anakin Skywalker, Obi-Wan Kenobi,
and Ahsoka Tano brings conflict between the Daughter and
her brother, the Son, who is aligned with the dark side. When
the Son attempts to murder their father, the Daughter takes
Obi-Wan to retrieve the Dagger of Mortis, the only weapon that
can stop him. The Son gains control of the dagger from the Jedi
and strikes at the Father. The Daughter shields him from the
blow and is mortally wounded.

THE FATHER

APPEARANCES CW **SPECIES** Force wielder **HOMEWORLD** Mortis
AFFILIATION The Force

A powerful family of Force wielders, known as the Ones, resides
in the mysterious realm of Mortis. There, the Father maintains
balance between his daughter, who has an affinity for the light
side of the Force, and his son, who aligns with the dark side.
When Anakin, Obi-Wan, and Ahsoka arrive on Mortis, Anakin
encounters the Father at his monastery and is given a test to
determine if he truly is the prophesied Chosen One. When Anakin
succeeds, the Father admits he is dying and asks Anakin to take
his place on Mortis to maintain the balance of the Force.

The Chosen One
The Father helps Anakin use
the fading powers of the dying
Daughter to heal Ahsoka.

THE SON

APPEARANCES CW **SPECIES** Force wielder
HOMEWORLD Mortis **AFFILIATION** The Force

The Son seeks to escape Mortis and wreak havoc in
the galaxy. His ambitions are hindered by the Father,
who has bound his children to Mortis, where he can
maintain balance between the two. With the arrival of
Anakin, the Son sees an opportunity to escape. He
corrupts Ahsoka, but the Padawan's brief fall to the
dark side fails to turn Anakin—he and Obi-Wan refuse
to harm Ahsoka. The Son then tries to kill the Father,

Escape
The Son believes
Anakin Skywalker,
the prophesied
Chosen One, is the
key to his escape
from Mortis.

instead inadvertently slaying his sister, the Daughter.
The Father forsakes his own life, thereby robbing the
Son of his immortality and allowing the Chosen One,
Anakin, to kill the dark one.

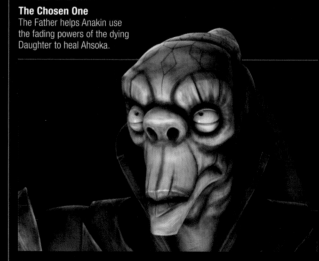

OSI SOBECK

APPEARANCES CW **SPECIES** Phindian **HOMEWORLD** Phindar
AFFILIATION Separatist

Osi Sobeck is the warden of the infamous Separatist prison
known as the Citadel. He specializes in torturing and breaking
Jedi prisoners of war. Count Dooku assigns Sobeck the
responsibility of learning the coordinates of a well-hidden
hyperspace lane, information Jedi Even Piell and Captain
Wilhuff Tarkin had memorized prior to their capture.

"You may fire when ready." GRAND MOFF TARKIN

Birth of a superweapon
At the end of the Clone Wars, Admiral Tarkin, Emperor Palpatine, and Darth Vader survey the early construction of the Death Star.

GRAND MOFF TARKIN

APPEARANCES CW, III, R, IV   **SPECIES** Human
HOMEWORLD Eriadu
AFFILIATION Republic, Empire

An ambitious, ruthless proponent of military power, Wilhuff Tarkin becomes a favorite of Supreme Chancellor Palpatine. While serving alongside Jedi General Even Piell during the Clone Wars, Tarkin undertakes a mission with Piell to find the strategic hyperspace lane known as the Nexus Route. Attacked by Separatist forces, each man memorizes half of the Route's coordinates before erasing them from the ship's computer files. Tarkin and Piell are imprisoned at the Citadel, a Separatist facility on Lola Sayu, but are freed by a Jedi strike team. After General Piell is killed during the rescue operation, Tarkin learns that Piell shared his half of the intelligence with Ahsoka prior to his death.

Arriving back on Coruscant, Tarkin insists that his orders strictly forbid him from sharing the information with anyone other than Chancellor Palpatine. Likewise, Ahsoka had promised Piell she would share her half of the information only with the Jedi Council.

Later in the war, Tarkin recommends gradually phasing out the Jedi from military command. He fears that the Republic would inevitably lose the war under the leadership of the Jedi's strict moral code. After the bombing of the Jedi Temple hangar, Tarkin transfers the accused perpetrator, Letta Turmond, into military custody. Tarkin informs Ahsoka that Turmond wishes to speak with her. While Ahsoka is alone in the cell with her, Turmond is strangled to death with the Force. Ahsoka is arrested but soon escapes. When she is recaptured, Tarkin appears before the Jedi Council on behalf of the Senate to demand that Ahsoka be expelled from the Jedi Order so that she

can stand trial in a military tribunal. The Jedi Council concedes. Ahsoka is tried before a jury of senators, with Tarkin arguing for the prosecution and Padmé Amidala for the defense. Before the verdict can be read, however, Barriss Offee confesses to the crimes.

Shortly after the Empire's creation, the Emperor puts Tarkin in charge of the construction of the Death Star. Tarkin views the superweapon as a means to crush all dissent against the Empire's rule. After the Rebel Alliance steals plans to the Death Star, Tarkin demonstrates the station's power by destroying Princess Leia's homeworld of Alderaan. Tarkin dies soon afterward when the Death Star is destroyed by the Rebel Alliance during the Battle of Yavin.

Empire's might
Tarkin and his Imperial strategists meet aboard the original Death Star *(left)*. Princess Leia must reveal the location of the secret rebel base or watch Alderaan be destroyed *(below)*.

THE CLONE WARS

Helpful friend
Chewbacca's repair skills assist Anakin Skywalker's apprentice, Ahsoka Tano, in escaping Trandoshan captivity.

▲ Jedi ally
When Yoda is betrayed after Order 66, Chewbacca delivers the Jedi Master to an escape pod.

▼ First mate
Obi-Wan Kenobi consults Chewbacca before hiring Han Solo for passage from Tatooine to Alderaan.

Solo's conscience
Han wants to take the rebels' reward payment and leave, but Chewbacca openly questions him.

▲ Furry jester
Chewbacca's amusement at Han's poorly concealed jealousy sparks the retort, "Laugh it up, fuzzball."

THE EMPIRE ERA

▲ Repairing "Goldenrod"
Han may think C-3PO is obnoxious, but Chewbacca gently rebuilds the de-limbed protocol droid.

Loyalty honored
Chewbacca submits to temporary imprisonment by Jabba the Hutt as part of the plan to rescue Han.

Hungry Wookiee
A slab of meat gets the rebels' Endor strike team captured when Chewbacca cannot resist the bait.

Big and small
Chewbacca teams with the diminutive Ewoks to capture an Imperial AT-ST walker.

timeline

"Let the Wookiee win." C-3PO

CHEWBACCA

Best friend of Han Solo and co-pilot of the *Millennium Falcon*, Chewbacca takes up the fight against the Empire, which has made his fellow Wookiees suffer unimaginable horrors.

APPEARANCES CW, III, IV, V, VI, VII **SPECIES** Wookiee **HOMEWORLD** Kashyyyk **AFFILIATION** Rebel Alliance

THE CLONE WARS
Chewbacca is captured by Trandoshan trophy hunters and taken to Wasskah, where Ahsoka Tano and Jedi younglings O-Mer and Jinx are already held as prey. In hopes of commandeering a flight off the moon, the Jedi attack the dropship delivering Chewbacca. Though the vessel crashes, they find a powerful ally in the mighty Wookiee, who cobbles together a transmitter from the crashed ship's remains and sends a distress call. When things look their bleakest, Chief Tarfful and a team of Wookiees arrive to rescue Chewbacca and his new friends. At the conclusion of the Clone Wars, Chewbacca fights by Tarfful's side during the Battle of Kashyyyk and aids Jedi Master Yoda's escape after Order 66.

Longtime partners
After learning Obi-Wan Kenobi is willing to pay for a fast ride, Chewbacca introduces the Jedi to his partner, Han Solo.

SMUGGLING PARTNERSHIP
During the dark times of Imperial tyranny, Chewbacca turns to a life of smuggling as co-pilot on Han Solo's *Millennium Falcon*. On one fateful spice run, they are forced to dump their cargo to escape Imperial pursuit, which puts them into debt with Jabba the Hutt, who seeks retribution for his lost contraband. Tempted by the sizable back-end payment for delivering Obi-Wan and his protégé plus two droids to Alderaan, Han and Chewbacca accept the job, unwittingly taking the first step toward new friendships with Luke Skywalker and Princess Leia Organa and a life with the Rebel Alliance.

REBEL WARRIOR
When Han Solo wants to leave with their reward for delivering Princess Leia to the rebel base on Yavin 4, Chewbacca provokes his friend's conscience, convincing him to turn around. The *Millennium Falcon*'s shot at Darth Vader's TIE fighter buys Luke Skywalker the time to fire the torpedo that destroys the Death Star. When the second Death Star again threatens the galaxy, Chewbacca joins the strike force that destroys its shield generator.

Wookiee intimidation
Chewbacca helps the Jedi convince Trandoshan hunter Smug to call the main lodge for help.

Two against the Empire
On Hoth, Han and Chewbacca scout for Imperial threats outside Echo Base.

Loyal friend
Typical of many Wookiees, Chewbacca values honor and friendship above all else. He does not hesitate to put his life on the line for his smuggler partner Han Solo.

CHIEF TARFFUL

APPEARANCES CW, III **SPECIES** Wookiee
HOMEWORLD Kashyyyk
AFFILIATION Galactic Republic

Tarfful is a Wookiee chieftain and general. During the Clone Wars, he leads the rescue of his friend Chewbacca, held captive with Ahsoka and other young Jedi by Trandoshan hunters. In the Battle of Kashyyyk, the two Wookiees serve alongside Jedi Generals Yoda and Luminara Unduli and help Yoda escape the Order 66 massacre.

NOSSOR RI

APPEARANCES CW **SPECIES** Quarren
HOMEWORLD Mon Cala
AFFILIATION Separatists, Galactic Republic

The Quarren chieftain on Mon Cala, Nossor Ri plots to switch the planet's allegiance to the Separatist side of the Clone Wars. When he realizes Count Dooku is merely exploiting the situation for his own ends, however, he leads his people to rejoin the Mon Calamari, supported by Jedi and clone troopers, and expel the Separatists.

LEE-CHAR

APPEARANCES CW **SPECIES** Mon Calamari
HOMEWORLD Mon Cala
AFFILIATION Galactic Republic

The rightful heir to the crown after his father's assassination, the Mon Calamari prince Lee-Char faces opposition from Separatist sympathizers who wish to see a Quarren king of Mon Cala instead. Despite assistance from Senator Padmé Amidala and Jedi Knight Anakin Skywalker, Riff Tamson instigates a violent uprising. Trusting the wisdom of his father's adviser, Captain Ackbar, Lee-Char overcomes his self-doubt and leads the Mon Calamari warriors into battle. Afterward, he is crowned king.

Crown prince
Denied a peaceful succession to the throne, Lee-Char is forced to pick up a weapon and fight alongside his people to reclaim his crown.

RIFF TAMSON

APPEARANCES CW **SPECIES** Karkarodon
HOMEWORLD Karkaris
AFFILIATION Separatists

One of Count Dooku's vicious Separatist warlords, Riff Tamson's Karkarodon physiology makes him the perfect choice to lead military operations on aquatic worlds. He secretly assassinates the king of Mon Cala, then openly leads agitators, urging a civil war between its Quarren and Mon Calamari populations. He hunts the rightful heir, Prince Lee-Char, who ultimately kills Tamson with one of his own exploding knives.

Adaptable
An aquatic species, Mon Calamari can breathe and work both underwater and on land.

Mission commander
Admiral Ackbar explains the battle plan for the assault on the second Death Star *(left)*, and later commands the battle from the bridge of his flagship, *Home One (below)*.

ADMIRAL ACKBAR

APPEARANCES CW, VI
SPECIES Mon Calamari
HOMEWORLD Mon Cala
AFFILIATION Galactic
Republic, Rebel Alliance

Admiral Ackbar's esteemed military career spans decades. During the Clone Wars, he holds the rank of captain of the Mon Calamari Guard. Trying to provoke a civil war on the planet Mon Cala, Separatists use Quarren insurgents to obstruct the succession to the throne of the rightful heir, Prince Lee-Char. After aqua battle droids led by Separatist Riff Tamson lay siege to the capitol, the Republic responds with underwater clone troopers and several Jedi to bolster the Mon Calamari forces. The Separatist attack nonetheless proves overwhelming, and Ackbar advises the prince to order a strategic retreat into caves on the sea floor. Tamson betrays the Quarren, however, leading them to reunite with the Mon Calamari, and Ackbar helps lead the counterassault to drive out the unwelcome invaders.

By the time of the Battle of Endor, Admiral Ackbar is the leader of the Rebel Alliance fleet. He personally commands the attack on the second Death Star. Seeing the size of the Imperial fleet massed to protect the space station, which is still under construction, Ackbar realizes the rebels have been led into a trap. With Imperial Star Destroyers engaging the rebels and the Death Star's superlaser blasting capital ships to smithereens, Ackbar prepares to order a retreat. At the last moment, Lando Calrissian convinces him to give Han Solo and Princess Leia more time. Their mission to take down the Death Star's shields succeeds, and Ackbar leads the rebel fleet in routing the Imperials.

SENATOR MEENA TILLS

APPEARANCES CW, III **SPECIES** Mon
Calamari **HOMEWORLD** Mon Cala
AFFILIATION Galactic Republic

A female Mon Calamari, Meena Tills is a Galactic senator during the Clone Wars. When Quarren insurgents on Mon Cala threaten to ally with the Separatists, Tills returns to her homeworld to assist the Jedi and clone army intervention that ultimately defeats the Separatist uprising. Tills joins the delegation of senators who oppose Chancellor Palpatine's continuation of his emergency powers, which later puts her at risk.

Jedi traitor
When clone troopers attempt to arrest Jedi General Krell, he fights back.

HYDROID MEDUSA

APPEARANCES CW **HOMEWORLD** Karkaris
AVERAGE SIZE 22 m (72 ft) long
AFFILIATION Separatists

Hydroid medusas are gargantuan jellyfish weaponized with cybernetic enhancements. Impervious to blasters and lightsabers, they wreak havoc on underwater battlefields with their electrified tentacles. In the Battle of Mon Cala, the Gungan Grand Army uses boomas to short-circuit the hydroid medusas.

BOSS LYONIE

APPEARANCES CW **SPECIES**
Gungan **HOMEWORLD** Naboo
AFFILIATION Gungan
High Council

Boss Lyonie bears an uncanny resemblance to Jar Jar Binks. He is hypnotically controlled briefly by an aide, Rish Loo, who is in league with Count Dooku to start a civil war. When Lyonie is gravely injured, Jar Jar poses as him to restore trust between the Gungans and the Naboo.

PONG KRELL

APPEARANCES CW **SPECIES** Besalisk
HOMEWORLD Ojom **AFFILIATION** Jedi Order

The only thing more imposing than Pong Krell's Besalisk physique is his reputation as a Jedi general in the Clone Wars. Renowned for his ruthlessness on the battlefield and intolerance of insubordination, he wields two double-bladed lightsabers but rarely chooses to fight alongside his troops. With war dragging on, Krell foresees the demise of the Jedi Order and the Republic and chooses the dark side of the Force in self-preservation.

On Umbara, Krell tricks two legions of clone troopers into attacking each other. After his treason is discovered by Captain Rex, Krell is killed by a devoted trooper named Dogma.

C-21 HIGHSINGER

APPEARANCES CW **SPECIES** Assassin droid
HOMEWORLD Unknown **AFFILIATION** Bounty hunter

A heavily modified assassin droid of unknown origin, C-21 Highsinger is presumably the only one of his kind. Serving no master, his autonomous programming is well suited to a bounty-hunting career. Most vicious among his capabilities is a rotator assembly that spins his upper torso at high speed, allowing him to unleash his blasters in a devastating circle of laser fire. His servomotors are optimized for swift reflexes, giving him proficiency in movement and hand-to-hand combat. On the planet Quarzite, during the Clone Wars, he dispatches many Kage Warriors in combat on a subtram; he is only stopped when they propel him overboard.

Team Boba
Highsinger and Latts Razzi *(below)* join Boba Fett to protect a locked box being delivered by tram.

MORALO EVAL

APPEARANCES CW **SPECIES** Phindian
HOMEWORLD Phindar
AFFILIATION Separatists

A heartless and deranged criminal, Moralo Eval brags that he killed his mother because he got bored. He escapes Republic prison alongside Cad Bane and Rako Hardeen, who is actually Obi-Wan Kenobi undercover. Bane and Hardeen compete in Eval's skill challenge, the Box, earning spots on a team that will attempt to kidnap Chancellor Palpatine.

OLD DAKA

APPEARANCES CW **SPECIES** Dathomirian
HOMEWORLD Dathomir
AFFILIATION Nightsisters

Old Daka is the oldest and wisest of the elders in Mother Talzin's Nightsisters clan, and her mastery of ancient magic is unparalleled. When General Grievous's forces attack the clan, Daka's incantation conjures an undead horde of Nightsister zombies to fight the battle droids. Grievous personally tracks down Daka in her hidden cave and slays her with his lightsaber.

LATTS RAZZI

APPEARANCES CW **SPECIES** Theelin
HOMEWORLD Unknown
AFFILIATION Bounty hunter

Even more distinctive than Latts Razzi's bright red hair is her primary weapon of choice, the grappling boa. Razzi spars with opponents by either cracking the green, scaled boa like a whip or using it as a lasso to ensnare them. One of Razzi's capers involves joining Boba Fett's cargo delivery job on the planet Quarzite, where she fends off attacking Kage Warriors. Later, Razzi takes work from the Hutts.

MIRAJ SCINTEL

APPEARANCES CW **SPECIES** Zygerrian
HOMEWORLD Zygerria
AFFILIATION Separatists

Queen of Zygerria Miraj Scintel seeks to restore her planet's former glory as the center of a slave-trading empire. She allies with the Separatists in the Clone Wars, leading the Jedi to intervene. Scintel attempts to romance Anakin Skywalker but is rebuffed. Later, when she turns against Count Dooku, he kills her.

BO-KATAN KRYZE

APPEARANCES CW
SPECIES Human **HOMEWORLD** Mandalore
AFFILIATION Death Watch

Like her sister, Duchess Satine, Bo-Katan Kryze is faithfully devoted to her homeworld of Mandalore. Rejecting Satine's commitment to pacifism, Kryze joins the Death Watch, an outlawed warrior sect that seeks to return Mandalore to its glorious past. However, she is skeptical of Pre Vizsla's alliance with Darth Maul to depose Satine. When the Sith Lord slays Vizsla, Kryze sees her worst fears for her planet come true.

DERROWN

APPEARANCES CW **SPECIES** Parwan
HOMEWORLD Parwa
AFFILIATION Bounty hunter

Derrown is a ruthless bounty hunter who has earned the nickname "The 'Exterminator.'" He has the innate ability to electrify his body with crackling energy, and his tentacled physiology, containing lighter-than-air gases, enables him to float to positions others would struggle to reach. These advantages help him successfully pass the Box, Count Dooku's bounty-hunter challenge.

DENGAR

APPEARANCES CW, V, VI **SPECIES** Human
HOMEWORLD Corellia **AFFILIATION** Bounty hunter

Dengar is one of the most dangerous bounty hunters in the galaxy. Wearing plated battle armor and a turban, he pursues targets with his blaster rifle and mini grenades. During the Clone Wars, he undertakes a mission organized by Boba Fett to safeguard a locked chest being shipped by tram on the planet Quarzite. When Kage Warriors attack, Dengar fights off as many as he can until he is thrown from the tram. Another time, while in the service of the Hutts, they are attacked by forces commanded by Darth Maul and Pre Vizsla. Dengar flees with his fellow mercenaries when it becomes clear defeat is inevitable. Years later, Dengar is one of the bounty hunters summoned by Darth Vader to hunt for the *Millennium Falcon*.

Train battle
On board a subterranean tram, Dengar battles a Kage Warrior to defend Boba Fett's team.

DEATH STAR ESCAPE

"When you came in here, didn't you have a plan for getting out?"
PRINCESS LEIA

Trapped inside the Death Star, the *Millennium Falcon*'s passengers attempt to liberate Princess Leia and make a daring getaway.

The *Millennium Falcon*'s crew—Han Solo and Chewbacca—are hired to bring Obi-Wan Kenobi, Luke Skywalker, R2-D2, and C-3PO to Alderaan. However, they are shocked to discover that Alderaan has been blasted to rubble, and pursue a TIE fighter toward what appears to be a small moon, but is actually an enormous Imperial battle station, the Death Star. A tractor beam snares the *Falcon* and draws her into a docking bay, but the *Falcon*'s crew and passengers avoid capture and infiltrate the bay's control room. After Obi-Wan leaves to shut down the tractor beam, R2-D2 learns that Princess Leia is imprisoned on the Death Star, and scheduled for execution. Luke hastily proposes a rescue mission.

BOLD BREAKOUT
Disguised as stormtroopers, Luke and Han pretend to escort their Wookiee "prisoner" to the detention area where Leia is being held captive. They manage to free Leia, but the arrival of real stormtroopers forces them all to dive into a chute that empties into a trash compactor. Fortunately, R2-D2 and C-3PO shut down the compactor before it crushes their human compatriots. Luke and Han rush Leia back to the *Falcon*, while Obi-Wan disables the tractor beam. However, when the Jedi warrior returns to join his allies at the Death Star docking bay, he encounters Darth Vader, who engages his former Master in a duel. To ensure that Luke, Leia, and the others escape, Obi-Wan allows Vader to strike him down, but becomes one with the Force.

Final duel
Their lightsabers brightly flashing as they clash, Vader and Obi-Wan duel for the last time outside the Death Star docking bay that holds the *Millennium Falcon*.

Fateful adventure
After exiting the trash compactor, Luke, Leia, and Han keep an eye out for stormtroopers as they make a dash for the *Falcon*. In the heat of the moment, they have little idea that their adventures together are just beginning.

KING SANJAY RASH

APPEARANCES CW **SPECIES** Human **HOMEWORLD** Onderon **AFFILIATION** Separatists

After King Ramsis Dendup refuses to commit Onderon to the Clone Wars, Sanjay Rash deposes him, assuming the crown. Some Onderon citizens successfully rebel against the Separatist droid army occupation requested by Rash. Before the Separatists' retreat, however, Rash is killed by super tactical droid Kalani on Count Dooku's command.

SAW GERRERA

APPEARANCES CW **SPECIES** Human **HOMEWORLD** Onderon **AFFILIATION** Onderon rebels

Saw Gerrera leads the Onderon rebels in their formative era. He and Lux Bonteri request assistance from the Jedi, who agree to train them. During the rebel victory, Saw shoots down a Separatist gunship that crashes near his sister Steela, causing her to fall off a cliff to her death. Saw later becomes a key figure in the rebellion against the Empire.

STEELA GERRERA

APPEARANCES CW **SPECIES** Human **HOMEWORLD** Onderon **AFFILIATION** Onderon rebels

After the Onderon rebels destroy a key power generator, Steela is elected their leader. Her courageous speech to the people of Onderon prompts Sanjay Rash to set a trap: former king Dendup's public execution. With the help of Stella's brother Saw, the rebels succeed in rescuing Dendup and restoring him to power.

GENERAL TANDIN

APPEARANCES CW **SPECIES** Human **HOMEWORLD** Onderon **AFFILIATION** Royal Onderon Militia

Although General Tandin initially supports King Rash, he disagrees with super tactical droid Kalani on how to deal with the Onderon rebels, and a conversation with captured rebel Saw Gerrera reinforces his doubts. The general leads the palace guard to stop Dendup's execution and pledges his support to the rightful king.

WAC-47

APPEARANCES CW **SPECIES** DUM-series pit droid **HOMEWORLD** Unknown **AFFILIATION** Galactic Republic

WAC-47 serves as D-Squad's pilot when they infiltrate a Separatist dreadnought to steal an encryption module. After crash-landing on Abafar, D-Squad uncovers a plot to blow up a space station using a stolen Republic cruiser. To foil the plan, WAC-47 has to leave R2-D2 behind to destroy the cruiser.

MEEBUR GASCON

APPEARANCES CW **SPECIES** Zilkin **HOMEWORLD** Unknown **AFFILIATION** Galactic Republic

Meebur Gascon was a tactical adviser during the First Battle of Geonosis. Later he led a D-Squad mission to steal an encryption module. Diminutive in stature, he often rides inside the droid M5-BZ. Gascon devises the daring plan to stop the Separatists from destroying a space station.

GREGOR

APPEARANCES CW **SPECIES** Human **HOMEWORLD** Kamino **AFFILIATION** Galactic Republic

A clone commando designated CC-5576-39, Gregor serves as a captain in the Grand Army of the Republic. He suffers amnesia when Republic forces are defeated on the planet Sarrish and ends up on Abafar, where the Sullustan, Borkus, employs him as a dishwasher. When D-Squad runs into Gregor, they help him recover his memory and enlist his help. At the local Separatist mining facility, Gregor dispatches battle droids and provides cover for D-Squad. After Gascon and M5-BZ get separated from the group, Gregor retrieves them. When D-Squad escapes aboard the shuttle, Gregor is overrun by the droid forces as the facility is destroyed.

ZITON MOJ

APPEARANCES CW **SPECIES** Falleen **HOMEWORLD** Falleen **AFFILIATION** Shadow Collective, Black Sun

Ziton Moj is Captain of the Guard for the Black Sun crime syndicate during the Clone Wars. After Savage Opress kills Black Sun leader Xomit Grunseit, Moj joins Darth Maul's Shadow Collective. During the takeover of Sundari, he leads disruptions throughout the Mandalorian city, before his capture by Bo-Katan Kryze.

LOM PYKE

APPEARANCES CW **SPECIES** Pyke **HOMEWORLD** Oba Diah **AFFILIATION** Shadow Collective, Pyke Syndicate

Hired by Tyranus, Lom Pyke kills Jedi Master Sifo-Dyas and captures his companion, Silman, who is Chancellor Valorum's aide. During the Clone Wars, Pyke joins the Shadow Collective. When Obi-Wan Kenobi and Anakin Skywalker confront Pyke during their investigation of Sifo-Dyas' death, Pyke reveals that Dooku is Tyranus. He is then killed by Dooku.

Selfless hero
On the planet Sarrish and again on Abafar, Gregor acts bravely, putting the lives of others before his own. He ensures D-Squad's escape, enabling them to later thwart a terrorist strike in the Carida system.

QUEEN JULIA

APPEARANCES CW **SPECIES** Bardottan
HOMEWORLD Bardotta
AFFILIATION Dagoyan Masters

Queen Julia rules over the peaceful planet Bardotta. After the Dagoyan Masters mysteriously vanish, she requests help from her old friend Jar Jar Binks. When Julia also is kidnapped by the Frangawl Cult, Jar Jar and Mace Windu track down and rescue her before Mother Talzin can steal her life essence.

DARTH BANE

APPEARANCES CW **SPECIES** Human
HOMEWORLD Unknown **AFFILIATION** Sith

Darth Bane is the sole survivor when the Jedi Order destroys the Sith a thousand years before the Clone Wars. Recognizing that infighting has weakened the Sith, Bane creates the Rule of Two when he reforms the order, mandating that there can be only a Master and an apprentice.

SIFO-DYAS

APPEARANCES II, CW **SPECIES** Human
HOMEWORLD Cassandran Worlds
AFFILIATION Jedi/Galactic Republic

Some time prior to the Invasion of Naboo, Master Sifo-Dyas takes a seat on the Jedi Council. Foreseeing a coming galactic war, he advocates for the creation of an army for the Republic. He is removed from the Council because his ideas are considered too extreme. Sifo-Dyas nevertheless proceeds with his plan, secretly commissioning the clone army from the Kaminoans while pretending to act with authorization from the Galactic Senate and the Jedi Council. Under this subterfuge' Chancellor Valorum covertly dispatches Sifo-Dyas to negotiate with the Pyke Syndicate. However, after initially mediating a tribal dispute on Felucia, Sifo-Dyas is killed when the Pykes are paid by the Sith to shoot down his shuttle.

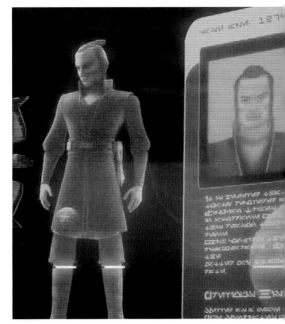

FORCE PRIESTESSES

APPEARANCES CW **SPECIES** Unknown
HOMEWORLD Unknown **AFFILIATION** Force

These mysterious Force-entities represent five emotions: serenity, joy, anger, confusion, and sadness. They test Yoda with daunting trials as a Jedi Master, including visiting the Sith homeworld. When the trials are complete, the priestesses deem Yoda worthy of retaining his identity in the Force beyond death, thus granting him immortality.

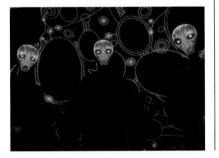

VARACTYL

APPEARANCES III **HOMEWORLD** Utapau
SIZE 15 m (49.2 ft) long **HABITAT** Arid scrubland, Utapauan sinkholes

Reptavian herbivores native to Utapau, the varactyl are known to be loyal and obedient steeds. To track down General Grievous in Pau City, Obi-Wan Kenobi rides a particularly swift varactyl named Boga. They quickly reach the tenth level and chase General Grievous on his wheel bike through the city. Along the way, Boga smashes several battle droids before the Jedi Master fights and kills Grievous. After Palpatine gives the command for Order 66, the clone troopers turn against Obi-Wan. Boga and her Jedi rider are caught in an AT-TE cannon blast that strikes a nearby wall, forcing the pair to plummet into the water at the bottom of the sinkhole.

ROOK KAST

APPEARANCES Other **SPECIES** Human
HOMEWORLD Mandalore
AFFILIATION Shadow Collective

Rook Kast leads the Mandalorian supercommandos in Darth Maul's Shadow Collective. At Ord Mantell, Kast boards General Grievous' command ship with Maul to capture the Separatist leader. Later, Kast and Gar Saxon combat clone troopers led by Jedi Aayla Secura, escaping with Maul and Count Dooku.

GAR SAXON

APPEARANCES Other **SPECIES** Human
HOMEWORLD Mandalore
AFFILIATION Shadow Collective

Gar Saxon is a Mandalorian supercommando in the Shadow Collective. On orders from Mandalorian Prime Minister Almec, Saxon and Rook Kast liberates Darth Maul from The Spire prison. Saxon leads Maul's ground forces during General Grievous' attack on the Shadow Collective base at Ord Mantell.

"There is no war here unless you've brought it with you." **TION MEDON**

TION MEDON

APPEARANCES III **SPECIES** Pau'an
HOMEWORLD Utapau
AFFILIATION Galactic Republic

As Port Administrator of Pau City, Tion Medon welcomes and offers his services to guests. When Obi-Wan Kenobi arrives at the sinkhole spaceport in search of General Grievous, Medon discreetly divulges helpful information about the Separatist presence on Utapau. Obi-Wan suggests that Medon gather the planet's warriors for the coming battle.

"I am a Jedi, like my father before me." LUKE SKYWALKER

LUKE SKYWALKER

Hidden on Tatooine after his mother's death, Luke emerges as a rebel hero and redeems his father on the way to becoming a Jedi Knight.

APPEARANCES III, IV, V, VI, VII **SPECIES** Human **HOMEWORLD** Tatooine **AFFILIATION** Jedi

CALL TO ADVENTURE

In need of new droids to work on his moisture farm, Luke's uncle Owen Lars purchases R2-D2 and C-3PO from Jawa traders. Little does Owen know that the Empire is scouring Tatooine for the two missing droids. When R2-D2 takes off in search of Jedi Knight Obi-Wan Kenobi, C-3PO accompanies Luke to chase down the determined astromech. R2-D2 delivers Princess Leia's message to an old hermit named Ben, who reveals his Jedi past as Obi-Wan and gives Luke the lightsaber that belonged to Luke's father, Anakin.

Wistful dreamer
Bored with the humdrum life of a moisture farmer, Luke dreams of unknown adventures awaiting him across the galaxy.

JEDI APPRENTICE

A spectral Obi-Wan appears to Luke, instructing him to journey to Dagobah and train with Jedi Master Yoda. After crashing his X-wing in a Dagobah swamp and being harassed by a mischievous creature, Luke despairs until his tormentor reveals his true identity—he is Yoda. The Jedi Master expresses doubt as to whether Luke is ready for Jedi training, but Luke persists, and Yoda accepts him as his new apprentice *(see also p. 200)*. As Luke's powers grow, he sees a vision of his friends in peril and abandons his training to mount a rescue.

Unexpected tutor
Luke arrives at Dagobah seeking to train with a legendary Jedi Master. The Master he finds isn't quite what he expects.

Trust in the Force
Goaded by the Emperor, Luke gives in to temptation and has to fight his father Darth Vader *(left)*. Later, with his life-sustaining suit damaged by Palpatine's Force lightning, Anakin Skywalker asks to see his son with his own eyes before he dies *(below)*.

REBEL HERO

Luke joins Obi-Wan on his mission to deliver the stolen Death Star plans to rebels on Alderaan. After the *Millennium Falcon* is trapped in the Death Star's tractor beam, Luke teams up with the freighter's captain, Han Solo, and first mate, Chewbacca, to free Princess Leia, who is imprisoned on the space station. After sabotaging the tractor beam, Obi-Wan sacrifices his life to let Luke and the others escape with the Death Star plans *(see also p. 106)*. Luke joins the rebel fleet and makes a daring X-wing run through the superweapon's trench, torpedoing the exhaust shaft and triggering a chain reaction that destroys the Death Star.

REDEEMING ANAKIN SKYWALKER

In his first lightsaber duel, Luke learns the truth about his father. Darth Vader had not betrayed and murdered Anakin Skywalker; Darth Vader *is* Anakin Skywalker. When Luke next crosses paths with Vader on the Endor moon, he surrenders peacefully. Although the temptation of the dark side is great, Luke resists Emperor Palpatine's overtures. In response, the vengeful Emperor pours Force lightning into Luke, inciting Vader to kill his Sith Master and save his son. With that act, Anakin is redeemed *(see also p. 146)*.

Redeeming hero
With the rise of the Empire,
Luke is one of the last hopes
of the Jedi Order. Raised in
secret on remote Tatooine,
ultimately he must face his
destiny to redeem his father,
Anakin Skywalker, and restore
balance to the Force.

timeline

▲ **Luke's birth**
When Padmé Amidala dies after childbirth,
Obi-Wan delivers Luke to Owen and
Beru Lars on Tatooine.

Message from a princess
Luke follows R2-D2 to the home of
Ben (Obi-Wan) Kenobi, where they hear a
desperate plea from Princess Leia.

Death of Owen and Beru
Orphaned again, Luke heads for Alderaan with
Obi-Wan and the droids on board the
Millennium Falcon.

▲ **Inside the beast**
Luke and his new friends free Leia from her cell,
then escape from the Death Star.

Battle of Yavin
Luke's torpedoes hit the Death Star exhaust
port, which destroys the superweapon.

Voice from the past
A vision of Obi-Wan impels Luke to seek out
Yoda on Dagobah.

Yoda trains Luke
Luke learns the ways of the Force from the
wise Jedi Master, Yoda.

▲ **Luke discovers the truth**
After an intense lightsaber duel, Darth Vader
reveals that he is Luke's father.

▲ **Rescue of Han Solo**
Jedi Luke Skywalker demands Jabba release
Han Solo. The Hutt and his minions are defeated
by the reunited friends.

▲ **Another Skywalker**
Before leaving to confront his father, Luke
reveals to Leia that she is his sister.

Anakin redeemed
Luke lays down his weapon, refusing to fight his
father. Darth Vader turns on the Emperor
as he attempts to kill Luke.

THE EMPIRE ERA

"Would it help if I got out and pushed?" PRINCESS LEIA

PRINCESS LEIA

A leader of the Rebel Alliance, Princess Leia challenges the Emperor's oppressive reign. Along the way, she finds love with Han Solo and rediscovers her long-lost brother Luke Skywalker.

APPEARANCES III, IV, V, VI, VII SPECIES Human HOMEWORLD Alderaan AFFILIATION Rebel Alliance

PRINCESS OF THE PEOPLE

An Imperial Star Destroyer captures the *Tantive IV* with Princess Leia aboard. With her mission to deliver the stolen Death Star plans to the rebels in jeopardy, Leia records a holographic message and tasks R2-D2 with seeking out Jedi Master Obi-Wan Kenobi on the nearby planet Tatooine. She distracts stormtroopers searching her ship while R2-D2 and his companion C-3PO jettison in an escape pod. Her brave refusal to reveal the rebels' location marks Alderaan as the Death Star's first target. With the planet's destruction, Leia becomes a princess without a home. Her duty to the peoples oppressed by the Empire carries on despite her loss. Escaping Imperial custody, Leia helps deliver the stolen plans to the rebel fleet, and the Death Star is eventually destroyed.

Critical mission
By way of a recorded message in R2-D2, Princess Leia delivers a desperate plea for help to her father's old ally, Obi-Wan Kenobi.

REBEL LEADER

Although Leia is a senator and diplomat, she is also a warrior. An excellent markswoman, she assumes command during her rescue from the Death Star. As the *Millennium Falcon* rockets away from the space station, Leia assists Chewbacca in flying the freighter while Luke and Han operate the quad lasers to fend off TIE fighters. On Hoth, Leia briefs the pilots as the Empire closes on Echo Base. She remains in the command center overseeing the evacuation until Han Solo insists it is time to go.

Hoth briefing
In Echo Base's icy hangar, Princess Leia briefs rebel pilots on their roles in the impending emergency evacuation.

Fixing things
Repairs on the *Millennium Falcon* put Han and Leia in tight quarters, where they share their first kiss.

MATTERS OF THE HEART

Unable to reach her rebel transport off Hoth, Princess Leia escapes on the *Millennium Falcon*. Barely eluding Imperial Star Destroyers, Han Solo decides the best option for needed repairs is the planet Bespin. During the journey, Leia and Han confront their feelings for each other. Once at Cloud City, the attraction flourishes. Their romantic interlude is short-lived, however, when they are captured by Darth Vader, who uses them as bait to lure Luke Skywalker into a trap. Leia admits she loves Han just before he is frozen in carbonite. She later frees him at the palace of Jabba the Hutt.

GALACTIC DIPLOMAT

Serving on General Solo's command squad for the rebel strike team planning to destroy the second Death Star's shield generator on the Endor moon, Leia is separated from the others after she pursues biker scouts who might report their presence. Leia encounters Wicket, a short, furry native, in the forest and is kind and patient with him despite her predicament. She and her unlikely ally take out a pair of biker scouts together. Wicket and the other Ewoks of Bright Tree Village agree to help the strike team against Imperial forces and later even free the team when they are captured.

Dinner surprise
Leia discovers her Ewok hosts have brought home new captives for dinner, and happen to be Luke, Han, and Chewbacca.

Unassuming aristocrat
The simple white robes of a princess keep Leia's enemies off-guard. She is just as handy with a blaster or at piloting as she is versed in royal protocol.

▲ **Leia's birth**
When Padmé Amidala dies after childbirth, Senator Bail Organa of Alderaan adopts Leia.

Buying time
After entrusting R2-D2 with the stolen Death Star plans, Leia distracts stormtroopers while the droid escapes with C-3PO.

Destruction of Alderaan
While a captive Leia watches in horror, Tarkin destroys her homeworld, Alderaan, to display the Death Star's might.

▲ **Escape from the Death Star**
Luke, Han, and Chewbacca free Leia and dodge stormtroopers to escape the space station.

Battle of Hoth
With the Empire closing in, Leia escapes on the *Millennium Falcon* and is separated from the fleet.

▲ **Cloud City**
Instead of refuge, Leia, Han, and Chewbacca find a trap set by Darth Vader on Cloud City.

Declaration of love
Before Han is encased in carbonite by Darth Vader, Leia admits she loves him.

▲ **To the rescue**
Disguised as a bounty hunter named Boushh, Leia joins her friends at Jabba's Palace to rescue Han Solo.

▲ **Slaying Jabba**
Captured by Jabba, Leia strangles the criminal with the chains of her captivity.

Mission to Endor
Leia volunteers for General Solo's strike team to destroy the Endor moon's shield generator.

Destruction of Death Star
The strike team blows up the shield generator, allowing the rebels to destroy the Death Star.

THE EMPIRE ERA

CAPTAIN ANTILLES

APPEARANCES III, IV **SPECIES** Human
HOMEWORLD Alderaan
AFFILIATION Republic, Rebel Alliance

Captain Raymus Antilles is commander of Bail Organa's fleet of diplomatic cruisers. Under the Empire, Antilles serves as captain of the *Tantive IV* for Organa's daughter, Leia Organa. In the battle over Tatooine, Darth Vader boards the ship and demands the stolen Death Star plans. When Antilles refuses, Vader kills him.

KANAN JARRUS

APPEARANCES R **SPECIES** Human
HOMEWORLD Coruscant
AFFILIATION Rebels

Caleb Dume (alias Kanan Jarrus) is raised on Coruscant and mentored as a Jedi Padawan by Depa Billaba. While at the Jedi Temple, he also receives lessons from various Jedi, including Obi-Wan Kenobi and Yoda. Kanan is only 14 years old when Chancellor Palpatine issues Order 66, branding the Jedi traitors and ordering their assassinations. Caleb's Jedi Master, Depa Billaba, sacrifices her own life to get him to safety, after which Caleb goes into hiding and assumes a new name, Kanan Jarrus. To avoid detection by the Empire, he abandons his Jedi teachings and drifts from world to world, taking odd jobs but never staying long enough to form attachments.

Eventually Kanan settles on the planet Gorse, where he lives in a modest room at the Asteroid Belt, a cantina owned by Okadiah Garson. Kanan works for a company called Moonglow Polychemical, which mines volatile thorilide in the crystal interior of Cynda, the moon above Gorse. Kanan leads a day-to-day existence until two people change the status quo: Count Denetrius Vidian and Hera Syndulla. The amoral Count is sent by the Emperor to improve thorilide production, and does so with catastrophic consequences. Renegade Twi'lek Hera, on the other hand, is intent on combating the Empire's atrocities.

Kanan is attracted to Hera, who sparks a gradual change in him, steering Kanan back toward the values of his Jedi past. After thwarting Vidian's dark plans, he

Jedi missions
Kanan chases Ezra on a stolen Imperial speeder outside Lothal's capital *(top)*. Kanan is on a mission with Sabine and Zeb *(above)*.

joins her on the *Ghost*. Their new rebel crew grows with the addition of Sabine Wren and Garazeb Orrelios. The team gravitates to the Outer Rim world of Lothal, where the Empire is pillaging local mineral resources to build new military machines.

During a mission, Kanan encounters Ezra Bridger, a Force-sensitive orphan living on the streets of Capital City. Sensing Ezra's potential, Kanan invites him to join them and become his Jedi apprentice. Kanan is reluctant to train Ezra, however, because he never finished his own training to become a full Jedi Knight.

On a mission to Kessel, Kanan is finally forced to reveal himself as a Jedi to the Imperials. Agent Kallus of the Imperial Security Bureau (ISB) then informs a servant of Darth Vader, known as the Inquisitor, who begins a relentless hunt for Kanan and Ezra. This results in a series of epic confrontations between the two Jedi and the dark-side assassin, leading to Kanan's eventual capture and a fateful duel.

Ship's captain
Hera is one of the best star pilots this side of the Outer Rim *(left)*. She handles the *Ghost*'s controls better than anyone on board *(below)*.

HERA SYNDULLA

APPEARANCES R **SPECIES** Twi'lek **HOMEWORLD** Ryloth
AFFILIATION Rebels

Hera Syndulla is a scion of an influential family on Ryloth. She saw her planet ravaged by violent conflict during the Clone Wars, only to see the clone troopers who once helped Ryloth's freedom fighters turn and enslave them for the Empire. Her own world is now oppressed by the Empire and drowning in corruption at the highest levels. Inspired by her revolutionary father, Cham Syndulla, Hera leaves her world behind in a quest to find other like-minded individuals and build a movement to oppose the Empire.

On a scouting mission to Gorse, Hera meets three misfits: a Sullustan, Zaluna Myder, manager at a surveillance company, Transcept Media Solutions; a disgruntled demolitions expert and Clone Wars veteran named Skelly; and a gun-slinging Jedi-in-hiding named Kanan Jarrus. Though she is not keen on any of them as potential rebel teammates, circumstances throw them all together when an Imperial efficiency expert, Count Denetrius Vidian, arrives on Lothal with a diabolical new plan.

When Kanan plays a key role in thwarting Vidian's scheme, Hera realizes his potential as a partner and invites him to join her aboard her ship, the *Ghost*. Over several adventures, Hera adds other members to her rebel crew, including ex-cadet and weapons expert Sabine Wren, a Lasat survivor named Zeb Orrelios, and an orphaned Force-sensitive named Ezra Bridger. Together with her astromech droid, Chopper, the team forms a surrogate family.

Hera is the nurturing mentor of the group, encouraging the others to do their best. She also functions as the team's ace pilot and getaway driver in their struggles against the Empire.

Hera conducts many of the team's missions in cooperation with a mysterious contact called "Fulcrum." As their mission objectives become increasingly ambitious, the crew of the *Ghost* becomes increasingly curious about Fulcrum's identity. Sabine in particular questions Hera's cooperation with Fulcrum, but when the two are shipwrecked on an asteroid with deadly fyrnocks, they reach a new understanding of mutual trust and reliance. Though not evident at first, Hera is the motivating force behind the group. Kanan allows himself to be captured so that the rest of the crew can escape when they are caught sabotaging an Imperial communications tower on Lothal. When Kanan is taken prisoner by the Empire, Hera's reliance on him becomes more obvious.

Attraction?
There is a special bond between Kanan and Hera, though it's not always visible on the surface.

Freedom fighting
Hera carries a Blurrg-1120 holdout blaster, manufactured by Eirriss Ryloth Defence Tech. It is named for a local creature on Ryloth.

RESCUE ON HOTH

"Artoo says the chances of survival are seven hundred and twenty-five... to one." C-3PO

When Luke Skywalker fails to return from his patrol of the rebel base's perimeter on the ice planet Hoth, a determined Han Solo ventures into the subfreezing night to find his friend.

After helping the Rebel Alliance destroy the Death Star, Han Solo continues to work with the rebels. He helps them to establish their new top-secret headquarters, Echo Base, on the frozen world of Hoth. Teaming up with Luke Skywalker, Han takes charge of placing security sensors around the base to prevent the infiltration of predatory wampa ice creatures. However, a run-in with a bounty hunter on the planet Ord Mantell reminds Han that his former client, the gangster Jabba the Hutt, has placed a price on his head for failing to recompense him for a lost shipment of spice. This prompts Han to leave Hoth and settle up with Jabba, but before his departure, he learns that Luke has not returned to the base from his last patrol.

SAVING LUKE

Ignoring the protests of Echo Base's deck officer, Han rides a tauntaun out of the base and into the bitter night. After hours of searching for signs of life amidst the frozen wastes, he eventually finds Luke collapsed against a snowdrift, suffering from wounds inflicted by a wampa. Han dismounts his tauntaun to check on his friend's condition, but the exhausted creature almost immediately falls dead. Undeterred, Han uses Luke's lightsaber to cut open the tauntaun's belly, and places Luke within the carcass for protection while he hastily sets up a shelter and a distress beacon. The following morning, a rebel pilot locates Han and helps him deliver Luke to Echo Base, where medical droids heal the future Jedi.

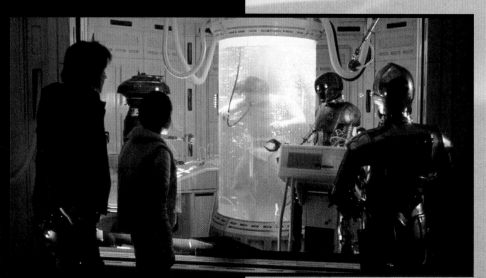

Recovery room
Inside Echo Base's medical center, Han, Leia, and C-3PO view surgical droids, who monitor Luke as he's immersed in a bacta tank. Thanks to Han and his allies, Luke makes a full recovery from his injuries.

Rebel hero
Although he exudes cynicism and mercenary tendencies, Han Solo values friendship, and readily risks his own life for his allies. When he rides out to find the missing Luke Skywalker on Hoth, he's determined to bring Luke back alive.

> "Stop whining. We're here to protect you." **LOTHAL STORMTROOPER**

STORMTROOPERS

Stormtroopers have replaced the clone armies of the Republic as expendable foot soldiers of the Empire. Their endless numbers serve across the galaxy, enforcing the Emperor's will.

APPEARANCES R, IV, V, VI **SPECIES** Human **HOMEWORLD** Various **AFFILIATION** Empire

RECRUITMENT AND TRAINING

Though not necessarily the army's deadliest weapons, beneath their white armor, stormtroopers are loyal Imperial citizens. They are mostly naturally born men, and occasionally women, who volunteer (or are conscripted) and rigorously train in Imperial academies. After the rise of the Empire, clone soldiers are gradually phased out due to their accelerated aging process. Most clones retire, but a few remain as advisers and trainers. Clone soldiers, though genetic copies, vary in personality and are surprisingly individualistic. Naturally born soldiers, in contrast, are trained and conditioned to forsake both individualism and empathy. In many ways, stormtroopers function like human droids.

Recruitment poster
This common propaganda poster on Lothal, used to recruit stormtroopers, reads "Galactic Empire: Help end the rebellion—Enlist today!" *(right)*. A garrison of stormtroopers attacks the rebel forces *(below)*.

Behind the mask
Apart from their alphanumeric designations, stormtroopers appear anonymous in their armor. This leads to an overall lack of accountability and also creates occasional opportunities for spies to impersonate soldiers.

Search for the droids
Obi-Wan Kenobi uses his Jedi powers of persuasion to get past a stormtrooper roadblock in Mos Eisley.

Officious gatekeeper
A stormtrooper officer manages the cell block where Princess Leia is held on the first Death Star.

MAINTAINING SECURITY AND ORDER

Stormtroopers are stationed on strategic worlds throughout the galaxy. On planets like Lothal, Tatooine, and Coruscant, they serve a variety of functions. They guard mining operations, factories, and commercial interests important to the Empire. They maintain societal order and monitor politically sensitive areas—stamping out all signs of rebellion. Their power, built on fear within local populations, creates an atmosphere of abuse and corruption. Some use their positions for personal gain, taking advantage of the helpless citizens in their charge. Others, whether due to blind obedience or brainwashing, carry out atrocities in the name of their Emperor, Palpatine.

DIVERSITY OF STORMTROOPERS

Stormtroopers include human men and women, but very rarely, if ever, nonhuman individuals. Outside of combat and security details, stormtrooper officers wear distinctive black caps, boots, and dress tunics. Their code cylinders, rank plaques, officers' discs, and uniform style conform to the Imperial Navy's standards. Officers in field units wear orange, black, and white pauldrons to indicate rank (unfortunately for stormtroopers, this boldly visible formality puts them at risk and many lose their lives to snipers). There are specialized units of stormtroopers, such as snowtroopers, scout troopers, and sandtroopers. Each may employ unique armor to support its niche combat roles. Army pilots may also be promoted from within their ranks.

Overwhelming numbers
An Imperial walker and stormtroopers surround Han and Chewbacca during the Battle of Endor.

TIE FIGHTER PILOTS

APPEARANCES R, IV, V, VI **SPECIES** Human
HOMEWORLD Various **AFFILIATION** Empire

The Empire's black-suited pilots fly the full range of TIEs, including fighters, bombers, interceptors, and experimental models. Only a small minority of cadets in the academy's pilot training program actually graduate with commissions. They comprise an elite class within the Imperial Navy and have a notorious superiority complex. Nonetheless, they make great sacrifices. TIE fighter pilots are trained to complete their missions at all costs, disregarding their own survival.

ON THE BATTLEFIELD

Stormtroopers are the backbone of the Imperial Army, waging war on rebel insurrection. In battle, stormtroopers are equipped with BlasTech's E-11 blasters and DLT-19 heavy blaster rifles, a thermal detonator, grappling hook, comlink, and surplus ammunition. Stormtroopers are dreaded by civilian populations—not only for their brutality but also their fanaticism to press on regardless of cost. They are trained to disregard fallen comrades in battle and to engage the enemy no matter the odds. When the Republic transitions into the Empire, stormtroopers are summoned to bring the remaining Separatist worlds into line. Later skirmishes are mostly small in size—the results of isolated rebel cells, indigenous politics, Jedi sightings, piracy and other underworld activity—until the dawn of the Rebel Alliance. As the Galactic Civil War expands, so does the involvement of stormtroopers in warfare, culminating in the Empire's defeat at the Battle of Endor.

The Navy's best
A TIE fighter pilot is seated in the cockpit during a dogfight at the Battle of Yavin.

CHOPPER (C1-10P)

APPEARANCES R **MANUFACTURER** Unknown
TYPE Astromech droid **AFFILIATION** Rebels

Chopper (C1-10P) is owned by Hera Syndulla and is an integral member of her rebel cell, despite his cantankerous, self-centered, and eccentric nature. Chopper is largely made of replacement parts. On the outside, his leg cowlings are mismatched and his paint is worn. His internal circuitry is a bit of a mess as well. Yet Hera refuses to part with him because of his resourcefulness, and perhaps because of her own sentimentality.

In addition to being the ship's chief mechanic, Chopper has also proven himself on missions. He often aids the crew of the *Ghost* as a lookout, and for such a diminutive droid, he is unusually brave, facing stormtroopers and even going undercover at Lothal's Imperial Academy.

Chopper is quite different from recent astromechs like R2-D2. He is unconcerned with what others think about him or his obligations to duty. He is fiercely independent, argumentative, and more interested in pulling pranks on Ezra, surfing the holonet, or playing dejarik than doing menial tasks aboard the *Ghost*.

Chopper has a long history and Hera isn't his only owner. For a short time, he was the property of Lando Calrissian, who won him from Zeb Orrelios in a game of sabacc. Nevertheless, Chopper has ensured his role among the crew of the *Ghost* by customizing the ship to such an extent that he is the only one aboard who can keep it operational.

Chopper doesn't mix well with other droids, often treating them with disdain. Yet he does demonstrate empathy on occasion, such as when he donates his own parts for Ezra's lightsaber construction or when he aids in the hijacking of an Imperial communications tower, at great risk to himself.

Chopper is always ready for challenges. Like every astromech, he has an extendable arm to interface with computers, manipulate doors, and fly ships. Like other C1 models, Chopper also has three robotic arms to manage objects like handles, buttons, and even blasters. Unlike later models, he has a retractable wheel instead of a third leg, and he can even activate a booster rocket from the same socket. Chopper also has an electric prod—his favorite feature—which he uses to shock friends and enemies alike.

A versatile droid
Chopper's mechanical arms not only allow him to manipulate the ship's controls but also engage TIE fighters.

SABINE WREN

APPEARANCES R **SPECIES** Human
HOMEWORLD Mandalore **AFFILIATION** Rebels

Sabine Wren is the resident weapons specialist aboard the *Ghost*. She is feisty, clever, and highly independent. Her courage and confidence are key traits of her Mandalorian heritage, though her concern for the plight of the downtrodden across the galaxy arises from her own personal journey.

Sabine develops her weapons expertise at the Imperial Academy on Mandalore before leaving and joining her rebel friends.

She is fond of explosions and creates them with artistic flair, in bright colors and unusual shapes, marked with her signature pattern, the rebel starbird. Sabine is not obsessed with violence, though, and her art is a significant part of her personal identity. Her stylish graffiti leaves its mark on TIE fighters and propaganda posters and on Lothal's allies. Her own room is likewise decorated with cartoons of the bounty hunters Embo and Cad Bane, as well as various animals and anti-Imperial symbols. Zeb and Ezra find their own room isn't immune to Sabine's creations either. Sabine's clothes and armor are often splattered with paint from successive bouts of artistic inspiration. She wears a quasi-traditional Mandalorian helmet and sports a pair of WESTAR-35 blasters. Similar gear is often used by Mandalore's notorious Death Watch, but she has customized hers with colorful designs all her own. Feared bounty hunters prefer Mandalorian gear as well, and the association tends to deter would-be aggressors.

Sabine's relationships aboard the *Ghost* are important to her, and she relies heavily on her friends, despite her strong-willed and self-sufficient nature. They have become the family that she lost on Mandalore. She looks up to Hera and Kanan as mentors and considers Zeb an older brother. She gets along with Chopper well enough, and she attributes Ezra's awkward teenage mannerisms to attraction. Her bad experiences while at the Imperial Academy mean that Sabine doesn't like being kept in the dark about things. However, a shared experience on a monster-filled asteroid helps her to put more faith in Hera's leadership.

Purpose driven
Sabine descends upon a TIE fighter airfield where she sabotages the Lothal fleet and leaves her starbird calling card.

ZEB (GARAZEB ORRELIOS)

APPEARANCES R **SPECIES** Lasat **HOMEWORLD** Lasan
AFFILIATION Rebels

Garazeb "Zeb" Orrelios is a vital member of the rebel crew aboard the *Ghost*. Despite his large size and brutish appearance, Zeb is thoughtful and sensitive, particularly to the plight of the weak and helpless. Nonetheless, Zeb gruffly speaks his mind, often not as tactfully as he should. The Lasat's tendency to act before he thinks leads Zeb and the crew into a lot of Imperial entanglements, although fighting with stormtroopers becomes one of his favorite pastimes. His impulsiveness also contributes to a sporadic gambling problem, which at one point leaves Zeb in debt to Lando Calrissian and leaves the rest of the crew to help him sort things out.

Lasat anatomy gives Zeb distinct physical advantages over humans. His digitigrade legs allow him to generally jump farther, run faster, and move more quietly than his human friends. His heavy build makes him stronger, and his large finger pads aid in climbing. Even his sizable eyes and ears offer improved senses over humans. Zeb's facial hair is a status symbol in Lasat culture.

Zeb gets along well with Kanan, Hera, and Sabine, but he's not particularly fond of Chopper. He reluctantly shares a bunk aboard the *Ghost* with Ezra (their room is sparsely furnished, but a poster of a YT-1300 freighter on the wall demonstrates Zeb's fondness for big ships). The two begin with a volatile relationship, but, over time, form a friendship much like competitive siblings. Stealing a TIE fighter in the town of Kothal establishes a positive milestone in their bond.

Zeb has a tragic past. The Empire razed his home planet of Lasan and ruthlessly murdered nearly all of its citizens. When Zeb encounters Kallus and

discovers that the Imperial Security Bureau (ISB) agent participated in the atrocity, it immediately sparks an intense rivalry between the two, leading to a series of violent confrontations.

Zeb doesn't talk about what happened to his friends and family on Lasan, but this trauma motivates him to fight for freedom for all from the Empire's tyranny. Zeb's own tragedy makes him sympathetic to the suffering of others. Even in a desperate situation, he refuses to use the Empire's own brutal weapons against them, having witnessed the effects of their horrific T-7 disruptors firsthand on Lasan.

Nonetheless, Zeb never runs from a fight. He is a former member of the Lasan Honor Guard on his home planet, and the only member of the crew with any significant combat training (apart from Kanan's early days as a Jedi Padawan). Zeb carries a Lasan bo-rifle, which is a traditional weapon unique to the Honor Guard. He is equally adept at fighting with his fists.

Handsome brute
With his green eyes and prominent purple stripes, Zeb is considered attractive for a Lasat, but few on Lothal have seen others of his species for comparison.

The guardian
Zeb has a soft spot for the small and helpless. When an Ugnaught vendor is bullied by stormtroopers, he can't resist stepping in *(above)*. During a chat with Ezra, Zeb knows that he will repay Ezra for saving his life during a duel with Agent Kallus *(left)*.

Zap!
In Lothal's capital city, Zeb pulverizes a group of stormtroopers with his bo-rifle. The shock will leave them unconscious for quite some time.

Full of surprises
Ezra carries a cadet helmet that will someday be painted by Sabine. He employs a number of gadgets, some of which he's snatched from Imperials, including the comlink on his belt, a shin-guard armor plate, a cadet's scouting pack, and a wrist-mounted slingshot. His sticky fingers always seem to acquire new items.

"It's only gonna get worse... unless we stand up and fight back." EZRA BRIDGER

EZRA BRIDGER

Born on Lothal the day the Empire was founded, Ezra Bridger is a 15-year-old orphan. His future is bleak until he meets a group of renegades who change his life forever.

APPEARANCES R **SPECIES** Human **HOMEWORLD** Lothal **AFFILIATION** Rebels

On the run
Zeb, Ezra, and Kanan flee an Imperial freighter.

A NEW REBEL FAMILY
Ezra falls in with a group of rebels (Kanan Jarrus, Hera Syndulla, Zeb Orrelios, Sabine Wren, and their droid, Chopper) when he tries to steal the same Imperial speeder shipment they are stealing. Having boarded their ship, the *Ghost*, to escape pursuing TIE fighters, they embark on a mission to rescue some Wookiee prisoners. Ezra learns to trust the crew and care for others, to the point of risking his own life. The rebels become like a family to Ezra and help give his life an exciting new purpose. Ezra makes other valuable friends along the way as well, notably Zare Leonis at the Imperial Academy of Lothal.

JEDI PADAWAN
Kanan Jarrus recognizes Ezra's keen abilities to sense things before they happen and perform extraordinary physical feats. When Ezra finds Kanan's lightsaber and activates his Jedi holocron with the Force, Hera encourages Kanan to take Ezra on as his Padawan. Ezra shows promise right away, but he is undisciplined and impatient, and his ability to manipulate the Force is erratic, coming in powerful bursts that concern Kanan. With Kanan's help, Ezra locates a hidden Jedi temple where Ezra confronts his fears, attachments, and his desire for revenge against those responsible for his parents' disappearance. He finds a kyber crystal in the temple and builds his own unconventional lightsaber. The Inquisitor, however, looms as a continuing threat.

A new life
Kanan welcomes Ezra as a member of the crew aboard the *Ghost* and as his new Jedi Padawan.

SURVIVAL INSTINCTS
Ezra's parents, Mira and Ephraim Bridger, disappear when he is 7 years old, taken by the Empire for sending illegal broadcasts over the holonet. Ezra resents their friend, a Rodian named Tseebo, for being unable to save them. Ezra changes his mind, however, when he learns Tseebo has received a cyber implant and a job with the Empire in the hopes of discovering the fate of his parents. Ezra manages on his own, taking odd jobs for shady characters like Ferpil Wallaway or Bossk the bounty hunter and stealing to survive. He lives in an abandoned communications tower just outside of Capital City, where he keeps his Imperial helmet collection, a small speeder, and pilfered gadgets. He has little hope for the future until he encounters a group of rebels.

Ezra's speeder
Ezra steals a surplus Imperial speeder bike and repaints it. He and Kanan run missions on their speeders, but mostly Ezra likes to run it through obstacles and shoot at Loth-rats.

BARON VALON RUDOR

APPEARANCES R **SPECIES** Human
HOMEWORLD Corulag **AFFILIATION** Empire

Baron Valon Rudor, code name "LS-607," is a highly decorated TIE fighter pilot of Lothal's Imperial Navy. He is cocky, self-obsessed, and insufferably arrogant. Nonetheless, he has terrible luck and is increasingly bitter about it. His constant run-ins with the rebels always end badly. On his first encounter, he is shot down by the *Ghost*, and when Ezra Bridger finds his crashed TIE, he steals Rudor's helmet and flight gadgets. Zeb Orrelios also separates Rudor from his ship more than once, and his chance to fly the latest TIE Advanced is sabotaged on Empire Day.

> "You'll be sorry! Or dead, you'll be dead!" **VALON RUDOR**

MYLES GRINT

APPEARANCES R **SPECIES** Human
HOMEWORLD Lothal **AFFILIATION** Empire

Taskmaster Myles Grint is a man of few words who relies on his size to intimidate others on Lothal. He follows Commandant Aresko's lead and bullies both citizens and officers of lower rank. Fortunately, his incompetence contributes to the rebels' ability to operate successfully on Lothal. When Governor Tarkin arrives, he orders the Inquisitor to put a decisive end to Grint's succession of mistakes.

Bullying the locals
Grint samples a jogan fruit while he and Commandant Aresko harass a vendor in one of the capital's open markets.

Unpleasant demeanor
Grint is always ready to bully lower ranking officers and the citizens of Lothal when asked.

Imperial uniform
The officer's disc on his hat and the insignia plaque on his chest, proudly displayed by Aresko, convey to all his status and rank.

CUMBERLAYNE ARESKO

APPEARANCES R **SPECIES** Human
HOMEWORLD Lothal **AFFILIATION** Empire

Commandant Cumberlayne Aresko is an egotistical and unsympathetic manager of military operations on Lothal. Together with Taskmaster Grint, he oversees the local Imperial Academy and ceremonies on Empire Day. Aresko overestimates his own importance, however. He is not as clever as he imagines himself, which is a failing that contributes to his eventual downfall. He first informs Agent Kallus of the rebel activity in the capital, and when he repeatedly fails to put a stop to it, the Inquisitor hastens the end of his career.

Man of duty
Aresko briefs Agent Kallus on the rebel theft of several Imperial speeder bikes and related weapons shipments in the capital.

> "This is LRC-01. I am bringing in a citizen under a charge of treason." **CUMBERLAYNE ARESKO**

IMPERIAL COMBAT DRIVER

APPEARANCES R **SPECIES** Human **HOMEWORLD** Various **AFFILIATION** Empire

Imperial combat pilots are well trained at the academy and envied by stormtroopers for their lofty, protected positions in their well-armored vehicles. These overly confident pilots are required to drive any number of vehicles, including speeders and Imperial troop transports. The competent drivers wear body armor to protect them from potential armed resistance.

YOGAR LYSTE

APPEARANCES R **SPECIES** Human **HOMEWORLD** Garel **AFFILIATION** Empire

Supply Master Yogar Lyste is an ambitious young Imperial officer posted on Lothal, charged with overseeing imports and exports as well as regulating, maintaining, and distributing products from the local Imperial-controlled industries. He also occasionally transports prisoners. His duties are continuously disrupted by the rebels, which only inspires him to redouble his efforts.

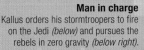

Man in charge
Kallus orders his stormtroopers to fire on the Jedi *(below)* and pursues the rebels in zero gravity *(below right)*.

Battle ready
Though concerned primarily with security and investigations, Agent Kallus relishes any opportunity to engage in combat, utilizing his bo-rifle.

AGENT KALLUS

APPEARANCES R **SPECIES** Human
HOMEWORLD Coruscant
AFFILIATION Empire

Agent Kallus (codename "ISB-021") is a member of the Imperial Security Bureau (ISB), a secret police organization charged with monitoring loyalty to the Empire and stamping out all signs of dissent. Kallus has a steadfast sense of duty to the Empire, and as such, he detests the rebels and all forms of insubordination. His superiority complex and enormous ego also feed his disdain for nonhuman races. Kallus is sent to Lothal to investigate increasing rebel activity, which Commandant Aresko informs him includes the recent theft of Imperial speeder bikes and a related weapons shipment.

Agent Kallus has both Imperial Navy and Army forces at his disposal. He maintains an office in Lothal's Capital City, but he also has command of his own Star Destroyer. He first encounters the *Ghost* and its crew when they attempt to rescue Wookiee prisoners. Kallus later runs into them again on Kessel, where he discovers Kanan Jarrus is a Jedi and Ezra Bridger is his presumed Padawan. Kallus contacts the Inquisitor to aid in the hunt for the two Jedi.

As an officer in the ISB, Kallus has received rigorous combat training. He is a formidable opponent, his physical prowess demonstrated by his ability to wield a heavy bo-rifle. His ISB helmet is a status symbol meant to intimidate as much as to protect him in conflict.

Agent Kallus participates in the sacking of Lasan and takes a bo-rifle from a fallen Lasat Honor Guard, which infuriates the Lasat Zeb Orrelios when the two cross paths. Kallus considers the opportunity to best Zeb in combat a point of pride, but Ezra saves Zeb at the last possible moment with a Force-push, and the rebels quickly escape. When they clash again, Zeb is better prepared for the conflict.

Despite his efforts, Agent Kallus is unable to destroy the rebel cell on Lothal and eventually earns Governor Tarkin's displeasure. Kallus is given another chance to prove himself, however, and participates in the capture of Kanan when the rebels boldly attempt to hijack a holonet broadcast.

CIKATRO VIZAGO

APPEARANCES R **SPECIES**
Devaronian **HOMEWORLD** Devaron
AFFILIATION Broken Horn Syndicate

Kingpin of Lothal's underworld, Cikatro Vizago is head of the Broken Horn Syndicate. Vizago deals in black market goods, particularly stolen Imperial weapons shipments such as E-11 blasters and T-7 ion disruptors. The Devaronian travels with an entourage of IG-RM thug droids aboard his C-ROC *Gozanti*-class cruiser, the *Broken Horn*. The crew of the *Ghost* often runs missions and trades with him for cash, supplies, or valuable information.

Discreet gangster
Vizago examines a stolen shipment of E-11 blasters brought to him by Kanan Jarrus.

Gadget ready
Vizago hides the various gadgets he needs for his black market business in his belt.

Chains of command
The Inquisitor is a skilled fighter, and his standing allows him to command stormtroopers and most Imperial officers.

THE INQUISITOR

APPEARANCES R **SPECIES** Pau'an
HOMEWORLD Utapau **AFFILIATION** Empire

The Inquisitor is personally instructed by Darth Vader to hunt down the last remaining Jedi. His task is to investigate Force-sensitive individuals and execute swift judgment. Among the young and willing, he takes promising individuals to be trained in the dark side. To committed Jedi and the unwilling, however, he shows no mercy. The Inquisitor is a servant to the dark side of the Force, but he is not technically a Sith. His cold, analytical mind is his most powerful weapon. He analyzes Jedi fighting styles and capabilities, as well as the Jedi traditions they follow. He can even identify a Jedi's mentor. He then uses this information to prey upon their weaknesses.

Due to the vital importance of the Inquisitor's secret missions, he is provided with an experimental TIE Advanced v1 prototype. He also carries a unique, double-bladed lightsaber and a fearsome, black-and-red helmet. Like fellow Pau'ans in the sinkhole cities of Utapau, the Inquisitor prefers darkness. Red dark-side tattoos cover his head, striking fear into targets and subordinates alike.

After Agent Kallus discovers the Jedi Kanan Jarrus and his presumed Padawan, Ezra Bridger, he notifies the Inquisitor. When Imperial Senator Gall Trayvis claims that Jedi Luminara Unduli is being held on Stygeon Prime, the Inquisitor waits at the Imperial prison, laying a trap for Kanan and Ezra. Despite having never met Kanan, the Inquisitor immediately identifies Kanan's fighting style; his Master, Depa Billaba; and, most important, the weaknesses of his form. The Inquisitor exploits this knowledge to great effect, and Kanan and Ezra barely escape. The Inquisitor confronts them once more on Empire Day. During the conflict, Ezra brushes with the dark side in order to save his Master from the villain. Later, Kanan allows himself to be captured in order to save his friends. Kanan finally proves himself a Jedi Knight when he defeats the Inquisitor in an epic lightsaber duel.

The Inquisitor's trap
Kanan Jarrus and the Inquisitor duel in the crypt of Jedi Luminara Unduli at the Imperial prison on Stygeon Prime.

MAKETH TUA

APPEARANCES R **SPECIES** Human
HOMEWORLD Lothal
AFFILIATION Empire

Minister Maketh Tua is a government official who often serves as a stand-in for Lothal's Imperial governor, Arihnda Pryce, where she is charged with protecting the Empire's industrial interests. She is also a graduate, with honors, of the Imperial Academy. Tua presides over Lothal's Empire Day celebrations when the governor is invited to Coruscant for the occasion. She introduces Sienar Fleet Systems' new advanced TIE fighter and its pilot, Baron Valen Rudor, but things go horribly wrong when the rebels attack.

Imperial proxy
Though patriotic, Maketh Tua is nonetheless a self-absorbed and ineffectual leader.

GALL TRAYVIS

APPEARANCES R **SPECIES** Human
HOMEWORLD Unknown **AFFILIATION** Empire

Gall Trayvis is a renegade senator who transmits anti-Imperial broadcasts over the holonet. He appears to be in hiding and to live on the run. He is an inspiration and hero to many would-be rebels, as well as the crew of the *Ghost*. At times, he encourages protest, such as boycotting Empire Day; at other times, he passes on valuable information. He delivers the message that Jedi Luminara Unduli is being held prisoner by the Empire at the Imperial prison, Stygeon Prime. Later, he hints at a secret visit he plans to make on Lothal. During his visit, however, Trayvis reveals he is a double agent, serving the Empire.

ZARE LEONIS

APPEARANCES R **SPECIES** Human
HOMEWORLD Uquine
AFFILIATION None

Zare Leonis is the son of Leo and Tepha Leonis, both scientists with Lothal's Ministry of Agriculture. The family is originally from a core planet, but finds a comfortable place in their new world. After Zare enters the Junior Academy for Applied Sciences, his sister Dhara, training at Lothal's Academy for Young Imperials, mysteriously disappears. The following year Zare enters the Imperial Academy, secretly hoping to discover her fate. When Ezra Bridger goes undercover at the Academy, Zare helps him steal an Imperial decoder.

Proud display
Zare wears a cadet uniform and helmet from the Imperial Academy. The gray and white uniforms are symbols of unity, solidarity, discipline, and prestige.

FYRNOCK

APPEARANCES R **HOMEWORLD** Asteroids
SIZE Variable **HABITAT** Shadows, caves

Fyrnocks are silicon-based life forms that live on large asteroids with thin atmospheres. Afraid of the light, they dwell in shadows and hibernate for long periods until disturbed, when they spring awake and attack prey with their sharp claws and teeth. Their meals are infrequent; they feed mostly on mynocks, small space slugs, and other creatures of the asteroid belts.
When Sabine Wren and Hera Syndulla are stranded on an old Republic asteroid base, they are swarmed by fyrnocks that have infested the facility. The two barely escape, but Kanan Jarrus notes the location in case the creatures could be useful later.

OLD JHO

APPEARANCES R
SPECIES Ithorian
HOMEWORLD Ithor
AFFILIATION None

Owner of Old Jho's Pit Stop, the Ithorian is one of the first settlers to arrive on Lothal, and there is little about the planet's history that he doesn't know. From a species notable for having mouths on either side of its head, Jho carries special headgear that translates Ithorian speech into standard Basic. The wise and fascinating pub owner has no love for the Empire and gives the crew of the *Ghost* safe harbor at his docking bay. He also occasionally passes valuable information on to Kanan and the crew.

In the Dark Lord's Clutches
Standing at the edge of a catwalk in Cloud City's reactor shaft, Darth Vader believes he finally has Luke Skywalker in his grasp, and that the young rebel has no opportunity for escape. But Luke refuses to yield to the dark side.

VADER'S REVELATION

"No. I am your father!"
DARTH VADER

After defeating Luke Skywalker on Cloud City, Darth Vader discloses his true identity, and invites Luke to ally with him so that they can bring order to the galaxy.

Darth Vader senses the power of the Force in the rebel pilot who destroys the Death Star, and subsequently learns that the pilot's name is Luke Skywalker. When he also realizes that Luke and Obi-Wan Kenobi lived on the planet Tatooine at the same time, he becomes obsessed with capturing Luke. Shortly after the Battle of Hoth, the Emperor confirms that Luke is, in fact, the son of Vader's alter ego, Anakin Skywalker, and encourages Vader to turn Luke to the dark side. Vader promptly places a bounty on Luke's allies, the crew of the *Millennium Falcon*, and it isn't long before the bounty hunter Boba Fett leads Vader to capture the crew at Cloud City in the Bespin system. When Luke arrives to rescue his friends, he walks right into Vader's trap.

A DARK DESTINY
Vader lures Luke to a Cloud City carbon-freezing chamber, and they engage in a furious duel with lightsabers. Their fight proceeds through a gas-processing vane and onto a maintenance gantry that extends to a balcony laden with atmosphere sensors. They continue to trade blows until Vader's blade severs Luke's right hand. Dazed and battered, Luke clings to a cylindrical atmosphere sensor as Vader urges him to give in to the dark side. Because Luke never questioned Obi-Wan's claim that Vader killed Luke's father, he is stunned when Vader tells him the truth. Vader also proclaims that Luke's destiny is to destroy the Emperor, and that together they can rule the galaxy as father and son. With nowhere to run, but determined to escape the Sith Lord, Luke releases his hold on the sensor, and plunges into the shaft.

Horrifying Truth
Having been told by Obi-Wan Kenobi years ago that Darth Vader killed his Jedi father, a distraught Luke Skywalker refuses to accept that Obi-Wan lied and Vader is his father.

"Smuggler? Such a small word.
I'm more of a... galactic entrepreneur." LANDO CALRISSIAN

LANDO CALRISSIAN

Beginning as a hustler, ending as a galactic hero, Lando Calrissian comes out on top, thanks to a winning smile, charm, and a little flattery.

APPEARANCES R, V, VI SPECIES Human HOMEWORLD Socorro AFFILIATION Rebel Alliance

A CHARMING CON MAN

Lando Calrissian is a charismatic smuggler, swindler, and womanizer with a serious gambling habit. His constant scheming results in a series of unlikely adventures across the galaxy. On Lothal, he buys land from local kingpin Cikatro Vizago to set up an illegal mining operation. Later, after winning the astromech Chopper from Zeb Orrelios, he bargains with the crew of the *Ghost* to help him con the slaver Azmorigan out of a puffer-pig, which is necessary for his convoluted scheme. Sometimes Lando's schemes don't pay off. Most famously, he loses his prized ship the *Millennium Falcon* to Han Solo in a game of sabacc.

New responsibilities
As Baron Administrator, Lando's decisions impact the entire population of Cloud City.

False front
Lando welcomes his friend Han Solo with a jovial facade to hide the Empire's presence on Cloud City.

BARON ADMINISTRATOR OF CLOUD CITY

After having gambled away his ship, Lando's fortune changes when he wagers big and wins control of Cloud City on the planet Bespin. His life takes a dramatic turn toward more reputable pursuits as he becomes Baron Administrator of the gas mining and luxury destination. His situation sours, however, when the Empire arrives and he is forced to turn his friend Han and his companions over to Darth Vader in exchange for the city's freedom. He watches as Han is frozen in carbonite, but when it appears that Vader intends to dishonor their deal, Lando implements a city-wide evacuation with the aid of Lobot, helping his friends escape. Nonetheless, the frozen Han is taken by the bounty hunter Boba Fett and delivered to Jabba the Hutt.

IN JABBA'S EMPLOYMENT

Lando helps orchestrate an elaborate mission to rescue Han, who is frozen in carbonite and hanging from a palace wall, from the Hutt gangster on Tatooine. Gaining employment as a skiff guard in Jabba's palace thanks to an underworld contact, Lando waits for Chewbacca and Leia Organa (disguised as the bounty hunter Boushh) to arrive on the desert world. However, the plan falls apart when Leia is discovered freeing Han from the carbonite, and she and Han are taken prisoner. Luke Skywalker arrives and attempts to persuade Jabba to release Han and Leia, but is captured, too, forcing the friends to resort to their last contingency plan. When Jabba takes Han, Luke, and Chewbacca out to the Dunes Sea to feed them to the Sarlacc, Lando is aboard one of Jabba's skiffs to help them escape. At the last moment, he and Han, Luke, and Chewbacca fight off Jabba's henchmen, while Leia Organa kills the Hutt. Afterward they all depart Tatooine.

Skiff guard
Lando disguises himself as just another vibro-wielding thug in Jabba's service. His ruse brings him fearfully close to the jaws of a Sarlacc.

In the war room
Lando and his friends listen intently to the mission briefing aboard *Home One*.

GENERAL CALRISSIAN

Wanted by both the Empire and the Hutt crime family, Lando decides to wholeheartedly commit to the rebellion. Now a general, he attends the rebel briefing on *Home One*, the Mon Calamari flagship, where Mon Mothma, Admiral Ackbar, and General Crix Madine detail plans to sabotage the shield generator on Endor, destroy the Death Star, and kill the Emperor. Lando and his co-pilot, Nien Nunb, fly the *Millennium Falcon,* accompanied by X-wing escorts, into the Death Star, where they detonate the battle station's core, bringing the long war with the Empire to a triumphant end *(see also p. 308).*

Living by his wits
Lando's smooth-talking and magnetic personality are infamous, and his charms have stolen more than just hearts. He is particularly adept at talking his way out of difficult or dangerous situations.

timeline

Arrival on Lothal
Lando Calrissian lands on Lothal, where he acquires a plot of land from Cikatro Vizago, which he plans to mine.

Winning hand
Lando meets Garazeb Orrelios, who loses the droid Chopper to him in a game of sabacc at Old Jho's Pit Stop.

Mining days
After using the crew of the *Ghost* to help him acquire precious cargo from Azmorigan, Lando tries his hand at mining.

▲ **Losing the *Millennium Falcon***
Lando bets his famous ship in a game of sabacc with smuggler Han Solo and loses.

▲ **Cloud City**
Lando turns to more respectable endeavors and becomes the Baron Administrator of Cloud City, a wealthy mining facility and luxury destination.

▲ **Betrayal of Han Solo**
When Darth Vader arrives on Cloud City, Lando is forced to make a deal to hand his friend over to the Empire.

▲ **Rescuing Han Solo**
Lando helps his new friends rescue Han Solo from the gangster Jabba the Hutt on Tatooine.

Battle of Tanaab
Lando defeats a pirate fleet at Tanaab. His "little maneuver" makes a big impression on rebel leadership.

Death Star assault
Flying his old ship, Lando leads the mission to destroy the second Death Star during the Battle of Endor.

AZMORIGAN

APPEARANCES R
SPECIES Jablogian
HOMEWORLD Nar Shaddaa
AFFILIATION Slaver

Lando Calrissian makes a deal with the repulsive kingpin, Azmorigan, to acquire a puffer pig in exchange for a slave. Lando manipulates the crew of the rebel starship *Ghost* into playing along, and presses the ship's owner Hera Syndulla to fill the slave role. Hera escapes, however, and leaves Azmorigan holding a serious grudge against them all.

R5-D4

APPEARANCES II, IV
TYPE Astromech droid
MANUFACTURER Industrial Automation
AFFILIATION Rebel Alliance

R5-D4, also known as "Red," is a white, red, and blue droid scavenged by Jawas and carried aboard their sandcrawler on Tatooine. They sell R5-D4 to Owen Lars, but his motivator immediately malfunctions. This gives C-3PO the opportunity to recommend R2-D2 to Lars and Luke Skywalker instead.

SANDTROOPER

APPEARANCES IV **SPECIES** Human
HOMEWORLD Various **AFFILIATION** Empire

Sandtroopers are specialized Imperial stormtroopers, trained and equipped to serve in arid environments such as Tatooine. Their armor is equipped with cooling units, long-range comlinks, anti-glare lenses, extra rations, and a water supply. All sandtroopers wear colored pauldrons to indicate their rank—black indicates enlisted troopers, white is for sergeants, and orange is for unit leaders.

> "These are not the droids we're looking for."
>
> **SANDTROOPER**

GENERAL TAGGE

APPEARANCES IV
SPECIES Human
HOMEWORLD Tepasi
AFFILIATION Empire

Born into nobility and privilege, General Tagge is chief of military operations aboard the first Death Star, under the command of Grand Moff Tarkin. Unlike some of his colleagues, he has cautious respect for the Rebel Alliance and expresses concern when the plans for the Imperial battle station are stolen. Prior to the Battle of Yavin, Tagge departs the Death Star, surviving that debacle to become a shining star in the profoundly reshuffled Imperial military hierarchy.

ADMIRAL MOTTI

APPEARANCES IV **SPECIES** Human
HOMEWORLD Seswenna
AFFILIATION Empire

Admiral Conan Antonio Motti hails from a wealthy and powerful family in the Outer Rim. He commands the Star Destroyer *Steel Talon*, and is also the head of naval operations aboard the *Death Star*, under Grand Moff Tarkin. He foolhardily challenges Darth Vader on his failure to discover the secret Rebel Alliance base, which earns him a Sith Force-choke. His arrogant overconfidence in believing the battle station to be invincible, results in his death.

WUHER

APPEARANCES IV **SPECIES** Human
HOMEWORLD Tatooine **AFFILIATION** None

Wuher is a bartender at the Mos Eisley Cantina. As an orphan, he works his way off the streets by studying the biochemistries of various species and mixing them the most desirable drinks. He has a strong dislike of droids and installs a droid detector to keep them out.

PONDA BABA

APPEARANCES IV **SPECIES** Aqualish
HOMEWORLD Ando **AFFILIATION** Smuggler

Ponda Baba is the pirating partner of Doctor Evazan. He rescues Evazan from a bounty hunter and the two begin smuggling spice for Jabba the Hutt. A drunken thug, Baba picks a fight with Luke Skywalker in the Mos Eisley Cantina, and loses his arm when Obi-Wan Kenobi intervenes.

DOCTOR EVAZAN

APPEARANCES IV **SPECIES** Human
HOMEWORLD Alsakan
AFFILIATION Smuggler

Doctor Cornelius Evazan is a murderous smuggler and partner of Ponda Boba. Once a promising surgeon, he is now notorious for conducting cruel medical experiments. Hideously scarred by a bounty hunter, Evazan has death sentences in 12 systems hanging over him. Obi-Wan Kenobi and Luke Skywalker encounter the troublemaker in the cantina on Tatooine.

MOMAW NADON

APPEARANCES IV **SPECIES** Ithorian
HOMEWORLD Ithor
AFFILIATION Rebel Alliance

Momaw Nadon is a male Ithorian ("Hammerhead") and rebel sympathizer exiled on Tatooine. His presence there is punishment for revealing the secrets of Ithorian agricultural technology to the Empire, even though doing so also saved his homeworld from destruction. On Tatooine he cultivates a hidden garden in the mountains south of Mos Eisley, where he conceals rebel operatives. He is present at the Mos Eisley Cantina on the fateful day Luke Skywalker and Obi-Wan Kenobi first meet Han Solo and Chewbacca.

THE MODAL NODES

APPEARANCES IV **SPECIES** Bith
HOMEWORLD Bith
AFFILIATION None

The Modal Nodes are a popular band that brings in the crowds at the Mos Eisley Cantina. Regular band members include Figrin D'an (on Kloo horn), Nalan Cheel (on Bandfill), Doikk Na'ts (on Fizzz, aka Dorenian Beshniquel), Tedn Dahai (on Fanfar), Tech M'or (on the Ommni box), Ickabel G'ont (on the Double Jocimer), and Sun'il Ei'de (on drums). The wholly instrumental band specializes in jazzy musical forms.

They are performing at the cantina when Luke Skywalker and Obi-Wan Kenobi enter the establishment looking for a pilot to take them to the Alderaan system.

"Whoever heard of a bander who didn't gamble?"

FIGRIN D'AN

FIGRIN D'AN

APPEARANCES IV **SPECIES** Bith
HOMEWORLD Bith **AFFILIATION** None

"Fiery" Figrin D'an is the overbearing band leader of the Modal Nodes. As a Bith, his brain has a fine aptitude for music and his high manual dexterity is well suited to playing a range of instruments. Though he favors the Kloo horn, D'an also plays a mean Gasan string drum.

"I expect to be well paid.
I'm in it for the money."

HAN SOLO

HAN SOLO

From a smuggler, gambler, and rogue to general, lover, and hero, Han Solo's life is transformed by the love of a woman whose stubborn independence is matched only by his own.

APPEARANCES IV, V, VI, VII **SPECIES** Human **HOMEWORLD** Corellia **AFFILIATION** Rebel Alliance

THE SCOUNDREL

In his younger years, Han Solo is an unsavory character, but not without heart. On one of his shady ventures he meets a Wookiee named Chewbacca, and the two become lifelong friends. A compulsive risk-taker, Han wins the *Millennium Falcon* from Lando Calrissian in a game of sabacc. With a fast and powerful new ship, he and Chewbacca engage in larger and riskier smuggling operations. However, business turns sour when Han is forced to dump a shipment owned by the notorious gangster, Jabba, which leaves him in dangerous debt to the Hutt. One way or another, he knows he must pay the crime lord's price soon.

Rogue trader
A wary Han Solo sizes up the odds at the Mos Eisley Cantina *(above)*. In a corner of the cantina, Han and Chewbacca meet Luke Skywalker and Obi-Wan Kenobi to negotiate their safe passage to Alderaan *(left)*.

THE RELUCTANT REBEL

Han Solo agrees to transport Luke, Obi-Wan, and the droids purely as a business deal; he has no interest in their rebel mission. When plans change, Han only agrees to rescue Princess Leia because of the promise of a big financial reward. When they reach Yavin 4, he intends to leave before the impending battle so he can pay off Jabba the Hutt. At the last moment, however, he has a change of heart and returns to help his newfound friends. On Hoth, Han tries to leave the rebels once again, but Leia averts it. Until now, the quest for money and saving his own skin were his primary motivations, but everything changes when he falls in love.

Love and war
Despite his mercenary, cynical approach to life, in the heat of battle on the new Death Star Han falls for Princess Leia and, ultimately, the rebel cause.

IMPRISONED IN CARBONITE

When Han finally comes to care deeply for Leia Organa, his world is turned upside down. On Cloud City, he is captured by Darth Vader and used as a test subject in a carbon-freezing chamber. Incapacitated and frozen in carbonite, he is handed over to Boba Fett and finally delivered to Jabba the Hutt on Tatooine *(see also p. 218)*. As a trophy hanging on the gangster's palace wall, Solo's plight seems hopeless until Leia and Han's friends orchestrate a successful rescue attempt. Once a die-hard rascal used to going it alone (apart from his Wookiee sidekick), the former rogue is now helpless and temporarily blinded by hibernation sickness. Han becomes entirely dependent on his compatriots, and through this humbling experience learns to trust others.

Frozen solid
Darth Vader uses Han to test whether a human would survive Cloud City's carbonite-freezing process before attempting it with Luke Skywalker.

GENERAL SOLO

After his rescue on Tatooine, Han fully embraces his place in the Rebel Alliance. Now a general, he leads a team to destroy the second Death Star's shield generator on the moon of Endor. Meanwhile, he reluctantly loans the *Millennium Falcon* to its previous owner, Lando Calrissian, to spearhead the attack on the Death Star. During the mission on Endor, Han becomes a prisoner of the Ewoks and once again must place his faith in others to survive. When the shield generator is destroyed and the Empire overthrown, Leia breaks the news that Luke is actually her brother. Han is delighted to discover that Luke is not a rival for Leia's affections.

Born leader
A newly commissioned general in the Rebel Alliance, Han Solo leads his friends on a successful raid against the Death Star's shield generator.

Corellian birth
Han Solo is born on Corellia and orphaned at a young age. He lives on the street as a petty thief.

Debt to Jabba
Han dumps the illicit cargo he is carrying for Jabba the Hutt before the *Millennium Falcon* is boarded by Imperials.

Kessel Run
Han Solo and Chewbacca fly the infamous smuggler's route in less than 12 parsecs, breaking a long-held distance record.

▲ Meeting at Mos Eisley Cantina
Han meets Luke Skywalker and Obi-Wan Kenobi on Tatooine, an encounter that changes his life forever.

▲ Medal of honor
After rescuing Princess Leia and aiding in the Battle of Yavin, Solo is awarded a medal by the Rebel Alliance.

Incident on Ord Mantell
Han encounters a bounty hunter, which reminds him that his troubles with Jabba are far from over.

▲ Battle of Hoth
Now a captain in the Rebel Alliance, Han rescues Luke Skywalker and helps Leia and the droids escape from the Empire.

▲ Incident on Cloud City
Captured by Darth Vader, Han is frozen in carbonite and turned over to Boba Fett.

Jabba's debt collected
The Hutt finally has his prize. Han hangs in Jabba's palace until sentenced to death by way of the Sarlacc.

▲ Battle of Endor
As General Solo, Han successfully leads the Endor mission to destroy the second Death Star's shield generator.

Guns and confidence
Han Solo believes that he doesn't need much more than a good blaster at his side, especially his trusty, customized DL-44 pistol.

GARINDAN

APPEARANCES IV **SPECIES** Kubaz
HOMEWORLD Kubindi **AFFILIATION** Various

Garindan is an informant in Mos Eisley who works for the highest bidder. Imperial authorities hire the spy to locate R2-D2 and C-3PO. He quickly picks up their trail and uses a comlink to alert the Empire that Luke Skywalker, Obi-Wan Kenobi, and the droids plan to meet Han Solo in docking bay 94.

DIANOGA

APPEARANCES IV **HOMEWORLD** Vodran
AVERAGE SIZE 7 m (23 ft) long
HABITAT Sewers, swamps

Dianogas spread themselves across the galaxy by climbing aboard starship bilges and stowing away in their garbage tanks. They can now be found in sewers in many spaceports. Luke encounters a dianoga in the trash compactor on the Death Star and is nearly drowned and eaten by the beast.

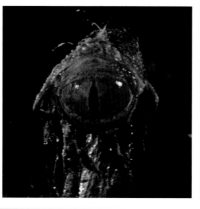

JAN DODONNA

APPEARANCES IV **SPECIES** Human
HOMEWORLD Commenor
AFFILIATION Rebel Alliance

General Jan Dodonna commands the assault on the Death Star during the Battle of Yavin. He identifies the Imperial battle station's only flaw: a thermal exhaust port that leads directly to the fragile main reactor. Dodonna provides the rebel pilots with tactical support from Yavin's command center during the battle.

Briefing
The general details the Death Star's trench run and instructs the rebel starfighter pilots. The visuals come directly from the plans R2-D2 carried.

JON VANDER

APPEARANCES IV **SPECIES** Human **HOMEWORLD** Onderon
AFFILIATION Rebel Alliance

Jon "Dutch" Vander is a former Imperial pilot who defects when he is ordered to bomb rebel-friendly areas of his home planet. He questions General Dodonna during their briefing, but leads the rebel's Gold Squadron of Y-wing fighters during the assault on the Death Star at the Battle of Yavin. He is shot down and killed by Darth Vader during the mission.

GARVEN DREIS

APPEARANCES IV **SPECIES** Human **HOMEWORLD** Virujansi
AFFILIATION Rebel Alliance

Garven "Dave" Dreis is Red Leader of the X-wing Red Squadron in the assault on the Death Star during the Battle of Yavin. When the Y-wing Gold Squadron fails in their trench run, Dreis attempts to fire his proton torpedo into the battle station's exhaust port. He fails, however, and his X-wing is blown to bits by Darth Vader.

BIGGS DARKLIGHTER

APPEARANCES IV **SPECIES** Human **HOMEWORLD** Tatooine
AFFILIATION Rebel Alliance

Biggs Darklighter is a childhood friend of Luke Skywalker. They often fly T-16 skyhoppers in Beggar's Canyon together. Biggs leaves Tatooine to attend an Imperial Academy and become a TIE pilot. After graduation he abandons his commission and joins the Rebel Alliance. He returns to Tosche Station on Tatooine to tell Luke of his plans, before traveling to Yavin 4. There he meets Luke again, and the two fly as part of X-wing Red Squadron in the mission to destroy the Death Star. Biggs is one of the last pilots killed in the battle, his ship destroyed by Darth Vader.

Old friends
Luke tells Biggs about watching a space battle above Tatooine, unaware at the time that it was Darth Vader's Star Destroyer intercepting Princess Leia's *Tantive IV*. In turn, Biggs relays his plan to join the Rebel Alliance and encourages Luke to come *(left)*. Biggs flies with Red Squadron *(below)*.

JEK PORKINS

APPEARANCES IV **SPECIES** Human
HOMEWORLD Bestine IV
AFFILIATION Rebel Alliance

Jek Porkins is a heavy-set pilot and trader who abandons his homeworld when the Empire moves in and develops a new military base there. He flies as Red Six during the Battle of Yavin. His X-wing is struck by debris, causing computer and mechanical malfunctions that leave his ship slow and unresponsive. His X-wing then explodes when it is hit by TIE fighter laser fire.

Death Star assault
Wedge is the only pilot to fly in and survive all of the rebellion's major battles since Yavin.

"Copy, Gold Leader. I'm already on my way out."

WEDGE ANTILLES

WEDGE ANTILLES

APPEARANCES IV, V, VI **SPECIES** Human
HOMEWORLD Corellia
AFFILIATION Rebel Alliance

Wedge Antilles grows up on Corellia, where he works as a pilot and mechanic. After joining Red Squadron, Wedge immediately begins flying raids on Imperial convoys and reconnaissance missions to discover Imperial research facilities. Over the course of his career, Wedge becomes a renowned pilot in the Rebel Alliance, recognized for his bravery and ace fighting skills. He also becomes fast friends with fellow pilots Jek Porkins, Biggs Darklighter, and Derek Klivian.

Wedge attends the briefing on Yavin, where General Dodonna details the mission to destroy the Death Star by exploiting the weakness of its exhaust vent. He expresses scepticism that their X-wings can hit such a small target, but Luke, seated beside him, reassures him. Wedge flies as Red Two in the X-wing squadron that meets the approaching Imperial battle station. In the course of the battle, Wedge saves Luke's life by destroying a TIE fighter that has locked on to his ship. Wedge is one of the three pilots who survives to participate in the final trench run, but his X-wing is damaged, forcing him to retreat. He and Luke are the only two survivors of Red Squadron.

At the Battle of Hoth, Wedge flies a T-47 airspeeder as part of Rogue Group, led by Luke. He and his gunner, Wes Janson, successfully bring down the first AT-AT by tripping the walker with a tow cable. Wedge and Janson both survive the Imperial attack on Echo Base.

Later, Wedge attends the Rebel Alliance briefing at *Home One* and is charged with leading Red Squadron during the Battle of Endor. He is one of several X-wing pilots to fly into the second Death Star, accompanying the *Millennium Falcon*. They narrowly escape after destroying the battle station's main reactor. Afterward, Wedge joins the celebration on Endor at the Ewoks' Bright Tree Village.

Rogue Squadron
Wedge and the other rebel pilots launch their T-47 airspeeders in an assault on the Empire's approaching AT-ATs.

DAVISH "POPS" KRAIL

APPEARANCES IV **SPECIES** Human
HOMEWORLD Dantooine
AFFILIATION Rebel Alliance

Davish Krail is a veteran Y-wing pilot who flies as Gold Five under Jon Vander in Gold Squadron during the Battle of Yavin. He accompanies Tiree and Vander in the first trench run to the Death Star's exhaust port. He aborts the unsuccessful attempt after his friends are killed, but his ship is likewise blown up by Darth Vader, though after he manages to alert Red Squadron.

DEX TIREE

APPEARANCES IV **SPECIES** Human
HOMEWORLD Onderon
AFFILIATION Rebel Alliance

Dex Tiree flies as Gold Two and Dutch Vander's wingman in the Y-wing Gold Squadron during the Battle of Yavin. While beginning the trench run in an effort to blow up the first Death Star, his ship is the first to be hit by Darth Vader's TIE Advanced, and he is electrocuted by a power surge just before his Y-wing explodes.

SAPONZA

APPEARANCES Other **SPECIES** Human
HOMEWORLD Tatooine **AFFILIATION** Mercenary

After the Battle of Yavin, Saponza and his partner return to Tatooine to set up a business. Hoping to leave their lives as mercenaries behind, they nonetheless become involved in a conflict with Jabba the Hutt. Eventually they are caught up in the Galactic Civil War and forced to choose a side.

JENNICA PIERCE

APPEARANCES Other **SPECIES** Human
HOMEWORLD Tatooine
AFFILIATION Rebel Alliance

Jennica Pierce is a Rebel Alliance special forces agent serving on Tatooine. With the help of a Jawa associate named Kekit, she has knowledge of threats to the rebellion on Tatooine, including information about Jabba the Hutt's operations. As the Galactic Civil War broadens, she is pulled into the conflict.

COMMANDER KOSH

APPEARANCES Other **SPECIES** Human
HOMEWORLD Tatooine **AFFILIATION** Empire

Captain Kosh is the commander of an Imperial garrison on Tatooine. His forces are caught up in a conflict with the local rebellion led by Jennica Pierce. Kosh manipulates both allies and enemies as pawns to achieve the goals of the Empire. He also has an unusual interest in ancient artifacts.

ANOTHER SKYWALKER

"The Force is strong in my family." LUKE SKYWALKER

Determined to face Darth Vader, Luke reveals to Princess Leia that she is his sister. If he fails to redeem their father, she will be the Jedi's only hope.

At the dawn of the Empire, former Jedi hero Anakin Skywalker pledges his allegiance to the Sith. Pregnant with twins, his wife Padmé Amidala makes a desperate bid at Mustafar to bring him back to the light side. Despite her heartfelt pleas, Anakin, now called Darth Vader, is too lost in darkness to see her words as anything but betrayal. When Padmé is gravely injured by Vader's Force choke hold, Obi-Wan Kenobi duels and defeats his lifelong friend. He rushes Padmé to Polis Massa, where she dies after giving birth to twins she names Luke and Leia. Yoda and Obi-Wan know they must immediately hide the children where Darth Vader and the Emperor Palpatine cannot discover them.

THE JEDI'S FUTURE

Luke is raised by his aunt and uncle on a Tatooine moisture farm, while Leia grows up as the adopted daughter of Bail Organa and his wife at the royal palace on Alderaan. Neither even knows of the other's existence until years later, when destiny reunites the twins during the Rebel Alliance's bold stand against the first Death Star. Afterward, Luke and Leia together play critical roles in the Rebellion without any clue of their true relationship. Only on his deathbed does Yoda ultimately reveal to Luke that there is another Skywalker who carries equal potential to become a powerful Jedi. Intuition, and confirmation from Obi-Wan's spirit, lead Luke and Leia to finally discover the truth of their sibling bond.

The legacy affirmed
Before becoming one with the Force, Yoda reveals to Luke the important role he is destined to fulfill. Yoda has waited patiently for the time when Anakin's children would be ready to restore the legacy of the Jedi Order.

Moments of truth
On the Endor forest moon, Luke reveals to Leia that Darth Vader is his father and that he must face him. He adds that if he doesn't make it back, then Leia is the only hope for the Alliance. Refuting her objections, he explains that the Force is strong within her—because she is his sister. "I know," she replies. "Somehow, I've always known."

TAUNTAUN

APPEARANCES V, VI **HOMEWORLD** Hoth
AVERAGE SIZE 2 m (9 ft) tall
HABITAT Snow plains

Rebel soldiers discover tauntauns living in ice caves while building Echo Base. Tauntauns are easily domesticated and used as pack animals. Well adapted for cold, they have thick scales and fur, and can slow their metabolism to survive Hoth's freezing nights. Han Solo keeps an injured Luke Skywalker alive by placing him inside a dead tauntaun.

> "I thought they smelled bad—on the outside!" **HAN SOLO**

FX-SERIES

APPEARANCES III, V, VI **TYPE** Medical assistant droid **MANUFACTURER** Medtech Industries **AFFILIATION** None

FX-series droids provide invaluable medical assistance to 2-1B surgical droids. Designed with multiple arms, they monitor patients, perform tests, operate equipment, and recommend procedures. An FX-9 supplies Darth Vader with a blood transfusion during his reconstruction. Later, an FX-7 monitors Luke Skywalker while he receives bacta treatments.

ADMIRAL OZZEL

APPEARANCES V **SPECIES** Human
HOMEWORLD Carida **AFFILIATION** Empire

Admiral Kendal Ozzel commands Darth Vader's flagship, the *Executor*. Ozzel displays poor judgment; first doubting evidence of life on Hoth, and then failing in a bid to surprise the rebels there. Vader accuses him of being "as clumsy as he is stupid," before executing him.

WAMPA

APPEARANCES CW, V **HOMEWORLD** Hoth
AVERAGE SIZE 3 m (10 ft) tall
HABITAT Snow plains

As the top predators on Hoth, wampas generally prey upon various species of tauntauns, but do not hesitate to attack humans or their settlements. Their thick white fur protects them from the intense cold and allows them to sneak up on prey undetected. Wampas drag victims back to ice caves where they are later torn apart at leisure.

ZEV SENESCA

APPEARANCES V **SPECIES** Human
HOMEWORLD Kestic Station
AFFILIATION Rebel Alliance

Zev Senesca locates Luke Skywalker and Han Solo when they become lost overnight on Hoth's ice fields. Zev flies as Rogue Two during the Battle of Hoth, but he and his gunner are both killed during the conflict when their snowspeeder is blasted by several Imperial walkers.

GENERAL RIEEKAN

APPEARANCES V **SPECIES** Human
HOMEWORLD Alderaan
AFFILIATION Rebel Alliance

A fighter for the Republic during the Clone Wars, General Carlist Rieekan becomes a founding member of the Rebel Alliance. Off-world when Alderaan is destroyed, he assumes command at Echo Base on Hoth. When Vader's forces strike, he delays them long enough for rebel transports to evade capture, and then escapes himself.

2-1B

APPEARANCES III, CW, V, VI
TYPE Surgical droid
MANUFACTURER: Industrial Automation **AFFILIATION** None

Popular since the days of the Republic, Model 2-1B surgical droids are equipped with an encyclopedic memory and a great bedside manner, whose removable hands support a variety of medical devices. 2-1Bs serve both Darth Vader and Luke Skywalker.

ADMIRAL PIETT

APPEARANCES V, VI **SPECIES** Human
HOMEWORLD Axxila **AFFILIATION** Empire

Firmus Piett hails from the Outer Rim Territories. He rises through Imperial ranks thanks to his quick thinking and ability to shift blame for his own mistakes. He serves as captain aboard Darth Vader's flagship, the *Executor*, until his commanding officer, Ozzel, is executed for incompetence. Promoted to Admiral by Vader himself, Piett pursues the *Millennium Falcon* through an asteroid field following the Battle of Hoth. His distinguished career ends abruptly when an A-wing crashes into the *Executor*'s bridge during the Battle of Endor.

GENERAL VEERS

APPEARANCES V **SPECIES** Human
HOMEWORLD Denon **AFFILIATION** Empire

General Maximillian Veers is the mastermind behind the Imperial assault on Echo Base during the Battle of Hoth. From the cockpit of his AT-AT, *Blizzard One*, he leads the attack that destroys the Rebel shield generator, before infiltrating their base with his snowtroopers.

MAJOR DERLIN

APPEARANCES V, VI **SPECIES** Human
HOMEWORLD Tiisheraan
AFFILIATION Rebel Alliance

Major Bren Derlin is security chief and a member of Alliance Intelligence at Echo Base on Hoth. He gives the order to close the base door when Han Solo and Luke Skywalker become lost outside, to avoid putting the whole base at risk. He later serves as the unit leader in the Battle of Endor.

DAK RALTER

APPEARANCES V **SPECIES** Human
HOMEWORLD Kalist VI
AFFILIATION Rebel Alliance

A rebel pilot in Rogue Squadron, Dak Ralter serves as Luke Skywalker's gunner during the Battle of Hoth. Born into a family of political prisoners in an Imperial penal colony, Ralter escapes, harboring bright ambitions that he will never realize—he is killed when his snowspeeder is destroyed by an AT-AT.

DEREK "HOBBIE" KLIVIAN

APPEARANCES V **SPECIES** Human
HOMEWORLD Ralltiir
AFFILIATION Rebel Alliance

Derek "Hobbie" Klivian is a distinguished pilot in Rogue Squadron. Klivian attends an Imperial Academy with Biggs Darklighter, but later mutinies after receiving his commission aboard the *Rand Ecliptic* and defects to the Rebel Alliance. Luke Skywalker's wingman in the Battle of Hoth, Klivian ejects just before his ship rams the lead walker.

WES JANSON

APPEARANCES V **SPECIES** Human
HOMEWORLD Taanab
AFFILIATION Rebel Alliance

Lieutenant Wes Janson flies as rear gunner for fellow pilot Wedge Antilles during the Battle of Hoth. They use their speeder's harpoon and tow cable to bring down the first AT-AT in the attack on Echo Base.

SNOWTROOPER

APPEARANCES V **SPECIES** Human
HOMEWORLD Various
AFFILIATION Empire

Snowtroopers are elite stormtrooper regiments equipped for combat and survival in the extreme cold. Modelled after the Republic's former clone cold assault troops, which served in frigid environments like Orto Plutonia, Rhen Var, and Toola during the Clone Wars, their insulated suits and heated breather masks are powered by battery packs that last up to two standard weeks. Deployed in General Veers' attack on Echo Base in the Battle of Hoth, and brandishing E-11 blaster rifles and E-Web heavy repeating blaster cannons, snowtroopers are a formidable match for rebel soldiers. Their equipment includes ice boots, an insulated belt cape, polarized snow goggles, grappling hooks, ion flares, and a homing beacon.

SPACE SLUG

APPEARANCES V **HOMEWORLD** Unknown
AVERAGE SIZE 900 meters (2,952 ft) long
HABITAT Asteroids

Space slugs are solitary, silica-based lifeforms that dwell in asteroid caves, living on the mineral-rich deposits found in their habitats. Largely dormant, these gargantuan slugs are also known to prey on passing ships. On one such occasion, Han Solo pilots the *Millennium Falcon* into an asteroid field in a desperate attempt to elude his Imperial pursuers, only to be swallowed by one of these opportunistic feeders.

"This is no cave."
HAN SOLO

Belly of the beast
A space slug uses all its energy to lunge at a passing ship. A view from the cockpit of the unlucky ship swallowed by the slug *(above)*.

MYNOCK

APPEARANCES V **HOMEWORLD** Unknown
AVERAGE SIZE 2 meters (7 ft) long
HABITAT Space slug stomach

Mynocks are space parasites that survive on a ship's power cables and energy conductors. If they are not cleared quickly, they can fully drain a craft's power. When mynocks are ingested by a giant space slug, they can live inside their host's gut, sharing its meals.

4-LOM

APPEARANCES V **MANUFACTURER** Industrial Automaton **TYPE** LOM-series protocol droid **AFFILIATION** Bounty hunter

4-LOM is a former protocol droid with an insect-like face made to resemble the species he once served. He overwrites his own programming and turns to a life of crime and bounty hunting. Darth Vader hires a team of bounty hunters, including 4-LOM, to locate the *Millennium Falcon* after it disappears in an asteroid field.

ZUCKUSS

APPEARANCES V **SPECIES** Gand **HOMEWORLD** Gand **AFFILIATION** Bounty hunter

Zuckuss, a bounty hunter who often works together with 4-LOM, is one of the first traditional findsmen to leave his planet. The air on his homeworld is thick and toxic to most off-worlders, and he wears a respirator to breathe ammonia in oxygen-rich atmospheres. Zuckuss also joins Vader's hunt for the *Millennium Falcon*.

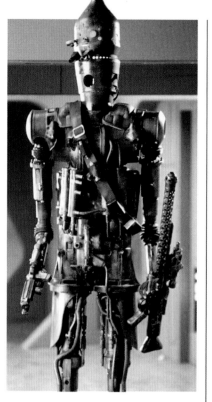

IG-88

APPEARANCES V **MANUFACTURER** Holowan Laboratories **TYPE** Assassin droid **AFFILIATION** Bounty hunter

Obsessed with hunting and killing, IG-88 is a rogue assassin droid turned bounty hunter who joins Vader's search for the *Millennium Falcon*. The droid is a chief rival of Boba Fett and tends to hunt alone. IG-88's head is ringed with sensors that allow him to see in all directions. He carries an arsenal of weapons, including blasters, pulse cannons, vibroblades, poison darts, and toxic gas dispensers.

CAPTAIN NEEDA

APPEARANCES V **SPECIES** Human **HOMEWORLD** Coruscant **AFFILIATION** Empire

Lorth Needa is a ruthless officer who serves the Republic in the Clone Wars when Chancellor Palpatine is kidnapped by General Grievous during the Battle of Coruscant. As commanding officer of the Imperial Star Destroyer *Avenger*, he takes part in the search for the rebels' secret base. After losing the *Millennium Falcon* while pursuing it through an asteroid field, Darth Vader Force-chokes him to death.

LOBOT

APPEARANCES V **SPECIES** Human cyborg **HOMEWORLD** Bespin **AFFILIATION** Rebel Alliance

Lobot is Lando Calrissian's chief administrative aide on Cloud City. With a cybernetic implant wrapped around his skull, he is able to continuously monitor the city's central computer and its vast array of systems. No friend of the Empire, he assists Lando in freeing Leia, Chewbacca, and C-3PO from Imperial custody.

MOFF JERJERROD

APPEARANCES VI **SPECIES** Human **HOMEWORLD** Tinnel IV **AFFILIATION** Empire

Tiaan Jerjerrod supervises construction of the second Death Star. When the project falls behind schedule, the Emperor sends Darth Vader to put additional pressure on the Moff. Jerjerrod commands the battle station's superlaser during the Battle of Endor. He perishes when the rebels detonate the Death Star's reactor core.

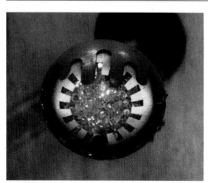

TT-8L/Y7

APPEARANCES VI **MANUFACTURER** Serv-O-Droid, Inc. **TYPE** Gatekeeper droid **AFFILIATION** Jabba's palace

Nicknamed the "tattletale," TT-8L/Y7s are security droids installed in entryways to screen visitors and scan for weapons. Considered obnoxious and invasive, they enjoy their position of control. Jabba the Hutt has a TT-8L fitted into a hole at his front gate that questions R2-D2 and C-3PO when they first arrive.

OOLA

APPEARANCES VI **SPECIES** Twi'lek **HOMEWORLD** Ryloth **AFFILIATION** Slave

Bib Fortuna kidnaps Oola and has her trained in exotic dancing. She becomes so enthralled with his stories of the grandeur of Jabba's palace that she turns down opportunities to escape. When Fortuna presents her to Jabba as his personal dancer, the Hutt lavishes unwanted attention upon her and keeps her chained to his throne. When she refuses his advances, he furiously drops her into his pet rancor's pit, where she meets a horrible end.

Save the last dance
A trained Ryloth dancer who is forced to entertain Jabba and his entourage, Oola is bound in chains and must obey Jabba's will.

SALACIOUS B. CRUMB

APPEARANCES VI **SPECIES** Kowakian
Monkey-Lizard **HOMEWORLD** Kowak
AFFILIATION Jabba's palace

Salacious Crumb is the jester of Jabba's
court. He begins his time with Jabba as
a stowaway thief aboard the Hutt's ship,
but Bib Fortuna manages to capture
him. Henceforth Crumb sits beside Jabba
and mercilessly teases captives. His shrill,
irritating laughter amuses Jabba immensely.

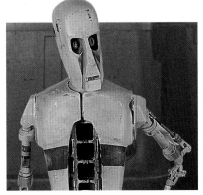

8D8

APPEARANCES VI **MANUFACTURER** Verpine
Roche Hive **TYPE** Smelter droid
AFFILIATION Jabba's palace

8D8 is a cruel industrial droid owned by
Jabba the Hutt. He tortures other droids
to ensure that they know their place in
the palace, sometimes tormenting just
for fun. The 8D-series droids resent
the more sophisticated protocol and
astromech droids and tend to be bullies.

EV-9D9

APPEARANCES VI **MANUFACTURER**
MerenData **TYPE** Supervisor droid
AFFILIATION Jabba's palace

EV-9D9 is Jabba's sadistic droid overseer.
Her programming is corrupted, but she
manages to avoid the manufacturer's
recall and continues working in the Hutt's
murky dungeons. She assigns R2-D2 to
Jabba's sail barge and C-3PO to be the
new interpreter.

DROOPY McCOOL

APPEARANCES VI **SPECIES** Kitonak
HOMEWORLD Kirdo III
AFFILIATION None

Droopy McCool is the lead horn player in
Jabba's house band. His real name is an
unpronounceable series of whistles, but
the band's manager, Max Rebo, gives him
his stage name. Lonely Droopy plays his
chidinkalu flute and longs for the company
of other Kitonaks.

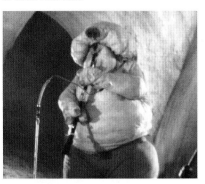

MAX REBO

APPEARANCES VI **SPECIES** Ortolan
HOMEWORLD Orto
AFFILIATION None

Max Rebo is the leader of his eponymous
band, famous for playing at Jabba's palace.
He ceaselessly plays keyboard for the Hutt
from atop his red ball jet organ, accompanied
by Sy Snootles, Droopy McCool, and the
other musicians. His large ears make him
sensitive to sound and an excellent
musician. His three passions are music,
money, and food, and the latter two make
him easily exploitable. When he brokers a
deal with Jabba to play for free meals only,
he infuriates the rest of the band.

RANCOR

APPEARANCES VI **HOMEWORLD** Dathomir
AVERAGE SIZE 5 m (16 ft) high
HABITAT Grottos, plains

Jabba's rancor is a birthday gift from Bib
Fortuna. The rancor lives in a chamber
below Jabba's throne room and is cared for
by Malakili, the resident monster handler.

When angry, Jabba likes to drop victims
through a trapdoor and into the rancor's
den, where they are eaten whole by the
beast. When Luke Skywalker finds himself
in the rancor's clutches, he is able to kill
the monster by dropping a secondary
gate on its head. Malakili has a bond with
the ferocious but semi-intelligent creature
and is heartbroken when it dies.

BARADA

APPEARANCES VI **SPECIES** Klatooinian
HOMEWORLD Klatooine **AFFILIATION** Slave

A slave and mechanic owned by Jabba
the Hutt, Barada is responsible for all
of the gangster's repulsorlift vehicles.
Despite his life of enforced servitude,
Barada is reasonably content with his
lot until Luke knocks him into the Pit of
Carkoon, where he will be digested by
the Sarlacc for 1,000 years.

SARLACC

APPEARANCES VI **HOMEWORLD** Tatooine
AVERAGE SIZE 3 m (10 ft) wide, 100 m
(328 ft) long **HABITAT** Desert

One of Jabba the Hutt's favorite pets, the
mighty Sarlacc nests in the Pit of Carkoon.
From above, only the Sarlacc's mouth is
visible. The rest of the enormous creature,
including its vast stomach, is buried deep
in the sand. When Jabba's prisoners are
dropped into the monster's pit, the Sarlacc's
tentacles grab them and drag them into its
mouth. Rows of hundreds of spear-like
teeth prevent the prisoner from climbing
out, and the Sarlacc swallows its prey
whole. Han, Luke, and Chewbacca are
taken to the pit for execution, but with
help from friends, manage to escape.

Fate worse than death
Jabba's slave Kithaba is snatched by the Sarlacc.

KLAATU

APPEARANCES VI **SPECIES** Kadas'sa'Nikto
HOMEWORLD Kintan
AFFILIATION Jabba the Hutt

Klaatu is one of several Kadas'sa'Nikto who serve Jabba the Hutt, repairing the crime lord's skiffs. A gambler, Klaatu enjoys watching the executions in the rancor pit beneath Jabba's throne. During the failed executions of Han Solo and Luke Skywalker at the Great Pit of Carkoon, he watches from the top deck of Jabba's sail barge as Luke Force-leaps from a skiff to the barge. The Jedi scales the side to confront Klaatu, slicing his weapon in half and forcing Klaatu to flee inside the vessel. Seconds later, Leia Organa fires the sail barge's cannon at the deck before escaping the barge with Luke. Klaatu is killed in the ensuing explosion.

Endor patrol
The environment on the forest moon of Endor suits the biker scouts' specialized light armor and swift, agile 74-Z speeder bikes.

SCOUT TROOPER

APPEARANCES VI **SPECIES** Human
HOMEWORLD Various
AFFILIATION Empire

Scout troopers are highly trained soldiers of the Imperial Stormtrooper Corps specializing in reconnaissance and sniping. The Imperial scout troopers were preceded by the clone scout troopers of the Galactic Republic. The scouts provide excellent long-range fire for their stormtrooper counterparts. Darth Vader's personal Death Squadron includes a complement of scout troopers, whose priority is to aid the Sith Lord in squashing the Rebel Alliance along with its sympathizers and secret allies. Scout troopers are stationed on Endor, where the second Death Star is under construction.

On the forest moon, scout troopers on patrol are taken by surprise and defeated by a small team of rebel soldiers. This same band of rebels attacks the bunker holding the shield generator that protects the Death Star in orbit. The scout troopers fight back, briefly subduing the rebels, before a tribe of Ewoks comes to the latter's aid. The defeated scouts are taken prisoner by the rebels, who successfully destroy the generator and the Death Star shortly thereafter.

GENERAL CRIX MADINE

APPEARANCES VI **SPECIES** Human
HOMEWORLD Corellia
AFFILIATION Rebel Alliance

Crix Madine is a general in the Rebel Alliance responsible for covert operations. After Bothan spies deliver intelligence on the second Death Star being constructed over the Endor moon, Madine devises the attack on the shield generator bunker. He enlists recently freed Han Solo to command this elite unit of highly trained commandos, which will be inserted onto the forest moon in a stolen Imperial shuttle. Solo's friends Luke, Leia, and Chewbacca accompany Han as the shuttle's flight crew. Although the mission requires some tactical modifications during execution, it is ultimately a success.

Rebel mastermind
General Madine briefs the strike team before they attack the second Death Star.

TEEBO

APPEARANCES VI **SPECIES** Ewok
HOMEWORLD Forest moon of Endor
AFFILIATION Bright Tree Village

After his scouting party captures the rebel strike team in a net trap, Teebo pokes Han with his spear to ensure compliance. In return, Teebo gets zapped twice by R2-D2 when he releases the droid from its bonds. During the Battle of Endor, Teebo sounds the Sacred Horn of the Soul Trees, giving the signal for the Ewoks to attack. In the celebration following the destruction of the second Death Star, Teebo plays percussion on stormtrooper helmets and bonds with R2-D2.

WICKET W. WARRICK

APPEARANCES VI **SPECIES** Ewok
HOMEWORLD Forest moon of Endor
AFFILIATION Bright Tree Village

Wicket discovers a human woman unconscious in the woods and remains wary until she offers him part of a ration bar to eat. Hearing the approach of Imperial scout troopers, he grabs his spear, ready for combat. When the troopers fire at them, Wicket and Leia hide behind a log. Wicket rolls out of sight as one of the scout troopers threatens Leia with his blaster. Wicket attacks the trooper's legs, giving Leia a chance to knock out her assailant, grab her blaster, and shoot the other Imperial trooper before he can escape.

Wicket brings his new friend Leia to the Ewok village, where she is treated as an honored guest. Wicket and Paploo accompany Leia and the rebel commando squad to a ridge overlooking the Imperial landing platform and reveal a "secret" entrance to the shield generator bunker on the other side of the ridge. The rebels mount a sneak attack on the bunker, but are outnumbered by the Imperial soldiers waiting for them. When the rebels are led back out of the bunker at gunpoint, Wicket returns with an army of Ewoks to free them.

First contact
After finding the woman who piloted the second crashed speeder bike, Wicket is suspicious of her intentions when she regains consciousness.

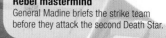

CHIEF CHIRPA

APPEARANCES VI **SPECIES** Ewok
HOMEWORLD Forest moon of Endor
AFFILIATION Bright Tree Village

At the time of the Battle of Endor, Chief Chirpa serves as the leader of the Council of Elders for the Bright Tree Village tribe. Scouts from the village capture key members of the rebel strike team sent to the forest moon, including C-3PO. Like the other Ewoks, Chirpa believes the shiny metallic droid is a prophesied golden god and initially agrees with the shaman Logray that several of the captives should be cooked alive in a sacrificial ceremony. Luke Skywalker tells C-3PO to order the Ewoks to release them, and when they refuse, Luke covertly uses the Force to levitate the droid into the air. Awed by this fearsome display of divine power, Chirpa orders the rebels freed immediately. C-3PO then tells the tribe the story of the rebels' struggles against the evil Empire, prompting Chirpa to declare the rebels honorary members of the tribe. Together, the Ewoks and rebels defeat the Imperial forces guarding the shield generator.

Bold leader
At first skeptical of the rebel intruders on the forest moon, Chief Chirpa allies with them to defeat the Imperial soldiers.

LOGRAY

APPEARANCES VI **SPECIES** Ewok
HOMEWORLD Forest moon of Endor
AFFILIATION Bright Tree Village

Logray is the head shaman for the Bright Tree Village tribe of Ewoks. He wears a distinctive headdress made from the skull of a large churi bird. When the captured members of the rebel strike team are brought to the village, Logray orders that Han, Luke, Chewbacca, and R2-D2 be cooked alive as a ritual sacrifice to "the Golden One," the shining protocol droid C-3PO, whom the Ewoks revere as a legendary deity.

PAPLOO

APPEARANCES VI **SPECIES** Ewok
HOMEWORLD Forest moon of Endor
AFFILIATION Bright Tree Village

Like his friends Teebo and Wicket, Paploo is a skilled Ewok scout. The trio leads the rebel strike team to the location of the bunker containing the planetary shield generator for the Death Star orbiting the forest moon. While others debate the best plan for seizing the bunker from the Imperial soldiers, Paploo sneaks forward and steals one of the Imperial scout trooper's speeder bikes. His diversion provides the strike team with the element of surprise as they launch their attack.

NIEN NUNB

APPEARANCES VI **SPECIES** Sullustan
HOMEWORLD Sullust **AFFILIATION** Rebel Alliance

Prior to the Battle of Endor, the Rebel Alliance fleet masses at the planet Sullust before launching into hyperspace to reach the site of the assault on the second Death Star. Many Sullustans serve as pilots for the rebels; one of them is Nien Nunb, a longtime friend of Lando Calrissian. Like others of his species, Nunb has large ears, big dark beady eyes, and enormous jowls. Lando plans to fly the *Millennium Falcon* inside the Death Star to make a direct attack on the vulnerable power core within the unfinished structure, and asks Nunb to be his co-pilot for the crucial mission. Nunb lives up to Lando's trust in him, displaying great skill at flying the highly customized freighter. During the mission, he chatters rapidly in the liquid tones of the Sullustan language.

Flying buddies
Nien Nunb *(above)* takes the co-pilot seat on the *Millennium Falcon*, alongside his friend and lead pilot Lando Calrissian, for a daring mission against the Death Star. With Nunb and Lando at the helm, the *Millennium Falcon* stages a direct assault on the Death Star's power core *(left)*.

Beneath Vader's mask
No longer seeking to dethrone the Emperor to gain personal
power (as he had previously planned), Darth Vader acts out of
selflessness—the antithesis of the Sith creed—to save his
son from certain death. Seriously injured, he asks Luke to
remove his mask, despite knowing this will hasten his death,
so he can look on his son.

LUKE REDEEMS HIS FATHER

"Just for once… let me look on you… with my own eyes." ANAKIN SKYWALKER

Like his mother, Padmé, Luke Skywalker believes that there is still some good in his father, Anakin. Luke resolves to use peaceful methods to turn him from the dark side.

After Luke Skywalker has received all of the Jedi training that Obi-Wan Kenobi and Yoda can provide, they charge him with one remaining task—to confront and kill his evil father Anakin, alias the dreaded Darth Vader. It appears that the old Jedi Order is now advocating violent methods in place of their traditional peace-keeping role. Luke rejects Yoda and Obi-Wan's instruction, and, going against strict Jedi teaching by acting out of love for his family, seeks to save his father.

A SECOND CHOICE
Luke travels to Endor to meet Darth Vader, who delivers him to the Emperor on the Death Star. Seeking a more powerful apprentice, the Emperor pits Luke against his father, hoping that Luke might kill Vader and then serve him. But Luke refuses to fight, and the Emperor tries to destroy him instead. When Vader sees the Emperor killing Luke, he finally has an opportunity to re-cast the original decision that set himself, Anakin Skywalker, on the path of evil. Anakin's former, selfish choice brought about Padmé's death, but his later sacrifice now saves the life of his son and his daughter. Padmé's belief in Anakin's inherent goodness is vindicated when he resolutely turns on the Emperor and casts him to his death. In doing so, Anakin is electrocuted, but has a final moment to speak with his son. Some time later, as the rebels celebrate the Empire's defeat, Anakin's Force spirit is peacefully reunited with Obi-Wan and Yoda.

History repeating
As Anakin once watched Palpatine, alias Sith Lord Darth Sidious, killing Mace Windu with Force lightning, Vader now watches the Emperor do the same to Luke. But unlike Anakin, who aided Sidious, Vader seizes the Emperor and throws him down the reactor shaft.

BEHIND THE SCENES

"[*Star Wars*] is finally about people and not finally about science... I think that's what makes it so accessible." Harrison Ford, 1977

It may be set in a galaxy far, far away, but it is the characters that have made *Star Wars* compelling for generations of fans. These people have fantastical origins, but they struggle with issues familiar to everyone: greed versus honor, duty versus desire, good versus evil. When combined with amazing practical makeup and groundbreaking visual effects, *Star Wars* has made space fantasy characters seem believable and relatable like never before.

Concept illustrator Ralph McQuarrie's first concept illustration for Deak Starkiller and Darth Vader's lightsaber duel on a rebel ship, was created in consultation with George Lucas, and helped hone the look of the characters **(1)**. Mark Hamill (Luke Skywalker) and Alec Guinness (Ben Kenobi) are shielded from the searing Tunisian sun while they take a welcome break from filming in March 1976 **(2)**. In *A New Hope*, the bantha was played by a trained elephant named Mardji in an elaborate costume **(3)**.

Makeup artist and creature designer Stuart Freeborn puts the finishing touches on a sculpture of Yoda, whose face was based on his own and that of Albert Einstein, as well as conceptual art by McQuarrie and Joe Johnston. Freeborn helped create several notable aliens for *Star Wars*, including some of the cantina aliens (many of whom were created by Rick Baker), Chewbacca, and Jabba the Hutt **(4)**.

Harrison Ford and Peter Mayhew, in his Chewbacca costume, on the set of *Star Wars: Episode V The Empire Strikes Back* **(5)**. Mark Hamill rehearses the Cloud City fight scene with Darth Vader swordmaster Bob Anderson, who played Darth Vader in the dueling scenes. **(6)**. Mask of the Mon Calamari leader, Admiral Ackbar, a part-puppet, part-mask creation for *Return of the Jedi,* developed by the ILM Monster Shop. The mask was controlled and performed by puppeteer Tim Rose, on loan from the Jim Henson Company **(7)**.

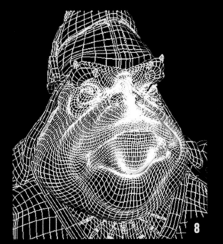

A wire frame rendering of Boss Nass, one of ILM's most challenging computer-generated creations (8). George Lucas directs Silas Carson as Nute Gunray for the Naboo Palace scenes in Italy (9). Ian McDiarmid and Natalie Portman film against a bluescreen for a Naboo scene in *The Phantom Menace* (10). Early costume concept art by Dermot Power for Anakin Skywalker for *Star Wars: Episode II Attack of the Clones* (11). On a vast bluescreen soundstage at Fox Studios in Sydney, Australia, Wookiees prepare for battle in *Star Wars: Episode III Revenge of the Sith* (12).

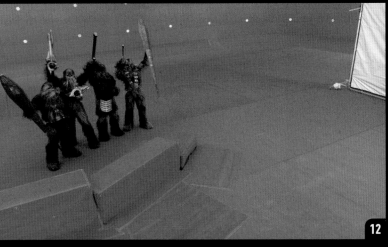

Dermot Power's concept art for *Attack of the Clones* depicts a female Sith warrior, a character who finally appears as the fierce assassin Asajj Ventress in the animated TV series *Star Wars: The Clone Wars* (13). Hayden Christensen in a pick-up shot from the final day of shooting *Revenge of the Sith* at Elstree Studios (14).

J.J. Abrams (top center) oversees the cast read-through of *Star Wars: The Force Awakens* at Pinewood Studios with (clockwise from right) Harrison Ford, Daisy Ridley, Carrie Fisher, Peter Mayhew, Producer Bryan Burk, Lucasfilm president and producer Kathleen Kennedy, Domhnall Gleeson, Anthony Daniels, Mark Hamill, Andy Serkis, Oscar Issac, John Boyega, Adam Driver, and writer Lawrence Kasdan (15).

LOCATIONS

Countless inhabitable worlds are scattered throughout the farthest reaches of the galaxy. Each one has its own geography, flora and fauna, secrets and surprises.

Long ago, hyperspace explorers established coordinates and trade routes for thousands of star systems, many of which have at least one inhabitable planet or moon. Since then, many new systems have been charted. Some of these far-flung worlds feature architectural wonders and are home to intelligent, indigenous civilizations, while others are undeveloped and populated almost entirely by wild creatures. Some worlds feature diverse terrain, while others are so dominated by a single geographical feature that they are described as sand, ice, jungle, or water planets.

More than a trillion citizens reside on the planet Coruscant, which is considered the heart of the Core Worlds, the galactic hub of culture, education, fine arts, technology, and finance. But because of economic or legal restrictions, or political oppression imposed by the prevailing government, many choose to live in the Outer Rim, beyond the civilizing influence of the Galactic Republic and the oppressive grasp of the subsequent Empire.

LOCATIONS TIMELINE

The galaxy is a vast and mysterious place. It contains countless star systems, and yet, whether by fate, design, or random chance, a mere handful of worlds witness the tumultuous events that shape galactic history.

● **CRISIS IN THE REPUBLIC:**
Spans Episodes I and II

● **THE CLONE WARS:**
Spans Episode II, CW, and Episode III

● **THE EMPIRE ERA:**
Spans Episode III, R, and Episodes IV to VI

Force testing
Qui-Gon Jinn brings Anakin Skywalker to the Jedi Temple on Coruscant to see if the boy can be admitted as a new member of the Jedi Order.

Invasion of Naboo
The Trade Federation sends battle droids to seize Naboo's capital city of Theed. Jedi Knights Qui-Gon Jinn and Obi-Wan Kenobi fear that they are too late to save Queen Padmé Amidala, but find an unexpected ally in Jar Jar Binks.

Beneath the waves
Jar Jar leads the two Jedi to the underwater city of Otoh Gunga, home of the Gungan people. A submarine trip through the planet's core allows the group to free the Queen and escape offworld.

Urgent plea
Inside the Galactic Senate chamber, Queen Amidala tries to win support for Naboo's liberation from the Trade Federation.

To Tatooine
On the desert planet of Tatooine the group meets Anakin Skywalker inside the junk shop of Watto the Toydarian. Young slave Anakin wins his freedom in a podrace held at the Mos Espa arena.

Republic capital
The Queen's starship journeys to Coruscant, capital of the Galactic Republic, a world covered with urban canyons and swarming with busy airspeeder traffic.

Visiting Dex

Obi-Wan looks up his old friend Dexter Jettster at Dex's Diner, a popular Coruscant eatery. Dex provides a clue that leads Obi-Wan to Kamino.

Clone origins

On watery Kamino, Obi-Wan tours the cloning laboratories of Tipoca City, where he visits bounty hunter Jango Fett, upon whose DNA the clones are based.

Tatooine return

Anakin Skywalker and Padmé Amidala travel to Tatooine in search of Anakin's mother, Shmi. At the Lars moisture farm, Anakin receives bad news concerning her fate.

Coruscant underworld

Obi-Wan Kenobi and Anakin Skywalker chase would-be assassin Zam Wesell into the lower levels of Coruscant. She tries to escape pursuit in the Outlander gambling club but is discovered.

Trouble on Geonosis

Obi-Wan learns that Geonosis is a hive of Separatist activity, with its droid factory operating at full capacity. He is captured and sentenced to die in the execution arena.

Failed assassination

As Count Dooku's Separatist movement gains in strength, Padmé Amidala, now Naboo's senator, becomes a target. In Padmé's apartment on Coruscant, venomous kouhuns are sent to kill her.

Start of the Clone Wars

The Republic and the Separatists clash inside the execution arena and later on the barren flats of Geonosis. The newly-deployed clone troopers enable the Republic to win the battle.

Battle of Naboo

The Trade Federation is defeated. Qui-Gon and Obi-Wan have a lightsaber duel with Darth Maul that starts in the Royal Palace's starship hangar and ends in the heart of the Theed power generator.

The war continues

On Teth, Anakin Skywalker and his new Padawan Ahsoka Tano fight their way through Separatist attackers to rescue Jabba the Hutt's son Rotta, and return him to his father on Tatooine.

Showdown on Utapau

Obi-Wan Kenobi and General Grievous battle to the death on the sinkhole planet of Utapau. Obi-Wan narrowly escapes the clone trooper ambush triggered by Order 66.

Fiery duel

The volcanic world of Mustafar is the scene of a lightsaber battle between Obi-Wan Kenobi and Anakin Skywalker. Anakin survives, badly injured, and is rebuilt on Coruscant by Darth Sidious into the cyborg Darth Vader.

Wookiee defense

In one of the last battles of the Clone Wars, the Wookiees of Kashyyyk repel a Separatist invasion on the beaches of Kachirho City.

Hidden away

Alderaan becomes the new home for Padmé's infant daughter Leia, where she will be raised by Bail Organa and his wife. Leia's twin brother Luke is brought to the Lars moisture farm on Tatooine.

Nightsisters

The witches of Dathomir become a thorn in the side of Count Dooku, who attacks the planet in retaliation. Savage Opress, a Nightbrother, leaves Dathomir to join forces with Darth Maul.

Rebels rise

As Imperial rule takes hold of the galaxy, a resistance cell on the agrarian world of Lothal causes headaches for the Inquisitor and other agents of the Empire.

Ultimate power

The Empire builds the Death Star, a moon-sized superweapon, and uses it to wipe out Alderaan. Luke Skywalker, Princess Leia, and Han Solo bring the Death Star plans to the Rebel Alliance to pinpoint the battle station's weakness.

Mandalorian intrigue

The planet Mandalore becomes one of the war's flashpoints when the Death Watch faction vows to overthrow the rule of Duchess Satine Kryze.

Way of the Force

Luke Skywalker seeks instruction from Jedi Master Yoda in the swamps of Dagobah. Despite an ominous vision in a dark side cave, Luke abandons his training to help his friends on Bespin.

A shocking reveal

Inside Bespin's Cloud City, Han Solo is frozen in carbonite and handed over to bounty hunter Boba Fett. Luke duels Darth Vader and is stunned to learn that the Sith Lord is his father.

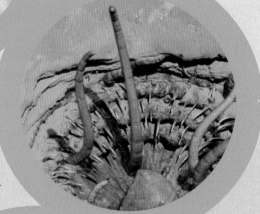

Going undercover

To free Han Solo from his carbonite slab, his friends infiltrate Jabba's palace on Tatooine. Jabba dies during a fight at the Great Pit of Carkoon.

Escape to Hoth

The rebels establish a new headquarters, Echo Base, on snowy Hoth. The Empire finds them there and obliterates the rebel stronghold.

Forest moon

The Rebel Alliance regroups and prepares for a final strike against the Empire. A secret mission to the moon of Endor wins the loyalty of the furry Ewoks, who ambush Imperial stormtroopers.

Battle of Yavin

Launching from the jungle-covered fourth moon of Yavin, rebel X-wing and Y-wing starfighters attack the Death Star. Luke fires the shot that destroys the station.

Death Star II

Above Endor, the Empire's second Death Star fires on rebel warships. Luke has his final showdown with Vader in the Emperor's throne room, and escapes just before the battle station explodes.

"The pride I feel for this planet cannot be put into words." SUPREME CHANCELLOR PALPATINE

NABOO

A small and geologically unique world, Naboo's surface consists of swampy lakes, rolling plains, and green hills. The river cities are resplendent with classical architecture and greenery, while the underwater Gungan settlements are exotic examples of hydrostatic bubble technology.

APPEARANCES I, II, CW, III, VI REGION Mid Rim SECTOR Chommell SYSTEM Naboo PRIMARY TERRAIN Plains, swamps, forests

Varykino
An island in Naboo's Lake Country, Varykino is also the name of the Naberrie family's villa, where Padmé and Anakin Skywalker secretly married.

ARCADIAN DESTINATION
Boasting some of the most idyllic meadows and scenic waterfalls on Naboo, the Lake Country is the planet's most remote inhabited region, with a sparse population of mostly farmers, shaak herders, and glass craftworkers. Sealed off from Naboo's underground waterways and caverns, the lakes here are safe from large aquatic monsters. In springtime, the Festival of Glad Arrival transforms the meadows into a setting for colorful pageants and musical performances. Although the fertile land is regularly flooded by its rivers, the area is pleasantly dry in summer. Padmé Naberrie's family maintains a retreat house on the island of Varykino in the Lake Country.

Peaceful planet
Although Naboo's sparse human population embraces peace and tranquillity, they and the indigenous Gungans navigate an uneasy relationship for hundreds of years until they ally to defend their verdant world.

THE CORE

Lacking a molten core, the small, ancient planet of Naboo is a conglomerate of large rocky bodies permeated by caves and tunnel networks. These largely water-filled networks cause numerous swampy lakes on the planet's surface, which lead deeper into its structure. The native Gungans have developed submersible transports to traverse the caves and tunnels, but most hesitate to venture deep into the planetary core, which is infested with enormous, ravenous sea beasts. However, hardy Gungan navigators regard certain networks through the core as time-honored trade routes and the most expedient avenues from one area of Naboo to another.

Trade routes
For generations, Gungans have used bongo submarines to explore and navigate the network of underwater tunnels that snake through the planet Naboo.

Urgent union
During the Trade Federation invasion of Naboo, Jar Jar Binks brings Queen Amidala to meet Boss Nass at the Gungan Sacred Place *(above)*. There, the Gungans and the Naboo agree to an alliance against their enemies. Little is known about the reptilian humanoids called the Elders *(right)*, who waged war with ancient Gungans and left numerous monuments on Naboo.

THE GUNGAN SACRED PLACE

Built by the Elders, the Gungan Sacred Place is an ancient monument north of the Lianorm Swamp. For generations, Gungans have gathered in this area during times of discord or when the leaders anticipate great danger. The monument is accessed by a hidden entrance, which leads to a path that emerges in a clearing beneath a dense forest canopy. The remains of gigantic statues and monolithic heads, some displaced by the roots of primeval trees, appear to alternately rise from and rest upon the hallowed grounds, which are restricted to outsiders.

FESTIVAL OF LIGHT

An annual event, the Festival of Light celebrates the anniversary of the planet Naboo joining the Galactic Republic. In the city of Theed, the celebration is traditionally observed with a public ceremony that includes an elaborate laser light show and fireworks display. During the Clone Wars, Supreme Chancellor Palpatine returns to his homeworld to attend the festival in its 847th year, even though he is aware he may be targeted for assassination. Knowing that to shrink from such duty would be to admit fear of the enemy, Palpatine trusts the Jedi to protect him during the festival.

Symbolic spectacle
The Festival of Light's fireworks are artfully controlled bursts that represent significant historic moments in Naboo's association with the Republic.

THE BATTLE OF NABOO

"We must not fail to get the viceroy." QUEEN AMIDALA

The tumultuous events of the Battle of Naboo unfold at four locations: the Great Grass Plains, Theed Palace, Theed's power generator, and the Trade Federation's Droid Control Ship.

Following a blockade by the Trade Federation, secretly directed by Darth Sidious as a cover for planetary invasion by a droid army led by Viceroy Nute Gunray, Queen Amidala returns to Naboo hoping to save her people. She leads the resistance with the help of Jedi Qui-Gon Jinn and Obi-Wan Kenobi, Anakin Skywalker, and the indigenous Gungans.

A SYMPHONY OF WAR

Boss Nass, leader of the Gungans, agrees to aid Amidala and the Naboo against the Trade Federation's invading droid army. With the Gungan military, he lures the droid army away from the capital and onto the Great Grass Plains for battle. This diversion allows Amidala and the Jedi to infiltrate Theed Palace, where Gunray is stationed. However, Sidious's apprentice, Darth Maul, appears and engages the two Jedi, leading them into the city's power generator for an epic duel.

Maul manages to separate Obi-Wan from his Master and slays Qui-Gon Jinn. However, Maul's overconfidence gives Obi-Wan a momentary opportunity to cut him in half. Meanwhile, young Anakin, who has obediently hidden in a starfighter cockpit, accidentally bumps the autopilot switch, and through unconscious use of the Force, finds his way to the Droid Control Ship, destroying it from the inside. Without further instructions from their ship, the battle droids automatically deactivate, giving the Gungan army a sudden, improbable victory. At the same time, in the Theed Palace throne room, Amidala arrests Gunray and forces him to sign a new treaty.

Although the people of Naboo have won the battle, their triumph is short-lived. The stage has simply been set for the terrible Clone Wars.

Duel in the power generator
Obi-Wan and Qui-Gon begin their duel with Maul in Theed's hangar, but quickly progress to the power generator, a perilous maze of machinery, deep shafts, conduits and energy beams.

Temporary protection
Normally a grazing area for shaak and other cattle, the lush grass plains of Naboo now feature reptilian fambaa's carrying shield generators. These protect the Gungan army from droid bombardment—though not from their advance.

Cultured capital
Theed's universities cultivate artists, educators, and politicians who are dedicated to public service.

THEED

APPEARANCES I, II, CW, III, VI
LOCATION Naboo

Originally a farming village nestled along the banks of the Solleu River, Naboo's capital city, Theed, is built at the edge of a great plateau where the Solleu runs toward a spectacular waterfall. Fed by underground tributaries that flow from the planet's core, the river travels through and around Theed so that nearly every vantage point in the city has water views. For generations, Naboo traders have used the waterways to occasionally meet with Gungans, but trade increases greatly after the two civilizations join forces during the Battle of Naboo. Most of the city's buildings have columned facades, domed roofs, and terraces with views of the river. Theed's harmonious architectural style reflects the peaceful ways and culture of the city's founders and citizens.

> "Theed is a beautiful city."
> **HEGO DAMASK**

> "If you like museums." **PALPATINE**

THEED ROYAL PALACE

APPEARANCES I, II, CW, III, VI
LOCATION Theed, Naboo

Resting serenely atop a plunging cliff face lined with waterfalls is the immense Theed Royal Palace, Naboo's seat of power. The city of Theed radiates from the palace, and it is often the terminus of grand parades. The ancient and majestic building serves as the residence of Naboo's elected sovereign, as well as the meeting place of Naboo's Royal Advisory Council. The palace is a mighty structure, with strong lines and an imposing presence, but it is also decorated with delicate, ornate finishes that are a testament to Naboo's sensitivity to art and culture. The palace is protected by the Naboo Palace Guard, although given Naboo's pacifist nature, the trained troops rarely need to mobilize.

Palatial sanctuary
Theed Palace enjoys commanding views from its cliff-face sanctuary (left). The city's main thoroughfare, the Palace Plaza, is a wide, pedestrian-only avenue that stretches from the Royal Palace to the Palace Courtyard (above).

ROYAL PALACE THRONE ROOM

APPEARANCES I, II
LOCATION Theed Palace, Theed, Naboo

The Royal Palace's original designers and contemporary curators eschew any display of bulky, inelegant machinery, but the building has many subtly blended technological features. The throne room is protected by ornate blast doors, an interplanetary communications system, and hidden compartments for weapons in case of an emergency. A composite holoprojector is built into the throne room's floor, along with a large viewscreen on the wall, which allows Queen Amidala and her Advisory Council to converse with dignitaries from other worlds.

Captured throne
During their occupation of Naboo, Neimoidians confer with Darth Sidious's hologram in the throne room.

OTOH GUNGA

APPEARANCES I, CW
LOCATION Lake Paonga, Naboo

Deep below the surface of Lake Paonga is the largest Gungan city on Naboo, Otoh Gunga. The city resembles a glittering cluster of jewel-like bubbles and is the crowning achievement of unique Gungan technology. The Gungans actually grow the building material of their cities, and the elegant structures contained within the bubbles consist of curving forms that appear alive. The bubbles are hydrostatic forcefields that contain breathable atmospheres for the city's inhabitants. Though the bubbles are rigid enough to keep the water out, they can be safely passed through by Gungans swimming to and from the city at special portal zones.

During the Trade Federation occupation of Naboo, the Gungan leader Boss Nass ignores the battle droid threat, believing Otoh Gunga is safe. But when the battle droids encroach on Gungan territory and invade Otoh Gunga, they force the Gungans to abandon their underwater city. The Gungans hide in the nearby forests containing the Gungan Sacred Place, and eventually ally with Queen Amidala and the Naboo people.

Following the defeat of the Trade Federation, overcrowding becomes a prime concern for Boss Nass and the Gungan Rep Council. The increased Gungan tolerance of visiting off-worlders results in Otoh Gunga becoming a tourist attraction and, surprisingly, a favored destination for honeymooning vacationers.

Gungan engineering
Gungans combine bubble wort catalyst and stabilized plasma in electrostatic field generators to create the permeable hydrostatic bubbles needed to keep their city dry *(above)*. Otoh Gunga's amphibious inhabitants use specially designed portal zones to enter and exit the submerged city *(right)*.

THEED HANGAR

APPEARANCES I, CW
LOCATION Theed, Naboo

Attached to one side of Theed Palace, a spacious hangar serves as the headquarters of the Royal Naboo Security Forces and Starfighter Corps, and houses the sleek yellow Naboo N-1 starfighters as well as the Queen's gleaming Royal Starship. Separated from the hangar by a heavy blast-proof door, the neighboring power generator supplies the hangar's spacecraft with plasma energy through underground conduits. The hangar is equipped with air-traffic control, tactical computer stations, and a secret subterranean tunnel link to the palace. During the Battle of Naboo, Queen Amidala and her allies use the tunnels to infiltrate Theed, allowing them to reach the hangar and liberate the air-traffic controllers and pilots from their droid captors. The pilots scramble to their N-1 starfighters and swiftly leave the hangar to join the fight.

Urgent exit
Ignoring blaster fire from battle droids, brave Naboo pilots launch their starfighters out of Theed Hangar.

> "Well, if there's a bright center to the universe, you're on the planet that it's farthest from."
>
> **LUKE SKYWALKER**

TATOOINE

Far from the Core Worlds, the inhospitable desert planet Tatooine is of little interest to either the Old Republic or the subsequent Empire. Ironically, this dusty world is home to two generations of Skywalkers, who are instrumental in bringing down both galactic governments.

APPEARANCES I, II, CW, III, IV, VI **REGION** Outer Rim Territories **SECTOR** Arkanis **SYSTEM** Tatoo **PRIMARY TERRAIN** Desert, mesas, buttes, canyons

Negotiations
Although Jedi have little reason to visit Tatooine, Obi-Wan Kenobi meets with Jabba the Hutt during the Clone Wars to discuss a delicate situation involving Jabba's abducted son, Rotta.

LAWLESS WORLD

Beyond the interests of the Republic or Imperial laws, Tatooine is largely controlled by the Hutts, whose shady operations bring many spacers, bounty hunters, and thieves to the planet's few port cities. Despite the planet's criminal activity and hardworking settlers' attempts to extract a living from the unforgiving environment, sporadic colonization efforts have resulted in only scattered communities, separated by vast gulfs of wilderness.

Sand planet

Isolated and almost entirely devoid of water, Tatooine is a world of dry air and parched soil. The planet's silicate surface reflects the light of its suns so intensely that legends tell of its original explorers first mistaking the planet for a third, smaller sun. Indigenous sentient life includes the scavenging Jawas and the fearsome Tusken Raiders. Creatures found roaming the desert include banthas, rontos, dewbacks, scurriers, womp rats, krayt dragons, and eopies.

Infinite wastes
Tatooine's surface is a seemingly endless desert environment cooked by the intense energy of twin yellow suns. Only the sporadic rocky mesas, canyons, and arroyos break up the monotony of seemingly endless shifting dunes.

DESERT SCAVENGERS

Long before the Hutts took control of Tatooine, mining colonies searched the sand planet for precious minerals and ores. When Tatooine metal proved to have unwanted metallurgic properties, the mines were shut down and the miners abandoned most of their equipment, including mobile transports used for hauling and refining ore. Much to the remaining colonists' surprise, the native Jawas quickly claimed and salvaged these "sandcrawlers," making them an important part of their culture. Jawas use the large, treaded vehicles not only as an armored defense against the elements and Tusken Raiders, but for transporting trade goods, including refurbished droids made from scavenged parts, to remote outposts. The sandcrawlers' smelting reactors, originally designed to melt processed ore, have been modified to produce salable ingots. Although Tusken Raiders have no interest in computer technology, they also scavenge—and more often steal—metal they can shape into weapons and masks.

Nomadic traders
Scurrying outside their sandcrawler, Jawas present various droids for sale to moisture farmer Owen Lars.

KRAYT DRAGONS

According to Jawa folklore, the great Tatooine desert known as the Dune Sea was once a true ocean. Ancient fossil-bearing rock and eroded canyons seem to confirm the Jawas' stories, but most of Tatooine's inhabitants still find it hard to believe water ever flowed on the planet's arid, sand-covered surface. Despite the scarcity of water, Tatooine boasts many indigenous creatures, the largest of which are krayt dragons, represented by two species: the relatively common canyon krayt, which dwells in rock caves and canyons, and the much larger greater krayt, which submerges itself in the shifting sands and uses its powerful limbs to swim through the dunes.

MOISTURE FARMS

Water vaporators are not only the most energy-efficient devices used to gather water on Tatooine, they are the most crucial piece of equipment for colonists' survival. Although a single vaporator may cost up to 500 credits, some colonists invest in multiple units to establish their own moisture farms. Independent farmers often use surplus water for their small hydroponic gardens, but few gardens yield enough to make substantial profits. Vaporators require frequent maintenance as well as security systems to deter Tusken Raiders.

Skeletal remains
Shortly after arriving on Tatooine, the droid C-3PO shuffles past the sand-scoured skeleton of a greater krayt dragon that rests in the Jundland Wastes.

Vaporator fields
Luke surveys his uncle's farm and vaporators *(right)*, which are strategically spaced to collect moisture *(above)*.

Crowded hovels
Abandoned by the mining companies that first colonized Tatooine, the cheap hovels in Mos Espa's Slave Quarter provide only the most basic shelter for downtrodden slaves.

MOS ESPA

APPEARANCES I, II
LOCATION Tatooine

On the lip of the Dune Sea, down a canyon called the Xelric Draw, the city of Mos Espa is a serpentine sprawl of low-level buildings with thick walls and domed roofs to defend against the scorching heat of the planet's twin suns. One of the few port cities on Tatooine, Mos Espa is larger than Mos Eisley spaceport and is known for its wide streets, bordered by many shops and stalls. Among the dwellings, workspaces, and commercial operations, the city also boasts many entertainment areas, including the famed Mos Espa Grand Arena, which can almost hold the city's entire population. Although wealthy Hutts, including Jabba, keep residences in Mos Espa, most of the inhabitants are settlers and subsistence earners who eke out meager livings as best they can.

Because neither the Galactic Republic nor the Trade Federation has any jurisdiction over Tatooine, and because Tatooine has few valuable natural resources, the only real wealth in Mos Espa is tied up in gambling and off-world trade, especially in the lucrative black market. The influx of commercial ventures fuels Mos Espa's growth, quickly transforming it into the largest city on Tatooine and the desert planet's de facto capital. Many outlanders believe they may avoid paying high tariffs by doing business in Mos Espa, but because Tatooine is controlled by the devious Hutts, few travelers save money at the spaceport. The inexpensive hotels and cantinas exist primarily to lure traders, spacers, and unwitting tourists into the Hutts' casinos and gambling dens, where they can easily lose their earnings and even life savings within hours. Few losers complain because they know the Hutt-owned establishments are staffed by security personnel who don't take kindly to troublemakers. However, the rise of the Empire prompts the Hutts to revise their business schemes, and

Tearful farewell
On the street outside their home, Anakin Skywalker says good-bye to his mother, Shmi.

Jabba shifts his interests to Mos Eisley, causing Mos Espa to decline.

Although slavery is outlawed in Republic space, it persists on worlds outside the Republic's authority. An entire section of Mos Espa's outskirts has been transformed into a slave quarter. Slaves function more as prestige possessions than cheap laborers, and owners part with them only reluctantly. Slaves are sometimes used as capital in business transactions. Nearly all slavery operations in Mos Espa are controlled by Hutt gangsters, who, as with all their illegal ventures, regard slavery as a useful institution.

Return to Mos Espa
Padmé Amidala's yacht delivers Anakin to a Mos Espa docking bay *(right)*, and the two take a droid rickshaw to Watto's shop *(above)*.

WATTO'S SHOP

APPEARANCES I, II
LOCATION Mos Espa, Tatooine

Although Watto promotes his establishment as a parts dealership, everyone in Mos Espa calls it a junk shop. The property is ideally situated near the spaceport's busiest docking bays and service hangars, and it is well known to many podracers. Originally, the shop's main building was an unremarkable squat dome, but Watto has added a distinctive bell-shaped top, which provides additional living and working space and attracts customers because of its unusual appearance and greater height than neighboring buildings. The dome's apex forms a comfortable perch for Watto and is similar to the muck nests of his home planet. The shop is one of the most successful of its kind in Mos Espa. Watto attributes his success to four things: inflated prices, stolen stock, slaves, and no questions asked. Like most Mos Espa merchants, Watto accepts only local currency.

Inside Watto's shop, merchandise ranges from desirable rare parts to fully operational droids. His selection of droids and droid parts includes GNK power droids, DUM-series pit droids, astromechs, and shell plating for Cybot Galactica protocol droids. An R1-type shopkeeping drone handles most of the routine business operations, while Watto's slave, Anakin, repairs and cleans machinery, allowing Watto to dedicate more time to his gambling interests.

Watto has also amassed a collection of podrace memorabilia, including many rare trophies. Outside the shop, an arched portal serves as the entrance to the scrapyard, where Watto stores the bulk of his merchandise, including larger items like podracer engines, landspeeder turbines, and empty cargo containers. Near the scrap yard's entrance, Watto maintains a constantly shifting pile of largely useless scrap, which he leaves outside for Jawa scavengers. Although Watto prefers paying customers, he has a certain respect for Jawas, as they have taught him much about salvaging ruined vessels and protecting technology from heat and sand.

Slave labor
Holding machinery for repairing and cleaning mechanical apparatus and technology, the curved tables inside Watto's shop double as display shelves for various parts for sale *(above)*. Anakin's natural talent for repairing machinery makes him one of Watto's most prized possessions *(left)*.

Tour of the scrap yard
Hoping to obtain an unusual hyperdrive component, the Jedi Qui-Gon Jinn follows Watto into the scrap yard behind Watto's shop.

"The entire planet is one big city." RIC OLIÉ

CORUSCANT

Situated in the heart of the galaxy, Coruscant is the seat of government for the Galactic Republic and the subsequent Empire. Completely covered by skyscrapers, the planet's population is over one trillion, including many powerful and influential politicians and industrialists.

APPEARANCES I, II, CW, III, VI **REGION** Core Worlds **SECTOR** Coruscant subsector, Corusca sector **SYSTEM** Coruscant **PRIMARY TERRAIN** Urban cityscape

Shimmering "surface"

Viewed from orbit, Coruscant resembles a great, glittering sphere and appears to promise prosperity for all. Sunlight dances across the gleaming skyscrapers' uppermost levels, which are home to the wealthiest citizens. But beneath this veneer, the city-world descends thousands of levels to impoverished, dangerous areas untouched by the sun for millennia.

SKYSCRAPER SPRAWLS

Over many thousands of years, Coruscant's surface has become completely buried under the foundations of immense, densely clustered skyscrapers. The enormous structures reach so high into the atmosphere that tenants require piped-in purified gases for breathing in upper-level complexes, a luxury only the affluent can afford. Several kilometers down, the lower levels are a worldwide maze of treacherous alleys where the most impoverished dwell. Citizens from above and below intermingle in myriad nightclubs, gaming houses, bars, and entertainment establishments that cater to alien species.

Urban growth
The crisis on Naboo and the Clone Wars dramatically impact Coruscant's Senate District, as the call to bolster the Galactic Republic's stability results in new buildings to house thousands of pro-Republic and war-effort departments.

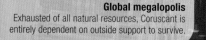

Global megalopolis
Exhausted of all natural resources, Coruscant is entirely dependent on outside support to survive.

AIR TRAFFIC

Coruscant's skies are filled with unending repulsorlift traffic. Most skylanes are autonavigated, with vehicles traveling on preprogrammed routes to minimize risk of collisions. Large passenger ships join the fastest traffic in the highest skylanes, while smaller air taxis crisscross these routes to take high-paying riders directly to their destinations. Tour operator pilots demand high fees for taking wide-eyed off-worlders on breathtaking cruises over the planet. Even in the depths of night, Coruscant is alive with glittering lights and rivers of traffic, a bustling megalopolis that refuses to sleep.

THE WORKS

A large sector and industrial area in Galactic City, the Works is a once-great manufacturing district, recognized as a major source of production for spacecraft parts, construction droids, and building materials. But centuries ago, increasingly high costs on Coruscant prompted most manufacturers to shift their operations to off-planet facilities. Now, the Works largely consists of long-abandoned buildings and empty warehouses, many appropriated by criminals. A derelict hangar in the Works is an ideal site for clandestine meetings between Darth Sidious and Darth Tyranus.

Freighter lanes
Unending streams of freighters deliver food and other necessities.

Abandoned towers
Toxic waste leaves large areas of the Works entirely uninhabitable.

MONSTER RAMPAGE

During the Clone Wars, Coruscant prepares numerous defenses against Separatist Alliance attacks. However, when a Republic ship delivers the enormous Zillo beast from the planet Malastare to the Coruscant laboratory overseen by Doctor Sionver Boll, no one anticipates that the creature will break its bonds and escape. Impervious to lightsabers, and with powerful claws and jaws that can bite through metal, the Zillo beast tears through Coruscant, leaving a trail of injured civilians and clone troopers as it cuts an apparently deliberate path to the Senate Building. The creature seizes a shuttle carrying Supreme Chancellor Palpatine, but thanks to the quick action of Anakin Skywalker and Republic forces, the monster is stopped.

Self-preservation
Realizing scientists intend to kill it, the Zillo beast runs amok across Coruscant's Senate District.

"Start your engines!" BEED

MOS ESPA GRAND ARENA

Financed by the Hutts, the Mos Espa Grand Arena is home to the Boonta Eve Classic, the largest annual podrace held on Tatooine. The arena's podracing track is one of the most famous in the Outer Rim Territories and attracts competitors and spectators from all over the galaxy.

APPEARANCES I **LOCATION** Outskirts of Mos Espa, Tatooine

Podrace fans

Over 100,000 beings fill the Mos Espa Grand Arena to capacity for the Boonta Eve Classic. They file into the grandstand seats, crowd into broad viewing platforms, or cluster into the upper tiers to witness the high-speed spectacle. Many hope to win big after hitting the betting windows and playing the odds.

PODRACER HANGARS

Originally constructed as a series of enclosed bays, each of which serviced a single podracer, the arena's hangars have been expanded as the sport has grown in popularity. The dividers between the bays have been removed to accommodate additional podracers and to keep up with the number of entrants. While the hangars are used for vehicle maintenance and last-minute tune-ups before a race, they also provide a place for podracer pilots, their wealthy fans, and their sponsors to place unregulated, high-stakes bets with one another.

Bustling pit droids
Inside a hangar, teams of pit droids are constantly on the move, assisting podracer mechanics in preparation for the Boonta Eve Classic.

Sand rock construction
Straddling the junction of the Xelric Draw and the Northern Dune Sea, the arena's amphitheater is built into the natural curve of a steep-walled canyon.

WATTO'S BOX

Mos Espa's wealthier residents and guests can afford private viewing boxes separated from the rest of the rabble. Toydarian junk merchant Watto hosts viewing parties for his friends and gambling partners in his own private box. Because only a small fraction of the racetrack passes the arena, Watto's box is equipped with viewscreens that broadcast transmissions from aerial cam droids, enabling Watto and his cronies to monitor each podracer's progress. The most opulent viewing box is reserved for the ruling Hutts, particularly Jabba, grandmaster host of the Boonta Eve Classic.

Heavy losses
Watto places huge bets on podracing champion Sebulba to win the Boonta. He is confident at first, but ends up a big loser when his own slave, Anakin Skywalker, wins the race.

No turning back
As the podracer pilots move into position on the arena's starting grid, none dwell on the fact that the Boonta Eve Classic has the highest mortality rate of all podrace competitions in the galaxy.

STARTING GRID

The formal race ceremony begins with a parade of flag-bearers, each carrying a racer's distinctive emblem as they line up before the starting grid. The system for determining the starting lineup at the Boonta is the subject of much speculation and argument among podracing aficionados. Allegedly developed by expert race officials, the system actually involves a baffling mix of performance statistics, outright bribery, and random chance. After the flag-bearers clear the grid, the podracers' massive engines roar to life, seemingly anxious at the chance to charge along at speeds exceeding 700 kilometers (435 miles) per hour. Eighteen podracers enter the fateful competition that results in a major upset for Sebulba the Dug and a great victory for Anakin, who wins not only the Boonta but also his freedom. Only seven pilots manage to cross the finish line.

PALPATINE'S APARTMENT

APPEARANCES I **LOCATION** 500 Republica, Galactic City, Coruscant

Within the upper levels of the most prestigious and exclusive residential tower in the Senate District on Coruscant, Senator Palpatine keeps an apartment that offers majestic views, yet is modest in comparison with the residences of other sectorial representatives. The apartment consists of an expansive suite of rooms, most of which are decorated in hues of scarlet, Palpatine's preferred color, and with unusual art objects that reflect his worldly point of view. To ensure the complete safety of his guests, Palpatine outfits each room with discreet surveillance and security systems, which enable him to know immediately whether his guests have any special requirements or require assistance.

Calming influence
Devoid of vibrant colors or ostentatious decorations, Palpatine's apartment is designed to pacify argumentative visitors and make every guest feel assured of their host's diplomatic authority.

"I'm on my way to the Jedi Temple to start my training, I hope." ANAKIN SKYWALKER

JEDI TEMPLE

For thousands of years, the Jedi Temple has been the home of the Jedi Order on Coruscant. Part school and part monastery, the temple houses facilities for training and meditation, dormitories, medical centers, and archives that contain extensive data from across the galaxy.

APPEARANCES I, II, CW, III, VI **LOCATION** Galactic City, Coruscant

Jedi dispatch
Standing in the center of the High Council chamber, Obi-Wan Kenobi and Anakin Skywalker receive orders from the Council.

HIGH COUNCIL CHAMBER

The Jedi High Council, the governing body of the Jedi Order, convenes within one of the Jedi Temple's outer spires. The circular High Council chamber holds a ring of 12 seats, one for each of the Jedi Masters who serve as Council members. Monitoring galactic events and contemplating the nature of the Force, the Council has final authority on Jedi missions on behalf of the Republic and also determines whether prospective Jedi candidates are worthy of training. While advanced communications networks keep the Council apprised of galactic events, its members also rely on the Force to sense disturbances and anticipate situations that may require their help. During the Clone Wars, the Council uses the High Council chamber to consider battle strategies and coordinate troops.

The temple
A massive ziggurat rising from one of the highest levels on Coruscant, the Jedi Temple is instantly recognizable by its distinctive crown of five spires. The Jedi Order also maintains chapter houses on numerous worlds throughout Republic space.

Giving instruction
While teaching Jedi younglings from the Bear Clan, Yoda confers with Obi-Wan.

TRAINING YOUNG JEDI

Prior to a Padawan's pairing with a Jedi Master, young Jedi—also known as Jedi younglings—are taught in a communal group called a clan. At any given time inside the Jedi Temple, 10 different clans undergo instruction in the ways of the Jedi under the tutelage of Jedi Master Yoda. Each clan consists of up to 20 younglings, ranging in age from 4 to 8 and comprising a number of different species. Anakin is a rare example of a Padawan student who skips the clan stage of training by joining the Jedi Order as an older child.

JEDI ARCHIVES

Inside the Jedi Temple, incredible amounts of data are stored electronically and holographically in the Jedi Archives, possibly the single largest source of information in the galaxy. Jedi scholars and investigators use the carefully organized data in their studies or their missions. Besides standard data tapes and holobooks, the Archives contain holocrons, which are cube-shaped devices that store phenomenal amounts of data. These are housed in a vault prohibited to non-Jedi.

Guardians of knowledge
Jocasta Nu, the chief librarian of the Jedi Archives, assists Obi-Wan *(above left)*, who searches the Archives for information about the mysterious Kamino system *(above)*.

Stalking Jedi
At Supreme Chancellor Palpatine's command, the newly appointed Sith Lord Darth Vader leads Anakin's former battalion, the 501st Legion, on a killing mission inside the Jedi Temple.

TEMPLE UNDER SIEGE

To help Palpatine conquer his enemies, his new apprentice, Darth Vader, storms the Jedi Temple with his elite clone trooper special forces in tow. They cut down the Jedi ranks within the temple, not sparing the younglings who cower in the empty Jedi Council chamber. Palpatine also broadcasts a false emergency transmission across space, notifying distant Jedi that the war is over and instructing them to return to the temple. Seeing through this trap, Jedi Masters Obi-Wan and Yoda infiltrate the temple and modify the transmission, warning the remaining Jedi to stay away. Subsequently, Palpatine rules his Empire from the Jedi Temple, which he renames the Imperial Palace.

Ultimate betrayal
Seeing Anakin enter the temple's High Council room, young Jedi realize too late that he has not come to help them.

Galactic representatives
Each box in the Galactic Senate Chamber contains a delegation from an important world or sector in the Republic. The democratic ideals of the Senate are put to the test every time the legislative process degenerates into arguing and pointless bureaucracy.

GALACTIC SENATE CHAMBER

APPEARANCES I, II, CW, III
LOCATION Senate District, Coruscant

The Galactic Senate Chamber is the nerve center of political activity on Coruscant. The huge open area is lined with 1,024 pods arrayed in concentric circles, each pod housing a delegation from an important planet, sector, or political body. The pods are outfitted with anti-gravity repulsorlifts, so that when a politician wishes to address the assembled Senate, his or her pod detaches from the wall and floats into the open air in the middle of the chamber. The entire structure is fitted with voice-amplifying microphones and automatic translators, and hovercams constantly flit about to record the proceedings for the official record. At the centermost point of the Galactic Senate Chamber is the podium of the Supreme Chancellor. This is where the elected leader of the Republic sits to hear arguments from every representative, usually joined in the podium by the Vice Chancellor and a senior administrative aide. The podium retracts into the floor when not in use, giving the chancellor access to a suite of rooms where business can be conducted between Senate sessions.

The Galactic Senate Chamber is the site of many of the most crucial events in the latter years of the Republic. It is where Queen Padmé Amidala of Naboo, upset over the lack of political help in ending the Trade Federation's blockade of her homeworld, calls for a Vote of No Confidence in the leadership of Supreme Chancellor Valorum. After the Battle of Naboo, Padmé joins the Senate as the representative from Naboo, playing a role in the debate over whether the Republic should adopt the Military Creation Act in response to the growing threat of Count Dooku's Separatist movement. At the end of the Clone Wars, Palpatine gives a speech in the Galactic Senate Chamber in which he declares himself Emperor. Jedi Master Yoda confronts Palpatine, and the two have a stunning clash of Force powers inside the chamber that results in Yoda fleeing the fight.

Power play

Senator Palpatine slyly manipulates Queen Amidala into pushing for Chancellor Valorum's removal from office. Amidala introduces the Vote of No Confidence in Valorum's leadership, leading to Palpatine's election as the new Supreme Chancellor. The Queen believes this will be a good move for Naboo, since Palpatine is a native of her homeworld, but it has dire consequences for the galaxy as Supreme Chancellor Palpatine slowly brings the Senate under his control and ensures that he is given stronger executive powers.

"Order! We shall have order!" MAS AMEDDA

Fight to the death
After the defeat of his Master Qui-Gon *(right)*, Obi-Wan Kenobi struggles to pull himself out of the reactor shaft while Maul attacks *(above)*.

THEED POWER GENERATOR

APPEARANCES I **LOCATION** Theed, Naboo

Located within the capital city of Theed on Naboo, the power generator is where the planet's natural plasma reserves are refined and used as a source of efficient energy. The building also houses hangar facilities for the starfighters of the Royal Naboo Security Forces. The power generator is a clean, brightly illuminated facility of towering columns and dangerous drops. During the Battle of Naboo, Obi-Wan Kenobi and Qui-Gon Jinn chase Darth Maul into the power generator and engage in a fierce lightsaber duel. A series of laser gates separates the Jedi, allowing Maul to get the upper hand and kill Qui-Gon. Obi-Wan defeats Maul and casts his body into a reactor shaft.

SENATE OFFICE BUILDING

APPEARANCES II, CW, III
LOCATION Senate District, Coruscant

The Senate Office Building houses administrative facilities used by legislators on Coruscant, including the offices of the Supreme Chancellor. Landing facilities constructed directly into the side of the building allow senators and guests to come and go freely. Senate Guards provide protection while senators such as Bail Organa, Padmé Amidala, and Onaconda Farr hold discussions with their allies and opponents concerning upcoming pieces of legislation. During the Separatist Crisis and the Clone Wars, many important meetings are held in the Senate Office Building, including debates on the wisdom of the Military Creation Act.

Legislative District
The Senate Office Building is close to the Galactic Senate Chamber for the convenience of its representatives.

Always busy
Starships and airspeeders are constantly arriving and departing, taking senators to important meetings.

CHANCELLOR PALPATINE'S OFFICE

APPEARANCES II, CW, III **LOCATION** Senate District, Coruscant

The office of the Supreme Chancellor of the Republic is located in one of the highest levels of Coruscant within the well-guarded Senate Office Building. It consists of several rooms, featuring red-paneled walls and decorated with bronze statues, bas-relief murals, and other rare and exotic artworks. One piece of sculpture on Palpatine's desk secretly contains his red-bladed lightsaber. During the Clone Wars, Mace Windu and three other Jedi Masters arrive in Palpatine's office to place the Chancellor under arrest. He defends himself using his dark-side powers. Palpatine's office is also where Anakin's conversion from Jedi to Sith takes place.

PADMÉ'S CORUSCANT APARTMENT

APPEARANCES II, CW, III
LOCATION Senate District, Coruscant

Padmé Amidala uses this apartment after she becomes Naboo's representative to the Galactic Senate. Spacious and luxurious, it is located in the upper levels of the Coruscant cityscape. Just prior to the Clone Wars, assassin Zam Wesell tries to kill Padmé by placing two venomous kouhuns in her apartment.

CORUSCANT UNDERWORLD

APPEARANCES II, CW
LOCATION Lower Levels, Coruscant

The Coruscant underworld is a term used to describe the lower levels of the city, where sunlight seldom reaches and crime is a constant danger. Nightclubs, taverns, and casinos are common in the better-trafficked areas of the underworld. Brightly colored signs offer illumination regardless of the time of day, while thugs and pickpockets lurk in dark corners preying on pedestrians. Senators and Jedi Knights rarely travel into the underworld unless they have good reason.

After dark
The Coruscant underworld is a dangerous place to travel for those who are alone or unarmed.

Mind trick
In the club, Obi-Wan is confronted by a patron offering him death sticks. With the Force, he convinces the dealer to go home and rethink his life.

OUTLANDER GAMBLING CLUB

APPEARANCES II **LOCATION** Entertainment District, Coruscant

One of the most popular gambling establishments in Coruscant's lower-level entertainment district, the Outlander Club is a busy place where patrons can place wagers on games of chance and the outcomes of sporting events across the galaxy. With so many people circulating in and out of the club's doors, it is a perfect spot for fugitives to escape unwanted attention or for criminals to sell illegal goods. Just prior to the Clone Wars, Obi-Wan and Anakin pursue assassin Zam Wesell into the Outlander Club. Wesell tries to blend in, but Obi-Wan finds her and cuts off her arm.

DEX'S DINER

APPEARANCES II **LOCATION** CoCo Town, Coruscant

The restaurant operated by Dexter Jettster is a stopover for residents of the CoCo Town neighborhood of Coruscant. The diner is small but usually jam-packed and offers a variety of filling, unhealthy foods and endless cups of Jawa juice. The droid WA-7 and the human Hermione Bagwa work in the diner as waitresses, and Dex himself often fills the role of chef. Just prior to the Clone Wars, Obi-Wan visits Dex's Diner to ask its proprietor about a dart used to silence bounty hunter Wesell. Dexter, who worked at a mining operation on Subterrel before opening his restaurant, identifies the weapon as a rare Kamino saberdart. This clue leads Obi-Wan to Kamino, where he discovers a secret clone army.

Foot traffic
Dex's Diner occupies a bustling location where customers can drop in at any time, day or night.

KAMINO

APPEARANCES II, CW **REGION** Outer Rim
SECTOR Unknown **SYSTEM** Kamino
PRIMARY TERRAIN Oceans

Kamino is a watery world located far beyond the Outer Rim, just south of the Rishi Maze. It is the home of the Kaminoans, tall, pale-skinned beings with large eyes who have a talent for genetic manipulation. Over the years, the Kaminoans developed cloning laboratories on their homeworld and their clone creations began appearing on outlying worlds, such as the mining planet of Subterrel. The weather patterns of Kamino are frequently rocked by storms and lightning blasts, but the stilt cities of the Kaminoans are built to withstand high winds and pounding waves. The capital of Kamino is Tipoca City, which also houses the most advanced cloning laboratories anywhere on the planet. Kamino is home to a wide variety of aquatic life, including aiwhas, flying cetaceans ridden by the Kaminoans as mounts.

Shortly after the Battle of Naboo, Darth Sidious sets in motion his plan to take control of the galaxy by setting off a false war. He ensures that Jedi Master Sifo-Dyas places an order with the Kaminoans for a massive clone army, then orders Count Dooku to find a suitable genetic template for the army's creation. Dooku recruits bounty hunter Jango Fett as the prime clone, and Fett agrees to live on Kamino for the next decade to provide samples and help train the newly grown soldiers. The deletion of Kamino's coordinates from the Jedi Archives ensures no one will interfere with the project until it is nearly complete.

Eventually Obi-Wan Kenobi tracks down Kamino's location and meets with Kaminoan Prime Minister Lama Su, who assumes he has come to take delivery of the clone army. Obi-Wan also encounters Jango Fett and his cloned son Boba Fett, who flee the planet so as not to attract Jedi attention. Obi-Wan's pursuit of them leads to the Battle of Geonosis that marks the start of the Clone Wars. The Republic happily accepts the clone soldiers grown on Kamino, and these troopers become the backbone of the newly formed Grand Army of the Republic. The Separatists quickly move to cut the clone army off at its source; General Grievous and Asajj Ventress lead a full-scale attack on Kamino, using *Trident*-class drill assault craft to damage the defenses of Tipoca City and aqua droids to execute an underwater assault. The mission ends in failure for the Separatists, but the Order 66 programming contained in the clone troopers soon leads to the downfall of the Jedi.

Isolated
Kamino's distant location keeps it safe until the Separatists target it during the Clone Wars.

"Kamino? It's not a system I'm familiar with." JOCASTA NU

Weather-proofed
All cities on Kamino have sloping roofs to deflect wind, rain, and ocean spray. The stilts that support the structures are strong, leaving little risk of damage to the Kaminoans or their delicate experiments *(right)*. A Kaminoan on an aiwha mount approaches the elevated expanse of Tipoca City *(above right)*.

TIPOCA CITY

APPEARANCES II, CW **LOCATION** Kamino

Tipoca City is the capital city of Kamino and the site of its most important cloning facility. As Kamino's governmental center, Tipoca City contains offices used by Prime Minister Lama Su and other high-ranking administrators, but many of its buildings are occupied by Kaminoan geneticists and filled with the advanced equipment needed to grow and train clones. The buildings of Tipoca City are constructed on stilts in the vast expanse of the Kaminoan oceans, made from reinforced materials with a streamlined architectural style designed to diffuse the impact of waves and the planet's storms. Landing platforms are usually exposed to the elements, but the doors leading to the city's interior are always watertight. The city's sloped roofs are topped with communications antennae and lightning rods.

The Kaminoans begin work on the Republic's clone army approximately 10 years before the Battle of Geonosis, and they alter each clone's genetic structure so that they age at twice the standard rate. With new batches of clones being produced every year, Tipoca City is soon filled with clones ranging from infancy to adulthood. Each age group requires a different set of instructional programs and training gear. The younger clones receive flash learning in the subjects of military strategy and galactic history, while older clones are permitted to suit up in armor and participate in simulated firefights.

These advanced training theaters are part of the Tipoca City Military Complex, which also houses the Central Armory, where thermal detonators, DC-15 blaster rifles, and other weapons are stored. War games held in the Military Complex can involve low-risk, holographic opponents or are set to live-fire settings in which severe injury is a real risk. Elsewhere in the Military Complex are testing facilities for heavy equipment, including six-legged AT-TEs, two-legged AT-RTs, AV-7 anti-vehicle cannons, and low-flying LAAT/i gunships.

Bounty hunter Jango Fett lives in Tipoca City for nearly a decade following

his selection as the prime clone for the Republic's clone trooper army. He abandons his apartment after Obi-Wan tracks him to Kamino.

Following the Battle of Geonosis, Tipoca City's cloning laboratories become one of

the Republic's most vital assets. Turbolaser emplacements are used to successfully defend Tipoca City during the Clone Wars, though the city does suffer structural damage from the drills of the Separatist attack craft.

Surprise inspection
Taun We and Prime Minister Lama Su take Obi-Wan on a tour of the city's cloning facilities *(above)*. Aging clone "99," a clone trooper who grew too rapidly, handles general maintenance duties *(left)*.

Attack on Kamino
Separatist *Trident* ships land near Tipoca City and unleash their droid passengers *(far left)*, while clone troopers scramble to intercept the threat and defend their birthworld from the Separatists *(left)*.

LAKE COUNTRY

APPEARANCES II **LOCATION** Naboo

The Lake Country is a very beautiful and extremely isolated area on Naboo. Surrounded by mountains, the locale is situated in a valley dotted with numerous picturesque lakes. Vacationers often visit the Lake Country to view its waterfalls and open grasslands filled with wildflowers. Herds of harmless shaaks graze openly in the bucolic meadows. Just prior to the Clone Wars, Padmé Amidala chooses the Lake Country as a safe hiding spot for herself and her bodyguard Anakin Skywalker following an attempt on her life.

NABOO LAKE RETREAT

APPEARANCES II
LOCATION Lake Country, Naboo

Located in the Lake Country area of Naboo, the lake retreat called Varykino has a long history of use by the Naberrie family. Before she became known as Queen Amidala, Padmé Naberrie spent her summers there. The villa occupies a small island in the center of a lake, reachable by gondola speeders, and an old man named Paddy Accu serves as its caretaker. Padmé and Anakin grow close while spending time at the retreat and later return to be married in secret.

JANGO'S APARTMENT

APPEARANCES II
LOCATION Tipoca City, Kamino

Bad feeling
Jango Fett isn't happy about Obi-Wan's intrusion into his apartment and the way he questions him.

Jango Fett's home for 10 years, this small apartment in Tipoca City on Kamino is given to the prime clone by the Kaminoans as compensation for his assistance in the cloning project. Jango keeps his accommodations simple, hiding his armor out of sight and displaying no trophies from his hunts. A large window on one wall offers a spectacular view of the churning ocean that stretches out to the horizon. Boba Fett also lives in the apartment with his father until Obi-Wan's investigation causes the pair to flee Kamino.

The central repository
In neat lines, hundreds of clones approach one
of the armor stations in Tipoca City to receive
their helmets. Because all clone troopers are
identical, one size of helmet fits all.

KAMINO'S CLONE ARMY

"Two hundred thousand units are ready, with another million well on the way."

LAMA SU

When Obi-Wan Kenobi arrives on Kamino, he has no idea of the surprise in store. A clone army is waiting, ready to fight for the Republic.

A saberdart left behind on Coruscant by bounty hunter Jango Fett leads Obi-Wan Kenobi to Kamino, where the weapon was made. The coordinates of the planet are mysteriously missing from the Jedi Temple's archives, increasing Obi-Wan's suspicions. When he finally finds the rain-soaked planet beyond the Outer Rim, Obi-Wan is prepared for anything. But he isn't expecting to be greeted as a paying client.

CLONED SOLDIERS

The Kaminoans assume that Obi-Wan has come as an official representative of the Jedi Council to check on the Republic's order of clone soldiers. Obi-Wan doesn't have any idea what they're talking about, but he subtly presses Prime Minister Lama Su for information. Su explains that the clone order was placed 10 years earlier by Jedi Master Sifo-Dyas, with Jango Fett serving as the genetic template. A tour of the cloning laboratories of Tipoca City takes Obi-Wan through the growth tanks where new clones are gestated and the education facilities where young clones receive instruction in military tactics. Kaminoan aide Taun We brings Obi-Wan to Jango Fett's apartment, where the new arrival questions the prime clone. Obi-Wan learns that Jango's "son" Boba Fett is actually another clone, created without genetic acceleration to age at a natural rate. Jango knows that the attention of the Jedi spells trouble, and he abandons Kamino as soon as possible.

A narrow escape
After discovering the existence of a secret clone army on Kamino, Obi-Wan Kenobi confronts Jango Fett as he tries to escape in his ship *Slave 1*, and a titanic battle between the two ensues.

"The droid foundry seems to be working at full capacity. I am going to go down and investigate." **OBI-WAN KENOBI**

GEONOSIS

An arid world of red skies and forbidding mountains, Geonosis is the Outer Rim home of an insectoid species known throughout the galaxy for its skill at manufacturing deadly battle droids.

APPEARANCES II, CW **REGION** Outer Rim **SECTOR** Arkanis **SYSTEM** Geonosis **PRIMARY TERRAIN** Rocky wastes, deserts

SEPARATIST STRONGHOLD

The Geonosians arm the Trade Federation before the Battle of Naboo, manufacturing the battle droids that fight the Gungans. When Count Dooku orchestrates the rise of the Separatist movement, he enlists Geonosian leader Poggle the Lesser's help to produce an automated army to make war with the Republic. In secret, the Geonosians help develop the plans for a planet-shattering battle station. Geonosis becomes one of the most valuable planets in Dooku's Confederacy and plays host to a meeting of top Separatist leaders before Obi-Wan discovers the scope of the threat and warns the Jedi Council.

Ultimate weapon
The Geonosians begin work on a battle station that can destroy planets, later called the Death Star.

ALL-OUT WAR

The Republic responds to Obi-Wan's summons with an attack force of Jedi and clone troopers. The Battle of Geonosis is the first conflict of the Clone Wars and sees the use of heavy artillery and other advanced war machines on both sides. After a fierce fight, the Republic emerges victorious, but many Separatist forces evacuate to fight another day. Dooku abandons Geonosis following a lightsaber duel with Master Yoda, then travels to Coruscant to report to Chancellor Palpatine (Darth Sidious) that the war has begun as planned.

Heavy equipment
Republic AT-TEs and clone troopers rout the Separatist defenders in the first Battle of Geonosis (above), assisted by gunships that are picking up troopers and Jedi commanders on the battlefield (left).

Tricky flying
The rocky rings surrounding Geonosis are a navigation hazard, but can be used as obstacle courses by those who wish to shake off their pursuers.

RETAKING THE PLANET

The triumphant Republic occupies Geonosis, but with flashpoints popping up all over the galaxy, clone troopers are needed elsewhere. As soon as the Republic relaxes its grip, the Separatists amass a force that sweeps in and seizes the planet. Republic war leaders have no choice but to plan the Second Battle of Geonosis to prevent the Separatists from bringing the factories back up to full capacity. By the time the Republic armada is ready, Poggle the Lesser has completed a new, advanced droid factory that becomes the primary target for the Republic invasion. Jedi warriors, including Anakin Skywalker, Ki-Adi-Mundi, and Ahsoka Tano destroy the factory and force Poggle to take shelter in the Geonosian cave network of Karina the Great. The Republic captures Poggle and reinforces its hold over Geonosis.

Return to Geonosis
When Poggle the Lesser and his Geonosians take back their homeworld, the Republic must fight a second time.

"It just isn't fair. I'm never gonna get out of here!" LUKE SKYWALKER

LARS MOISTURE FARM

A humble homestead in a desolate corner of Tatooine, the Lars moisture farm becomes a home for Shmi Skywalker and her grandson, Luke, before being destroyed by the Empire.

APPEARANCES II, III, IV **LOCATION** Near Jundland Wastes, Tatooine

Conference
Cliegg Lars informs Anakin Skywalker that his mother is a captive of the Tusken Raiders *(right)*. Later Anakin bids farewell to his slain mother at her graveside *(below)*.

Secret message
After his uncle purchases the droids R2-D2 and C-3PO from Jawas, Luke brings the pair to the garage, or tech dome, attached to the moisture farm. Here, he cleans the droids with equipment kept in his workshop, removing carbon scoring from R2's chassis and treating C-3PO to an oil bath. During his examination of R2-D2, Luke discovers a mysterious recording. R2-D2 claims the holographic vision of Princess Leia Organa is a private message for Obi-Wan Kenobi, and after Luke removes his restraining bolt, the little droid runs away in the dead of night. Luke and C-3PO follow him, hoping to recover the fugitive before Luke's uncle Owen realizes what has happened. They thus avoid the stormtrooper attack that destroys the homestead.

CLIEGG AND SHMI
Located near the Jundland Wastes, the Lars moisture farm belongs to Cliegg Lars in the years before the Clone Wars. With his son, Owen, Cliegg uses the vaporators installed on the property to draw water from the atmosphere and grow small food crops. Cliegg soon buys the slave Shmi Skywalker from Watto and marries her. Just prior to the Battle of Geonosis, Tusken Raiders kidnap Shmi while she is inspecting the vaporators on the homestead's perimeter. A search party finds no trace of her, and Cliegg loses his leg to a Tusken trap. Anakin finally locates his mother, but not in time to save her life.

Dreaming of something more
Luke Skywalker becomes a talented bush pilot in his T-16 skyhopper, fueling his hopes that his uncle will let him leave the moisture farm behind and begin a new life away from Tatooine as an Academy cadet.

CHANGE OF HANDS

After a funeral is held for Shmi, Anakin leaves Tatooine behind. Cliegg mourns the loss of his wife and soon follows her into death. This leaves the Lars moisture farm the property of Owen Lars, who maintains the estate with the help of his new wife, Beru. The couple gets a surprise when Anakin's former Jedi Master, Obi-Wan Kenobi, visits them, carrying Anakin's infant son, Luke. Owen doesn't want to get mixed up in any further complications involving the Jedi, but he and Beru reluctantly agree to take Luke in and become his guardians, acting as his aunt and uncle as he grows into adulthood. Obi-Wan remains on Tatooine to watch over the boy, despite Owen's disapproval.

Looking to the future
Beru and Owen agree to raise Luke as his aunt and uncle.

Providing sustenance
Beru Lars prepares a meal in the homestead's kitchen.

RAISING LUKE

Luke becomes a great pilot, racing his T-16 skyhopper through Beggar's Canyon and dreaming of joining the Academy. Owen tries to protect Luke by keeping him on the moisture farm year after year. Owen's purchase of the droids C-3PO and R2-D2 from Jawas leads Imperial stormtroopers to the homestead in search of the plans hidden in R2-D2's memory banks. A stormtrooper squad executes Owen and Beru and burns down their homestead.

GEONOSIS DROID FACTORY

APPEARANCES II **LOCATION** Geonosis

The planet Geonosis is of great value to the Separatists, primarily for the massive factories built into its crust that produce seemingly endless ranks of military-grade battle droids. The largest droid factory is capable of churning out B1 battle droids and their bulkier cousins, B2 super battle droids, all with minimal supervision by organic operators. The factory is almost entirely automated and rarely shuts down for any reason. This reduces the factory's safety margin to almost nothing and allows the Geonosians to make as many droids as possible. It also makes the environment a death trap for any unlucky beings who wander into its machinery. The factory is a whirl of activity and a clamor of noise at all hours, with assembly lines snaking from level to level and the constant motion of machinery stamping rigid patterns into metal sheets. Waste materials are continuously fed into the factory and

No place for visitors
The droid factory is a hazardous environment of extreme temperatures, corrosive chemicals, and industrial equipment.

melted down, only to be poured into new molds so the process can start again. Large cargo droids, propelled by anti-gravity repulsorlifts, ferry supplies from one assembly station to the next. The factory is located underground and is detectable at the surface only by telltale plumes of smoke wafting out of vents.

When Obi-Wan Kenobi arrives on Geonosis to investigate Separatist activity, the sight of the droid factory confirms his suspicions that Count Dooku is arming for war against the Republic. He informs the Jedi Council of his findings but is captured by Dooku's Geonosian allies. Anakin Skywalker and Padmé Amidala follow Obi-Wan to Geonosis and endure a terrifying trip through the factory. Anakin's lightsaber is destroyed by one of the stamping machines, while C-3PO suffers the indignity of having his head removed and placed on a battle droid frame.

> "Machines building machines! How perverse!"
>
> **C-3PO**

Automated assembly line
The factory largely runs itself and requires little supervision from the Geonosians.

> "Let the executions begin!"
>
> **POGGLE THE LESSER**

GEONOSIS EXECUTION ARENA

Also known as the Petranaki arena, this place is a source of entertainment for Poggle the Lesser and his Geonosians, who cheer as helpless victims are devoured by monsters like the acklay, nexu, and reek.

APPEARANCES II **LOCATION** Desert plains near droid foundry, Geonosis

Awaiting the end
Chained to tall, massive columns, Padmé, Anakin, and Obi-Wan look like easy prey for the execution monsters.

CRUEL SPECTACLE

An open-air amphitheater close to Poggle the Lesser's seat of power, the execution arena is the site of the scheduled execution of Obi-Wan, Anakin, and Padmé following their capture by Geonosian forces. While Count Dooku watches in satisfaction, the three captives are chained to posts and left to the mercies of a clawed acklay, a horned reek, and a sharp-toothed nexu. Though they manage to free themselves, it seems only a matter of time before they perish.

Arena beasts
Anakin uses the Force to tame a reek, which carries him on its back. He is pursued by Geonosian guards riding thick-skinned orrays.

JEDI RESCUE

Alarmed by the captives' plight and the news of a massive Separatist buildup, the Jedi launch a two-pronged rescue mission. First, Mace Windu gathers a squad of 200 Jedi to fly to Geonosis and slip into the execution arena. At Mace's signal, the Jedi ignite their lightsabers while Mace faces off against Count Dooku inside Poggle the Lesser's viewing platform. Any hope that the standoff might end without bloodshed vanishes when bounty hunter Jango Fett springs into action to defend Dooku. Geonosian warriors follow Fett's lead, and soon the stands erupt in chaos as the Jedi defend against their insectoid attackers. Anakin, Obi-Wan, and Padmé join the struggle as the battle spills onto the arena floor, where Mace beheads Jango Fett with his lightsaber.

Stopping the action
The sudden arrival of the Jedi brings a halt to the gruesome festivities.

REINFORCEMENTS ARRIVE

Just when the tide begins to turn against the Jedi, the second stage of their mission begins. Master Yoda, newly arrived from Kamino, leads an army of clone troopers into the arena aboard a fleet of LAAT/i gunships. The Separatists respond with more battle droids, and soon the violence cannot be contained within the confines of the arena—the desert plains become the next battlefield as the Battle of Geonosis kicks into high gear.

Air attack and ground assault
A Republic gunship takes aim at Separatist cannons *(far left)*. After gaining a new body in the droid factory, C-3PO marches into the execution arena as part of a legion of battle droids *(left)*.

> "Lando Calrissian and poor Chewbacca never returned from this awful place." C-3PO

JABBA'S PALACE

This iron-walled fortress beyond Tatooine's Dune Sea is home to one of the galaxy's vilest gangsters. But the palace isn't enough to protect Jabba the Hutt from Luke Skywalker.

APPEARANCES CW, VI LOCATION Northern Dune Sea, Tatooine

Nosy guardian
C-3PO is startled by the surveillance droid built into the palace's gate.

Built to last
The elevated position of Jabba's palace offers long-distance views of any approaching threats. In the shadow of the palace, a hungry worrt scans for passing prey animals.

IMPENETRABLE FORTRESS

Jabba the Hutt has attracted many enemies. His palace, designed to keep out unwanted visitors, is located in a remote part of Tatooine and protected by a huge gate guarded by a mechanical eyeball. These precautions don't keep out Darth Maul and Savage Opress, who invade the palace during the Clone Wars and force Jabba to join their Shadow Collective.

Walking into danger
C-3PO is right to be afraid of what awaits them in Jabba's palace. R2-D2 is as confident as ever, reassuring his friend that they have nothing to worry about.

A LIFE OF DECADENCE

Most of the time, Jabba carefully controls who has access to the interior of his palace. His majordomo Bib Fortuna screens anyone who gets past the gate. Most of the welcomed guests are bounty hunters, criminal associates, or entertainers. In his throne room, Jabba sits on a dais to watch his dancers move to the sounds of the Max Rebo Band. If anyone displeases him, Jabba hits a button that triggers a trap door, sending the victim tumbling into the rancor pit, where he is devoured by the beast.

Palace entertainment
The dancers and musicians of Jabba's court do not stop performing *(below)*, even when one of them is fed to Jabba's pet rancor. While his aide Bib Fortuna offers whispered advice, Jabba gleefully accepts C-3PO as his new interpreter droid and dresses Leia in the garb of a palace slave *(right)*.

Deep freeze
Disguised as the bounty hunter Boushh, Leia is determined to rescue Han from his carbonite prison.

TETH

APPEARANCES CW **REGION** Outer Rim **SECTOR** Baxel **SYSTEM** Teth
PRIMARY TERRAIN Cliffs, jungles

Teth is controlled by the Hutts. During the Clone Wars, Separatist agents kidnap Jabba the Hutt's son, Rotta, and retreat to a cliff-top fortress on Teth. Republic forces find them, triggering the Battle of Teth and securing Rotta's rescue. Later, Ziro the Hutt escapes from captivity on Nal Hutta and visits his father's grave on Teth to retrieve a secret holojournal. Ziro is betrayed by his companion, Sy Snootles, who shoots him and takes the journal.

RESCUE MISSION

Angry with Han Solo for dumping a valuable cargo of spice, Jabba the Hutt puts a price on the smuggler's head. When Boba Fett delivers a slab of carbonite containing Han Solo in hibernation, Jabba puts the trophy on display. Princess Leia and Luke Skywalker arrive at the palace to rescue their friend, but Jabba, one step ahead of them, captures the princess and drops Luke into his rancor pit. Luke manages to kill the beast, so Jabba decrees his prisoners will instead be executed at the Great Pit of Carkoon. Jabba and his entourage leave the palace in the luxury sail barge *Khetanna*, but Jabba meets a fatal end.

RYLOTH

APPEARANCES CW **REGION** Outer Rim **SECTOR** Gaulus
SYSTEM Ryloth **PRIMARY TERRAIN** Deserts, plains, mountains

Ryloth is inhabited by the Twi'leks, a species whose members include Jedi Aayla Secura and the criminal Bib Fortuna. During the Clone Wars, Orn Free Taa represents Ryloth in the Galactic Senate. When the Separatists invade, Mace Windu leads the effort to liberate Ryloth from Techno Union foreman Wat Tambor. Mace brokers an alliance between Orn Free Taa and his rival, insurgent Cham Syndulla, and ultimately wins a Republic victory.

Listening post
Rishi Station is filled with communications equipment designed to detect secure military transmissions.

Idyllic world
Maridun is a peaceful planet untouched by war, until the arrival of Separatist general Lok Durd.

RISHI STATION

APPEARANCES CW **LOCATION** Outer Rim **SECTOR** Abrion
SYSTEM Rishi **PRIMARY TERRAIN** Rocks, craters

This barren moon in the Rishi system is the site of a Republic outpost during the Clone Wars. It is staffed by a small team of clone troopers, who monitor transmissions to determine whether the Separatists plan to attack Kamino. When Separatist commando droids take control of Rishi Station, a squad of clones led by Captain Rex and Commander Cody recapture the base after suffering many losses.

MARIDUN

APPEARANCES CW **REGION** Outer Rim **SECTOR** Rolion
SYSTEM Maridun **PRIMARY TERRAIN** Grasslands, forests

The grassy world of Maridun is home to the peaceful settlement of Lurmen as well dangerous animals like mastiff phalones. During the Clone Wars, Anakin is among the Jedi and clone troopers who crash-land on the planet. The Jedi agree to help the Lurmen tribe defend themselves against the forces of Separatist general Lok Durd. Their coordinated effort destroys Durd's life-exterminating defoliator weapon.

> ## "I am sending you to the Mustafar system in the Outer Rim. You will be safe there." GENERAL GRIEVOUS

MUSTAFAR

A place of ashen skies and glowing lava, Mustafar is one of the harshest environments in the galaxy and the site of Anakin Skywalker's fateful duel with Obi-Wan Kenobi.

APPEARANCES CW, III, R **REGION** Outer Rim **SECTOR** Atravis **SYSTEM** Mustafar **PRIMARY TERRAIN** Volcanoes, lava flows

WORLD OF FIRE
Wishing to harvest rare minerals from the molten lava on Mustafar, the Techno Union builds mining facilities that incorporate energy shields to protect the machinery from the intense heat. During the Clone Wars, Darth Sidious orders bounty hunter Cad Bane to kidnap Force-sensitive children and take them to Mustafar, but Anakin and Ahsoka Tano foil his plans. Late in the war, General Grievous sends the members of the Separatist Council to Mustafar to stay hidden from the Republic.

Surrounded by fire
The administrative buildings on Mustafar offer spectacular views of erupting lava geysers. Mustafar's molten rock contains rare and valuable minerals, making mining in such a harsh environment worth the risks.

DUEL OF BROTHERS

With the Separatist Council now an easy target, Darth Sidious sends his new apprentice Anakin to Mustafar to execute them. After completing the evil deed, Anakin remains on the planet, where his wife Padmé Amidala finds him. Anakin accuses her of conspiring with Obi-Wan Kenobi to work against him, and when Obi-Wan emerges from Padmé's ship, Anakin believes his suspicions have been confirmed. Anakin and Obi-Wan engage in an epic duel of Force powers and lightsaber swordplay that spills from the control rooms out onto the precarious catwalks spanning the lava river. With its energy shields damaged, most of the mining facility is consumed by volcanic eruptions. Obi-Wan eventually reaches the safety of a rocky shore and warns Anakin not to attack him while he holds the high ground.

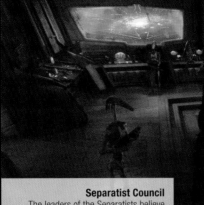

Separatist Council
The leaders of the Separatists believe they will be safe on Mustafar, not suspecting they have been led into a trap.

ANAKIN'S FATE

The former apprentice doesn't listen and leaps at Obi-Wan to kill him. Obi-Wan strikes, removing Anakin's legs and arm and leaving him defeated at the edge of a lava lake. The heat causes Anakin's clothing and skin to catch fire, and a heartbroken Obi-Wan departs the planet, believing Anakin has died *(see also p. 189)*. Darth Sidious arrives on the scene soon after, retrieving the critically injured Anakin and bringing him to a medical facility on Coruscant. There, Anakin receives treatments that save his life but transform him into the terrifying cyborg Darth Vader.

Barely alive
Emperor Palpatine arrives on Mustafar in time to save Anakin from death, rebuilding his new apprentice as a terrifying, armored cyborg.

Brothers at war
Obi-Wan Kenobi and Anakin Skywalker were brothers-in-arms, fighting side by side to bring peace to the Republic. But the Clone Wars destroy their bond, and now they battle for opposing sides—the light and the dark—on fiery Mustafar.

DUEL ON MUSTAFAR

"You have allowed this Dark Lord to twist your mind…" OBI-WAN KENOBI

Only Obi-Wan Kenobi can stop Darth Vader, Lord Sidious's new apprentice. Volcanic, hellish Mustafar hosts their final showdown.

The seething, fiery planet of Mustafar in the Outer Rim attracts dark factions, including the Separatist leaders, who have gathered in a mining facility to await instructions from their overlord, Darth Sidious. Word comes in the form of his new Sith apprentice, who mercilessly eliminates these pawns. Meanwhile, on Coruscant, Obi-Wan Kenobi confronts Padmé Amidala with the truth of the lengths his former apprentice Anakin Skywalker—now Darth Vader—will go to save the mother of his unborn children. Determined to end Vader's reign of terror, Obi-Wan sneaks aboard Padmé's ship before she races to Mustafar to face her husband. When Vader ignores her pleas to return to the light, Obi-Wan intervenes.

SPLIT IN TWO
While Mustafar is being torn apart by the opposing gravitational forces of two gas giants, Anakin's loyalties are likewise strained to the breaking point. Passionate emotions festering inside him have fueled his meteoric rise as a Jedi hero; now they finally erupt as his wife and his former Master turn against him. When Padmé's body slumps seemingly lifeless to the ground, Obi-Wan recognizes the point of no return. His lightsaber duel with Anakin is fierce and unrelenting, stretching out of the mining facility and across Mustafar's molten rivers. The master swordsmen are evenly matched until Obi-Wan outmaneuvers Vader and claims the high ground on the bank of a lava river. The dark side fueling his arrogance, Vader attacks, losing his limbs to his former Master's blade. Retrieving Anakin's lightsaber, Obi-Wan leaves the gravely wounded Vader behind.

Left for dead
After Obi-Wan Kenobi walks away from the dying shell of his former student, Darth Sidious reaches his new apprentice Darth Vader on the lava river's bank just in time to save his life.

— begin

MALASTARE

APPEARANCES CW **REGION** Mid Rim
SECTOR Dustig **SYSTEM** Malastare
PRIMARY TERRAIN Forests

Malastare is the homeworld of the Dug species, though humans and Grans have migrated there. The planet is known for both its dangerous podracing and vital fuel reserves. Ainlee Teem, a Gran from Malastare, is nominated in the election for Supreme Chancellor after the Invasion of Naboo. During the Clone Wars, Malastare's fuel deposits are fought over by the Republic and Separatists. During a massive ground battle, the Republic deploys an electro-proton bomb that immobilizes Separatist droids. The bomb awakens the last Zillo beast, which goes on a rampage. Fearing an apocalypse, the Dugs insist the Republic exterminate the monster. The Republic has other plans, capturing the virtually invulnerable creature for study on Coruscant.

Fuel wars
Across Malastare, vast fuel reserves flow into depots through an extensive network of pipelines *(left)*. When the Separatists and the Republic are drawn into fierce conflict over the fuel, the Republic detonates an electro-proton bomb to disable the Separatist droids *(below)*, but the blast also unleashes the Zillo beast, long believed to be extinct.

CATO NEIMOIDIA

APPEARANCES CW, III **REGION** Colonies
SECTOR Quellor **SYSTEM** Cato Neimoidia
PRIMARY TERRAIN Canyons

Famed for its bridge cities, Cato Neimoidia is the headquarters of the notorious Trade Federation. Several Jedi visit the planet briefly, including Anakin Skywalker, Obi-Wan Kenobi, Ahsoka Tano, and Plo Koon, who is shot down by one of his own clone pilots over the planet when Order 66 is executed.

SALEUCAMI

APPEARANCES CW, III **REGION** Outer Rim
SECTOR Suolriep **SYSTEM** Saleucami
PRIMARY TERRAIN Desert, swamps

A world of mixed terrain, from dank swamps to arid deserts, Saleucami hosts settlers wishing to avoid the Clone Wars. Clone deserter Cut Lawquane makes the planet his home, taking up farming with his adopted family. Saleucami is also the location of Stass Allie's final mission, after troops blast her speeder bike when Order 66 is given, killing the Jedi Master.

SCIPIO

APPEARANCES CW **REGION** Core Worlds
SECTOR Albarrio
SYSTEM Albarrio
PRIMARY TERRAIN Mountains

Enveloped in ice and snow, the planet Scipio's hardened mountain fortresses shield massive vaults, which secure the InterGalactic Banking Clan's wealth against all manners of threat. The clan is controlled by the Muuns, who constitute the managing Council of Five. In the Galactic Senate, the Banking Clan's interests are represented by Senator Rush Clovis from Scipio, until his plot with the Trade Federation's Lott Dod to construct battle droid factories for the Separatist Droid Army is revealed. Clovis returns to power by exposing corruption and fraud in the Council of Five, compelling the Muuns to name him the new head of the Banking Clan conglomerate. Both the Galactic Republic and the Separatists send ambassadors to Scipio to ensure their respective agendas are safeguarded from further corruption. Clovis's appointment ends quickly, however; he is killed during a Separatist attack on the planet.

Frozen assets
Senator Padmé Amidala's shuttle approaches the Clan's landing bay on a diplomatic mission to the frozen world *(above)*. The ice-bound fortress protecting the InterGalactic Banking Clan's vaults lies amidst Scipio's snow-capped mountains *(right)*.

MANDALORE

APPEARANCES CW **REGION** Outer Rim
SECTOR Mandalore
SYSTEM Mandalore
PRIMARY TERRAIN Deserts, urban

Centuries of war have made Mandalore a wasteland. Under the leadership of Duchess Satine Kryze, the New Mandalorians faction tries to leave behind the planet's violent past. Terrorist groups like the Death Watch, however, demand that Mandalore return to its warrior roots. When the Duchess declares Mandalore's neutral position in the Clone Wars between the Galactic Republic and the Separatists, the Death Watch, now aligned with Darth Maul and his Shadow Collective, stages a coup and seizes control of Mandalore. The fiercely independent planet nevertheless falls to the Galactic Empire at the end of the Clone Wars.

SUNDARI, MANDALORE

APPEARANCES CW **LOCATION** Mandalore

Sundari is the domed capital city of the planet Mandalore during the reign of Duchess Satine Kryze's New Mandalorian government. Situated in the desert, the bio-dome protects the city from the harsh environment that resulted from the Mandalorian wars. The Death Watch attacks the city during the terrorists' bid to regain control of Mandalore.

ALDERAAN

APPEARANCES CW, III, IV
REGION Core Worlds **SECTOR** Alderaan
SYSTEM Alderaan
PRIMARY TERRAIN Mountains

One of the most picturesque planets of the Core Worlds, Alderaan is home to wildflower-speckled grasslands that sweep upward into ancient mountain ranges capped with snow. Its cities, designed to enhance and preserve the planet's natural beauty, have become epicenters for culture and education, both highly valued by Alderaanians.

In the days of the Galactic Republic, Alderaan is a prominent planet in galactic affairs. When the Invasion of Naboo ends the tenure of Chancellor Valorum with a Vote of No Confidence in the Galactic Senate, one of the nominees to succeed him is Senator Bail Organa of Alderaan.

A decade later, as the Separatist crisis reaches its peak, Alderaan's Senator Bail Organa is a leading member of Chancellor Palpatine's Loyalist Committee, which strives to maintain the integrity of the Republic. When the Jedi and the Senate learn that an army of clones has secretly been created for the Republic, Bail speaks out against a rush to war. Unfortunately, the Senate votes emergency powers to Supreme Chancellor Palpatine and the Grand Army of the Republic invades Geonosis, beginning the Clone Wars.

During the war, Alderaan hosts a conference dedicated to the plight of the conflict's refugees. Senator Padmé Amidala is the keynote speaker. Jedi Padawan Ahsoka Tano has a vision of Padmé's murder and joins her on Alderaan, where she successfully prevents an assassination attempt by bounty hunter Aurra Sing.

Near the end of the Clone Wars, Bail joins Padmé and Mon Mothma as vocal senators opposed to the Chancellor's continually expanding powers. After Palpatine declares himself Galactic Emperor, Bail aids the fleeing Jedi and adopts Padmé's newborn daughter Leia to raise her as a princess of Alderaan.

The planet holds true to its peaceful beliefs, refusing armaments even as conflict troubles the galaxy. Alderaan supports the Rebel Alliance against the evil Galactic Empire in other ways, its leaders striving to maintain plausible deniability of their ties to the outlawed organization. But the Empire knows the truth. Grand Moff Tarkin, who heads the project to build the Death Star, needs to make a dramatic political statement with the initial demonstration of his newly operational weapon's power. For that reason, and inspired by the presence of Princess Leia Organa as a prisoner aboard the space station, he selects Alderaan as the first target. The Death Star's massive laser annihilates the planet. Now only an asteroid field remains of the once-proud world.

"Alderaan is peaceful.... You can't possibly—"

LEIA ORGANA TO GRAND MOFF TARKIN

Mountain palace
Skilled architects blend the cityscape design into the beautiful sweeping backdrop of the local snow-capped mountains.

"You will never find a more wretched hive of scum and villainy." **OBI-WAN KENOBI**

MOS EISLEY SPACEPORT

On the remote desert world of Tatooine, far from the bright center of the galaxy, the dingy city of Mos Eisley serves as the planet's principal spaceport.

APPEARANCES CW, IV, VI **LOCATION** Great Mesra Plateau, north of Anchorhead, Tatooine

DESERT OASIS

Southeast of the barren Jundland Wastes and not far from the palace of the ruthless crime lord Jabba the Hutt, Mos Eisley's wind-worn appearance belies its true nature as a thriving spaceport. Countless varieties of starships travel in and out of the city daily, bringing with them pilots, passengers, and cargo, both lawful and highly illegal. Goods traders and parts dealers share the dusty streets with dewbacks and wanted fugitives. Precious amid the desert, water is what binds Mos Eisley together. The main distribution plant sits in the heart of the city. From there, a patchwork of duracrete and plastoid buildings spreads outward, born of the lack of central planning in a spaceport that grew haphazardly and that does not even have a main landing facility.

City of hangars
With no main landing facility, arrivals must berth in one of the 362 hangars around the spaceport *(above)*. Between flights, travelers head for a local cantina *(right)*.

Quiet streets
The usually bustling streets become nearly deserted once Imperial stormtroopers take up posts around the city. No one wants to be scrutinized too closely by the Empire.

Den of iniquity
Cantina clientele hustle up their next paying job *(above)* or relax along the bar for a drink and some downtime *(left)*.

Evading capture
Obi-Wan's Jedi mind trick helps Luke and the droids evade a checkpoint *(above)*. Hunting for the stolen Death Star plans, Imperial stormtroopers patrol the streets *(right)*.

IMPERIAL OCCUPATION

Ordinarily such a pit of crime would attract little attention from the forces of the Galactic Empire, but all that changes when two droids carrying crucial stolen Imperial intelligence—the plans to the Death Star battle station—vanish in the nearby desert. A detachment of Imperial stormtroopers arrives to lock down the city. Obi-Wan Kenobi brings Luke Skywalker, C-3PO, and R2-D2 to the spaceport to seek passage to Alderaan. The Jedi Master's quick-thinking use of the Force allows them to slip past stormtroopers who are patrolling the streets. Then it is a matter of finding a pilot willing to risk Imperial entanglement.

Hunk of junk
At Docking Bay 94, Luke is not impressed with the *Millennium Falcon*.

SMUGGLER'S PARADISE

Amid the hustle and bustle of the spaceport, smuggling activities carry on with nary a second glance. Trafficking in spice and illegal weapons brings great rewards to those willing to take the risks involved, though corrupt customs officials are generally willing to overlook such transgressions for a fee. After a haul, Han Solo and Chewbacca secure the *Millennium Falcon* in Docking Bay 94 at the spaceport, little suspecting that their departure will be far more eventful—a narrow escape from the blaster fire of Imperial stormtroopers pursuing the freighter's passengers.

MOS EISLEY CANTINA

APPEARANCES CW, IV **LOCATION** Mos Eisley, Tatooine

The Mos Eisley Cantina is favored by star pilots laying over on Tatooine before their next journey into space. On any given day, aliens of numerous species relax within its dimly illuminated confines, whispering secrets over strong drinks. Patrons range from legitimate cargo haulers to all manner of criminals, gangsters, and bounty hunters, and among such a throng, sudden outbursts of violence are no surprise. During the Clone Wars, a vicious blaster fight breaks out when Chairman Papanoida, leader of the Pantorans, arrives to liberate his kidnapped daughter Chi Eekway, who had been taken by the bounty hunter Greedo on behalf of the Separatists. All of her captors die in the rescue, except for Greedo, who manages to escape. Later in the war, Sith-acolyte-turned-bounty-hunter Asajj Ventress is biding her time over a drink in the cantina when she notices a tremendous bounty posted for the fearsome brothers Savage Opress and Darth Maul. She locates their ship, inadvertently aiding the rescue and escape of Jedi Knight Obi-Wan. Two decades pass before desert hermit Obi-Wan needs swift passage to Alderaan to bring Luke and the stolen Death Star plans to the Rebel Alliance. In the cantina, he discovers an old friend of Master Yoda, the Wookiee Chewbacca, now first mate on the *Millennium Falcon*. In a grimy booth, captain Han Solo agrees to transport the passengers for a sizable fee. Moments later, Greedo accosts Han at gunpoint and Han shoots him dead under the table.

Hot spot
The Mos Eisley Cantina is the gathering place for patrons from all walks of life *(left)*, entertaining them with the rollicking tunes of the Modal Nodes *(below)*.

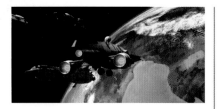

RAXUS

APPEARANCES CW **REGION** Outer Rim
SECTOR Tion Hegemony **SYSTEM** Raxus
PRIMARY TERRAIN Plains, hills, ocean

Raxus hosts the Separatist Parliament during the Clone Wars. Hoping for a peaceful resolution of the grievances stated by the Confederacy of Independent Systems, Padmé Amidala secretly travels to Raxus to meet with her longtime friend, former Republic senator Mina Bonteri. Padmé's bodyguard Ahsoka Tano is initially skeptical but soon recognizes the integrity of Mina and her son, Lux. Padmé and Bonteri strike an accord, but Count Dooku sabotages their pact.

MORTIS

APPEARANCES CW **REGION** Wild space
SECTOR Unknown **SYSTEM** Chrelythiumn
PRIMARY TERRAIN Caverns, forests, mountains

An ancient monolith of unknown origin, from the outside Mortis appears to be a black octahedron with red lines etched upon its surface. Once inside, visitors discover a seemingly terrestrial realm, ranging from verdant forests and stone fortresses to deep caverns and floating mountains. Disconcertingly, the terrain sometimes mutates as travelers cross it. On Mortis, the flow of the Force is especially strong; some believe Mortis may be the very origin of the Force itself.

Foreboding landscape
Dathomir's central star casts an eerie red glow across its fog-shrouded terrain covered in twisted vegetation.

DATHOMIR

APPEARANCES CW **REGION** Mid Rim
SECTOR Quelii **SYSTEM** Dathomir
PRIMARY TERRAIN Forests, swamps

Dathomir is a planet that few people visit willingly. Illuminated by the eerie scarlet light of its red sun, its continents are thick with swamps and forests. Its dominant inhabitants, the witches known as the Nightsisters, live in massive stone fortresses. The Nightsisters wield ancient magic fueled by the planet's power, and they are capable of supernatural feats rivaling the Force talents of the Jedi and Sith. Also dwelling on Dathomir, separate from the all-female witch clan, are Zabrak males known as Nightbrothers. When necessary, Nightsisters venture to the Nightbrother village to select the most suitable mates from among them.

At the time of the Clone Wars, Mother Talzin is the spiritual leader of the Nightsisters. She sells the services of her clan to the galaxy's wealthy, but is willing to betray clients in order to protect her people. Darth Sidious views Talzin as a growing threat to his plans for galactic domination, but she is not the only Nightsister who troubles the Sith Lord: his apprentice Count Dooku trains another, Asajj Ventress, and Sidious demands her death when her dark-side powers grow dangerously powerful.

On guard
Isolated from other tribes on the planet, wary Nightbrothers are cautious of visitors who approach their village.

Mother nature
The spiritual leader of the Nightsisters, Mother Talzin protects her clan by any means possible, even summoning the dead to rise.

After Dooku attempts to murder Ventress, she returns to Dathomir and enlists the aid of the clan to seek revenge upon the Sith. Mother Talzin uses her magic to turn Ventress's selected apprentice, Savage Opress, into a vicious, Force-powered warrior. Ventress and Opress are unable to defeat Dooku, who sends General Grievous and his droid army to annihilate the Nightsister clan. Despite their best efforts, including animating an undead horde of Nightsister zombies to fight the battle droids, all but Talzin and Ventress are massacred. Talzin and Sidious then wage a proxy war via Opress and Darth Maul, whose mental and physical prowess were restored by Talzin's magic, before Sidious finally triumphs.

LOLA SAYU

APPEARANCES CW **REGION** Outer Rim
SECTOR Belderone **SYSTEM** Lola Sayu
PRIMARY TERRAIN Volcanic

The purple hue of Lola Sayu might be considered beautiful, were it not for the fact that much of the planet's southern hemisphere consists of nothing more than a gaping hole where the spherical orb is shattered. Much of the planet's remaining crust is crisscrossed with countless cracks, like a broken eggshell. This inhospitable world, controlled by the Separatists during the Clone Wars, hosts the Citadel, an impenetrable prison.

THE CITADEL

APPEARANCES CW **LOCATION** Lola Sayu

Built centuries before the Clone Wars by the Galactic Republic, the Citadel prison is designed to hold the most difficult-to-restrain inmates—even rogue Jedi Knights. In Separatist hands, under the command of sadistic warden Osi Sobeck, it houses the Confederacy's highest-value detainees, including Captain Tarkin and Jedi Master Even Piell. In addition to the prison's imposing sheer walls and labyrinthine design, the Citadel is guarded by commando droids, electro-mines, and vicious anoobas.

WASSKAH

APPEARANCES CW **REGION** Mid Rim
SECTOR Mytaranor **SYSTEM** Kashyyyk
PRIMARY TERRAIN Forests

This verdant moon is controlled by a gang of Trandoshan hunters who kidnap individuals and release them into the dense foliage of the forests, after which hunting parties track and slay the desperate captives as trophies. Ahsoka Tano is briefly trapped on Wasskah, where she teams up with several kidnapped Jedi younglings, the mighty Chewbacca, and his Wookiee allies, to defeat the Trandoshans.

MON CALA

APPEARANCES CW **REGION** Outer Rim
SECTOR Calamari **SYSTEM** Calamari
PRIMARY TERRAIN Oceans

The oceanic world of Mon Cala is home to two sentient aquatic species: the Mon Calamari and the Quarren. Although the two share a long history of differences, mutual respect keeps their planet united under the reign of a single king and a single representative in the Galactic Senate. In the Clone Wars, Senator Tikkes, a Quarren, defects to the Separatists and is replaced by Tundra Dowmeia, a loyalist Quarren, and later Meena Tills, a Mon Calamari. During Prince Lee-Char's accession to the throne, civil war breaks out, but the young leader is able to heal the schism.

UMBARA

APPEARANCES CW **REGION** Expansion Region **SECTOR** Ghost Nebula **SYSTEM** Umbara **PRIMARY TERRAIN** Hills

The dangerous planet Umbara earns the moniker "the Shadow World" because so little sunlight reaches its surface. The near-human species that inhabit the planet are known for their advanced technology. During the Clone Wars, Umbara secedes from the Republic after the assassination of its senator, Mee Deechi, resulting in an invasion by the Grand Army to retake the planet.

THE BOX

APPEARANCES CW **LOCATION** Serenno

Criminal mastermind Moralo Eval designs the Box as the ultimate, deadly test of intelligence and skill. Housed at Count Dooku's palace on the planet Serenno, the gigantic cubical structure contains a constantly shifting series of obstacle courses and traps spanning five levels. Dooku invites 12 of the galaxy's finest bounty hunters to be tested, five of whom move on to undertake a mission to kidnap Supreme Chancellor Palpatine on Naboo.

ONDERON

APPEARANCES CW **REGION** Inner Rim
SECTOR Japrael **SYSTEM** Japrael
PRIMARY TERRAIN Jungles

To guard against the creatures that fill Onderon's jungles, the planet's primitive human inhabitants build fortified settlements that eventually expand into enormous walled cities like Iziz, the capital. At the start of the Clone Wars, King Ramsis Dendup is deposed by Sanjay Rash, who allies with Count Dooku. A citizen rebellion against Rash's rule receives covert aid from the Jedi and succeeds in overthrowing him. Insurgent leader Lux Bonteri pledges Onderon will rejoin the Republic.

ILUM

APPEARANCES CW **REGION** Unknown Regions **SECTOR** 7G **SYSTEM** Ilum **PRIMARY TERRAIN** Arctic

Entirely frozen over, the inhospitable world of Ilum is the principal source of the crystals found in many Jedi lightsabers. An ancient Jedi Temple marks the exit from the dim caverns where the crystals are found. Jedi younglings are brought to Ilum for a ritual in which they discover their own individualized crystals.

ABAFAR

APPEARANCES CW **REGION** Outer Rim
SECTOR Sprizen **SYSTEM** Unknown
PRIMARY TERRAIN Desert

Abafar's most memorable feature is the seemingly endless wasteland known as the Void. Uncannily flat and barren, its unnaturally uniform orange hue, due to particulates in the atmosphere, can drive even the most strong-willed individuals mad. The Galactic Republic's database file on Abafar notes large indentations crisscrossing the planet's surface. Settlements such as Pons Ora have grown up around mining operations that extract rhydonium, a rare, volatile fuel.

BARDOTTA

APPEARANCES CW **REGION** Unknown
SECTOR Unknown **SYSTEM** Unknown
PRIMARY TERRAIN Mountains

Bardotta is home to a spiritual order of peaceful mystics called Dagoyan Masters. Due to previous bad experiences with Jedi seeking to take younglings for training on Coruscant, the Bardottans distrust the Jedi Order. When Dagoyan Masters begin disappearing, Queen Julia fears an ancient prophecy is being fulfilled and seeks help from her friend Jar Jar Binks. He arrives with Mace Windu to vouch for the Jedi Master's honor, just before Julia vanishes. Jar Jar and Windu rescue Queen Julia and thwart the Frangawl cult's grim plan to drain the Force essence from the Dagoyan Masters.

DEATH ON MORTIS

"But... beware your heart." THE FATHER TO ANAKIN SKYWALKER

In the mysterious realm of Mortis, the Force-wielders' struggle for dominance affects the precarious balance of the Force.

During the Clone Wars, Anakin Skywalker, Obi-Wan Kenobi, and Ahsoka Tano respond to an ancient Jedi distress code and discover an immense monolith. They travel through its mysterious realm, where the seasons are ever-shifting. This constant cycle of renewal and destruction reflects the conflicting auras of two Force-wielders, Daughter and Son, who dwell on Mortis with their Father. In their supernatural forms of a griffin and a gargoyle, Daughter and Son abduct Obi-Wan and Ahsoka and bring them to the monastery. Father tells Anakin that he may only save one of the two Jedi, presenting Anakin with a near-impossible choice.

THE CHOSEN ONE
Rejecting the ultimatum, Anakin overpowers the Force to tame both winged creatures. Obi-Wan and Ahsoka are freed, and Daughter and Son return to their humanoid forms. Father declares that only the Chosen One could control both his children, the embodiments of selflessness and selfishness. When Anakin insists on leaving Mortis, Son and Daughter elevate their conflict. Both Ahsoka and Daughter are mortally wounded by Son, and Daughter's remaining essence is passed to Ahsoka, saving her life. When it appears not even the trio of Jedi can stop Son, Father impales himself with a mystical dagger. The act leaves Son vulnerable, and Anakin uses the distraction to slay Son with his lightsaber. Father's dying words reaffirm his belief that Anakin is the Chosen One, but warn Anakin about forming strong personal attachments.

Family tragedy
After seeing Son react when Daughter is mortally wounded, Father understands the

Taming the Force
On one side of the monastery arena, Obi-Wan
dangles in the clutches of the griffin form of
Daughter; on the opposite side, Ahsoka is the
captive of Son's gargoyle form. Father oversees
the conflict as Anakin is faced with the choice of
saving one of his friends, but not both.

"Mudhole?! Slimy?! My home this is!" YODA

DAGOBAH

Covered in swamps and dense jungles, Dagobah teems with life and the Force. Here, Luke Skywalker is trained in the ways of the Jedi by Master Yoda.

APPEARANCES CW, V, VI **REGION** Outer Rim **SECTOR** Sluis **SYSTEM** Dagobah
PRIMARY TERRAIN Swamps

Dangerous passage
Dagobah is unassuming from space, but the trip down to the planet's surface is treacherous, as vehicles must negotiate violent lightning storms and poor visibility.

Murky exile
Luke crashes his X-wing in a swamp during his dangerous descent to the planet's surface.

LIVING FORCE

Late in the Clone Wars, while meditating, Yoda hears the voice of the dead Jedi Master Qui-Gon Jinn, who claims he is part of the living Force. The other Jedi worry about Yoda's mental state, but Qui-Gon implores Yoda to travel to Dagobah alone. With the help of Anakin Skywalker, Yoda escapes the Jedi Temple in his Jedi starfighter. Upon reaching Dagobah, Yoda meditates and again hears Qui-Gon, who explains that Dagobah is one of the purest places in the galaxy with strong manifestations of the living Force.

Led by a cloud of fireflies to a dark cave, Yoda has a vision of Jedi being struck down by a shrouded Sith Lord. Yoda collapses in despair outside the cave. Qui-Gon consoles him with words of hope and offers to guide Yoda to an understanding of how the Jedi will ultimately prevail.

Force teachings
Qui-Gon passes along to Yoda and Obi-Wan Kenobi the secret of how a Jedi can retain consciousness within the Force after death (above). They then share their Jedi knowledge with the new hope, Luke Skywalker (left).

Awaiting his student
After the Clone Wars, Yoda returns to Dagobah to live in a small hut in the swamp while he waits to train Luke.

EXILE PLANET

After his trials by the mysterious Force Priestesses, Yoda understands that a victory over the Sith will not come during the Clone Wars. When Supreme Chancellor Palpatine is revealed as a Sith Lord, Yoda fights but does not defeat him. Yoda retreats with Bail Organa to Polis Massa, where they rendezvous with Obi-Wan and Padmé Amidala. Padmé gives birth to twins—the children of former Jedi Anakin Skywalker, now Sith apprentice Darth Vader—and then dies. Yoda and Obi-Wan decide to separate the children, keeping them hidden from the Sith until the time is right to reveal them. Before he departs for his exile on Dagobah, Yoda introduces Obi-Wan to the teachings of Qui-Gon. Yoda continues to study the Force while the children grow into adulthood.

TRAINING GROUNDS

Dagobah itself proves to be part of Luke's Jedi trials. Storms and dense fog create rough landing conditions, and his X-wing crashes into a swamp. A seemingly primitive life-form tests his patience at camp, but Luke is eager to meet Yoda, so he tolerates the interloper. Upon arriving at the creature's hut, Luke's irritation is unmistakable. The creature voices his concerns about training Luke to Obi-Wan's ghostly voice, thereby revealing that he is in fact the Jedi Master. Yoda reluctantly agrees to train Luke in the ways of the Force, despite sensing in him traits similar to his father. The swamps serve as the training grounds for Yoda's new apprentice. Deep in the jungle, Yoda tests Luke's readiness by sending him into the Cave of Evil that he had entered years before during the Clone Wars. As Luke's powers grow, he has a vision of his friends in danger. He resolves to leave Dagobah without completing his training, but promises to return.

Balance in the Force
To help Luke to further his Force abilities, Master Yoda guides him on stamina and balance.

TRAINING ON DAGOBAH

"Judge me by my size do you? Mm?" YODA

Compelled by Ben Kenobi's spirit to find a Jedi Master on Dagobah, Luke Skywalker begins his arduous Jedi training with Yoda.

After crash-landing their X-wing starfighter on Dagobah, Luke and R2-D2 become aware that the planet—which Luke describes as a "slimy mud hole"—is filled with many dangers. One wrong move could prove fatal. Luke is eager to find Yoda, the Jedi Master who taught Obi-Wan Kenobi the ways of the Force, and is at first relieved to meet the small, green-skinned alien who claims he will lead Luke to Yoda. But after the alien brings him to a hovel, Luke suspects the alien is more interested in preparing a meal than helping him, and loses his patience. Only then does the alien identify himself as Yoda, and Luke realizes that by failing to remain calm, he has failed his first test as a Jedi.

JUNGLE GYMNASIUM
From his years on Dagobah, Yoda is familiar with every gnarled root, muck-covered tree, slimy stone, and fetid pool in the area around his home, and he takes full advantage of his knowledge of the swampy terrain to train his new apprentice. He directs Luke to race through a series of natural obstacle courses, to seize long vines with which to climb towering trees, to swing from one tree to another, and to run farther and faster than he ever has before. Although Luke has already developed some ability with the Force to move objects without touching them, Yoda teaches him how to lift multiple heavy objects at the same time. When Luke leaves Dagobah, he is stronger than ever, but still has much to learn.

Up-close instruction
Riding in a pack strapped to Luke's back, Yoda guides his student through a vigorous exercise regime across the swamps while simultaneously imparting knowledge about the Force.

Gaining strength
While R2-D2 watches with interest, Yoda teaches
Luke to develop his physical strength and
coordination as well as his Force powers. Luke
not only levitates nearby objects without touching
them, but glimpses visions of the future.

CAVE OF EVIL, DAGOBAH
APPEARANCES CW, V **LOCATION** Dagobah

The cave is a hollow beneath a tree. Infused with dark-side Force energy, the cavern manifests visions of possible dark futures. Guided by the deceased Qui-Gon Jinn, Yoda enters the cave near the end of the Clone Wars and has a vision of the destruction of the Jedi Order that overwhelms him. Years later, Yoda tests Luke Skywalker by taking him to the cave. Luke has a vision in which he faces Darth Vader and strikes him down. The Sith Lord's helmeted head hits the floor, and the damaged face shield reveals Luke behind the mask.

Man in the mask
Luke sees his own face in the damaged helmet of Darth Vader after confronting the Sith Lord's apparition in the cave.

STYGEON PRIME
APPEARANCES Other, R **REGION** Unknown **SECTOR** Unknown **SYSTEM** Stygeon **PRIMARY TERRAIN** Mountains

Stygeon Prime is an inhospitable world with towering snow-capped mountain peaks. This fearsome terrain makes the planet the perfect location for a maximum-security facility to house the most dangerous, high-value prisoners. During his years as both Supreme Chancellor and Emperor, Darth Sidious exerts dominion over Stygeon Prime's prison, the Spire. After Darth Maul returns from exile during the Clone Wars to lead his criminal organization, the Shadow Collective, Sidious confronts his former apprentice on Mandalore and defeats him in single combat. Maul is then incarcerated at the Spire.

THE SPIRE
APPEARANCES Other, R
LOCATION Stygeon Prime

The Spire is one of the galaxy's most imposing prisons. During the Clone Wars, Mandalorian commandos are able to break Darth Maul out of his confinement there, but only because Darth Sidious permits the escape in order to set a trap for Maul's patron, Mother Talzin. Years later, the Spire is under Imperial control when former Jedi apprentice Kanan Jarrus is lured there with the promise of rescuing Jedi Master Luminara Unduli from captivity. The Inquisitor is waiting for him, however, and they fight a vicious duel.

Planned escape route

Prison break
Kanan leads his team of Zeb, Sabine, and Ezra (left) in a mission to infiltrate the Spire (above).

ORD MANTELL
APPEARANCES V **REGION** Mid Rim **SECTOR** Bright Jewel **SYSTEM** Bright Jewel **PRIMARY TERRAIN** Mountain chains

Ord Mantell orbits the blue star Bright Jewel. The planet's thick clouds glow with a pinkish cast when viewed from space. Every land mass on the planet is dotted with mountain chains. Ord Mantell houses a base of operations for the Black Sun crime syndicate, which joins the Shadow Collective led by Darth Maul during the Clone Wars. The Separatists attack the planet as part of Darth Sidious's plot to drive a wedge between Maul and his Shadow Collective allies.

Many moons
One sun and nine moons give Utapau a distinctive skyline *(below)*. Tidal effects on the planet's subterranean oceans vary wildly depending on the positions of the moons in relation to one another *(right)*.

UTAPAU

APPEARANCES CW, III **REGION** Outer Rim
SECTOR Tarabba **SYSTEM** Utapau
PRIMARY TERRAIN Sinkholes

Located in the remote Tarabba sector of the Outer Rim, the arid, windswept planet Utapau is pitted with enormous sinkholes and surrounded by numerous moons. Its surface is mainly desert terrain, but the bottoms of the sinkholes contain pools of water that support life on the planet. Utapau is home to the Pau'an and the Utai, collectively referred to as Utapauns, and also a more primitive lifeform, the Amani. Utapauns dwell in cities that line some of the sinkholes, while the Amani are often found in villages out on the plains. The cities, which expand into the caves and crevasses beneath the planet's surface, are supported by mining operations that excavate valuable minerals.

Although the planet tries to remain neutral during the Clone Wars, the death of a Jedi in Pau City brings Obi-Wan Kenobi and Anakin Skywalker to Utapau. They uncover a Separatist plot to purchase a rare enormous kyber crystal from Sugi arms dealers. Crystals of this size were believed to be the stuff of legend, but Obi-Wan and Anakin witness its incredible power firsthand. Before General Grievous can take the crystal from the Utapau system, Obi-Wan and Anakin destroy it rather than let it fall into Separatist hands.

In the final days of the Clone Wars, Darth Sidious orders key Separatist leaders to gather on Utapau. When Obi-Wan returns to Utapau in search of Grievous, Tion Medon, the port administrator of Pau City, tips the Jedi off to the Separatists' presence. Obi-Wan sends his astromech droid R4-G9 back to the Republic fleet in his starfighter. With the help of the varactyl Boga, Obi-Wan tracks down Grievous and challenges him to a duel. During their battle, Republic forces arrive and battle the droid army. Obi-Wan defeats Grievous, only to be attacked by the clones in his command when Order 66 is issued.

> # "Chancellor Palpatine thinks Grievous is on Utapau." **KI-ADI-MUNDI**

Sinkhole city
Obi-Wan's Jedi starfighter descends into the sinkhole of Pau City when he is searching for General Grievous, who is rumored to be on the planet.

GALAXIES OPERA HOUSE

APPEARANCES III **LOCATION** Coruscant

The Galaxies Opera House is located in the upper levels of the Uscru District on Coruscant. The venue is favored by Supreme Chancellor Palpatine, who has a private box in a premier viewing location in the main theater. During a performance of the acrobatic opera *Squid Lake* by a Mon Calamari troupe, a pivotal meeting between Anakin and the Chancellor takes place. Palpatine tells Anakin the Sith legend of Darth Plagueis the Wise, who sought to control death.

"Good relations with the Wookiees, I have." YODA

KASHYYYK

The Wookiees of Kashyyyk are fierce warriors loyal to the Republic and the Jedi. Their determination and courage has made their homeworld a battleground for galactic domination.

APPEARANCES III **REGION** Mid Rim **SECTOR** Mytaranor **SYSTEM** Kashyyyk **PRIMARY TERRAIN** Forests

REPUBLIC LOYALISTS

For many years Kashyyyk has been a prominent world represented by respected members of the Galactic Senate. Renowned for their strength and ferocity in battle, Wookiees do not hesitate to fight when the need arises. However, they are also firm believers in peace and justice. Their arboreal homeworld of Kashyyyk reveals the Wookiees' technical prowess and artistic vision. Wookiee cities are built upon the planet's mighty trees, their architecture interwoven with the beauty of the canopy. Wookiee aircraft, such as an ornithopter resembling a fearsome insect, also reflect the planet's hues, as do their weaponry and battle armor. Anyone who believes a Wookiee is merely a primitive beast will soon discover the folly of such a mistake.

Battle ready
Captain Merumeru and his Wookiee warriors prepare to defend Kashyyyk.

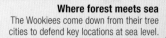

Where forest meets sea
The Wookiees come down from their tree cities to defend key locations at sea level.

Under attack
As Republic forces arrive to assist the Wookiees *(left),* fierce warriors rally to defend their homeland from the droid army *(below).*

BATTLE OF KASHYYYK

Its location on key hyperspace lanes makes Kashyyyk a strategic objective in any galactic conflict. Late in the Clone Wars, the Separatists launch a massive invasion of the planet with battle droids and heavy artillery. The Jedi Council knows an immediate defensive response by the Grand Army of the Republic is required, and Yoda volunteers to lead the counteroffensive, based on his strong relationships with Wookiee leaders. The clone troopers and war droids engage in a vicious battle on the beaches outside the vital city of Kachirho.

RISE OF THE EMPIRE

When Chancellor Palpatine, alias Darth Sidious, gives the command to execute Order 66, Kashyyyk is one of many worlds where the Republic's clone troopers turn against the Jedi. Yoda senses the nearly simultaneous deaths of hundreds of Jedi across the galaxy. When the previously reliable Commander Gree approaches, the Jedi Master senses the danger and cuts him down in self-defense. With clones still swarming the planet, Tarfful and Chewbacca escort Yoda to an escape pod. As a consequence of the Wookiees' long-standing loyalty to the Galactic Republic and the Jedi Order, the new Galactic Empire visits great brutality upon Kashyyyk. Imperial soldiers conquer the planet, and many Wookiees are enslaved. Some are taken to the spice mines of Kessel, where the harsh working conditions dramatically shorten the Wookiees' life spans.

Order 66
Yoda defends himself when the clones turn against the Jedi on Chancellor Palpatine's command.

KACHIRHO

APPEARANCES III **LOCATION** Kashyyyk

Kachirho is a coastal city on Kashyyyk that spirals around the trunk of an enormous wroshyr tree near the Wawaatt Archipelago. Two piers and docks extend out from the city into the freshwater lagoon. The center of Wookiee hyperspace mapping, Kachirho is led at the time of the Clone Wars by the chieftain Tarfful. Most other cities on the planet are protected by dense foliage, but the wide-open area around Kachirho makes it an optimal landing site when the Separatists attack Kashyyyk late in the Clone Wars. Kachirho's neighbors come by the thousands from land and sea to defend the city from the droid invasion.

Tree city
In Kachirho, Wookiee architects blend their designs into the curving majestic trunks of the wroshyr trees.

POLIS MASSA

APPEARANCES III **REGION** Outer Rim **SECTOR** Subterrel
SYSTEM Polis Massa **PRIMARY TERRAIN** Asteroid

Polis Massa is the field of asteroids that remains following the destruction of a planet of the same name. The Archaeological Research Council of Kallidah settles Polis Massa Base and begins an archaeological mining project to uncover the mysteries of the cataclysm. The Kallidahin eventually become known as Polis Massans. Far from important hyperspace lanes, Polis Massa Base serves as an emergency sanctuary for the Jedi after Order 66. There, Padmé Amidala gives birth to the twins Luke and Leia and then dies. Along with Senator Bail Organa, Yoda and Obi-Wan Kenobi determine their plans for the future of the Jedi Order.

Remote hideaway
The asteroid field proves an ideal location for the Jedi to regroup after Order 66 *(below).* Obi-Wan brings Padmé to Polis Massa Base, where she delivers twins *(right).*

Technological terror
Although the Death Star is the most fearsome
weapon in the Empire's arsenal, Darth Vader
reminds its gathered military commanders that its
might cannot compare to the power of the Force.

That's no moon
Hyperdrive systems propel the moon-sized
Death Star's lightspeed jumps to cross the galaxy.

Planet buster
The superlaser's blast is
powerful enough to shatter
a planet into chunks of rock.

IMPERIAL MIGHT

Even before the birth of the Empire, preparations
for its ultimate weapon are underway. On
Geonosis, engineers working at the behest of the
Sith Lord Darth Sidious create the first designs
for the Death Star. When Jedi Knights and clone
troopers attack the planet, beginning the Clone
Wars, Count Dooku retrieves the designs
for safekeeping in the hands of the Sith.
By the time the war ends and Sidious
has declared himself Emperor of
the galaxy, the battle station's
construction has begun in
secret under Admiral Tarkin's
supervision. Two decades
later, Grand Moff Tarkin
commands the
Death Star when
it obliterates the
peaceful world
of Alderaan.

"This station is now the ultimate power in the universe." ADMIRAL MOTTI

THE DEATH STAR

With the embers of rebellion simmering in the Empire, Grand Moff Tarkin believes fear will keep its many planets in line. Who would dare stand against the Death Star with its power to destroy entire worlds?

APPEARANCES II, III, IV **AFFILIATION** Empire

Princess rescued
Refusing to divulge the rebel base's location, imprisoned Leia Organa faces Darth Vader's interrogation droid *(above)*. She is liberated from her cell by Han and Luke, and together they escape through the trash compactor *(right)*.

DETENTION BLOCK AA-23
Among the Death Star's many facilities is a detention block where prisoners are held for interrogation, temporary detention pending transfer to planetary prisons, and execution. As the block is impossible to penetrate with a direct attack, Han Solo and Luke Skywalker don stolen stormtrooper armor and simply walk right in, posing as escorts for a newly arrived captive Wookiee— Chewbacca—destined for one of the cells. Once inside the guard station, Chewbacca helps them to overpower the guards and break Princess Leia out of her cell. Pinned down in the corridor by stormtroopers, Leia blasts open a grating and jumps down—into the space station's foul-smelling trash compactor. Chewbacca dives in next, albeit reluctantly, followed by Luke and Han. Foreshadowed by an ominous clang, the walls of the compactor begin to close. A desperate Luke contacts C-3PO via comlink and gives R2-D2 the information the astromech needs to shut down the compactor and release the door lock.

Size matters not
The Death Star's primary weapon combines multiple laser beams *(far left)* to form a single massive blast. But two small proton torpedoes fired down a thermal exhaust port merely 2 meters (6.6 feet) wide *(left)* prove catastrophic for the battle station.

FATAL FLAW
Engineers designing the Death Star expect threats will come from an enemy fleet bombarding the space station with the heavy cannons of capital ships. They never anticipate the kind of attack launched by the Rebel Alliance: a small number of single-pilot starfighters making a bombing run at a seemingly inconsequential exhaust port in the Death Star's meridian trench. Used to hitting womp rats on Tatooine with the pneumatic cannons on his T-16 skyhopper, Luke Skywalker fires the fatal shot with the added guidance of the Force. The proton torpedoes explode when they reach the main reactor and the resulting chain reaction blows the Death Star apart.

"Lothal is just as important to our Empire as any world in the galaxy."

MAKETH TUA

LOTHAL

Lothal would seem to be just another insignificant, sparsely populated backwater in the Outer Rim. However, the Imperial Star Destroyer in orbit, as well as the Sienar Fleet Systems factories and a stormtrooper garrison in the capital, all suggest otherwise.

APPEARANCES R **REGION** Outer Rim Territories **SECTOR** Lothal **SYSTEM** Lothal
PRIMARY TERRAIN Prairies, mountains, seas

Tarkintown

Impoverished refugees find shelter in run-down Tarkintown, named after Grand Moff Tarkin, the governor of the Outer Rim Territories. Tarkin evicts farmers from their homes when he appropriates their land for new industries to benefit the Empire. The shantytown is a haven for smugglers and criminals as well, many of whom take advantage of the desperate locals. However, the crew of the *Ghost* likes to donate supplies—stolen from the Empire—to the needy townspeople.

Home on the range
Prairie grass dances in Lothal's afternoon winds, hiding Loth-cats hunting Loth-rats below ancient rock formations *(right)*. Near the remote settlement of Jhothal, smoke rises from a Lothal homestead's chimney under a double moonrise *(below right)*.

QUIET LIFE ON THE OUTER RIM

Before the arrival of the Empire, Lothal is an agricultural society. Farmers cultivate rolling prairies and moisture vaporators draw water to grow jogan, melons, gourds, grains, and other crops. Towns like Kothal, Jalath, and Tangletown are small and the citizens diverse, including humans, Feeorins, Bardottans, Xexto, Balosars, Anx, Ruurians, and Ithorians. While gangsters, bounty hunters, and slavers are a problem, and gladiator matches are frowned upon in Lothal culture, most early settlers are more concerned with Loth-wolves and sabercats. There is a small Jedi presence to keep the peace, their temple hidden among ancient catacombs in the mountains. Lothal is peaceful and quiet, of little concern to major powers in the galaxy.

Serve and protect whom?
Stormtroopers are concentrated in Capital City, where they guard the Empire's headquarters, government buildings, the Imperial Academy, and Sienar Fleet Systems factories. Meanwhile, average citizens struggle to maintain their own safety and security, sometimes even at odds with corrupt stormtroopers and Imperial officials.

THE EMPIRE ARRIVES

Everything changes when the Empire, pushing farther into the Outer Rim, arrives on Lothal, which lies on their new trade route. They establish a port and base on Lothal, but also come to exploit the planet's mineral wealth. The citizens—those in smaller towns and the farmers in the countryside—receive no benefit from the Empire's presence, especially when the Empire starts appropriating land and evicting settlers to build mines and factories. Those who speak out are imprisoned, and some are never seen again. Mines strip the land bare, leaving gaping holes in the landscape. Meanwhile, the Imperial Governor Arihnda Pryce manages everything from the shadows.

Policing the city
Stormtroopers chase rebels after they steal speeder bikes and an important weapons shipment.

A SPARK OF REBELLION

The Empire is quick to move on any sign of dissent from the locals. Merchants who resist are immediately arrested. Mira and Ephraim Bridger, who run dissident broadcasts on the holonet, are among the many citizens taken away by authorities. At the Imperial Academy, students who stand out with unusual abilities—believed to be Force-sensitives—mysteriously disappear. Despite the risks, some citizens do their part to resist, and a small rebel cell begins to stand out. Led by Hera Syndulla and Kanan Jarrus, the rebels fight against the Imperial machine managed by Minister Maketh Tua and military officers Grint and Aresko. Their activities draw the attention of the ISB's Agent Kallus, the Inquisitor, Governor Tarkin, and eventually Darth Vader himself.

CAPITAL CITY

APPEARANCES R **LOCATION** Lothal

Some of Lothal's citizens are thrilled when the Empire first arrives. Land barons, government officials, the wealthy elite, and those with military ties all benefit handsomely. Trade is tightly regulated, which creates many new opportunities for smugglers, organized crime, and corruption within the local government.

The economy of Capital City booms as mining operations bring back valuable minerals, metals, and crystals to refineries in the city. Processed materials in turn supply the factories building TIE fighters, Imperial troop transports, and AT-DPs. The factories in and out of the city, however, spew toxic gases and slowly poison the rivers and seas.

Those who live in the capital—humans, Rodian, Aqualish, Gotals, Ugnaughts, Ithorians, Chagrians, Houks, and others—face constant surveillance, excessive taxation, and harassment. Propaganda campaigns dominate the media to control public opinion, while citizens are forced to attend mandatory displays of Imperial patriotism and participate in rigged local elections.

Travel and communications are monitored, and patrols of stormtroopers, AT-DPs, and ITTs ensure everything stays in order within Capital City.

Apart from risky pursuits like bounty hunting or podracing, a young person's best hope is getting accepted by Lothal's Academy for Young Imperials and graduating as a commissioned officer. Some, however, turn to illegal activities, like smuggling, piracy, or joining a rebel cell. Others get along as best they can, buying and selling in open markets, working in the Empire's factories, and trying not to be noticed.

Nonetheless, leisure pursuits continue in the shadow of the city's Imperial Command Center. The shopping district offers art from Naboo, Alderaan, and Bith, the latest fashions imported from Coruscant, as well as restaurants with chefs from all over the galaxy. For the wealthy, luxury housing is available in skyscrapers above the shops. Nearby stadiums are popular for fans of grav-ball, too.

Aesthetic influence
Citizens walk among the curved towers and stadiums of Lothal (right). Lothal's Capital City (below) has a lot of architectural similarities to other mining economies, like those found on Bespin and Garel.

EZRA'S ROOST

APPEARANCES R **LOCATION** Lothal

Ezra Bridger lives in an abandoned communications tower outside Lothal's Capital City. The tower is entered through a room at the base, where Ezra stores his speeder. An elevator shaft leads to the top, exiting onto a circular balcony where Ezra can see all the way to the city and the sea beyond. The balcony encircles several empty rooms, one of which holds the bunk where Ezra sleeps and stores his helmet collection and various pilfered gadgets. The roost also has a toilet and a cooler for food storage.

Vantage point
Ezra has a great view from his tower, but it is so isolated that he would be trapped if the Empire ever discovered him there.

KESSEL

APPEARANCES R **REGION** Outer Rim Territories **SECTOR** Kessel
SYSTEM Kessel **PRIMARY TERRAIN** Rocks, mines

The spice mines dominate one half of the paradise world of
Kessel. The opposite side, marked by lush forests and the palatial
estates of its royal family, is kept at a distance from the infamous
slave mines, where conditions are harsh. The spice is a valuable
commodity traded by the galactic criminal underworld.

GAREL

APPEARANCES R **REGION** Outer Rim Territories **SECTOR** Lothal
SYSTEM Garel **PRIMARY TERRAIN** Mountains, deserts

Garel is a rocky world dominated by large spiral cities built amid
mesas and desert plains. Situated directly on the Empire's newly
established trade route through the Outer Rim, Garel is a primary
exchange point for weapons shipments. The droids R2-D2 and
C-3PO become entangled with the crew of the *Ghost* when they
intercept one such Imperial shipment there.

BEN KENOBI'S HOME

APPEARANCES IV **LOCATION** Jundland Wastes, Tatooine

Obi-Wan "Ben" Kenobi lives in an abandoned moisture
prospector's home on a bluff surrounded by the Western Dune
Sea. The house is built on top of a sheltered cave, which Obi-Wan
uses as a little workshop and cellar to store food. Obi-Wan spends
most of his time above, in a simple dwelling with one main room.

> "The moon with the
> rebel base will be in
> range in 30 minutes." **DEATH STAR INTERCOM**

YAVIN 4

**Yavin 4 is the fourth moon of an uninhabitable red gas
giant. No native sentient life inhabits the moon, and with
no known mineral resources of significance, Yavin 4 has
avoided the attention of the Empire.**

APPEARANCES IV **REGION** Outer Rim Territories **SECTOR** Gordian Reach **SYSTEM** Yavin **PRIMARY TERRAIN** Jungles

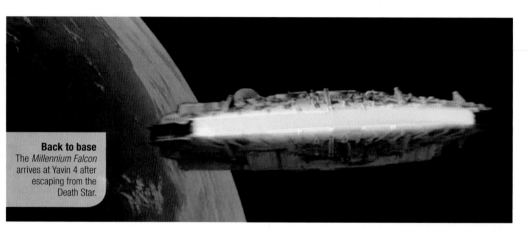

Back to base
The *Millennium Falcon*
arrives at Yavin 4 after
escaping from the
Death Star.

PRISTINE ENVIRONMENT

Yavin 4 is covered by an impenetrable rain forest of purple-barked
Massassi trees, climbing ferns, grenade fungi, and bioluminescent orchids.
Woolamanders cradle their young in the canopy above, and their mating
calls echo through the forest late at night. Stintaril rodents hunt in packs
through the trees, overwhelming the roosting golden whisper birds. Runyip
forage on the floor below, harassed by ravenous piranha beetles. Below
ground, leviathan grubs feed on Massassi roots for 300 years before
emerging as one of the largest carnivores in the forest. In the swamps,
armored eels prey on brightly colored lizard crabs, which are caught and
absorbed by bulbous anglers perched on buttress tree roots above the
muck. Unspoiled by industry, pollution, or colonies of settlers, Yavin 4
retains one of the galaxy's richest and most diverse ecosystems.

Canopy cover
A rebel soldier
stationed above the
forest canopy scans
for incoming ships.
Allies are signaled for
landing instructions
inside the base of the
temple ruins.

SECRET REBEL BASE

Seeking to avoid detection by the Empire, the rebels abandon their former base on Dantooine and move to Yavin 4. There they find ancient towering ruins left by the Massassi, an extinct slave race once ruled by the Sith. Rebel engineers convert the largest structure into a base of operations for the entire Rebel Alliance. Inside are living quarters, meeting and services rooms, and landing bays for the fleet. A hidden power station 2 kilometers (1.2 miles) away supplies the base and provides shields and ion cannons sufficient to hold off an attack from most battleships.

Arrival at the rebel base
The crew of the *Millennium Falcon* waits outside the Rebel Alliance headquarters, hidden in the dense jungles on Yavin 4.

Protecting the Alliance
At the Battle of Yavin, pilots of new X-wings fly as Red Squadron while pilots of the older Y-wings fly as Gold Squadron. Thirty rebel pilots fly past the red gas giant, but only three return.

THE BATTLE OF YAVIN

When the *Millennium Falcon* delivers Princess Leia to Yavin 4, the rebels discover her freedom comes at a high price. A tracking device has been attached to the ship and the approaching Death Star has forced their hand. The rebel fleet must launch an attack on the Imperial battle station before their base and Yavin's moon are both destroyed. With R2-D2 aboard, Luke Skywalker joins the X-wing flight team in an attempt to detonate the Death Star's reactor core via an unprotected shaft. If this mission fails, the Empire will destroy Yavin 4 with its superlaser and utterly destroy the Rebel Alliance.

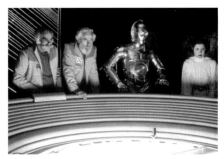

Monitoring the battle
From their strategy center, Commander Bob Hudsol, General Jan Dodonna, Princess Leia Organa, and C-3PO monitor the assault on the Death Star.

Hail the heroes
Instrumental in the success of the rebellion, the Heroes of Yavin attend the Royal Award Ceremony.

"Set your course for the Hoth system. General Veers, prepare your men." **DARTH VADER**

HOTH

Once the Empire becomes aware of the rebels' base of operations on Yavin 4, the freedom-fighters must relocate to a new secret hideaway. In their search for unlikely homes, they settle upon the cold, barren world of Hoth.

APPEARANCES V **REGION** Outer Rim Territories **SECTOR** Anoat
SYSTEM Hoth **PRIMARY TERRAIN** Plains, mountains

A FROZEN WORLD

Hoth is a frozen, inhospitable world. Rocky mountains give birth to winding glaciers, spilling into vast fields of snow and icy tundra. Surrounded by a precarious asteroid belt, the planet is barraged by meteors. Still, life exists on the planet. Several species of tauntauns feed on lichens in glacier caves and grottos formed by the planet's heated core. Wampas hunt tauntauns and drag them back to their caves to feed their young. At night, the wind howls haunting melodies through winding burrows of sapphire ice worms.

Frozen wastes
From space, Hoth appears bleak and barren. There are no signs of civilizations or significant life, making it an ideal hiding place.

Probe droids
The Empire disperses spies across the galaxy, looking for the rebels' secret base. Eventually a droid discovers curious signs of life on Hoth.

Ice monsters
Wampas are a hazard of being stationed on this frozen world. They have even been known to attack Echo Base in small groups.

PERILS AT THE DOORSTEP

Hoth is fraught with dangers. While on patrol, Han Solo and Chewbacca discover one of the Empire's Viper probe droids. It self-destructs when struck by blaster-fire, but only after alerting the Imperials. Meanwhile, Luke Skywalker is attacked by a ferocious wampa and pulled back to its den. The beasts are a frequent problem for the rebels, and several remain captive at Echo Base. Though Luke escapes, he nearly freezes to death in a blizzard afterward. Yet the rebels' worst struggles are faced once the Imperial military arrives.

Race to the *Falcon*
Chewbacca, Han, Leia, and C-3PO narrowly escape Echo Base.

Inevitable defeat
Imperial walkers descend upon the rebel forces *(top)*. At best, the rebels know they can only slow down the Empire's assault. Their real goal is to give the evacuation effort more time *(above)*.

THE BATTLE OF HOTH

General Veers is tasked with destroying the shield power generator at Echo Base. Forced to steer clear of the shield perimeter, Imperial dropships set down on the precarious Moorsh Moraine, well north of the heavily fortified rebel base. Having surrendered all element of surprise, but augmented with legions of snowtroopers, the Empire's AT-ATs, AT-STs, and speeders begin their march toward the rebel stronghold. As they move south to the foot of the Clabburn Range, they are met by the rebels' Rogue Squadron of modified T-47 airspeeders.

EVACUATION

Once Veers destroys the shield power generator, the rebels must evacuate. As their ion cannon disables the Star Destroyers above, transport ships launch the evacuation from below the South Ridge. Virtually unarmed, the rebel transports rely on starfighter escorts led by Wedge Antilles, "Hobbie" Klivian, and Wes Janson. The *Millennium Falcon* takes off with the last transport, *Bright Hope*. Luke and the remaining survivors scramble to take off in their X-wings, leaving Darth Vader and his snowtroopers to scrounge through the wreckage for clues to the fleet's destination.

Tired troops
Rebel soldiers wait for the oncoming battle.

"That's it. The rebels are there."

DARTH VADER

ECHO BASE

APPEARANCES V **LOCATION** Hoth

Following the Battle of Yavin, the Rebel Alliance begins searching for a new location to base its secret operations. The rebels settle on the icy planet Hoth, which is so remote that it is absent from most navigational charts. Rebel engineers carve the command center from the ice and clear out several natural caverns, excavating vast bays to hold their rebel fleet of starfighters and a contingent of GR-75 medium transports, in addition to quarters for more troops and other personnel. Establishing a military installation buried in snow and ice proves challenging: frequent ice melts, shrinkage, and cave-ins require constant maintenance. The rebels are resolute, however, and name their new home Echo Base after its remarkable acoustics.

Rebels must not only deal with harsh environmental conditions and the eventual ground war with the Empire, but also wampa attacks, itchy tauntaun lice, and even meteor showers. To keep personnel healthy, Echo Base has a well-equipped medical center with physicians and medical droids.

Though vital for defense, the shield generators, visible from a great distance due to their large size, guarantee eventual detection by the Empire. General Rieekan orders extra defenses to be constructed, including heavy blast doors, infantry

trenches surrounding the base, and anti-personnel batteries in key locations. The base's chief defense is a sizable Kuat Drive Yards v-150 ion cannon, which fires gigantic charged-plasma bursts powerful enough to penetrate the shields of an Imperial Star Destroyer and disable its shields, weapons, and engines.

All these precautions prove necessary when an Imperial probe droid discovers the rebel presence on Hoth and the Empire launches an AT-AT assault. This eventually captures Echo Base and puts the rebels on the run once again. Instrumental in the evacuation, the base's ion cannon disables the Imperial fleet above while the GR-75 transports ferry rebel personnel away from Hoth to temporary safety.

Danger comes to Echo Base
The rebel fleet prepares in the hangar bay *(above)*. R2-D2 wanders the corridors of Echo Base *(right)*.

Mounting tension
Leia Organa monitors progress from the Echo Base control room, expressing concern about the impending battle.

HOTH ASTEROID BELT

APPEARANCES V **REGION** Outer Rim Territories **SECTOR** Anoat **SYSTEM** Hoth **PRIMARY TERRAIN** Rocks, gas pockets

The planet Hoth suffers constant meteor bombardment from the surrounding asteroid belt. The chaotic region is a favorite hiding place for pirates and smugglers, as well as a legitimate

source of metal ore and minerals.

Following the battle of Hoth, the *Millennium Falcon* hides inside the belt, where the crew finds that the asteroids harbor life. Giant space slugs have formed a colony, with some specimens large enough to swallow entire starships. Mynocks infest the rocky caverns, feeding on passing starships and the wreckage of vessels that don't survive.

YODA'S HUT

APPEARANCES V, VI **LOCATION** Dagobah

When Yoda returns to the planet Dagobah after the ascension of Emperor Palpatine, he initially makes a camp in the E3-standard starship lifeboat that brings him there. Though the craft is small, it affords reasonable living space for a being of Yoda's diminutive size, providing shelter from the constant threat of Dagobah's unrelenting rains and persistent pests and predators. Within a year, however, the craft begins to degrade as it is slowly consumed by the swamp.

Yoda sets about building a new home made of mud, gnarltree wattle, and stones. He constructs his house at the base of a great gnarltree on a knoll beside a murky lagoon. The humble dwelling includes a sitting room, kitchen area, and sleeping loft, with several windows and two circular entries. The interior is surfaced in smooth, white clay adobe, providing a clean, attractive, and dry shelter.

Yoda cooks at a small stove in the middle of his home, behind which is a storage area with windowsills covered in drying seeds, berries, and herbs. In the back of the shelter is a sink with running water, a few clay bowls and pots, and Yoda's spice collection. A loft hangs above, with sleeping mats and blankets, though Yoda sleeps on the ground level during his final years. Tools and keepsakes are stored in a nook. The rest comprises a sitting area with a wooden stump for a table.

Being so close to the lagoon, with open doors and windows, means Yoda's home is visited by many creatures. Yoda frequently finds snakes, lizards, butcherbugs, and spiny bograts scampering across the floor. He doesn't mind the company and only sweeps the venomous ones back out the door.

Yoda lives in his home for more than 20 years before Luke visits him there, twice. On his first visit, Yoda agrees to train Luke as a Jedi, and during the second, Yoda tells Luke that he must confront his father, Darth Vader. Advanced in years, Yoda then passes away in the comfort of his bed. Yoda's vacant hut is reclaimed by the swamp and the many creatures he befriended over the years.

Cozy in the swamp
R2-D2 waits outside Yoda's home, which is too small and cluttered for him to move easily about inside *(above)*. After Luke mentions his desire to find Yoda on Dagobah, Obi-Wan Kenobi's voice speaks to Yoda and Luke inside the hut *(above left)*.

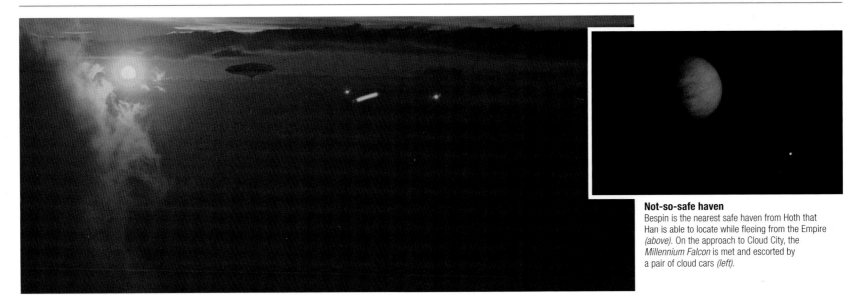

Not-so-safe haven
Bespin is the nearest safe haven from Hoth that Han is able to locate while fleeing from the Empire *(above)*. On the approach to Cloud City, the *Millennium Falcon* is met and escorted by a pair of cloud cars *(left)*.

BESPIN

APPEARANCES V, VI **REGION** Outer Rim Territories **SECTOR** Anoat **SYSTEM** Bespin **PRIMARY TERRAIN** Gas giant

The planet Bespin is a gas giant isolated from two sister worlds by an asteroid belt known as Velser's Ring. Bespin has no landmasses, but its upper, habitable atmosphere has a layer of breathable air, and this zone hosts a number of orbital cities, gas-mining facilities, and unique life forms. Bespin has an unusual abundance of life for a gas planet, and the night skies are lit with bioluminescent organisms that look like twinkling stars.

In the lower atmosphere, giant beldons float in large herds. They range in size from 0.8 to 10 kilometers (0.5 to 6.2 miles) wide, filled with numerous orange gas bladders and propelled by fleshy fins. Long tendrils fall from their bodies, gathering atmospheric plankton and chemicals, which they metabolize into tibanna gas, a valuable commodity and the foundation of Bespin's economy.

Algal "trees" form floating mats with stalks that descend to the lower atmosphere to gather nutrients. These algal forests produce most of the oxygen in the planet's life zone. They also provide a habitat and food source for an untold number of creatures.

Large thrantas, transplanted from Alderaan, dive majestically through the clouds, ridden by only the bravest thrill-seekers. Blue-and-red-tipped rawwks flit among the algal trees, chasing schools of air shrimp that shimmer in rainbow colors to warn others of a predator. Flocks of velkers attack beldons and feast on their buoyant flesh, attracting carrion-eating crab gliders, until the corpse slowly drifts toward the toxic planet core.

"We're a small outpost here and not very self-sufficient."

LANDO CALRISSIAN

CLOUD CITY

Floating 59,000 kilometers (37,000 miles) above Bespin's gaseous core, Cloud City is both a gas-mining facility and a luxury destination. Founded by Lord Ecclessis Figg of Corellia, it is presently overseen by Baron Administrator Lando Calrissian.

APPEARANCES V, VI **LOCATION** Bespin

Seeking refuge
The *Millennium Falcon* approaches Cloud City at sunset, hoping to hide from the Empire. Little do those aboard know that Darth Vader lies in wait for them.

Refining in the clouds
An automated tibanna gas refinery hovers outside Cloud City.

MINING THE SKIES

Cloud City is built around a central column that rises from a gas-processing reactor at its base, below the city. The city's otherwise hollow core contains giant directional vanes that control the facility's ever-floating location. Plants around the city's outer ring process Bespin's tibanna gas for export.

Cloud City employs countless freelance gas prospectors to navigate Bespin's breathable upper atmosphere. They are hired to pinpoint pockets of tibanna using their flying craft before larger contractors can locate gas eruptions.

Rare and valuable tibanna gas has a variety of uses. Its anti-gravitational properties are utilized across the galaxy for numerous types of airborne craft. It is also a key component in some blasters as a conducting agent and power-output amplifier. On some worlds, the gas is even employed as a heating fuel, while non-spin-sealed tibanna is used as hyperdrive coolant.

A LUXURY DESTINATION

Cloud City is an exclusive resort, attracting elite clientele and wealthy tourists who stay in stylish casino hotels and enjoy Bespin's legendary two-hour sunsets. Visitors include well-to-do politicians, celebrities, industry tycoons, gangsters, and the occasional high-ranking Imperial officer. Fortunes are made and lost in this city renowned for its nightlife, scandals, and excess.

Cloud City's five million residents and visitors dwell atop its 16-kilometer- (10-mile-) wide mining facility levels. The City floats in the planet's breathable upper atmosphere, known as the "Life Zone," which is shielded and infused by a layer of airborne algae and other photosynthetic organisms.

A city for fun
The promenade of Cloud City is lined with designer shops full of imported goods, fine restaurants, bars and cafes, cinemas, and gaming rooms.

Unsettling beauty
Princess Leia discusses her anxiety about their situation with Han Solo. Her suite is typical of the luxury resorts on Cloud City. It is coincidentally designed in white synthstone, after the architecture of her homeworld, Alderaan, and crafted in honor of Lord Figg's Alderaanian wife.

Ugnaughts are a small species of humanoids with tusks and upturned noses. Lord Ecclessis Figg builds Cloud City with the aid of three Ugnaught tribes. When the city is complete, Figg allows the Ugnaughts to remain in residence and maintain the city for a share in its mining profits.

Sith subterfuge
Darth Vader discusses arrangements regarding the capture of Han with Boba Fett and Lando.

THE IMPERIAL OCCUPATION

In anticipation of the arrival of Han Solo and the *Millennium Falcon*, Boba Fett infiltrates Cloud City and alerts Darth Vader. Vader, in turn, quietly arrives with a contingent of stormtroopers and forces Lando Calrissian to cooperate. Lando agrees to turn Han over to Vader in exchange for a guarantee that the Empire will not interfere with Cloud City in the future.

Leia Organa notices something is amiss when her droid, C-3PO, goes missing. Chewbacca discovers the droid has been dismantled and set to be destroyed by Ugnaughts (in fact, he has been shot and memory-scanned by stormtroopers) and brings C-3PO back to their room.

Lando then leads his friends to Vader under the ruse that they are going to dinner. Upon capture, Han is tortured and interrogated regarding the whereabouts of Luke Skywalker, before being taken to the carbon-freezing chamber. Darth Vader then uses the rebels to lure Luke into a confrontation.

Chamber of horrors
As Han is led to the carbon-freezing chamber, Lando has second thoughts about his deal with Darth Vader to ensure the safety of his Cloud City.

CARBON-FREEZING CHAMBER

APPEARANCES V **LOCATION** Cloud City, Bespin

Carbonite storage repulsor sleds are designed for use with the carbon-freezing chamber on Cloud City to safely store and transport high-pressure gases like tibanna. The gas is stored within a super-strong block of frozen carbonite inside the sled. Darth Vader hopes to immobilize his son, Luke, in carbonite and transport him to the Emperor.

To determine whether a human will be able to survive the carbon-freezing process, Vader decides to use Han as a test subject. After he freezes Han, Vader hands him over to bounty hunter Boba Fett, who in turn delivers him to Jabba the Hutt for a substantial reward. Although a success, the process causes chronic hibernation sickness, which afflicts Han with temporary blindness and severe disorientation when he is eventually freed. Ultimately, however, Vader fails to trap Luke.

CLOUD CITY CAPTURE

"This facility is crude, but it should be adequate to freeze Skywalker for his journey to the Emperor."

DARTH VADER

After capturing Luke Skywalker's allies on Cloud City, Darth Vader sets a trap for Luke in a carbon-freezing chamber.

Intent on collecting the bounty that Darth Vader has placed on the crew of the *Millennium Falcon*, bounty hunter Boba Fett tracks the *Falcon* and calculates that her destination is the gas planet Bespin. As the *Falcon* is traveling at sublight speed, Boba concludes that the ship's hyperdrive is damaged, and that Han Solo will attempt to repair it at Bespin's Cloud City. Boba promptly informs Vader of the *Falcon*'s course, and they arrive on Cloud City in advance of the fugitive rebels. This allows Vader to command the city's administrator, Lando Calrissian, to help him capture the *Falcon* crew, as he knows Luke Skywalker will come to the aid of his friends. And so Vader lays a trap for Luke.

BATTLEGROUND

Although Lando promotes Cloud City as a luxury resort with hotel casinos, the city remains a floating gas-mining facility, processing and carbon-freezing exotic gases for transport to other worlds. Vader schemes to lure Luke into a carbon-freezing chamber before delivering him to the Emperor. Although he knows from personal experience in the Clone Wars that humans can theoretically survive carbon freezing, Vader decides to use Han Solo as a test subject, and freezes him in a slab of carbonite. When Luke arrives to help Han, he evades Vader's trap, and the carbon-freezing chamber becomes a battleground.

Clash of lightsabers
Finding Vader in the carbon-freezing chamber, Luke realizes the Dark Lord has lured him into a deadly trap, but he bravely engages Vader in a lightsaber duel.

Freezing time
After learning that Darth Vader intends to freeze him in carbonite and turn him over to Boba Fett, Han Solo urges Chewbacca to protect Princess Leia. Han survives the freezing process, but his friends are unable to stop Boba Fett from escaping with Han aboard his ship.

THE GREAT PIT OF CARKOON

"Victims of the almighty Sarlacc: His Excellency hopes you will die honorably." C-3PO, TRANSLATING FOR JABBA THE HUTT

Furious with Luke Skywalker for slaying his prized rancor, Jabba decrees that the Jedi and his allies will be fed to the enormous Sarlacc.

R2-D2, C-3PO, Princess Leia, Chewbacca, and Luke Skywalker infiltrate Jabba the Hutt's palace on Tatooine in order to rescue Han Solo, but are captured by Jabba's minions. Jabba chooses to keep the droids as his servants and Leia as his slave, and looks forward to seeing the others die for his own amusement. Traveling in his sail barge with accompanying skiffs, he brings his captives to the Great Pit of Carkoon in the Dune Sea, at the base of which rests a gruesome creature known as the Sarlacc. Almost entirely concealed beneath the desert sands, the omnivorous, immobile beast extends only its foul mouth to the surface. The mouth is ringed with grasping tentacles that readily seize any prey that falls its way.

BATTLE OVER THE PIT
Although Jabba's calculating mind serves him well as a career criminal, he fails to anticipate that Lando Calrissian is disguised as a guard on the skiff that carries the rebel captives, and that Luke's lightsaber is concealed inside R2-D2. The astromech launches the lightsaber to Luke, who makes short work of Jabba's guards, most of whom wind up tumbling into the Sarlacc. Even the notorious bounty hunter Boba Fett cannot escape the creature, as an out-of-control rocket pack deposits him into the Sarlacc's gullet. Leia strangles Jabba with the same chain that binds her to his dais before she escapes with Luke and their allies on a skiff. Having rescued Han, the heroes quickly rejoin the rebel fleet.

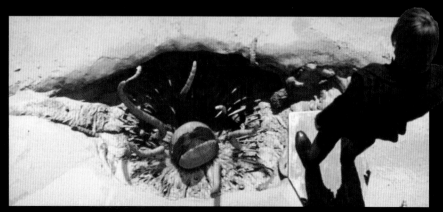

Walking the plank
Perched at the end of a plank extending from a sand skiff, Luke gazes down into the maw of the Sarlacc, who lives in a sand hole deep below Tatooine's surface.

Rendezvous with the Sarlacc
Under the blazing suns of Tatooine, Jabba the
Hutt watches from his luxury Ubrikkian sail
barge, *Khetanna*, while his henchmen position
a sand skiff carrying Han Solo and Chewbacca
above the Pit of Carkoon.

"A small rebel force has penetrated the shield and landed on Endor." DARTH VADER

ENDOR

The fate of the galaxy is determined on a peaceful forest moon, where the Rebel Alliance obtains the aid of the most unlikely allies to defeat the Empire.

APPEARANCES VI **REGION** Outer Rim Territories **SECTOR** Moddell **PRIMARY TERRAIN** Forests, savannahs, mountains

Captured by Ewoks
The Ewok Wicket senses a scout trooper approaching *(left)*. A group of Ewoks comes to investigate the rebels caught in their net *(above)*.

HOMEWORLD OF THE EWOKS

The Moon of Endor is a sanctuary of pristine temperate forests and primitive societies that thrive there. The primeval landscape remains relatively undisturbed until the arrival of the Empire. Ewoks dwell in family huts connected by terraces, ladders, and suspension bridges. Villages are overseen by wise chiefs and tribal elders. In warm summer months, Ewoks may stay in fishing villages or hunting and farming lodges on the forest floor. Well versed in forest survival, they travel long distances on shaggy spotted ponies and use friendly bordoks to haul loads of supplies. Ewoks soar through valleys on gliders with leather wings, but must be careful to avoid vicious blue-and-gold condor dragons.

SECRET IMPERIAL BASE

Bothan spies steal information about the second Death Star and deliver it to the rebel leadership. Not only do they discover the existence of a new Death Star, but also that it is protected by a shield generator located on Endor. Believing they can strike before the new battle station is fully operational, a team of rebel commandos led by General Han Solo sneaks past the Imperial blockade in the stolen shuttle *Tydirium*. Their mission is to destroy the Empire's facility on the moon's surface. The Imperial command bunker is located below a relay dish and guarded by Imperial walkers and a garrison of stormtroopers, scout troopers, and other officers under the command of Colonel Dyer, Commander Igar, and Major Hewex.

Imperial landing zone
Lambda-class shuttles *(left)* fly to a landing platform with turbolifts running up the legs of the installation *(below)*. AT-ATs are loaded at gates below.

RESIDENTS AND EXPATRIATES

Endor is rich with life, and Ewoks are not the only creatures of significance. Yuzzums are Endor's dreamy wanderers. Two of them catch a ride on visiting ships, making their way to Jabba's palace on Tatooine. One works there as a singer and the other as an exterminator. Aggressive duloks dwell in the swamps, emerging to hunt Ewoks and lantern birds. The songs of munyips and ruggers can be heard as they climb through Ewok villages. Giant gorax, though rarely seen, descend from the mountains and terrorize villages.

Yuzzums
The rifle-carrying Endor native Wam Lufba tends to the pests—some quite menacing—in Jabba's palace on Tatooine.

Bait
C-3PO and R2-D2 lure a group of troopers into an ambush, where Ewoks pummel them with stones during the Battle of Endor.

CLIMACTIC BATTLE

Though they initially meet after the rebels are captured by the Ewoks, C-3PO eventually persuades the Ewoks to join their cause, in order to save their own homes and families as well as the rest of the galaxy. The rebel success at the Battle of Endor, which decisively ends the rule of the Emperor, can largely be attributed to the bravery and ingenuity of the Ewoks. Their primitive culture is able to overthrow the technologically advanced Imperial army with spears and arrows, rock-throwing catapults, wooden battering rams, and rolling logs.

Change in the primeval forest
The evergreen forest of Endor is peaceful until the Empire arrives. Songs of churi and lantern birds are replaced by speeder bike engines and the clanking of AT-STs.

DEATH STAR II

APPEARANCES VI
REGION Outer Rim Territories
SECTOR Moddell **SYSTEM** Endor
PRIMARY TERRAIN Space battle station

Emperor Palpatine constructs the second Death Star, in part as an elaborate ruse. He hopes to destroy the Rebel Alliance by feigning a critical vulnerability in the Death Star, thus luring the rebels into a conflict they cannot win.

The Emperor devises a plan to let the rebels' Bothan spies obtain false information about the progress and status of the Death Star's construction. The rebels presume the battle station's superlaser will not be in operation at this stage, while in fact, the superlaser, powered by massive green kyber crystals (the same crystals which, in smaller form, are utilized in Jedi lightsabers), is fully functional. During the battle of Endor, Palpatine surprises the rebels by ordering the Death Star to fire on one of the large Mon Calamari cruisers.

However, once the rebel strike team manages to destroy the shield generator on Endor that protects the Death Star, a small flight team, led by General Lando Calrissian on the *Millennium Falcon*, is able to enter the Death Star and destroy the battle station's main reactor core. Meanwhile, Luke Skywalker barely escapes after his father, Darth Vader, sacrifices himself to destroy the Emperor and save his son.

The second Death Star is significantly larger than the first. Its diameter is more than 160 kilometers (99.4 miles), compared to the original battle station's 120 kilometers (74.5 miles). In fact, the Death Star is nearly 3 percent the size of the moon of Endor itself. Since the Death Star is stationary and not in a synchronous orbit, it requires tremendous force to counter Endor's gravity. It utilizes a repulsorlift field created by the shield generator on Endor to maintain its position. The force generated by the Death Star creates earthquakes, tidal imbalances, and other geological disturbances on the surface below.

The Death Star has considerable defenses. Batteries include a complement of 15,000 heavy turbolasers, 15,000 standard turbolasers, 7,500 laser cannons, and 5,000 ion cannons, all of which are installed on the station's outer surface. Thousands of TIE starfighters of various models are ready to deploy at all times, in addition to shuttles and ground assault vehicles such as AT-ATs and AT-STs.

Chain reaction
The Death Star's reactor core is its one vulnerability. When the rebel ships fly through the battle station's coolant shafts and detonate the core, a massive chain reaction occurs that destroys the Death Star.

EMPEROR'S THRONE ROOM

APPEARANCES VI **LOCATION** Death Star II

Emperor Palpatine's throne room is his command center and ceremonial seat of power aboard the second Death Star. Its gleaming industrial design, devoid of decorations and symbols of lavish comfort (unlike his personal offices and chambers, both here and on Coruscant), are meant to intimidate the dignitaries, subjects, and prisoners brought before him. His throne is a simple, contoured swiveling chair set in front of a viewport with enhanced magnification scanners. The dais before him is flanked by viewscreens linked to the station's computers and communications systems.

EWOK VILLAGE

APPEARANCES VI **LOCATION** Endor

Bright Tree Village perches 15 meters (49.2 feet) above the forest floor, where nest-like bunches of thatched huts housing nearly 200 Ewoks cling to the trunks of evergreen trees. At the village center are communal meeting areas, as well as homes for tribal elders and Chief Chirpa's family. Large huts for extended families huddle along the outer edges of the village. All are tied together by rope bridges, ladders, and platforms. In the canopy above, watchers look out for marauding gorax and condor dragons. Ewoks also launch gliders from the canopy to patrol the forests and valleys beyond. Bachelors maintain small huts below the village proper, where they keep watch for even greater dangers below.

Ewok huts are cozy inside. A cooking fire is located at the center, where meat is roasted on a spit and soups boiled in clay pots. Storerooms of food and kindling lie under the floor and woven sleeping mats and furs are stacked in lofts above. Wooden stools and baskets sit on the floor, while Ewok hoods, capes, and tools hang on the walls. Fires and torches light the village at night. The bark of the conifer trees where the Ewoks live not only provides a good insect repellent but is also highly fire resistant. The boughs also make excellent spears, bows, slingshots, glider frames, and catapult arms.

Ewoks spend much of their time in the trees, but descend to the forest floor to forage for berries, gather herbs, and hunt. A few Ewoks, such as the Warrick family, even maintain huts and lodges on the ground.

When the Rebel Alliance arrives on Endor, it is Leia Organa who first befriends the Ewok Wicket and walks with him back to Bright Tree Village. There she is welcomed with Ewok hospitality, fed, and clothed. Her rebel friends are then captured and brought to the village to be the main course in a banquet in C-3PO's honor—the Ewoks believe that the timid protocol droid is a god. Luke cleverly uses the Force to play on their superstitions and win the rebels' freedom. That night, C-3PO explains their plight to the Ewoks and persuades them to join the fight. After the battle is won, the Ewoks and the rebels return to the village to celebrate.

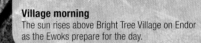

Village morning
The sun rises above Bright Tree Village on Endor as the Ewoks prepare for the day.

Village evening
Bonfires burn at night in the Ewok village, where the inhabitants are safe and secure from the dangers of battle elsewhere in the forest *(left)*. Meanwhile, Han and Leia share a private moment *(below)*.

Dinner party
The Ewoks carry the rebels back to their village, all of them bound except C-3PO, who receives royal treatment *(above)*. Later, the Ewoks prepare Han, Luke, and Chewbacca for a feast in C-3PO's honor *(left)*.

"Wonderful. We are now a part of the tribe." C-3PO

ENDOR BUNKER SECRET ENTRANCE

APPEARANCES VI **LOCATION** Endor

When Han Solo and the rebel forces debate how to infiltrate the secret entrance to the Empire's shield generator bunker, an Ewok named Paploo takes it upon himself to steal an Imperial speeder bike and create a diversion. The rebels then attempt to take the bunker and a back-and-forth ensues in which the Ewoks once again prove their worth. They are instrumental in winning the ground battle that rages outside the bunker entrance. The rebels are eventually able to trick the officers inside the bunker into opening the blast doors. Once inside, they place charges and destroy the entire complex.

Entering the bunker
Biker scouts stand guard outside the bunker entrance *(left)*. Han, Leia, and the rebel strike team invade the bunker *(above)*.

BEHIND THE SCENES

"*Star Wars* is very plot driven. Every minute and a half we're on to a new set. So you have to instantly believe in it."   Rick McCallum, producer of the Prequel Trilogy

Space fantasy and science-fiction films may live or die as based on their locations, as dubious scenery and/or obvious props can spoil the illusion. *Star Wars* has always used a combination of beautiful, real-world locations and incredible production design. From the Death Star's cavernous hangar and Tatooine's burning deserts, to the snows of Hoth, the jungles of Dagobah, and the vertigo-inducing skyline of Coruscant, fans have marveled at the amazingly lifelike worlds created for the movies.

A blueprint by Alan Roderick-Jones of production designer John Barry's Mos Eisley Cantina set, showing the bar, for *Star Wars:* Episode IV *A New Hope* (1). Anthony Daniels (C-3PO), Mark Hamill, Alec Guinness, and Kenny Baker (R2-D2) filming on location for Episode IV, with the Tunisian desert standing in for Tatooine (2).

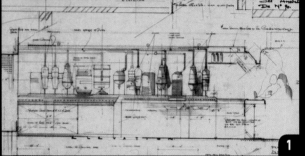

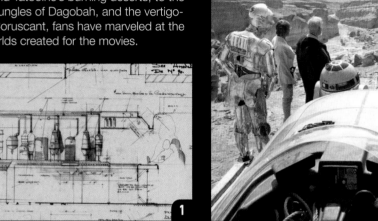

Shooting Han Solo's rescue of Luke Skywalker from the icy wastes of planet Hoth in Finse, Norway, for *Star Wars:* Episode V *The Empire Strikes Back*; a tauntaun puppet stands in the foreground (3). At Elstree Studios, UK, the crew shoots a scene on Episode V's Dagobah jungle set, production designed by Norman Reynolds (4), where Yoda trains Luke Skywalker in the ways of the Jedi.

A detail of this production painting by Ralph McQuarrie visualizes the key elements of an entire scene: Darth Vader stands on the bridge of an Imperial Star Destroyer, a crewman, other Star Destroyers, and a distant planet lend perspective in the background (5). Industrial Light & Magic matte artist Frank Ordaz works on a painting of the interior of the Death Star docking bay in *Star Wars:* Episode VI *Return of the Jedi* (6).

Production designer Gavin Bocquet and director George Lucas examine a maquette model of Mos Espa on Tatooine for *Star Wars: Episode I The Phantom Menace* **(7)**. The spectacular Palace of Caserta in southern Italy becomes the setting for Episode I's Theed Palace on Naboo **(8)**, where several scenes were shot.

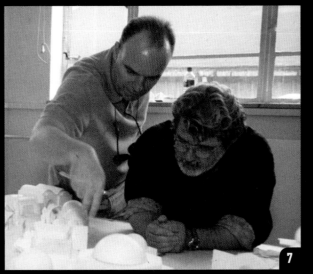

ILM model maker Grant Imahara works on the miniature set for the Coruscant street chase in *Star Wars:* Episode II *Attack of the Clones* **(9)**. ILM chief grip Tom Cloutier helps to light the Geonosis arena miniature set **(10)**.

Concept art by ILM art director Aaron McBride for Anakin and Obi-Wan's duel in the Mustafar collection plant, created during postproduction work on *Star Wars: Episode III Revenge of the Sith* **(11)**. Concept artist Warren Fu's pre-production painting of the Imperial rehabilitation center in *Revenge of the Sith*; Darth Sidious in the background **(12)**.

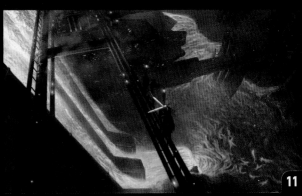

Like much of the design for the animated series *Star Wars Rebels*, artist Andre Kirk's depiction of Lothal's sprawling Capital City was inspired by concept artist Ralph McQuarrie's production paintings for the original *Star Wars* trilogy **(13)**.

TECHNOLOGY

Although some cultures eschew technology, most embrace everything from basic tools and droids to sophisticated sensors and weapons systems.

Throughout the galaxy, most beings rely on various types of technology, whether advanced or primitive, to help them in their work duties as well as their everyday lives. Many utilize sensors to collect and examine data, and use energy shields and weapons for protection. They may also depend on droids for a multitude of tasks, ranging from running simple diagnostics to performing complicated medical procedures, or sending communications to flying starships.

While interplanetary trade eventually yields myriad technological developments, wars also spur innovation, as manufacturers and armorers are conscripted or compelled to develop new defensive and offensive weapons. Historians frequently cite the Jedi lightsaber as the most remarkable energy weapon ever made, and the planet-shattering Death Star as the most fearsome. However, while many technologically advanced civilizations believe that they are superior to comparatively primitive cultures, and confident that they will easily prevail in any conflict, the Battle of Endor attests to the fact that technology alone does not guarantee victory.

TECHNOLOGY TIMELINE

Hyperdrives, lightsabers, and blasters—all were invented millennia ago. But the outbreak of galactic warfare, first in the Clone Wars, and later the rebellion against the Empire, sparks rapid technological development on a massive scale.

CRISIS IN THE REPUBLIC:
Spans Episodes I and II

THE CLONE WARS:
Spans Episode II, CW, and Episode III

THE EMPIRE ERA:
Spans Episode III, R, and Episodes IV to VI

Battle droids
The Trade Federation's invasion of Naboo heralds a terrible new era in galactic warfare—armies of battle droids will become a common sight across the galaxy for years to come.

Invasion of Kamino
A Separatist fleet attacks the cloning facility with underwater attack vessels, aqua droids, and Trident drill assault craft. Simultaneously, a droid army invades Tipoca City, birthplace of the clone army.

Podracing
When the Queen of Naboo is stranded on Tatooine, Anakin Skywalker offers to race in the Boonta Eve Classic to secure the necessary repairs for her ship. He wins not only the podrace, but his freedom.

Electro-proton bomb
An electro-proton bomb detonated on Malastare inadvertently unleashes a gargantuan Zillo beast. Because the creature's scales are nearly indestructible, Chancellor Palpatine orders the monster's corpse hidden for further military research.

Cloning
The Kaminoans' advanced cloning technology fosters warfare on a galactic scale. Legions of identical soldiers march into battle for the Republic, giving the Clone Wars their name.

Death Star designs
Count Dooku flees Geonosis on his solar sailer, taking with him the schematics for a new superweapon called the Death Star. Arriving on Coruscant, he delivers them to his Sith Master, Sidious.

Droid operatives

R2-D2 and four other Republic droids infiltrate a Separatist facility to steal a crucial encryption module, and then foil an enemy plot to load a stolen Republic destroyer with the deadly explosive rhydonium.

Bombing investigation

When a bomb explodes in a Jedi Temple hangar, Anakin Skywalker and Ahsoka Tano use three-dimensional forensic imaging holograms to determine the exact point of the explosion and the nanobots that caused it.

Kyber crystal

When General Grievous seizes an enormous Kyber crystal on Utapau, Obi-Wan Kenobi and Anakin Skywalker go to great lengths to claim the crystal for the Jedi before ultimately destroying it.

Bounty

At the planet Quarzite, Boba Fett and his team of bounty hunters protect a chest that is being shipped by subtram, a levitating, train-like subterranean conveyance propelled by thousands of kilometers of anti-grav strips.

Ion cannon

The rebels' Echo Base ion cannon plays a crucial role in the Battle of Hoth. By disabling the Empire's Star Destroyers, it gives the rebel forces a vital chance to escape.

The Box

Designed by mastermind Moralo Eval, the Box is located in Count Dooku's palace. An enormous structure filled with deadly mazes and tests of skill, the Box determines the best bounty hunters.

Vader's meditation chamber

Darth Vader's flagship, *Executor*, features a unique piece of technology. It is a specially built chamber that allows him to remove his helmet and meditate beyond the claustrophobic confines of his armor.

Battle of Umbara

Fearing that highly advanced technology, such as the Umbaran millicreep, hover tank, crawler tank, and MHC tank, would be handed over to the Separatists, the Republic Army attacks the planet Umbara.

Death Star II's superlaser

When the Rebel Alliance attacks the second Death Star, they are unaware that the Emperor has set a deadly trap—a fully operational superlaser ready to destroy their fleet. The second Death Star's superlaser is far more advanced than that of its predecessor. Improved targeting sensors and power regulators enable it to destroy individual ships, rather than only planet-sized targets.

"Roger, roger."
BATTLE DROID

BATTLE DROID

Easily controlled, unquestioningly obedient, and inexpensive to mass-produce, battle droids are the primary troops in the Trade Federation's mechanized armies.

APPEARANCES I, II, CW, III **MANUFACTURER** Baktoid Combat Automata **MODEL** B1 Battle Droid
TYPE Battle droid

Starship crew
General Grievous's flagship, the *Malevolence*, is crewed by 900 battle droids, who receive commands from the shipboard Central Control Computer to carry out complicated technical duties.

TECHNICAL CAPABILITY

The Trade Federation commissions battle droids with humanoid physiques for practical reasons, as this allows the droids to operate existing machinery, vehicles, and weapons originally designed for organic operators and pilots, saving the Federation unnecessary production costs or expensive retrofitting. The battle droid infantry pilots STAPs, MTTs, and AATs, as well as Trade Federation battleships and other vessels. Federation vessels that operate beyond the range of a Droid Control Ship have inboard Central Control Computers that coordinate the droid crews, enabling them to operate tactile computer consoles and communications stations.

INVASION FORCE

With their tall, gaunt, humanoid design, exposed joints, and metal finishes, battle droids bear an eerie resemblance to animated skeletons. Essentially mindless, lethal puppets, they are operated via a Central Control Computer housed in an orbital Droid Control Ship, a modified Trade Federation battleship that transmits both direct orders from the Federation's leaders and computer-automated commands. Peaceful civilizations and worlds without military defenses are easy targets for the Trade Federation. However, if a Droid Control Ship is destroyed, battle droids enter a stand-by hibernation mode that leaves them totally vulnerable.

Armor plating
Inexpensive but durable metal protects signal receiver assembly.

Identical soldiers
Frightening in their uniformity, battle droids are only distinguished by numerical markings on the back of their comlink booster packs. Droids with specialized functions have distinct colored markings on their armor. Blue denotes pilot droids. Red denotes security droids. Yellow denotes command droids.

E-5 blaster rifle
Lightweight blaster rifles are ideally suited to battle droids' never-surrender programming.

Robotic army
Cheap to make, quick to assemble, battle droids roll off the production line at Baktoid Combat Automata's factories.

Covert agents
Three reprogrammed battle droids, painted blue to maintain their guise as innocuous pilots from a Separatist shuttle, follow their commander, R2-D2.

ASSEMBLY LINE

In choosing to rely on Central Control Computers to operate large armies of droids simultaneously, the budget-minded Trade Federation saves the astronomical costs that would have been required for the production of thousands of individual droid brains. The Federation contracts Baktoid Combat Automata to mass-produce B1 battle droids in the foundries-turned-factories on Geonosis.

REPROGRAMMED B1S

During the Clone Wars, Republic forces capture and disable three B1 battle droids, which are subsequently refurbished and reprogrammed to serve the Republic. After Separatists apprehend Jedi Master Even Piell and place him in a deadly prison known as the Citadel, Anakin Skywalker devises a rescue plan that involves conscripting the reprogrammed B1s to infiltrate the prison. Under the command of the astromech droid R2-D2, the B1s pilot a shuttle to deliver the other members of the rescue team to the Citadel. When a large number of enemy droids attack, the trio of B1s sacrifice themselves holding off the attack.

Calculated assault
Utilizing motion-capture data from highly trained organic soldiers, battle droids demonstrate an array of combat stances, positions, and maneuvers while fighting the newly formed Republic Army at the Battle of Geonosis.

IMAGECASTER

APPEARANCES I, CW, III
MANUFACTURER SoroSuub Corporation
MODEL SoroSuub Imagecaster
TYPE Personal holoprojector

Commonly carried by members of the Jedi Order, the Imagecaster is a handheld, disc-shaped hologram projector, which displays three-dimensional images formed by the interference of light beams. The Imagecaster can be tuned with a comlink to carry a hologram transmission for face-to-face contact or can be used as an independent image recorder and projector. The device is sturdily constructed for field use and can hold up to 100 minutes of images. Jedi Master Qui-Gon Jinn loads his holoprojector with selected images of Queen Amidala's starship before he proceeds to the junkyard on Tatooine, where he hopes to obtain repair parts for the ship's hyperdrive.

Holographic image
Anakin Skywalker watches Qui-Gon Jinn using an Imagecaster to project a three-dimensional representation of Queen Amidala's starship.

Utilitarian design
The Imagecaster's casing ring has three curved arms that rotate downward, allowing the device to stand on a level surface or link to a larger image projector.

Deflector shield

DROIDEKA (A.K.A. DESTROYER DROID)

APPEARANCES I, II, CW, III
MANUFACTURER Colicoids **TYPE** Battle droid

Unlike the spindly battle droid, whose humanoid frame allows a degree of versatility, the droideka is engineered with the sole function of completely annihilating its targets. Insectoid in its mix of curves and sharp angles, the droideka has heavy arms that carry immense twin blasters, which unleash destructive energy at a pounding pace. Compact deflector shield

Rolling mode
A droideka barrels across a starship's deck before opening fire on its target.

generators envelop the droid in a globe of protective energy. Although its three-legged gait is slow and awkward, the droideka can curl its body into a disc-shaped form, which can roll on smooth surfaces at great speed. The Trade Federation uses droidekas aboard its starships for security, as well as on the ground during combat operations.

E-5 DROID BLASTER

APPEARANCES I, II, CW, III
MANUFACTURER Baktoid Armor Workshop
MODEL E-5 **TYPE** Blaster rifle

The standard-issue armament of B1 battle droids and BX-series droid commandos, the E-5 blaster rifle is a lightweight weapon with a large gas chamber that allows for powerful blasts. Based on a

Droid grip
The blaster is equipped with a continuous-fire trigger.

BlasTech design, the rifle has been reverse-engineered by Baktoid Armor for use by robotic soldiers, which will not feel the excessive heat it produces when it is repeatedly fired.

OBI-WAN KENOBI'S FIRST LIGHTSABER

APPEARANCES I
CREATOR Obi-Wan Kenobi
MODEL Lightsaber
TYPE Single-blade

Based on the simple design of Qui-Gon's weapon, Obi-Wan's first lightsaber is lost during his duel with Darth Maul when it falls into a Naboo generator shaft.

Handgrip
The notched grip surrounds the diatium power cell.

T-14 HYPERDRIVE

APPEARANCES I **MANUFACTURER** Nubian Design Collective **CLASS** 1.8 **TYPE** Hyperdrive

T-14 hyperdrive generators, which propel starships smoothly into hyperspace, are commonly used aboard ships produced by the Nubian Design Collective, such as the J-type 327 Nubian starship assigned to Queen Amidala of Naboo.

GX-8 WATER VAPORATOR

APPEARANCES I, II, III, IV **MANUFACTURER** Pretormin Environmental
MODEL GX-8 water vaporator **TYPE** Moisture vaporator

Essential for survival on the desert planet Tatooine, GX-8 water vaporators coax moisture from the air by means of refrigerated condensers. Captured water accumulates on the condensers and is pumped or gravity-directed into storage cisterns. Vaporators are capable of collecting up to 1.5 liters (1.5 quarts) of water per day.

PIT DROIDS

APPEARANCES I, II, CW **MANUFACTURER** Serv-O-Droid
MODEL DUM-series pit droid **TYPE** Repair droid

Standing just over 1 meter (3.2 feet) tall, pit droids maintain podracer engines and cockpits, and are capable of lifting objects many times their own weight. The cheap, expendable droids run onto the racetrack to repair still-cycling superheated engines without hesitation. When not in use, they fold up into a compact stowed mode.

Tough construction
Hardened alloy casings can endure harsh Tatooine weather.

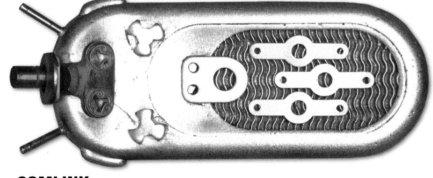

COMLINK

APPEARANCES I, CW, III **MANUFACTURER** SoroSuub
Corporation **MODEL** Hush-98 **TYPE** Handheld comlink

Comlinks are used for standard communication and to transmit and receive data. Many Jedi Knights are equipped with the Hush-98 comlink, which features a 100-kilometer (62-mile) range and complex security devices to prevent unauthorized interception. Built-in silence projectors allow Jedi to maintain stealth while communicating with their allies. Other components include a reception antenna, variable frequencies, encoding, and a sound-reproduction matrix. The Hush-98 is also capable of transmitting complex information such as blood sample data used to determine midi-chlorian levels.

ADVENTURER SLUGTHROWER RIFLE

APPEARANCES I, CW **MANUFACTURER**
Czerka Arms **MODEL** Adventurer
TYPE Slugthrower rifle

A projectile rifle with excellent aim over long distances, the Czerka Adventurer floods its chamber with a rich oxidizer as it detonates its shell, giving the projectile added punch and extra range. The weapon can be easily dismantled for concealed transport.

Long range
This projectile rifle can hit targets from up to 450 meters (1,476 feet).

TUSKEN RAIDER SNIPER RIFLE

APPEARANCES I, IV
MANUFACTURER Tusken Raiders
MODEL Tusken Cycler
TYPE Slugthrower

Built from stolen and scavenged parts, the Tusken Cycler is the standard projectile weapon used by Tatooine's Tusken Raiders for ranged combat. As a Slugthrower-class rifle, it fires solid shots enveloped in energy instead of blaster bolts.

Killing time
After years of extensive martial arts training, Maul relishes the opportunity to finally use his weapon against two Jedi on the planet Naboo (left).

Two against one
Maul's savage prowess with two blades (below) is not enough to defeat Obi-Wan's single-bladed weapon.

DARTH MAUL'S DOUBLE-BLADED LIGHTSABER

APPEARANCES I, CW **CREATOR** Darth Maul
MODEL Handcrafted **TYPE** Double-bladed Sith lightsaber (two joined lightsabers)

The Sith Lord Darth Maul's primary weapon is a pair of identical red-bladed lightsabers connected at their respective pommels to form a double-bladed lightsaber. Crafted by Maul himself, the weapon contains two sets of internal components, allowing one set to act as backup for the other if necessary. Activator controls can ignite both blades simultaneously or one at a time, and each lightsaber also features blade modulation controls. The double-bladed lightsaber is traditionally used as a training device, but because it can be much more dangerous to its wielder than an enemy, most Sith have historically eschewed the weapon in favor of the single-bladed lightsaber. In Maul's expert hands, it becomes a whirling vortex of lethal energy.

When Darth Maul attacks the Jedi Knight Qui-Gon Jinn on the planet Tatooine, Maul uses a single blade from his lightsaber during their duel but fails to strike down his opponent. Soon after, when Maul confronts Qui-Gon and his Jedi apprentice, Obi-Wan Kenobi, on Naboo, he activates both blades to fight the two Jedi at the same time. Maul slays Qui-Gon, but Obi-Wan's lightsaber cleaves through the joined pommels of Maul's weapon, leaving Maul with a single operational lightsaber. Despite Maul's deadly proficiency, Obi-Wan cuts Maul in half. Incredibly, Maul survives and manages to retain his one functional lightsaber. Years later, during the Clone Wars, Maul still possesses his weapon when he emerges from obscurity, and with it, he duels Obi-Wan and also his own former Master, Darth Sidious.

Violent reunion
Wielding his sole remaining lightsaber, Maul resumes his duel with Obi-Wan during the Clone Wars.

GUNGAN PERSONAL ENERGY SHIELD

APPEARANCES I **MANUFACTURER** Otoh Gunga Defense League **MODEL** Standard issue personal energy shield
TYPE Personal energy shield

This handheld shield carried by soldiers of the Gungan Grand Army defends against light physical attacks as well as blaster fire. The ovoid-framed shield uses hydrostatic bubble technology and can deflect blaster bolts back at the shooter.

ENERGY BALL (BOOMA)

APPEARANCES I, CW **MANUFACTURER** Otoh Gunga Defense League **MODEL** Gungan energy ball **TYPE** Energy weapon

Using the plasmic energy found deep in Naboo's porous crust, the Gungans have crafted a spherical grenade-type weapon they call a booma, or boomer. Made in many different sizes, these grenades are either thrown by hand, sling, or falumpaset-towed catapult. When they hit their target, their protective shells burst, releasing the plasma and a powerful electric shock.

Snap trigger
A firm squeeze is needed to prevent misfires.

NABOO ROYAL PISTOL

APPEARANCES I, CW **MANUFACTURER** Merr-Sonn Munitions, Inc. **MODEL** ELG-3A blaster pistol **TYPE** Hold-out blaster

Lightweight, elegant, and functional, the SoroSuub ELG-3A is practically a standard accessory for diplomats and nobles who require a personal blaster. Padmé Amidala and each of her handmaidens carry the slim royal pistol. Designed for practical use and easy concealment.

GUNGAN ATLATL

APPEARANCES I, CW **MANUFACTURER** Otoh Gunga Defense League **MODEL** Otoh Gunga standard issue atlatl
TYPE Bludgeoning/ranged weapon

Used by Gungans to launch energy balls at a greater distance than an unassisted arm can achieve, the atlatl is essentially a throwing stick that also serves as a highly effective blunt weapon. Atlatls are carved from a naturally isolating wood and can be wielded with one hand. They have a maximum range of 100 meters (328.1 feet) and an optimal range of 30 meters (98.4 feet).

KAMINO SABERDART

APPEARANCES II **CREATOR** Kaminoans
MODEL Handcrafted Kamino saberdart **TYPE** Toxic dart

Recognized by few experts outside the Outer Rim, the Kamino saberdart is a rare artifact. A small, fork-shaped dart with distinctive cuts on its side, it is used to deliver a deadly toxin. Although highly lethal, saberdarts may attract suspicion because they are so unique to the Kamino system.

Poison chamber
The toxins Malkite themfar and Fex-M3 can cause death in less than 10 seconds.

REMOTE

APPEARANCES II, CW, IV **MANUFACTURER**
Industrial Automaton **MODEL** Marksman-H
TYPE Training remote

Typically used as combat training tools, training remotes are small floating spheres equipped with relatively harmless blasters and an array of sensors. Jedi use remotes to hone their lightsaber skills, as well as their attunement to the Force. Jedi younglings usually wear vision-obscuring blast shields and use the Force to visualize a remote's location and actions, wielding lightsabers to block any incoming shots. As training sessions intensify, the remote begins to move more and more quickly and attacks with increasingly intense bursts of energy. Remotes are also extensively used by sharpshooters who want to polish their skills.

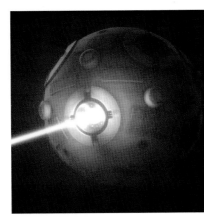

Lethal variation
Remotes can be modified to be defensive security weapons capable of firing deadly blasts of energy at intruders.

Learning tool
Ahsoka inspects Jedi initiates training with remotes *(above)*. A remote hovers before initiates *(right)*.

DC-15 BLASTER RIFLE

APPEARANCES II, CW, III
MANUFACTURER BlasTech Industries
MODEL DC-15A blaster rifle **TYPE** Blaster rifle

A standard-issue weapon for clone troopers in the Grand Army of the Republic, the DC-15 blaster rifle uses a replaceable tibanna gas cartridge that yields up to 500 shots of charged plasma bolts when the weapon is set on low power. On maximum power, the DC-15A yields 300 shots and can leave a .05-meter (1.6-foot) hole in any ferroconcrete wall.

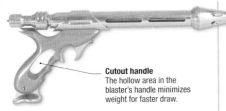

Cutout handle
The hollow area in the blaster's handle minimizes weight for faster draw.

WESTAR-34 BLASTER PISTOL

APPEARANCES II, CW **MANUFACTURER**
WESTAR, custom-made **MODEL** WESTAR-34
TYPE Blaster pistol

Designed for brief but intense surprise attacks at close range, and custom fit for the bounty hunter Jango Fett, the WESTAR-34 blaster pistol is made of an expensive dallorian alloy that can withstand sustained-fire heating that would melt most ordinary blasters.

CLONE TROOPER ARMOR

APPEARANCES II, CW, III, R
MANUFACTURER Kaminoan armorsmiths
MODEL Phase I armor **TYPE** Body armor

Full-body protection
Armor allows clone troopers to march through deflector shield barriers and withstand hails of deadly projectiles or explosive blasts with impunity.

Design flaw
Inexperienced with human ergonomics, Kaminoans unintentionally built Phase I armor to be uncomfortable to sit in. Subsequent generations of armor correct this flaw.

Various armor has been developed for clone troopers to operate in different environments and atmospheres. The first series of clone troopers, which were deployed at the Battle of Geonosis, wore Phase I armor, which consists of 20 form-fitting plastoid-alloy composite plates sealed to a temperature-control body glove via magnatomic gription panels. In creating the armor, Kaminoan designers took inspiration from armor worn by the clones' genetic source, the bounty hunter Jango Fett, including his helmet with its distinctive T-shaped visor. The pressurized body glove also provides temporary protection against the vacuum of space.

GEONOSIAN SONIC BLASTER

APPEARANCES II, CW **MANUFACTURER**
Gordarl weaponsmiths **MODEL** Geonosian sonic blaster **TYPE** Sonic blaster

The standard sidearm of Geonosian soldiers uses oscillators to produce a powerful omnidirectional sonic blast. The weapon's energy is enveloped in a plasma-containment sphere shaped by emitter cowls that channel the sonic beam.

MACE WINDU'S LIGHTSABER

APPEARANCES II, CW, III **CREATOR** Mace Windu **MODEL** Handcrafted **TYPE** Jedi lightsaber

During his long career as a Jedi, Mace builds and uses at least two lightsabers, both of which incorporate the same violet crystal that produces a purple-hued blade. After many years of experience with his first lightsaber, and after being appointed a senior member of the Jedi Council, he crafts his second lightsaber using the highest standards of precision, creating a superior weapon that represents his mature abilities as a Jedi leader. Regarded as one of the best lightsaber fighters of the Jedi Order, Mace is a master of combat techniques that sometimes tread dangerously close to dark-side practices.

Modulation circuitry for amethyst blade

Electrum finish denotes a senior Council member

Handgrip

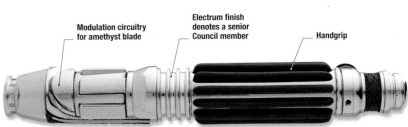

"The planet is secure, sir. The population is under control."

SUPER BATTLE DROID G21

SUPER BATTLE DROID

The bulkier, stronger, and more advanced version of the standard B1 battle droid, the super battle droid is equipped with a built-in laser cannon and can operate without a command signal.

APPEARANCES II, CW, III   **MANUFACTURER** Baktoid Combat Automata
MODEL B2 super battle droid   **TYPE** Super battle droid

Durable
The reinforced elbow-joint
bearings are hermetically sealed.

Secret weapon
Initially built in secret for the Trade Federation,
the military-grade super battle droid violates
Republic regulations on private security forces.

Flexible armored midsection

BUILT-IN WEAPONS
The standard B2 battle droid has built-in dual laser cannons mounted on its right forearm, which is modular and can be replaced with a rocket launcher and other weapons. Because the B2's armored monogrip hands lack fingers, it has difficulty handling standard blasters. However, the hands have built-in signal emitters that trigger the firing mechanism on specialized blaster rifles, making it easy for the droids to squeeze off shots.

IMPROVED MODEL
After the Trade Federation loses thousands of B1 battle droids at the Battle of Naboo, Federation leaders begin researching concepts for an improved battle droid. The result is the B2 battle droid, which is designed by the Techno Union. The B2 incorporates many components from the standard B1, but packages them in a much sturdier shell. The droid's delicate signal receptor— identical to B1 components—is built into its heavily armored upper chest, which also houses a basic cognitive processor. This limited intelligence enables the B2 to function semi-independently of a Droid Control Ship. However, because the B2 is not capable of complex thinking, a link with a Control Ship is required for optimum performance. Because the B2 has a high center of gravity, it utilizes programmed movement algorithms to maintain balance. The B2 also has strap-on foot tips that can be replaced with climbing claws or buoyant pods to traverse different terrains.

Jedi killers
Deployed on Geonosis to defend leaders of the Trade Federation against an invasion of Republic forces, armored B2 battle droids *(right)* deflect blaster bolts as they join B1 battle droids in an unrelenting attack on Jedi targets. But for all their ferocity, B2 battle droids can be defeated by a dauntless astromech *(below left)*.

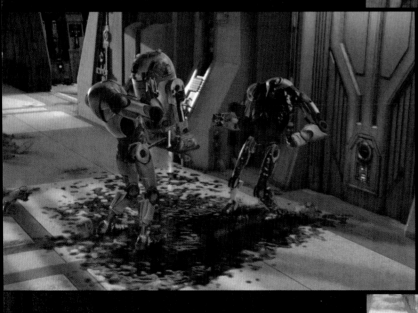

JETPACK VARIANT

Techno Union engineers design a powerful jetpack for propelling the B2 battle droid through the air. To economize on fuel, increase range, and compensate for the B2's weight, the jetpack incorporates a compact repulsorlift. Commonly referred to as rocket droids or jetpack droids, this variant B2 is officially designated the B2-RP (Rocket Pack) and is distinguished from other B2s by blue-white markings on its torso, arms, and legs. During aerial conflicts, vessels in the Confederacy of Independent Systems deploy B2-RPs, which launch themselves directly at enemy ships.

Airborne B2
A super battle droid hurtles toward its target.

Rocket trooper
A platoon of upgraded B2s *(top)* fire wrist-mounted blasters. An upgraded B2-RP *(above)* fights at the Battle of Ringo Vinda.

B2-RP UPGRADE

Introduced late in the Clone Wars, the upgraded B2-RP is dubbed the super battle droid rocket trooper, featuring a larger jetpack with two bulky thrusters that attach to the droid's shoulders and small additional thrusters secured to the ankles. The design and configuration of these thrusters give the droid greater control over its aerial maneuvers, as well as increased speed. The upgraded B2-RP also features wrist-mounted blasters on both arms.

DWARF SPIDER DROID

APPEARANCES II, CW, III
MANUFACTURER Baktoid Armor Workshop
TYPE DSD1 dwarf spider droid
AFFILIATION Separatists

The DSD1 dwarf spider droid is also known as the burrowing spider droid for its ability to invade narrow spaces. Frequently used by the Commerce Guild, it becomes a mainstay of Separatist ground forces during the Clone Wars. The dwarf spider droid's primary weapon is a long blaster cannon capable of both rapid-fire and high-intensity bursts. The legs of the dwarf spider droid are designed to affix securely to the sides of cliffs, and the droids are used by the Separatists during the Battle of Teth to fire at Republic AT-TE walkers trying to gain the high ground. In other engagements, dwarf spider droids provide heavy backup for squads of battle droids.

On the beach
Dwarf spider droids attack a coastal city on Kashyyyk, blasting the Wookiee defenders.

DC-15A BLASTER

APPEARANCES II, CW, III **MANUFACTURER** BlasTech Industries **MODEL** DC-15A blaster **TYPE** Blaster

One of the standard-issue weapons for clone troopers during the Clone Wars, the DC-15A is a reliable blaster rifle capable of both sustained fire and slower, long-range accuracy. The variable power output can be controlled by the clone trooper and includes a low-powered stun setting. The weapon can be mounted on a tripod. DC-15A rifles can be outfitted with sniper scopes and also work in conjunction with the holographic data readouts inside a clone trooper's helmet. During the Battle of Teth, clone troopers use ascension cables attached to their DC-15A rifles to scale high walls.

ANAKIN'S MECHNO-ARM

APPEARANCES II, CW, III, IV **MANUFACTURER** Republic **MODEL** Custom mechno-arm **TYPE** Cybernetic prosthetic

After Count Dooku cuts off Anakin's right arm on Geonosis, the Jedi Knight receives a mechanical prosthetic as a replacement. It resembles a droid arm with exposed gears and joints, and it greatly boosts Anakin's gripping strength. Electrostatic fingertips allow Anakin to retain his sense of touch.

Exposed armature
Mechanical servos are not covered by artificial skin.

T-SERIES TACTICAL DROID

APPEARANCES CW **MANUFACTURER** Baktoid Combat Automata **MODEL** Tactical droid **AFFILIATION** Separatists

T-series tactical droids serve an important advisory role among Separatist forces during the Clone Wars. Far smarter than most battle droids, tactical droids are designed to stay away from the frontlines and plan battle strategies from the security of a flagship or fortified headquarters. Due to tactical droids' intelligence, many commanders allow them to have full authority over Separatist military elements. This leads many T-series droids to express their superiority over all other droid models.

COUNT DOOKU'S LIGHTSABER

APPEARANCES II, CW, III **CREATOR** Count Dooku **MODEL** Handcrafted **TYPE** Sith lightsaber

Count Dooku considers himself a sophisticated duelist and builds his lightsaber with an unusual, curved hilt for greater finesse at executing precise slashes and lunges. During a confrontation on Geonosis, Dooku easily dispatches both Anakin Skywalker and Obi-Wan Kenobi, but proves unable to gain the upper hand when facing Master Yoda. Dooku carries the lightsaber throughout the Clone Wars. He faces Anakin and Obi-Wan a second time aboard the *Invisible Hand* during the Battle of Coruscant. This time his dueling skills fail him, and he loses his head to a vengeful Anakin.

YODA'S LIGHTSABER

APPEARANCES II, CW, III **CREATOR** Yoda **MODEL** Handcrafted **TYPE** Jedi lightsaber

Yoda's lightsaber has a shorter-than-average hilt and a blade proportioned to match the Jedi Master's smaller size. Despite his age, Yoda is one of the best combatants in the Jedi Order, executing dizzying attacks from every direction. The green-bladed lightsaber serves Yoda well throughout the Clone Wars, but he loses his weapon while fighting Emperor Palpatine inside the Senate Chamber.

Scarlet blaze
Sith crystals produce a red blade.

Unusual shape
The hilt's curved shape adds control when dueling.

OCTUPTARRA DROID

APPEARANCES III **MANUFACTURER** Techno Union
TYPE Octuptarra combat tri-droid **AFFILIATION** Separatists

Octuptarra droids are found among Separatist forces during the Clone Wars, often fielded by the Techno Union. These tall, three-legged automatons have large heads containing operational software and sensory equipment. Three laser turrets are mounted equidistantly beneath the droid's three photoreceptors. Because the octuptarra looks in every direction at once, it has virtually no blind spots. Despite its omnidirectional field of fire, the octuptarra droid is slow-moving and vulnerable to tripping. The Techno Union produces a number of different-sized droids during the war, some of them large enough to take on heavily armored Republic AT-TEs.

Three laser cannons for offensive punch

Three spider-like legs

360-degree attack
The octuptarra can swivel its head to easily cover any angle.

DATAPAD

APPEARANCES I, CW, III **MANUFACTURER** Various **MODEL** Various **TYPE** Datapad

Datapads are common devices used for a variety of informational purposes across the galaxy. Most datapads have a display screen and an input mechanism and are capable of storing holographic data and playing it back on command.

Blade stabilizing ring

Like his father
Luke has never held a lightsaber before, but knows how to wield the weapon.

ANAKIN/LUKE'S LIGHTSABER

APPEARANCES CW, III, IV, V
CREATOR Anakin Skywalker
MODEL Handcrafted **TYPE** Jedi lightsaber

This lightsaber, a legacy from one generation to the next, comes into existence after the Battle of Geonosis when Anakin builds a replacement for his original Jedi weapon. Anakin's second lightsaber has a blue blade and a silver hilt featuring black handgrips. He wields the weapon against the Separatists throughout the Clone Wars and uses it to defeat Count Dooku aboard the *Invisible Hand* during the Battle of Coruscant. Later, to defend Supreme Chancellor Palpatine,

Anakin cuts off Mace Windu's hand. The action marks Anakin's transformation into Darth Vader, and he uses this lightsaber during the massacre at the Jedi Temple and his battle with Obi-Wan on Mustafar.

Obi-Wan takes the lightsaber from his defeated opponent and holds onto it for nearly two decades while he watches over Anakin's son, Luke, on Tatooine. He eventually passes the weapon on to Luke, who studies under Yoda on the planet Dagobah before facing his father on Cloud City. Luke's inexperience is no match for Vader's mastery, and Vader uses his lightsaber to cut off Luke's hand, sending the blue-bladed weapon tumbling into the depths of the floating metropolis.

Last Actions
Anakin uses his lightsaber to confront Palpatine. Very soon, he will replace this weapon with a red-bladed saber.

ASAJJ VENTRESS'S LIGHTSABERS

APPEARANCES CW **CREATOR** Unknown **MODEL** Handcrafted **TYPE** Sith lightsaber

Asajj Ventress wields a pair of curved-hilt lightsabers during her apprenticeship to Count Dooku. Extremely skilled with the red-bladed weapons, Ventress fights the Jedi Master Luminara Unduli to a standstill during her assault on the attack cruiser *Tranquility*. Late in the Clone Wars, Ventress helps Ahsoka Tano escape from Republic authorities on Coruscant, but loses her twin lightsabers when she is ambushed by Barriss Offee.

DC-17 BLASTER

APPEARANCES CW, III **MANUFACTURER** BlasTech Industries
MODEL DC-17 hand blaster **TYPE** Blaster pistol

This heavy blaster pistol is carried by most Republic clone troopers, particularly high-ranking captains and commanders. The BlasTech DC-17 can also be outfitted with an ascension hook for scaling walls and has a built-in stun setting. The weapon is often worn in a quick-draw holster allowing for rapid response to sudden threats. Both Commander Bly and Captain Rex prefer to wield two DC-17 blaster pistols at the same time.

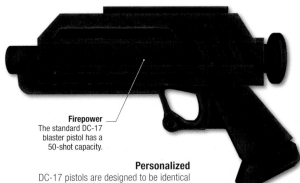

Firepower
The standard DC-17 blaster pistol has a 50-shot capacity.

Personalized
DC-17 pistols are designed to be identical and interchangeable, but commanders often customize them with unique paint jobs.

REPUBLIC ANTI-VEHICLE CANNON (AV-7)

APPEARANCES CW **MANUFACTURER** Taim & Bak **MODEL** AV-7 Anti-vehicle Artillery Cannon **TYPE** Artillery cannon

The AV-7 is a self-propelled artillery unit that moves on anti-grav repulsorlifts. It can be operated by a single clone trooper who sits behind the gunnery controls located on the side of the central assembly. When an AV-7 is in position, it stabilizes itself with its four widely spaced legs. The blasts from an AV-7 can take out both tanks and battle droids.

AHSOKA'S LIGHTSABER

APPEARANCES CW **CREATOR** Ahsoka Tano **MODEL** Handcrafted **TYPE** Jedi lightsaber

Ahsoka Tano's green-bladed lightsaber sees heavy use during the Clone Wars. The young Jedi Padawan develops a unique fighting style that incorporates a non-standard reverse grip for holding the weapon. Under Anakin Skywalker's instruction, she becomes a skilled duelist and wields her lightsaber in battles on Teth, Geonosis, and Lola Sayu, briefly losing it to a thief in the underlevels of Coruscant. Ahsoka builds a short-bladed saber to use in conjunction with her primary weapon.

Double duty
Both ends of an electrostaff can be activated to deliver a debilitating shock.

Adjustable charge
Electrical charge can be dialed up to lethal levels.

Always watching
MagnaGuards stay vigilant, scanning their surroundings for threats.

MAGNAGUARD

APPEARANCES CW, III
MANUFACTURER Holowan Mechanicals **TYPE** Bodyguard droid
AFFILIATION Separatists

MagnaGuards, the robotic bodyguards assigned to General Grievous, share his fearsome reputation. The IG-100 MagnaGuard is manufactured by Holowan Mechanicals and is distantly related to the IG assassin droid from the same company. Each MagnaGuard excels at close-quarters fighting, using its two-handed electrostaff to stun or kill attackers. The MagnaGuards that work with Grievous wear cloaks, a nod to the traditions of the general's homeworld. Grievous knows he will be facing many Jedi Knights during the Clone Wars and trains his MagnaGuards in dueling techniques that allow them to gang up against a single target. Backup systems allow MagnaGuards to keep fighting even after they lose a limb. While Grievous doesn't expect his MagnaGuards to be able to kill every Jedi who challenges them, he knows his bodyguard screen will exhaust most attackers and leave them vulnerable to a finishing blow delivered by Grievous himself. Aboard Grievous's flagship, *Invisible Hand*, Obi-Wan Kenobi and Anakin Skywalker tangle with a number of MagnaGuards.

ELECTROSTAFF

APPEARANCES CW, III **MANUFACTURER** Holowan Mechanicals
MODEL Electrostaff **TYPE** Two-handed staff

The MagnaGuard electrostaff is built from a material that conducts energy, allowing it to intercept lightsaber strikes without being cut in half. Each end of an electrostaff incorporates an electromagnetic module sheathed in energy tendrils that can incapacitate most organic beings. MagnaGuards can spin their electrostaffs so quickly they appear to be circular blurs.

First line of defense
General Grievous orders his MagnaGuards to intercept Jedi attackers.

MagnaGuard uniforms
The ceremonial cloak is pushed behind the shoulder when fighting.

High-ranking droid
A MagnaGuard automatically outranks any battle droid. Their presence indicates an elite Separatist commander must be close by.

TRACTOR BEAM

APPEARANCES CW, R, IV, V, VI
MANUFACTURER Various **MODEL** Tractor beam **TYPE** Starship equipment

Tractor beams are a fundamental piece of technology for starships and space stations. They project a force field that can seize an object in a near-unbreakable grip and pull it into a hangar bay. Aboard warships like the Separatist heavy cruiser *Malevolence*, tractor beams are classified as offensive weapons; these beams are aimed at a fleeing craft to slow its escape or to immobilize it entirely, making it easy prey for the warship's turbolasers. Tractor beams have peaceful applications as well. Space stations use tractor beams to guide arriving vessels to safe landings, and space tugs are outfitted with powerful tractor beams for towing disabled ships.

Powerful pullers
Most of the equipment inside a space tug, which needs to be able to move a large ship, is devoted to keeping its tractor beam generators working.

COMMANDO DROIDS

APPEARANCES CW **MANUFACTURER** Baktoid Combat Automata **TYPE** Battle droid
AFFILIATION Separatists

Commando droids are advanced, sturdier versions of B1 battle droids, programmed with improved combat tactics and battlefield awareness and equipped with glowing white photoreceptors. Captains and other high-ranking commando droids bear white identifiers on their heads and chests. Due to a more compact head size than the B1, commando droids can fit inside clone trooper armor to execute infiltration missions. Most commando droids carry blaster rifles and stun batons, and command units wield vibroswords for one-on-one combat.

Agile adversary
A commando droid is able to move and react much faster than a standard battle droid.

Heavy armor
The droids are designed to withstand blaster fire.

Airborne
Piloting speeder bikes, commando droids blast away at their targets.

LM-432 "MUCKRAKER" CRAB DROID

APPEARANCES CW, III **MANUFACTURER** Techno Union
TYPE Droid tank **AFFILIATION** Separatists

The LM-432 crab droid, also known as the muckraker, is a Separatist military unit that excels at navigating swampy environments. Its six armored limbs provide secure purchase when clambering over uneven terrain, and teeth at the tips of the limbs combined with gripping prongs at the joints allow crab droids to scale steep inclines. The LM-432's face is dominated by three glowing red photoreceptors, while communications antennae keep the droid in contact with its Separatist commanders. Two blaster cannons underneath the droid's body serve as long-range threats.

Lethal limbs
The droid's heavy claws can punch through vehicle armor.

Weak points
By exploiting a crab droid's blind spots, an attacker can slip past its claws and strike its vulnerable central processor.

Droid slaves
R2-D2 finds many strange droids aboard the Jawa sandcrawler, including astromechs, power droids, and servant droids. All are scavenged or stolen and then sold to farmers. Owen and Luke buy R2-D2 after their first choice malfunctions.

FAITHFUL DROID

"He says he's the property of Obi-Wan Kenobi, a resident of these parts." C-3PO

In desperation, Leia Organa entrusts R2-D2 with the Rebel Alliance's greatest secret, sending the droid on a wild odyssey.

When Darth Vader captures the *Tantive IV*, Princess Leia uses her last moments of freedom to load the stolen Death Star plans into R2-D2. She quickly tells the little droid to deliver the plans to the Jedi Obi-Wan Kenobi on Tatooine, just before she is captured. Together with his compatriot C-3PO, R2-D2 then boards an escape pod and descends to the planet below.

DROID ADVENTURES

R2-D2 and C-3PO disagree over what they should do next and temporarily part ways. Continuing on his own, R2-D2 encounters a group of Jawas, who immobilize him with an ion blaster and bring him on board their sandcrawler, where he meets an array of other droids. R2-D2 is also reunited with C-3PO, who has similarly been taken captive. The two are soon sold by the Jawas to Owen Lars and his nephew, Luke Skywalker, but it isn't long before R2-D2 sets out alone to find Kenobi once again. When Luke pursues the droid he finds Kenobi, and together they take R2-D2 and C-3PO back to the Jedi's home, in Luke's landspeeder. There, Kenobi gives Luke his father's lightsaber and reveals to the moisture farmer his true Jedi lineage. R2-D2 finally shares Leia's holographic message. Having faithfully fulfilled his duty, it is now up to Obi-Wan and Luke to safely deliver R2-D2 to the rebel authorities.

Double act
C-3PO and R2-D2's different personalities complement each other. Protocol droid C-3PO is diplomatic and cautious, while R2-D2 never hesitates to take action. Because of his command of language, C-3PO likes to feel that he's the boss of the partnership, but he usually ends up reluctantly following R2-D2 into danger.

JEDI HOLOCRON

APPEARANCES CW, R **CREATOR** Various
MODEL Handcrafted **TYPE** Jedi holocron

Holocrons are information-storage artifacts primarily used by the Jedi, though the Sith have their own holocron traditions. They act as repositories of vital and sensitive knowledge. Most of the data contained on a holocron is related to the nature and applications of the Force, so sharing this knowledge outside the Jedi Order is discouraged. For this reason, many holocrons are constructed with a security mechanism that permits access only to those who exhibit Force sensitivity. It is common for holocrons to resemble evenly

proportioned polyhedrons, with the sides made from a crystalline material that glows when in use. A holocron's lessons are typically relayed in the form of an interactive hologram that resembles the Jedi Master who recorded the information.

Hundreds of holocrons have been created by long-vanished Jedi Masters over the centuries. The Jedi Order values these artifacts for their historical significance and their insights into teaching methods. The Order isn't willing to take chances with its holocrons and keeps them in the Jedi Archives in the Jedi Temple, with the rarest specimens locked away behind the movement-triggered lasers and heavy blast doors of the Holocron Vault. Many

holocrons will not react unless paired with a specific memory crystal, and for added security, the Order does not store these items together.

During the Clone Wars, bounty hunter Cad Bane raids the Jedi Temple with the intent of penetrating the Holocron Vault. The Jedi detect his intrusion but misidentify his target, allowing Bane to slip through the temple's ventilation shafts. When the shape-shifter Cato Parasitti, Bane's compatriot, impersonates Chief Librarian Jocasta Nu, the ruse distracts the Jedi long enough for Bane to pocket the kyber holocron and exit the temple with little difficulty.

Guarded secrets
A special chamber in the Jedi Archives hosts the most valuable holocrons in the history of the Order.

> "The Holocrons contain the most closely guarded secrets of the Jedi Order."
>
> **JOCASTA NU**

Retrieval
Data playback often takes the form of interactive holograms.

Members only
Holocrons can detect if the user is a Force wielder.

Ornamentation
The transparent outer shell of this holocron allows its user to perceive its inner mechanisms.

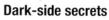

Dark-side secrets

The Sith have their own holocrons, usually identified by their pyramidal shapes. Similar to Jedi holocrons, Sith holocrons are often accessible only to those who can control the dark side of the Force. The Jedi Order considers these holocrons to be some of the most dangerous artifacts in the galaxy.

KYBER CRYSTAL

APPEARANCES CW **CREATOR** Jedi Order
MODEL Handcrafted **TYPE** Memory crystal

Kyber crystals are rare, naturally occurring gems found on scattered planets across the galaxy. They concentrate energy in a unique manner and resonate with the Force. A kyber crystal forms the heart of a lightsaber, focusing energy into the weapon's characteristic blade. The Empire develops a method of weaponizing massive kyber crystals to become the basis of the Death Star superlaser.

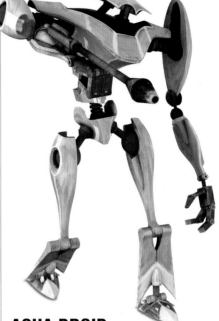

Dark weapon
No other lightsaber is known to have a black blade.

THE DARKSABER

APPEARANCES CW **CREATOR** Unknown **MODEL** Handcrafted **TYPE** Specialty lightsaber

The darksaber is a unique lightsaber with a sinister black blade that glows with an eerie halo. Many decades before the Clone Wars, the Jedi Order loses possession of the darksaber during a fight with the Mandalorians. The artifact eventually falls into the hands of Pre Vizsla, leader of the Mandalorian Death Watch. Vizsla opposes the pacifist leader of Mandalore, Duchess Satine, and uses the darksaber as his personal weapon. After Vizsla stages a coup to take control of Mandalore, Darth Maul kills him and takes the weapon.

Deadly duels
Obi-Wan battles Pre Vizsla, lightsaber against darksaber (above right). Pre Vizsla is skilled enough with the darksaber to keep a Jedi at bay (right).

AQUA DROID

APPEARANCES CW, III **MANUFACTURER** Techno Union **TYPE** Droid tank
AFFILIATION Separatists

The Separatists use aqua droids for underwater fighting on oceanic planets such as Kamino and Mon Calamari. The droids have retractable laser cannons and can move speedily while submerged, using propellers in their feet. For surprise attacks, the Separatists deploy aqua droids by hiding them in underwater starship wreckage, where they ambush their targets.

SEPARATIST ASSASSIN DROID

APPEARANCES CW
MANUFACTURER Techno Union
TYPE Assassin droid
AFFILIATION Separatists

Assassin probes are spider-like droids programmed for quiet killing. Each assassin probe moves on eight clawed legs and has multiple photoreceptors for scanning its surroundings. If cornered, it can release dozens of smaller droids through pores on its head that swarm a target and stab it with their sharp limbs. During the Clone Wars, three Separatist assassin probes attack Duchess Satine Kryze aboard the spaceliner Coronet, but Anakin Skywalker and Obi-Wan Kenobi successfully stop the threat.

NIGHTSISTER CRYSTAL BALL

APPEARANCES CW **CREATOR** Mother Talzin
MODEL Handcrafted
TYPE Nightsister artifact

The Nightsisters of Dathomir have strange traditions for tapping into the Force, including the use of crystal balls to give glimpses of future events. During the Clone Wars, Nightsister shaman Mother Talzin uses a crystal ball to locate Savage Opress, and later to find his brother Darth Maul.

ZYGERRIAN ELECTRO-WHIP

APPEARANCES CW **MANUFACTURER** Unknown **MODEL** Zygerrian electro-whip
TYPE Shock whip

Zygerrian slavers, such as the notorious Miraj Scintel, are known throughout the galaxy for their cruelty. Their weapon of choice is the electro-whip: a metal grip with an extendable wire that glows when powered up.

GAMORREAN AX

APPEARANCES CW, VI **MANUFACTURER** Various **MODEL** Two-handed vibro-ax
TYPE Vibro-ax

The Gamorrean guards in Jabba the Hutt's palace carry intimidating axes as their primary weapons, a display that lets visitors know they mean business. Many of these axes contain vibration generators that improve their cutting ability, though they are just as deadly without them.

NIGHTSISTER ENERGY BOW

APPEARANCES CW **CREATOR** Nightsisters
MODEL Handcrafted **TYPE** Energy bow

The Nightsister energy bow's strings are made from plasma that emits a bright pink glow, and is designed to fire arrows made from a similar plasma material. A special group of Nightsisters, known as the Hunters, use energy bows to track down and eliminate enemies on Mother Talzin's orders.

Triple eyes
Three optical receptors allow sight in a variety of spectrums.

"I am programmed to resist intimidation."

KRAKEN

Drill
The drill's twisted teeth inflict maximum damage.

SUPER TACTICAL DROID

APPEARANCES CW **MANUFACTURER** Baktoid Combat Automata
TYPE Tactical droid **AFFILIATION** Separatist

Super tactical droids are an upgraded line based on the T-series tactical droids. They serve as generals in the Separatist Droid Army during the Clone Wars. They are not only an advancement on the previous model, but also consider themselves superior to their biological counterparts. As a result, they are both arrogant and argumentative to a fault and operate without sympathy or morality, executing ruthless strategies. Notable individuals include General Kalani, assigned to Onderon; Aut-O, a Separatist fleet commander defeated by D-Squad; and Kraken, assigned to aid Admiral Trench.

BUZZ DROID

APPEARANCES CW, III **MANUFACTURER** Colicoid Creation Nest
TYPE Pistoeka sabotage droid **AFFILIATION** Separatist

Swarms of small buzz droids attack Republic ships during the Clone Wars. Vulture droid starfighters and droid tri-fighters fire jet-powered discord missiles at Republic targets, containing up to seven buzz droids, each in a shock-absorbing, spherical casing. The droids dodge their way through enemy defenses with maneuvering thrusters until they reach their targets and hatch open. Mechanical arms and cutting tools then dismantle enemy ships and droids to inflict as much damage as possible. The droids are difficult to remove from ships, and while the Republic has not developed adequate defenses against buzz droids, Jedi have found ways to work around them.

DARTH SIDIOUS'S LIGHTSABERS

APPEARANCES CW, III
CREATOR Darth Sidious
MODEL Handcrafted
TYPE Sith lightsaber

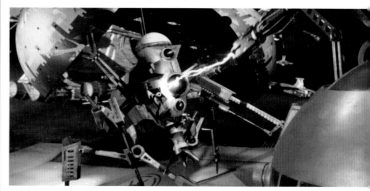

Secret weapon
One of Sidious's lightsabers is normally hidden inside a neuranium sculpture displayed in his office within the Senate building.

Darth Sidious has discerning tastes and constructs his lightsabers using nearly indestructible phrik, a metallic compound, and an aurodium emitter, all finished with electrum. At the core is a synth-focusing crystal. Sidious creates his lightsabers during his apprenticeship under Darth Plagueis. Sidious rarely uses his lightsabers—only when absolutely necessary—as it would immediately reveal his identity as a Sith. He prefers instead to exercise his powers of manipulation and use servants to carry out his dark deeds.

Weak spot
When a buzz droid lands on Anakin Skywalker's starfighter, R2-D2 zaps it in its most vulnerable spot: the main photoreceptor.

IMPERIAL TURBOLASER

APPEARANCES R, IV, V, VI **MANUFACTURER** Taim & Bak **MODEL** XX-9 heavy turbolaser
TYPE Anti-ship emplacement weapon

The XX-9 heavy turbolaser features a rotating double laser cannon turret mounted on a square base. The weapons are typically installed on the surface of Star Destroyers and the Death Star. On the Death Star, turbolasers are divided into four sections. The top level includes the turbolaser battery, while the second, lower level, houses rows of capacitor banks to store energy. The third contains the support crew and maintenance stations, and the lowest level encloses gunnery stations and control computers.

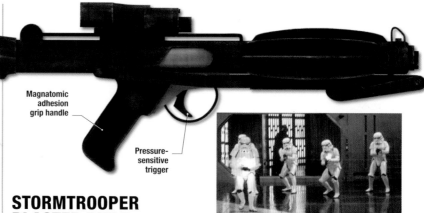

Magnatomic adhesion grip handle

Pressure-sensitive trigger

STORMTROOPER BLASTER RIFLE

APPEARANCES R, IV, V, VI
MANUFACTURER BlasTech Industries
MODEL E-11 **TYPE** Stormtrooper blaster rifle

The BlasTech E-11 is standard issue for Imperial stormtroopers. It combines lethal firepower with an impressive range in a versatile design. Most visible of the E-11's features is the telescopic range-finding sight and the folding three-position stock, which converts the pistol-sized blaster into

Assault weapon
Stormtroopers fire at the crew of the *Millennium Falcon* as they escape from the first Death Star.

a full-length rifle. Standard power cells carry energy for approximately 100 shots. Plasma cartridges last for more than 500 shots. Replacement power cells and gas cartridges are carried on the stormtrooper's utility belt, and the blaster also features an advanced cooling system for superior performance.

Audio pickup

Favorite Tatooine pistol
Luke confronts Jabba the Hutt with a DL-18 blaster.

Storming ships
Stormtroopers raid the *Tantive IV*, over Tatooine.

STORMTROOPER ARMOR

APPEARANCES R, IV, V, VI **MANUFACTURER**
Imperial Department of Military Research
MODEL Stormtrooper armor **TYPE** Body armor

Stormtroopers are anonymously shielded in white plastoid composite armor worn over a black body glove. While most armor is fitted for humans, other forms may be manufactured to suit different body types. Armed with the most powerful weapons and finest armor in the Empire, stormtroopers are among the most dreaded opponents of rebel freedom fighters.

This armor protects stormtroopers from inhospitable environments, projectile weapons fire, and blaster bolts. Stormtrooper helmets have built-in filtration systems that extract breathable atmosphere from polluted environments. For operation in the vacuum of space or the filtration of potent toxins, troopers wear backpacks with extended life-support capabilities.

Stormtrooper armor is generally impervious to most blast shrapnel and projectiles. It can be punctured by a powerful blaster bolt, but the armor will generally withstand glancing blasts.

Stormtroopers are equipped with a utility belt containing a variety of equipment, including a compact toolkit, power packs, and energy rations. The belt may also contain a comlink, macro binoculars, and a grappling hook. Field troops are allowed additional ammunition and comprehensive survival equipment. Backpacks can include field communicator sets, mortar launchers, and blaster components.

Stormtroopers usually carry a thermal detonator on the back of their utility belt. Controls on the detonator are not labeled, to prevent enemy troops from activating them, but include settings for arming, blast intensity, and timing. While detonators are not normally used within ships or bases, troopers carry a full complement of such field gear to be prepared for any situation.

Reinforced alloy plate ridge

Sniper position knee protector plate

> ## "I can't see a thing in this helmet!"
> **LUKE SKYWALKER**

DL-18 BLASTER

APPEARANCES R, VI
MANUFACTURER BlasTech Industries
MODEL DL-18 **TYPE** Blaster pistol

The DL-18 is so popular among Tatooine's underworld that it is known as the "Mos Eisley special." Many of Jabba the Hutt's employees are armed with this versatile blaster pistol. The weapon is also favored by the renegade Jedi Kanan Jarrus, whose pistol bears a dewback skin handle. The weapon weighs approximately 1 kilogram (2 pounds) and carries enough charge for approximately 100 shots. It has a range of accuracy up to 120 meters (394 feet).

Ubiquitous pistol
One of Jabba's barge guards draws his weapon.

KANAN'S LIGHTSABER

APPEARANCES R
CREATOR Kanan Jarrus **MODEL** Handcrafted **TYPE** Jedi lightsaber

Kanan originally builds his lightsaber as a Jedi Padawan. Following the enactment of Order 66, Kanan must hide his Jedi identity for 15 years, and thus keeps his lightsaber disassembled in a secret compartment until Ezra discovers it. Every time Kanan uses it, he makes himself a target for the Empire and draws the Inquisitor closer.

TIE FIGHTER PILOT HELMET

APPEARANCES R, IV, V, VI **MANUFACTURER**
Imperial Department of Military Research
MODEL TIE fighter pilot's helmet
TYPE Pilot's helmet

TIE fighter pilots rely on their flight suits and helmets in case of hull damage to their unshielded fighters. Their reinforced black flight helmets are connected to a life-support pack hanging on their chest via a pair of gas transfer hoses. The helmet also includes ship-linked communications systems and enhanced visor displays.

SABINE WREN'S HELMET

APPEARANCES R **MANUFACTURER** Unknown
MODEL Mandalorian Nite Owl helmet
TYPE Lady's helmet

Sabine wears a Nite Owl–styled Mandalorian helmet, popular among the notorious Death Watch faction. Other notable wearers of the helmet include Bo-Katan, sister of Duchess Satine Kryze, whose helmet features a targeting range finder, macro binocular viewplate, and comlink. Sabine's helmet is painted purple-pink to match the rest of her armor.

SABINE WREN'S TWIN BLASTERS

APPEARANCES R **MANUFACTURER**
Concordian Crescent Technologies
MODEL WESTAR-35 **TYPE** Blaster pistols

Sabine Wren uses a pair of custom-painted WESTAR-35 blasters. The blasters, which are popular on her homeworld, Mandalore, are used by everyone from the local police to the infamous Death Watch. They feature a high-precision barrel, rapid-fire mode, magnetic-grip handle, flash suppressor, and pressure-sensitive trigger.

ZEB'S BO-RIFLE

APPEARANCES R **MANUFACTURER**
Lasan-Malamut Firearms Corporation
MODEL AB-75 **TYPE** Lasan Honor
Guard bo-rifle

The Lasan bo-rifle, which is highly specialized and has a long tradition in Lasat culture, is the signature weapon of Garazeb Orrelios. Bo-rifles are used exclusively by the Lasan Honor Guard, of which Zeb is a former member. They come in a variety of forms, some using ethnic design, while others are

constructed more pragmatically. Since the Empire razed Lasan, bo-rifles are rarely seen around the galaxy; much like Jedi lightsabers during the years of the Empire, bo-rifles are relics of antiquity.

Bo-rifles are nonetheless versatile weapons for violent times, as they are not only robust and reliable blaster rifles, but also powerful melee weapons. A bo-rifle quickly transforms into a deadly electrostaff—ideal for a powerful Lasan to pummel a squad of stormtroopers.

The rifle component's power supply and discharge are similar to an EE-3 carbine rifle. The bo-rifle tips emit electromagnetic pulses that stun opponents and neutralize ray shields. The bo staff is activated by twisting the top handle downward, pressing both handles inward, and then activating both EMP tips. In staff mode, the weapons measure 2 meters (6.5 feet) long. Zeb's bo-rifle weighs 19 kilograms (41 pounds), requiring considerable strength to wield.

EMP staffs with similar technology are used in other militaries as well. IG-100 MagnaGuard droids, for example,

carry electrostaffs during the Clone Wars. The ISB's Agent Kallus also carries a bo-rifle, taken from a fallen Lasan Honor Guard during the sacking of Lasan. His black model J-19 is a more recent and less artfully designed version. A bayonet sits along the top edge, and a folding stock is situated along the back.

> "Only the Honor Guard of Lasan may carry a bo-rifle."
>
> ZEB

EMP generator tips
The tips carry a maximum adjustable voltage of 11,000V.

Brute force
Zeb leaves a pile of stunned and pummeled stormtroopers in his wake.

EZRA'S SLINGSHOT

His best shot
Ezra fires his energy slingshot at Agent Kallus on the planet Kessel.

APPEARANCES R **CREATOR** Xexto tinkerer
MODEL Handcrafted **TYPE** Wrist-mounted
energy slingshot

Ezra Bridger acquired his energy slingshot from his friend Ferpil Wallaway, who owns a pawnshop on Lothal. It was constructed by another Xexto friend of Ferpil's. Slingshots of various kinds are popular on their home planet, Troiken,

where having extra arms makes them more convenient to use. Slingshots are now favored by children on Lothal as well. Pulling the virtual line back builds a low-voltage charge that can be launched accurately for long distances, and like a Jawa ion blaster, the power is sufficient to disable droids and computer systems. Although the self-charging firing mechanism is not engineered to be lethal, it can stun a living being.

IG-RM DROID

APPEARANCES R **MANUFACTURER** Holowan
Laboratories **MODEL** IG-RM **TYPE** Thug droid

Designed by the same corporation that created the IG-86 sentinel droids and the IG-100 MagnaGuards (the latter preferred by General Grievous), IG-RMs are the next line in aggressive security automatons. More stable than assassin droids, they

require frequent instructions from their masters and are less likely to go rogue than other models. The droids are popular with underworld organizations; Cikatro Vizage owns quite a few IG-RMs, which are colorfully painted and armed with DLT-18 laser rifles. Within his Broken Horn Syndicate, the droids do much of the hard labor, fighting, and strong-arming, while Vizago manages them at a distance.

INQUISITOR'S LIGHTSABER

APPEARANCES R **MANUFACTURER** Unknown
MODEL Unknown **TYPE** Double-bladed
spinning lightsaber

Like all emissaries of the dark side, the Inquisitor uses his lightsaber not to defend the weak, but to kill without deliberation. His lightsaber is designed pragmatically to hasten confrontation and extinguish life with absolute efficiency. The Inquisitor's style of confrontation—particularly his use of a spinning, double-bladed lightsaber—is meant to intimidate. In the face of this unorthodox technique, inexperienced Jedi become apprehensive, presenting the Inquisitor with the perfect opportunity to strike.

The process of construction for the Inquisitor's lightsaber is unknown. It is possible that he built it himself, though it may have been issued to him by Darth Vader. Like standard Sith lightsabers, it is made using a red lightsaber crystal, and, fully extended, it measures 1 meter (3.2 feet).

The Inquisitor's unique lightsaber functions in several modes. In crescent mode, the single-bladed lightsaber is wielded in a standard manner. In disc mode, a second blade is drawn, allowing broader fighting strokes, ideal for battling multiple combatants simultaneously. Both blades are capable of spinning around the disc by detaching from the central handle, forming an impressive wall of red lightsaber energy. The Inquisitor wields the spinning lightsaber single handedly or throws it at opponents, recalling it with the Force.

It is unknown how many Jedi the Inquisitor has extinguished in lightsaber duels; before Kanan Jarrus and Ezra, none have survived to tell the tale. He also uses the weapon to execute non-Jedi. In relying on such a mechanical lightsaber model, the Inquisitor betrays one weakness: his fighting skills are not as potent as his analytical skills.

Lightsaber handle
The ribbed handle grip and lightsaber controls are set for crescent mode.

EZRA'S LIGHTSABER

APPEARANCES R **CREATOR** Ezra Bridger **MODEL** Handcrafted
TYPE Jedi lightsaber-blaster hybrid

During the dark times of the Empire, many traditions of the Jedi Order are abandoned for the sake of survival. Though some wayward Jedi do make use of them, blasters have never been condoned by the Jedi Council. A Jedi would never have built a blaster into his or her own lightsaber in the past, as Ezra does. Ezra, however, is not a typical Jedi.

When he first begins his Jedi training under Kanan Jarrus, Ezra must borrow his Master's lightsaber for practice. When he is ready, Ezra uses the Force to locate an ancient Jedi temple on Lothal. There, in the underground ruins, Ezra faces a series of challenges and confronts his own fears and weaknesses. When he does overcome them, a Jedi voice guides him to a blue kyber crystal—the key component required to build a lightsaber.

Ezra takes several weeks to construct his lightsaber aboard the *Ghost*. He uses a combination of spare lightsaber parts from Kanan, modulation circuits and an energy gate from Sabine, a donated power cell from Chopper, some extra tech Hera finds for him, and perhaps a part or two secretly acquired from Zeb's supplies. His double-bar design is unconventional for a lightsaber, but the outer bar is necessary to hold the blaster components. Having such an unusual and unproven design does pose some risk of a short-circuit at crucial moments. Since Ezra learned to build his lightsaber through trial and error, the blaster component is easily removed from the lightsaber to facilitate maintenance and repairs.

Ezra must be careful not to use his lightsaber unless there is no alternative. Doing so always draws the attention of the Empire, so having a built-in blaster function gives Ezra a safer option in violent confrontations. Ezra first uses his new lightsaber when the crew of the *Ghost* is attacked by the slaver Azmorigan on Lothal.

Battle ready
Ezra draws his novel new lightsaber. Opponents are taken by surprise when he not only slashes and blocks, but also returns fire. When the blade is not drawn, it merely looks like a blaster, so he avoids the unwanted scrutiny of Imperials.

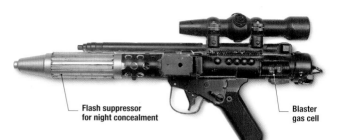

Flash suppressor
for night concealment

Blaster
gas cell

DH-17 BLASTER PISTOL

APPEARANCES IV, V **MANUFACTURER** BlasTech Industries
MODEL DH-17 **TYPE** Medium-range blaster

Though not as versatile as Imperial military blasters, the DH-17 pistol is a well-made close-combat weapon commonly used by rebel forces for shipboard combat. Though the E-11 is favored by the Empire, sometimes their officers use the DH-17. The DH-17 is dependable on a semiautomatic setting, firing in short bursts; on automatic, the power is drained in 20 seconds.

DEFENDER SPORTING BLASTER

APPEARANCES IV, VI **MANUFACTURER** Drearian Defense Conglomerate **MODEL** Satine's Lament **TYPE** Hunting pistol

DDC's Defender sporting blasters are low-powered weapons intended for small-game hunting and self-defense. The blasters are popular with nobility and aristocrats for their lightweight design, ease of disassembly and reassembly, and their ability to be concealed. Broken down into three components, the blasters can pass through most security scans undetected. This model is named after Duchess Satine Kryze of Mandalore, who might have fared better in the Clone Wars had she been properly armed. The power cell allows 100 shots per charge, though only a direct hit to vital organs is lethal. Princess Leia Organa uses the blaster when Darth Vader boards the *Tantive IV* looking for the stolen Death Star plans.

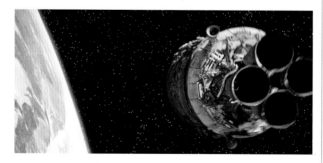

ESCAPE POD

APPEARANCES IV **MANUFACTURER** Corellian Engineering Corporation **MODEL** Class-6 **TYPE** Six-passenger pod

CEC's Class-6 escape pods are fitted with four retro escape thrusters and six smaller maneuvering jets for fast, controlled evacuations. The emergency pods are designed to carry a maximum of six living passengers of average size. They employ a simple design with minimal equipment. The fore and aft cameras and proximity sensors aid the autopilot. They also optionally route camera feeds to the single viewport display screen. Though pods are normally off-limits to droids, during the attack on the *Tantive IV*, R2-D2 accesses an escape pod. Together, he and C-3PO flee to Tatooine. Darth Vader allows them to escape because neither he nor his Star Destroyer sensors are able to detect that the droids are on board.

Saber fight
Darth Vader duels with his long-lost son Luke Skywalker in Cloud City.

DARTH VADER'S LIGHTSABER

APPEARANCES III, IV, V, VI **CREATOR** Darth Vader
MODEL Handcrafted **TYPE** Sith lightsaber

When Darth Vader first pledges loyalty to Darth Sidious, he continues to use his own Jedi lightsaber. After being disarmed by Obi-Wan Kenobi during their duel on Mustafar, Vader loses his lightsaber. He later constructs a new weapon with a red lightsaber crystal provided by his Master. The resulting lightsaber resembles his original Jedi weapon, but it is made with a darker alloy. The new lightsaber features a black-ridged handgrip, a black power cell chamber and beveled emitter shroud, a dual-phase focus crystal, a high-output diatium power cell, and the customary power and length adjustment switches.

After his transformation, Darth Vader draws his lightsaber only when dueling Jedi. He dispatches other combatants and victims using the dark side of the Force. In lightsaber combat, Vader favors bursts of powerful attacks and defense, followed by counterstrikes.

With this new lightsaber, he kills Obi-Wan and cuts off the hand of his son, Luke Skywalker, in Cloud City. In their final duel, Luke momentarily succumbs to his anger and cuts off his father's hand. Thus Vader's lightsaber falls into the same energy well in which Sidious perishes.

Handgrip ridges

Sith crystal chamber

Power indicator

Blade power
adjustment casing

Emitter shroud housing

Feared throughout the galaxy
Not as limber in his new cyborg form, Darth Vader is nonetheless the Emperor's deadliest servant.

Safety button

IONIZATION BLASTER

APPEARANCES I, CW, IV, VI **MANUFACTURER** Jawas
MODEL Handcrafted **TYPE** Ion blaster pistol

Jawas construct their own ion blasters using whatever scraps they can scrounge. They begin with a stripped-down blaster power pack. An accu-accelerator from a ship's ion drive and a droid-restraining bolt are added to the firing mechanism. The blasters may be fired accurately up to 12 meters (39 ft).

DLT-19 HEAVY BLASTER RIFLE

APPEARANCES IV, V **MANUFACTURER** BlasTech Industries
MODEL DLT-19 **TYPE** Blaster rifle

DLT-19 rifles are commonly carried by Imperial stormtroopers, though bounty hunters employed as snipers also use them. As a long-range rifle, the DLT-19 is commonly used by sandtroopers on Tatooine and by stormtroopers aboard the Death Star. The rifle has folding sights and bipod support. It may be fired in single shots and short bursts, or be fully automatic for brief periods.

GADERFFII (GAFFI) STICK

APPEARANCES II, IV **CREATOR** Tusken Raiders
MODEL Handcrafted **TYPE** Melee weapon (staff)

Gaffi sticks are staff weapons created by Sand People using a variety of scrounged materials, though preferably durable metals. They are roughly 1.3 meters (4 ft) long with a different weapon head on each end. One end is bent at a 90-degree angle with a club head tipped by a spear point. The other end is shaped like a mace with sharpened edges. Gaffis facilitate many attack forms, from crude clubbing and stabbing to the finer staff-fighting arts.

Wookiee weapons

The Wookiee language has more than 150 words for wood—and this easily available material is used in most of their weapons, shields, and armor. Wookiees fashion a large selection of blasters that blend both traditional materials, such as wood, bone, and horn, with advanced technologies. A few popular models are even mass-produced in workshops all over Kashyyyk.

WED TREADWELL DROID

APPEARANCES II, CW, IV, V, VI **MANUFACTURER** Cybot Galactica
MODEL WED-15 Septoid Treadwell Droid **TYPE** Repair droid

WED Treadwells are common droids used to repair ships, machinery, and other droids. The WED's binocular visual sensors are mounted on a telescopic stalk, and multiple tool-tipped arms can be purchased separately. The droids are relatively fragile and require frequent maintenance. Jawas offer a WED-15 for sale to Owen Lars and Luke Skywalker on Tatooine.

INTERROGATOR DROID

APPEARANCES IV **MANUFACTURER** Imperial Department of Military Research
MODEL IT-0 **TYPE** Interrogation droid

Illegal under the laws of the Republic, interrogator droids are one of the technological horrors constructed in Imperial secrecy. Used by the Imperial Security Bureau without mercy, this droid meticulously exploits a prisoner's mental and physical weaknesses by engaging its terrifying devices. It begins by injecting drugs that lessen pain tolerance and inhibit mental resistance while forcing the victim to remain conscious. Hallucinogens and truth serums ensure maximum effectiveness, and the experience is so unpleasant, most prisoners will confess on sight. Darth Vader subjects Princess Leia Organa to an IT-0 interrogation aboard the Death Star, but she is able to resist due to her training and fortitude.

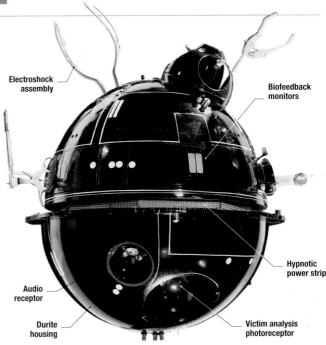

Electroshock assembly

Biofeedback monitors

Hypnotic power strip

Audio receptor

Durite housing

Victim analysis photoreceptor

CHEWBACCA'S BOWCASTER

APPEARANCES IV, V, VI **CREATOR** Chewbacca **MODEL** Handcrafted
TYPE Wookiee bowcaster

Bowcasters are a traditional weapon of Wookiees on their homeworld, Kashyyyk. They are based on ancient weapons of Wookiee culture that once employed poison darts and arrows. Bowcasters are more powerful and accurate than the average blaster, with a maximum effectiveness of up to 30 meters (98 ft). Designs vary depending on the materials used (usually wood and metal) and the craftsman's artistic approach. Bowcasters fire a metal quarrel enveloped in energy, while a polarizing orb, balanced on each end of the bow, creates a magnetic field that boosts the projectile's momentum. After the cocking spring is pulled back, the trigger speeds the quarrel forward, charged with plasma energy. Chewbacca crafts several bowcasters, his most recent an unconventional design making use of the frame and power pack of a stormtrooper blaster. At Han Solo's side, Chewbacca uses his weapon against a variety of foes, including Imperial stormtroopers, bounty hunters, and mynocks. Other fans of this weapon include the infamous Kyuzo bounty hunter Embo.

Hero of Endor
Chewbacca expertly wields his Wookiee bowcaster at the Battle of Endor to fight stormtroopers, biker scouts, and Imperial officers.

Solo modification
At one point, the barrel-scope is removed to improve fast draw.

Powerful shot
The pistol fires laser bolts strong enough to pierce stormtrooper armor.

Cooling unit

Steady grip
The grip emits a pulse warning when the weapon is low on power.

"Hokey religions and ancient weapons are no match for a good blaster at your side, kid."

HAN SOLO

HAN SOLO'S MODIFIED DL-44 HEAVY BLASTER PISTOL

APPEARANCES IV, V, VI **MANUFACTURER** BlasTech Industries **MODEL** DL-44 **TYPE** Heavy blaster pistol

A wide range of individuals make the DL-44 their blaster pistol of choice. It offers above-average firepower for a pistol, without compromising accuracy, making it ideal for use by military forces as well as bounty hunters and smugglers. The DL-44's capacitor can charge a double-power laser bolt without overheating.

Throughout his career, Han Solo keeps his trusty DL-44 handy at all times. Just as he did with his ship, the *Millennium Falcon*, Han made a number of personalized modifications to his blaster pistol. Confident in his own aim, Han removes the factory-issue motion-sensitive scope so that the pistol can be drawn faster from its holster.

Bounty denied
The bounty hunter Greedo tries to abduct Han at gunpoint in the Mos Eisley Cantina on behalf of Jabba the Hutt. Instead, Han covertly draws his DL-44 beneath the table, prepared to defend himself.

Trusty blaster
Han rarely goes anywhere without his customized DL-44 blaster pistol *(far left)*, although it proves of little use against Darth Vader when the Sith Lord captures the rebels at Cloud City. Han wields it to great effect against the Imperial forces on Endor during the raid on the shield generator bunker protecting the second Death Star *(left)*.

IMPERIAL PROBE DROID

APPEARANCES V, VI **MANUFACTURER** Arakyd Industries **MODEL** Viper probe droid **TYPE** Probe droid

Also called a probot, the Imperial probe droid is used to track down the enemies of the Empire almost anywhere in the galaxy. It can be launched from starships to travel through space in a hyperspace pod until arriving at the planet it is assigned to search. The probe droid's repulsorlift engine allows it to travel across any type of terrain, and its thrusters have silencers to prevent detection. At 2 meters (6.5 feet) in height, the probot contains numerous sensors, a holocam, six manipulator arms for taking samples, and a small mounted blaster for defense. The high-frequency holonet transceiver allows the probe droid to transmit information to Imperial forces even at great distances.

Rebels found
Darth Vader dispatches numerous probe droids across the stars to search for the rebel base. One of the droids discovers Echo Base on Hoth and transmits visual confirmation to Vader's flagship.

Double threat
The Z-6 model jetpack combines a powerful missile launcher with jumper-jet propulsion for short flights through the air. This enables Boba Fett to swoop down on bounties swiftly or to annihilate them from afar.

Homing missile
The jetpack supports several missile types, including a homing missile.

Reactant tank
The pack contains enough fuel for 20 controlled bursts.

Electronic scope

Modified stock

Fett favorite
The feared bounty hunter Boba Fett trusts his blaster rifle's deadly aim. The stock provides added stability, and the electronic scope ensures its accuracy, even at long range.

EE-3 BLASTER RIFLE

APPEARANCES CW, IV, VI
MANUFACTURER BlasTech Industries
MODEL EE-3 **TYPE** Blaster carbine

Shorter and lighter than the E-11 blaster rifle, which serves as the standard-issue weapon of Imperial stormtroopers, the EE-3 carbine rifle relies on a two-handed grip to compensate for the smaller handle attached to the barrel. The EE-3 has a quicker rate of fire but less accuracy and stopping power than larger rifles. Its size is its primary advantage, making it a favorite of bounty hunters across the galaxy. Boba Fett carries an EE-3 as his preferred blaster, and the Zabrak bounty hunter Sugi wields one during the Clone Wars.

Z-6 JETPACK

APPEARANCES II, CW, IV, V, VI **MANUFACTURER** Mitrinomon Transports **MODEL** Z-6 **TYPE** Jetpack

The notorious bounty hunter Boba Fett includes the Z-6 jetpack among his usual gear. Fuel burned by the personal transportation device produces significant thrust, providing a tactical advantage during combat situations but also creating personal risk for the wearer. Gyro-stabilizers ensure that the directional thrusters provide easy maneuverability. The launcher supports two uses: a projectile grappling hook with its cable attached to the internal winch, enabling Fett to snare and haul in bounties, or a powerful anti-vehicle homing missile. This functionality makes the Z-6 model a favorite for others, including Mandalorian commandos during the Clone Wars and Boba's father, Jango Fett.

BOBA FETT'S WRIST GAUNTLETS

APPEARANCES IV, V, VI **CREATOR** Boba Fett
MODEL Handcrafted **TYPE** Bounty hunter wrist gauntlets

Always careful to ensure he has many options at his disposal, Boba Fett wears wrist gauntlets stocked with numerous features. Their powerful weapons include the ZX miniature flamethrower from Czerka Corporation, capable of projecting a cone of fire 5 meters (16½ ft) long and 1 meter (3ft 3 in) in diameter, and the Dur-24 wrist laser from BlasTech Industries, which combines the full firepower of a standard blaster rifle with a range of up to 50 meters (164 ft). The MM9 mini concussion rocket launcher from Kelvarek Consolidated Arms fires various types of small homing missiles, such as stun rockets and anti-vehicle rockets. Fett's right gauntlet includes an extensible fibercord whip that can be fired to quickly bind up the target's limbs.

Crafty devices
Boba Fett has many tricks on his sleeves *(above left)*. At the Great Pit of Carkoon, he fires a fibercord whip from a wrist projector to ensnare Luke *(above)*.

GOLAN ARMS DF.9 ANTI-INFANTRY BATTERY

APPEARANCES V **MANUFACTURER** Golan Arms
MODEL DF.9 **TYPE** Anti-infantry battery

A fixed emplacement weapon, the DF.9's single laser cannon fires blasts capable of annihilating whole squads of approaching infantry. The cannon is effective at a distance of up to 16 kilometers (10 miles). The gunner in the 4-meter- (13-ft-) tall upper turret enjoys a full 180-degree rotation of fire. Within the durasteel armored turret, which can readily withstand blaster fire, a targeting computer technician assists with precision aim, while another ensures stable energy flow from the power generator.

LUKE SKYWALKER'S REBEL PILOT HELMET

APPEARANCES IV, V, VI
MANUFACTURER Unknown
MODEL X-wing flight helmet
TYPE Flight helmet

When Luke arrives at the secret rebel base at Yavin 4, he promptly volunteers to join the desperate attack mission against the Empire's approaching Death Star. Assigned to fly Red Five, Luke receives a standard-issue X-wing pilot's uniform for Red Squadron, including a helmet adorned with the Rebel Alliance starbird logo. The helmet has a plasteel exterior and insulated foam-lined interior. Among other features it also includes a retractable polarized visor, sensa-mic for communications, and localized atmospheric field generator. After he destroys the Death Star, Luke continues to wear his pilot helmet on other missions in his X-wing.

A280 BLASTER RIFLE

APPEARANCES V, VI
MANUFACTURER BlasTech Industries
MODEL A280 **TYPE** Blaster rifle

Considered one of the best armor-piercing blaster rifles, the A280 provides more power than other blaster rifles at long range. During the Republic's final years, A280s are commonly used by local planetary forces, which makes them readily available on the black market for rebel units rising up against the Empire.

Power charge system

Integrated muzzle compensator

E-WEB REPEATING BLASTER

APPEARANCES V
MANUFACTURER BlasTech Industries
MODEL E-Web **TYPE** Heavy repeating blaster

The Emplacement Weapon, Heavy Blaster, commonly known as an E-Web, is the most powerful repeating blaster in the Imperial arsenal. Rigid mounts counteract the kinetic energy created by the weapon's formidable firepower. Usually operated by a two-person crew, its set-up time limits its effectiveness, so some Imperial crews pre-charge the generator for faster assembly. This requires careful adjustment of the power flow to prevent an overload.

1.4 FD P-TOWER

APPEARANCES V
MANUFACTURER
Atgar SpaceDefense Corporation
MODEL 1.4 FD
TYPE Light anti-vehicle laser cannon

The 1.4 FD P-Tower is a fixed emplacement anti-vehicle laser cannon for use in all terrains. The single laser cannon fires from the center of the energy dish, which has 16 micropower routers spaced evenly along the edge and eight power conversion cells along the interior. The P-Tower is inexpensive, and quick and easy to produce.

Rotating base
The 1.4 FD P-Tower has 360° rotation for full range of fire.

Extreme conditions
The 1.4 FD P-Tower can operate in temperatures from -73°C (-100°F) to 49°C (120°F).

V-150 PLANET DEFENDER

APPEARANCES V
MANUFACTURER Kuat Drive Yards
MODEL v-150 **TYPE** Heavy ion-to-space cannon

The v-150 Planet Defender is a surface-based ion cannon designed to target starships orbiting above a planet. Often deployed in conjunction with planetary shields, it defends planets while the shields reach full power. The cannon has an optimum range of 4,000 kilometers (2,485 miles) and a maximum range of 180,000 kilometers (111,847 miles), and can disrupt Star Destroyers with a single ion bolt. However, being a stationary weapon makes the v-150 Planet Defender vulnerable to attack, and its blast shield must be retracted to utilize the cannon.

Permacite blast shielding

Surface-to-space firepower
The v-150 Planet Defender is equipped with an independent power generator buried some 40 meters (131 feet) below the weapon placement.

Activation panel
An internal fusion reaction is activated via the control panel.

Thermite shell
Volatile baradium is contained inside a thermite casing.

CLASS-A THERMAL DETONATOR

APPEARANCES VI
MANUFACTURER Merr-Sonn Munitions, Inc.
MODEL Class-A thermal detonator
TYPE Thermal detonator

The Class-A thermal detonator's power and range make it illegal for use other than for authorized military purposes. The detonator has a blast radius of up to 20 meters (65 feet), though it can be tuned to limit the radius depending on the situation. Posing as the bounty hunter Boushh, Leia threatens Jabba the Hutt with disintegration when she negotiates her fee for "capturing" Chewbacca. Impressed by the bounty hunter's boldness, Jabba agrees to her terms.

LUKE SKYWALKER'S GREEN LIGHTSABER

APPEARANCES VI **CREATOR** Luke Skywalker
MODEL Handcrafted **TYPE** Jedi lightsaber

The green lightsaber is the first one built by Luke Skywalker and the second he owned. Constructed three years after his fateful trip to the Death Star, Luke models the weapon on Obi-Wan's lightsaber, yet simplifies some design elements. For the rescue of Han Solo from Jabba's Palace, the young Jedi entrusts his lightsaber to his droid R2-D2. During their escape, R2-D2 launches the weapon across the Great Pit of Carkoon into Luke's hand. Aboard the second Death Star, Luke uses his lightsaber during his final confrontation with Darth Vader. Refusing to succumb to the Emperor's goading to kill his father, Luke deactivates his lightsaber.

SLD-26 PLANETARY SHIELD GENERATOR

APPEARANCES VI **MANUFACTURER** CoMar Combat Systems
MODEL SLD-26 **TYPE** Deflector shield generator

The SLD-26 shield generator can protect a small moon or a large space station with a nearly impenetrable energy shield for an indefinite period of time. The Galactic Empire installs such a generator on the forest moon of Endor to protect the second Death Star during its construction phase. The Rebel Alliance sends a strike team to the moon to disable the shield generator in advance of their fleet's attack on the Death Star. Unaware that the Emperor has set a trap for the rebels on Endor, most of the strike team, including Han Solo and Princess Leia Organa, is captured. However, with the help of the Ewoks, Chewbacca routs the troopers and frees the strike team, which destroys the shield generator, thus allowing the rebel fleet to demolish the second Death Star.

> "I'm afraid the deflector shield will be quite operational when your friends arrive."
>
> **EMPEROR PALPATINE**

Positioning antenna
The emitter antenna helps align the shield.

Force field
Shield projectors deliver an energy field that protects the Death Star.

Deep focus
A powerful focus dish enables large objects in space to be shielded.

Power station
The power core is by necessity efficient and sustainable.

Planetary protector
The shield generator is essential for the protection of the second Death Star, as is its destruction for the rebel victory during the Battle of Endor.

Short-range laser emitter

Pressure-sensitive grip

SCOUT TROOPER BLASTER

APPEARANCES VI
MANUFACTURER BlasTech Industries
MODEL EC-17 **TYPE** Hold-out blaster

A standard-issue weapon for Imperial scout troopers, this compact, one-handed weapon serves as a hold-out blaster, and is optimal for short-range targets. Holstered in a scout trooper's boot, the pistol has a pressure-sensitive grip instead of a trigger to account for the trooper's gloves. It also has a built-in targeting scope to assist its user's aim.

BEHIND THE SCENES

"It was crazy—spaceships, and Wookiees, and robots. It was just unlike anything that had ever been seen before." George Lucas, creator of the *Star Wars* saga

Technology is one of the hardest things in moviemaking to get right. Too much emphasis and it starts to overpower the characters, not enough and the film loses its otherworldly setting. Like much of the design that went into the *Star Wars* universe, the technology was created to be believable, but in ways that seem incredible. The use of robotics, cloning, and prosthetics anticipates real-world innovations, while lightsabers so pervade modern popular culture, it can be strange to realize that they don't exist!

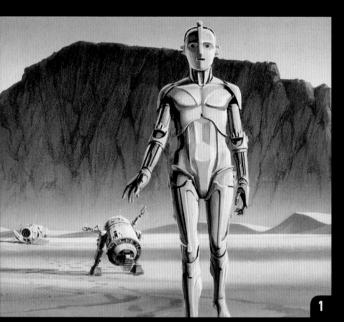

Star Wars concept illustrator Ralph McQuarrie's first production painting depicts droids R2-D2 and C-3PO on a desert planet after landing in their escape pod. At George Lucas's request, the protocol droid was redesigned to look less human and more mechanical **(1)**. Early concept costume sketches for Darth Vader by costume designer John Mollo for *Star Wars:* Episode IV *A New Hope* **(2)**.

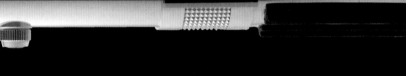

George Lucas shows Carrie Fisher (Princess Leia) how to hold a blaster on the Death Star set of *A New Hope* **(3)**. Inspired by the classic swashbuckling movie serials Lucas enjoyed as a boy, Luke Skywalker's lightsaber for *A New Hope* was fashioned in part from a camera flash attachment by set dresser Roger Christian **(4)**.

Irvin Kershner directs Dave Prowse as Darth Vader with the full-sized puppet of assassin droid IG-88 on the set of the Star Destroyer in *Star Wars:* Episode V *The Empire Strikes Back* **(5)**. Producer Howard Kazanjian with a model of an AT-ST walker, and a Boba Fett stunt double, with a miniature set on the ILM backlot for *Star Wars:* Episode VI *Return of the Jedi* **(6)**.

The prototype all-white super trooper armor for Boba Fett was revised in favor of a muted color scheme. Both versions of Fett's armor for *The Empire Strikes Back* were conceptually designed primarily by concept artist Joe Johnston and Ralph McQuarrie, and built by Norman Reynolds and his art department team **(7)**. A model of the second Death Star under construction, created by ILM model makers under the direction of Lucas and supervisor Lorne Peterson. The Death Star image was flipped horizontally for *Star Wars:* Episode VI *Return of the Jedi* **(8)**.

9

10

13

12

R2-D2 and an exposed C-3PO, operated by a puppeteer, take directions on a greenscreen soundstage at Leavesden Studios for *Star Wars: Episode I The Phantom Menace* (9). ILM's animation director Rob Coleman studies a CG rendering of Jar Jar Binks for *The Phantom Menace* (10). ILM's digital models of cyborg General Grievous and background droids in an animation or creature effects 'take,' which can be used for shape correctives or to fix interpenetrating pieces before final rendering, from *Revenge of the Sith* (11).

Obi-Wan Kenobi's elegant lightsaber from *The Phantom Menace* illustrates the look the *Star Wars* prequel concept design supervisors created with Lucas—a more Art Deco style that reflected the high civilization achieved by the Republic (12). Liam Neeson (Qui-Gon Jinn) and Ray Park (Darth Maul), rehearse their lightsaber duel at Leavesden's FS1 stage, with Ewan McGregor (Obi-Wan Kenobi) (13). Early concept art by TJ Frame for General Grievous's Tsmeu-6 personal wheel bike for *Star Wars: Episode III Revenge of the Sith* (14).

11

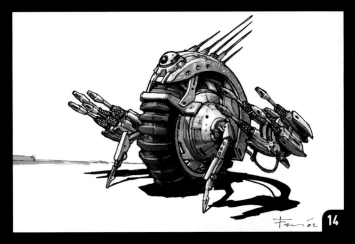

14

15

16

A Wookiee wields his low-tech yet lethal bowcaster during a bluescreen pick up for the Battle of Kashyyyk at Fox Studios, Sydney, Australia (15). A new model R2-D2, surrounded by (from left to right) director J.J. Abrams, droid builders Lee Towersey and Oliver Steeples, and Lucasfilm president Kathleen Kennedy at Pinewood Studios for *Star Wars: The Force Awakens* (16).

VEHICLES

Factories produce a staggering variety of vehicles for both peaceful and warlike purposes, from starships traveling at light speed to transporters moving with a slow, remorseless tread.

On thousands of civilized worlds, most atmospheric-propulsion vehicles utilize repulsorlift technology, which levitates vehicles and lightweight atmosphere craft via antigravitational emanations called "repulsor fields." Some repulsorlift craft are little more than engines with padded seats that travel close to the ground, while others are large luxury vessels that can skim a planet's atmospheric ceiling. For voyages between distant star systems, starships use hyperdrive technology that enables vessels to exceed lightspeed, and sublight engines for traveling at slower speeds.

During the Clone Wars and the subsequent war between the Empire and the Rebel Alliance, many manufacturers convert transports and freighters into combat craft, and also produce entirely new vehicles that are laden with weapons. To evade the Imperial ships that patrol the galaxy's best-known commercial routes, pirates and smugglers outfit their own vessels with powerful engines and exotic weaponry.

VEHICLES TIMELINE

In a dangerous and unpredictable galaxy, vehicles have defined the course of civilization. They have been used as the means of exploration, for transportation and entertainment, and as awesome weapons of war.

CRISIS IN THE REPUBLIC:
Spans Episodes I and II

THE CLONE WARS:
Spans Episode II, CW, and Episode III

THE EMPIRE ERA:
Spans Episode III, R, and Episodes IV to VI

Droid invasion of Naboo
The Trade Federation uses a fleet of illegally modified cargo vehicles to blockade and subsequently invade the peaceful world of Naboo. Landing ships and transporters ferry thousands of battle droids to the planet.

Hunted by the Sith
The Sith Lord Darth Sidious dispatches his apprentice, Darth Maul, to hunt down the queen. Maul flies to Tatooine using a cloaked Sith Infiltrator ship, allowing him to hunt his quarry in secrecy.

Journey through the Core
The Jedi Knights Qui-Gon Jinn and Obi-Wan Kenobi use a Gungan sub known as a bongo to navigate the submerged core of Naboo. They reach Queen Amidala's palace undetected and rescue her from the droid forces.

Boonta Eve Classic
In order to leave Tatooine, the queen and her companions are forced to bet on a high-stakes podrace. One of the pilots is a young slave boy named Anakin Skywalker, who uses his unusual podracer to win the race.

Escape from Naboo
Alongside Qui-Gon and Obi-Wan, Queen Amidala escapes from the Naboo blockade in her personal royal starship, but it is damaged, forcing the group to set down on the inhospitable planet of Tatooine.

Battle of Geonosis

The Clone Wars erupt in a massive battle on Geonosis. The newly formed Grand Army of the Republic crushes the Separatist forces with its advanced assault vehicles, but the Separatist leaders escape in their ships to fight another day.

Twilight adventures

Anakin Skywalker makes use of the battered Corellian freighter *Twilight* to perform secret missions for the Republic, including rescuing Jabba the Hutt's infant son.

Duel with Jango

While investigating a mysterious killing, Obi-Wan Kenobi stumbles on a secret cloning facility guarded by the bounty hunter Jango Fett. Obi-Wan pursues Jango's ship, *Slave I*, but becomes embroiled in an intense dogfight.

Destruction of the *Malevolence*

The Separatist superweapon, *Malevolence*, is attacked by Republic Y-wing starfighters, and subsequently infiltrated by a Jedi strike team. The ship is destroyed after colliding with the Dead Moon of Antar.

Battle of Coruscant

The Separatist fleet strikes at the heart of the Republic, the city-world of Coruscant. A gigantic battle erupts above the planet, with Republic Star Destroyers on one side, and Separatist frigates and destroyers on the other. The Separatist flagship, *Invisible Hand*, is destroyed.

Battle of Naboo

A battle rages for control of Naboo. Droid tanks battle Gungan forces on the grassy plains, while in space, Naboo starfighters engage the Trade Federation fleet. The destruction of their Droid Control Ship ends the Trade Federation's invasion.

Capture of the *Tantive IV*

Tatooine again becomes the focus of galactic events as Princess Leia's starship, the *Tantive IV*, is captured in orbit by an Imperial Star Destroyer. Two droids carrying secret plans to the Death Star superweapon escape to the planet's surface.

Escape from Tatooine

Luke Skywalker joins forces with Obi-Wan Kenobi, and together with the droids, escapes the Empire by fleeing from Tatooine aboard the star freighter *Millennium Falcon*. They set course for the planet Alderaan.

The *Ghost*

A nascent rebel cell forms on the planet Lothal, and makes use of a modified star freighter named the *Ghost* as their base of operations. Attacks by the *Ghost* seriously disrupt Imperial operations in the sector.

Destruction of Alderaan

In an attempt to terrify the galaxy into obedience, Grand Moff Tarkin uses the Death Star's superlaser to destroy Alderaan. Millions of innocent people are wiped out in an instant.

Invasion of Kashyyyk

The Separatists invade the Wookiee homeworld of Kashyyyk using new and powerful droid vehicles. Allied with fearsome Republic turbo tanks, the Wookiees fight back with indigenous aerial craft.

Aboard the Death Star

The *Millennium Falcon* arrives at Alderaan to find the planet has been blasted into dust. Shortly thereafter the ship is captured and brought aboard the Death Star, leading to a final confrontation between Obi-Wan Kenobi and Darth Vader.

Pursuit of the *Millennium Falcon*

Darth Vader launches a hunt across the galaxy for the *Millennium Falcon* and her crew. Han Solo is subsequently captured by the bounty hunter Boba Fett, frozen in carbonite, and taken to the gangster Jabba the Hutt aboard *Slave I*.

Jabba the Hutt

Han's friends mount a rescue mission to Jabba's palace on Tatooine. A battle aboard Jabba's sail barge, the *Khetanna*, ends with Han's rescue, the death of Jabba the Hutt, and the fiery destruction of the barge.

Battle of Hoth

The Empire discovers the new rebel base on the icy world of Hoth, and immediately mounts an overwhelming invasion using AT-AT walkers. The rebels manage to evacuate in their transports, but the base is destroyed.

Battle of Endor

In the climactic battle of the Galactic Civil War, the rebel fleet attacks the unfinished second Death Star. Although they have actually fallen into an Imperial trap, they succeed in destroying the superweapon, and the Emperor is killed.

Battle of Yavin

The Rebel Alliance makes a desperate attempt to destroy the Death Star using small X-wing and Y-wing starfighters. Almost the entire rebel fleet is wiped out, but Luke Skywalker succeeds in destroying the battle station.

Deflector shield

Jedi transport
Before the dark times, red was the color of neutrality
for spacecraft of the Galactic Republic.

Cockpit

Docking ring

REPUBLIC CRUISER

APPEARANCES I, CW **MANUFACTURER**
Corellian Engineering Corporation **MODEL**
Consular-class space cruiser **TYPE** Cruiser

Built in the great orbital shipyards of the
Corellian Engineering Corporation, the

115-meter- (377.2-foot-) long *Consular*-
class Republic Cruiser is used by the
Supreme Chancellor, members of the
Galactic Senate, and the Jedi Order for
diplomatic missions. The cruiser's striking
scarlet color scheme declares the ship's

diplomatic immunity. Typically
unarmed, the cruiser features three
powerful Dyne 577 radial atomizer engines,
a Longe Voltrans tri-arc CD-3.2 hyperdrive,
and sturdy deflector shields as protection.
The bridge is located in the cruiser's

forward section, just above an
interchangeable diplomatic salon pod,
which can eject from the cruiser in the
event of emergencies.

Federation flotilla
When the Republic's ambassadors emerge from
hyperspace and approach the blockaded world of
Naboo, they find a flotilla of Federation warships
surrounding the peaceful blue and green world.

Communications array
Control signals sustain
a mechanized army.

Centersphere
The main droid-control
computer support
systems are housed in
the ship's center.

Converted freighter
Cavernous hangar
bays carry an entire
invasion army.

Reinforced hull
Irregular armor plating
strengthens the ship's
overall structure.

TRADE FEDERATION BATTLESHIP

APPEARANCES I, II, CW, III **MANUFACTURER**
Hoersch-Kessel Drive Inc. **MODEL** Modified
Lucrehulk-class LH-3210 cargo freighter
TYPE Battleship (converted freighter)

Originally cargo freighters for the
Neimoidian Trade Federation's vast
commercial fleet, Trade Federation
Battleships are over 3 kilometers

(2 miles) in diameter and hold a central
sphere that contains the ship's bridge and
reactor assemblies. Each battleship can
carry 550 MTTs, 6,250 AATs, 1,500 troop
carriers, 50 C-9979 landing craft, and
1,500 droid starfighters. Converting the
freighters into warships was one of the
Neimoidians' first priorities when they
began secretly building their armed forces.

However, the conversion has not been
entirely successful, and these immense,
powerful vessels have a number of
weaknesses. The addition of retractable
turbolasers along the equator of the ship's
hull left large blind spots that small, speedy
enemy vessels could exploit.
The most important vessel in the Trade
Federation's fleet is the Droid Control Ship,

which is used to operate the droid armies.
A Control Ship is distinguished from other
Federation battleships by the large
communications array on its dorsal hull.
Neimoidian commanders typically seal
themselves in the ship's bridge while their
droids handle all ship operations.
Destroying a Control Ship can disable
every droid in the warship's service.

Droid pilots
The effectiveness of droid starfighters has been debated in strategic circles for generations. Although droid starfighters are capable of maneuvers that would pulp even the sturdiest organic pilot, they lack the resourcefulness and cunning that living pilots bring to combat.

Wing/leg
These are locked in starfighter mode during flight.

Droid head
This contains the pilot droid's brain components.

Tapered claw
The wings extend for walker mode.

Torpedo launchers
Energy torpedoes are fired from these channels.

Confederate colors
The blue and white insignia is clearly visible.

Laser armament
Each wing houses two blaster cannons.

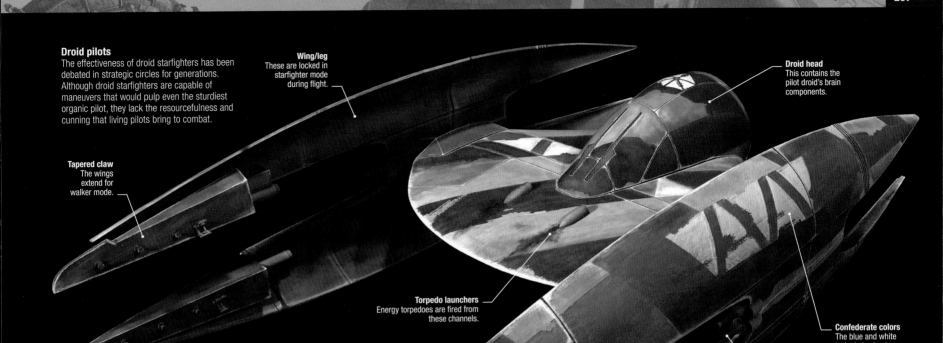

Aerial combat
Droid starfighters are engineered to operate in atmospheric environments as well as outer space.

Ambulatory starfighters
When not in flight mode, droid starfighters transform their configuration so that they can "walk" on their wings.

VULTURE DROID (DROID STARFIGHTER)

APPEARANCES I, CW, III
MANUFACTURER Xi Char Cathedral factories
MODEL Variable Geometry Self-Propelled Battle Droid, Mark I **TYPE** Droid starfighter

The Trade Federation's droid starfighters—also known as vulture droids—were designed and originally manufactured by the Xi Charrians. Like the ground-based battle droid infantry, droid starfighters are controlled by the Trade Federation's Droid Control Ship. When in starfighter mode, the droid carries four blaster cannons in its wings and two energy torpedo launchers

along its forward edge. When not in flight, the droid starfighter can transform into a walking mode, allowing them to be used in surface patrols. When reconfigured for walking, the launchers are angled for anti-personnel use.

Unconventional solid fuel concentrate slugs housed in the aft fuel chamber power the droids. These slugs burn rapidly when

ignited, giving the droid starfighter incredible bursts of energy but a very limited range of operation. As such, droid starfighters must operate from a nearby launch base or capital ship. When not deployed, these starfighters hang from overhead recharging racks. The Trade Federation attempts to counter any shortcomings in their automated vulture

droid designs by dispatching them en masse. The Trade Federation also jealously guards its new innovations and equips the droid starfighter to protect its trade secrets. Should it lose contact with the Droid Control Ship due to a malfunction or other catastrophe, the starfighter's self-destruct mechanism is engaged, preventing it from falling into enemy hands.

TRADE FEDERATION MTT

APPEARANCES I, CW, III
MANUFACTURER Baktoid Armor Workshop
MODEL Multi-Troop Transport (MTT)
TYPE Multi-troop transport

A giant armored repulsorlift vehicle, the MTT is capable of depositing over a hundred battle droid soldiers into the thick of combat. The MTT's bulbous front end

opens to reveal an articulated deployment rack, upon which rest dozens of compressed battle droids. The rack extends forward, releasing the droids into neatly organized rows. Upon activation from an orbiting Droid Control Ship, the droids unfold into their humanoid configuration. The hydraulically powered deployment rack can carry 112 battle droids in stowed configuration.

TRADE FEDERATION LANDING SHIP

APPEARANCES I, CW, III
MANUFACTURER Haor Chall Engineering
MODEL C-9979 landing craft
TYPE Landing craft

With its huge wingspan and imposing loading ramp, the Trade Federation landing ship is a daunting sight. The

ship can hold heavy armor, is capable of carrying a total of 28 troop carriers, 1,114 AATs, and 11 MTTs, and requires a crew of 88 droids. The wings are removable for ease of storage and docking, and when deployed, powerful tensor field generators bind the wings to the craft and strengthen the vessel's structural integrity. Additionally, large repulsorlifts keep the ship from sagging under its own weight.

Landing-zone patrol
During the Naboo invasion, STAP-mounted battle droids survey the Great Grass Plains and transmit data to their Droid Control Ship.

SINGLE TROOPER AERIAL PLATFORM (STAP)

APPEARANCES I, CW
MANUFACTURER Baktoid Armor Workshop
MODEL Single Trooper Aerial Platform
TYPE Patrol vehicle

Deployed by the Trade Federation army's battle droids, STAPs are slim, lightweight reconnaissance and patrol vehicles armed with a pair of blaster cannons. Trade Federation engineers drew inspiration for their design from similar civilian vehicles called airhooks, which they reengineered for greater performance and reliability, and to be specifically piloted by B1 battle droids. High-voltage energy cells fuel the tiny repulsorlift craft's drive turbines, which provide the STAP with impressive speed and maneuverability.

The STAP's greatest weaknesses are its pilot's exposure to enemy fire and its fragility. Though the craft is highly agile, and transmissions from Droid Control Ships skillfully guide droid pilots, a lucky shot can quickly bring down a STAP or its pilot. As such, the vehicles are primarily relegated to patrol, "mopping up" missions, and the occasional foray into battle to harry enemy forces, while the brunt of combat is borne by heavier vehicles.

BONGO

APPEARANCES I, CW
MANUFACTURER Otoh Gunga Bongmeken Cooperative **MODEL** Tribubble bongo sub
TYPE Submarine

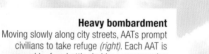

Organically grown through secret Gungan techniques, the bongo is a submersible vehicle used to travel the depths of Naboo's waters. Distinguished by a manta-shaped hull, the bongo's hydrostatic bubble shields keep the cockpit and cargo areas dry and filled with air. A semirigid assembly of tentacle-like fins spins to provide the bongo with thrust. In emergencies, the cockpit module can eject from the sub like an escape pod.

NEIMOIDIAN SHUTTLE

APPEARANCES I, II, CW, III
MANUFACTURER Haor Chall Engineering
MODEL *Sheathipede*-class transport shuttle
TYPE Transport shuttle

The *Sheathipede*-class shuttle is strictly used for short-range transit, either across a planetary surface or for ferrying passengers into orbital space where a larger ship or station awaits its arrival. The shuttle's curved insect-like landing gears lower from the ship's belly, giving the craft's legs a pincer-like appearance as it touches down. Neimoidian officials prefer models with automatic pilots because the absence of a cockpit allows for an expansive passenger cabin.

Heavy bombardment
Moving slowly along city streets, AATs prompt civilians to take refuge *(right)*. Each AAT is crewed by four battle droids: a commander, a pilot, and two gunners *(below)*.

ARMORED ASSAULT TANK (AAT)

APPEARANCES I, CW, III **MANUFACTURER** Baktoid Armor Workshop
MODEL Armored Assault Tank **TYPE** Repulsorlift battle tank

Studded with heavy artillery, the floating tanks known as AATs form the frontline of Trade Federation armored infantry divisions. The AAT's turret-mounted primary laser cannon has long-range destructive capability, and is bracketed by a pair of pylon-mounted secondary laser cannons. A pair of forward-facing short-range blaster cannons round out the AAT's energy-weapon complement. The tank also carries formidable additional weaponry: six energized projectile launchers that fire high-energy shells encased in a cocoon of plasma for incredible speed and penetrative power, specialized armor-piercing warheads, and high explosive "bunker-busting" shells.

Escape from Naboo
In orbit above Naboo, the Naboo Royal Starship's mirror surface reflects its planet of origin and its designers' desire to create a symbol of grace and beauty *(left)*. Sustaining damage after escaping the Trade Federation's blockade of Naboo, Amidala's ship makes an emergency landing on Tatooine *(below left)*.

NABOO ROYAL STARSHIP

APPEARANCES | MANUFACTURER Theed Palace Space Vessel Engineering Corps
MODEL Modified J-type 327 Nubian starship
TYPE Transport

Boasting a strikingly beautiful design that embodies the craftsmanship that prevails in the peaceful years of the Republic, the Naboo Royal Starship is at Queen Amidala's disposal for formal state visits to other planetary representatives and for royal events on Naboo. The streamlined J-type 327 Nubian vessel lacks any offensive weaponry, but does feature powerful shields and a high-performance hyperdrive. Although Naboo tradition encourages the reigning monarch to personally name the royal vessel, Amidala—by the time of the Battle of Naboo—has more important concerns than the ship's name.

The Royal Starship's unique spaceframe is handcrafted at Theed but designed around the imported Nubian sublight engine and hyperdrive propulsion system. Nubian systems are often sought by discriminating buyers and are easily acquired on most civilized worlds, but can be difficult to obtain on remote planets. The ship's gleaming finish is purely decorative and made of royal chromium, a substance usually reserved for vessels serving Naboo's monarch. The mirrored hull is hand-polished and crafted by fine artisans, not by automatons or factory equipment. The ship's interior is made with equal care and is quite spacious. From fore to aft, the vessel contains luxurious royal quarters; a forward hold; a main hold with tech station; the cockpit, which is accessible via turbolift; and the throne room, where Queen Amidala sits while in transit or to receive guests. Naboo citizens consider the entire ship a work of art.

Ready for action
Few pilots in Naboo's Space Fighter Corps have actual combat experience, but their rigorous training prepares them for the battle against the Trade Federation.

NABOO N-1 STARFIGHTER

APPEARANCES I, II, CW, III, VI
MANUFACTURER Theed Palace Space Vessel Engineering Corps **MODEL** Royal N-1
TYPE Starfighter

Starfighter hit!
Although N-1 starfighters are fast and agile, they are also prone to uncontrollable spins when the engines suffer damage.

Protecting the skies and space around Naboo, the N-1 starfighter—like the Royal Naboo Starship—exemplifies the philosophy of blending art and function seen throughout Naboo technology. Its twin radial J-type engines are capped in gleaming chrome and trail long delicate finials behind the ship's single-pilot compartment. Behind the pilot, a standard astromech droid plugs into a ventrally fed socket that requires the droid to compress its legs slightly and telescopically extend its domed head through a dorsal port. The fighter features twin blaster cannons, twin fire-linked torpedo launchers, and an automatic piloting system.

ANAKIN'S RADON-ULZER PODRACER

APPEARANCES | **MANUFACTURER** Radon-Ulzer (engines) **MODEL** Customized repulsorlift vehicle **TYPE** Podracer

Built in secret by the young slave Anakin Skywalker, the shiny blue and silver podracer is smaller and leaner than all the other competing podracers in the Boonta Eve Classic. Anakin's podracer follows the same basic design found throughout the sport: a pod with a cockpit pulled by two high-powered engines. Energy binders lock the engines to each other, and durable Steelton control cables connect the engines to the pod. Seated in the cockpit, a pod pilot operates thruster bars that control power to the engines, and speeds can reach well over 800 kilometers (497 miles) per hour.

Because podracer pilots differ greatly in shape, size, and weight, the pods are heavily customized to match the requirements of the individual pilots.

Pilots must have incredibly quick reflexes and very strong nerves. Anakin is the only known human to ever pilot a podracer and survive. Unlike other pilots, who invest in larger engines in the hopes of getting greater performance, Anakin salvages a pair of Radon-Ulzer 620C racing engines that his junk-dealer master, Watto, discarded, deeming them too burned out to be of any use.

Anakin develops a new fuel atomizer and distribution system that sends more fuel into the Radon-Ulzer's combustion chambers, radically increasing their thrust and his racer's top speed to almost 950 kilometers (590 miles) per hour, which is a testament to his engineering brilliance.

Race to the finish
Anakin's Radon-Ulzer engines are capped with a trio of bright yellow air scoops that provide additional control when braking and cornering. Despite the dastardly antics of his nemesis, Sebulba, Anakin remains focused on winning the Boonta.

SEBULBA'S PODRACER

APPEARANCES | **MANUFACTURER** Collor Pondrat (engines) **MODEL** Customized repulsorlift vehicle **TYPE** Podracer

If reputable podracing officials were to examine Sebulba's podracer closely, they would classify it as illegal. His oversized Collor Pondrat Plug-F Mammoth Split-X engines, 7.8 meters (25.6 feet) in length, can achieve a top speed of 829 kilometers (515 miles) per hour. The engines are fueled by tradium power fluid pressurized with quold runium and activated with ionized injectrine. Sebulba takes pleasure in using a concealed flamethrower against competitors who dare to pass him, blasting them off course and ensuring his victory.

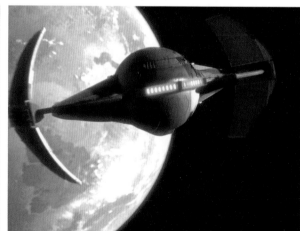

SITH INFILTRATOR

APPEARANCES | **MANUFACTURER** Republic Sienar Systems **MODEL** Heavily modified Star Courier **TYPE** Armed star courier

Customized in a secret laboratory, the Sith Infiltrator, dubbed the *Scimitar*, is the personal spacecraft for Darth Maul. The craft, 26.5 meters (86.9 feet) in length, with folding angular wings and a rounded bridge compartment, is equipped with many weapons and instruments of evil, including six laser cannons, spying and surveillance gear, interrogator droids, and Maul's speeder bike. Powered by a curious high-temperature ion engine sublight drive system, the craft's most impressive feature is its full-effect cloaking device, which makes it invisible.

SITH SPEEDER

APPEARANCES | **MANUFACTURER** Razalon **MODEL** Modified Razalon FC-20 speeder bike **TYPE** Speeder bike

A pared-down crescent-shaped conveyance, Darth Maul's Sith Speeder, alias the *Bloodfin*, lacks weapons or a sensor array, diverting all of the vehicle's energy to speed. Maul uses probe droids to find his prey, and then programs his speeder to decelerate and enter a "wait mode" should he suddenly dismount.

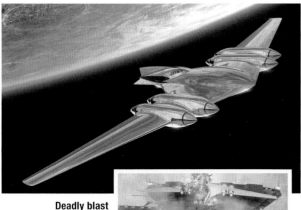

Deadly blast
The Royal Cruiser *(above)* takes a direct hit on Coruscant *(right)*.

NABOO ROYAL CRUISER

APPEARANCES II **MANUFACTURER** Theed Palace Space Vessel Engineering Corps **MODEL** Custom-built J-type diplomatic barge **TYPE** Transport (diplomatic barge)

Like the Royal Starship used by the Queen of Naboo, this chrome-hulled cruiser is a J-type vessel constructed by the Theed Palace Space Vessel Engineering Corps. The shortcomings of the previous Nubian J-type 327 are addressed with improved shield generators and paired S-6 hyperdrive generators providing adequate backup for the superluminal drive. The unarmed transport often travels under escort and can function as a fighter carrier craft, carrying up to four N-1 starfighters fitted into recharge sockets along the leading edge of its wing.

ZAM'S AIRSPEEDER

APPEARANCES II **MANUFACTURER** Desler Gizh Outworld Mobility Corporation **MODEL** Koro-2 all-environment Exodrive airspeeder **TYPE** Airspeeder

A lean getaway vessel with a pressurized cabin, Zam Wesell's airspeeder features an uncommon external electromagnetic propulsion system. The forward mandibles irradiate the air around them, inducing ionization and making it conductive. Paired electrodes electrify the airstream and magnetically propel it toward the rear of the craft, resulting in the air dragging the vessel through the skies at speeds of 800 kilometers (497 miles) per hour.

ANAKIN'S AIRSPEEDER

APPEARANCES II **MANUFACTURER** Custom special (Narglatch AirTech kit) **MODEL** XJ-6 **TYPE** Luxury airspeeder hot rod

On Coruscant, Anakin commandeers a sleek, open-cockpit airspeeder to pursue the assassin Zam Wesell. The speeder's owner, a wealthy representative of the Vorzyd sector, customized the vehicle with twin turbojet engines originally designed to function in groups of 50 aboard the gigantic bank-courier repulsor trucks of Aargau. The engines direct pressurized air through a series of thrust ducts to propel the craft.

Hyperspace booster
After the Delta-7 docks with the hyperdrive booster ring, the astromech transmits destination coordinates to the ring's navicomputer.

Enclosed cockpit
Modular options can accommodate human or alien pilots.

Bow sensors
Delta-7's bow houses scanning and communications technology.

Starfighter strikeforce
During the Clone Wars, Jedi pilots and their faithful astromechs fly Delta-7s on many missions throughout the galaxy.

JEDI STARFIGHTER

APPEARANCES II, CW, III
MANUFACTURER Kuat Systems Engineering
MODEL Delta-7 *Aethersprite*-class light interceptor **TYPE** Light interceptor starfighter

Although Jedi generally use Republic Cruisers for missions across the galaxy, some assignments call for less conspicuous transports. For this reason, and because Jedi cannot always depend on pilots to take them to their destination, all Jedi learn how to pilot starships as part of their training. Prior to the outbreak of the Clone Wars, Kuat Systems Engineering unveiled the Delta-7 Jedi starfighter. A wedge-shaped, single-person craft, the Delta-7 is equipped with dual laser cannons, two secondary ion cannons, and a powerful deflector shield. Despite the craft's armaments, most Jedi pilots prefer to rely on their cunning and attunement to the Force to avoid disputes and aggression, and they use weapons as a last resort.

Because the Delta-7 is too small to hold a standard navicomputer and hyperdrive, it relies on a truncated astromech droid, hard-wired into the starfighter's port side, for storing navigational data, and a TransGalMeg Industries booster ring for transit through hyperspace. The astromech also provides diagnostic and repair service to the craft, as well as managing the secondary scanning and communications gear. Kuat Systems Engineering also produced the variant design of the dart-shaped starfighter: the Delta-7B *Aethersprite*-class interceptor. The Delta-7B relocated the astromech socket from the port side to just fore of the cockpit, and had a slightly enlarged hull to accommodate a full-size astromech droid. Both Anakin and Obi-Wan piloted Delta-7Bs during the Clone Wars.

Unusual design

An antiquated and extremely rare *Firespray-31*-class patrol and attack craft, *Slave I* is a distinctive-looking vessel. A large engine cluster dominates the lower section of the ship when docked, with the cabin resting atop. Once airborne, *Slave I* pivots 90 degrees and its base becomes its trailing edge, while its top-mounted cockpit faces forward. *Slave I* is armed with twin blaster cannons, as well as concealed projectile launchers and a seismic charge deployer, a turret-mounted tractor beam projector, a pair of proton torpedo launchers, concussion missile tubes, and a powerful ion cannon.

"Get him, Dad! Get him! Fire!" BOBA FETT

SLAVE I

Inherited by the bounty hunter Boba Fett from his father Jango, the pursuit vessel *Slave I* has sophisticated anti-detection gear that ensures very few fugitives ever see their captor coming.

APPEARANCES II, CW, V **MANUFACTURER** Kuat Systems Engineering **MODEL** Modified *Firespray-31*-class patrol and attack craft **TYPE** Pursuit vessel

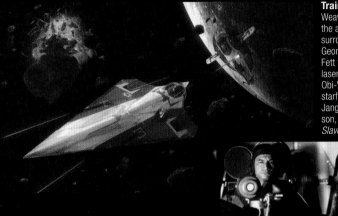

Training Boba
Weaving through the asteroid belt surrounding Geonosis, Jango Fett fires *Slave I*'s laser cannons at Obi-Wan's Jedi starfighter *(left)*. Jango teaches his son, Boba, to pilot *Slave I (below)*.

Getaway starship
After rescuing young Jedi from General Grievous on Florrum, Hondo Ohnaka commandeers *Slave I* into space.

FAMILY LEGACY

After an assassination assignment goes wrong for Jango Fett on Coruscant, the Jedi Obi-Wan Kenobi tracks Jango to Tipoca City on the water world Kamino. Jango and Boba board *Slave I* and escape to the Geonosis system, but when they realize the Jedi has pursued them, Jango launches seismic charges at Obi-Wan's starfighter. When Boba Fett eventually inherits *Slave I*, he remembers his father's deadly tactics and learns many more.

PIRATE PROPERTY

On the planet Florrum, a team of Jedi captures Boba, and Aurra Sing crashes *Slave I* while attempting to escape. The Weequay pirate Hondo Ohnaka salvages the vessel, repaints it, and adds it to his collection of starships. But after General Grievous and his droid army invade Florrum and capture Ohnaka, the Jedi Ahsoka Tano and a band of Jedi younglings rescue Ohnaka, and they escape in *Slave I*. Eventually, Boba regains ownership of *Slave I* and modifies it to transform it into the ultimate vessel for bounty hunting.

Airlock
Standing in *Slave I*'s airlock, Bossk and Aurra Sing wait for Boba to exit the clone cadets' escape pod.

Valuable cargo
Anticipating a big payout from Jabba, Boba oversees the Bespin guards who load Han onto *Slave I*.

BOBA FETT'S CREW

After the Battle of Geonosis, Boba seeks vengeance against Mace Windu, the Jedi who struck down his father. He forms an alliance with the bounty hunters Aurra Sing and Bossk, who help him infiltrate a group of clone cadets scheduled to meet Mace on the Republic Star Destroyer *Endurance*. Boba fails to kill Mace, but critically damages the *Endurance* and winds up in an escape pod with a group of cadets. Sing and Bossk rescue Boba from the pod, and together they set another trap for Mace on the planet Vanqor.

CAPTURING HAN SOLO

On Tatooine, Boba is present when Jabba the Hutt threatens to put a bounty on the smuggler Han Solo unless he pays arrears. Shortly after the Battle of Hoth, Darth Vader also places a bounty on Han, and Boba sees an opportunity to profit twice. Piloting *Slave I*, Boba stalks Han's freighter from the Anoat system and alerts Vader that Han is heading for Cloud City. Boba and Vader arrive on Cloud City before Han and easily capture the smuggler, along with his rebel allies. After Vader freezes Han in carbonite, he allows Boba to load Han's frozen form onto *Slave I* and proceed to Tatooine, where Boba delivers Han to Jabba and collects the second bounty.

Staying in touch
The ship contains a communications chamber for conducting important senatorial business.

Royal sheen
The unmistakable silver finish of Padmé's ship announces her status as a former monarch and a highly influential politician. Here she touches down on Rodia on a diplomatic visit.

Silver finish indicates
Naboo royalty

PADMÉ'S STARSHIP

APPEARANCES II, CW **MANUFACTURER** Theed Palace Space Vessel Engineering Corps **MODEL** H-type Nubian yacht **TYPE** Luxury space yacht

The sleek yacht used by Padmé Amidala during the Clone Wars lacks weapons, but has a powerful engine bank and a strong deflector shield generator. Padmé receives the vessel after a failed assassination attempt on Coruscant destroys her royal cruiser. Senator Amidala uses her new starship to travel with Anakin Skywalker to Tatooine and Geonosis, where she witnesses the opening battle between the Republic and the Separatists. Padmé's original starship is lost when she intentionally overloads its engines to disable the Separatist cruiser *Malevolence*.

Long range
Padmé's starship is both speedy and capable of sustained travel across the galaxy, a necessity when making political visits in person.

Scrap heap
The main hold of a sandcrawler is full of half-fixed machinery and random junk.

SANDCRAWLER

APPEARANCES II, IV **MANUFACTURER** Various **MODEL** Sandcrawler **TYPE** Mobile desert base

Sandcrawlers are massive vehicles that crisscross the deserts of Tatooine on their wide treads. They are operated by tribes of glowing-eyed Jawas, who use the sandcrawlers as homes, workshops, and trash repositories. If a Jawa locates a droid that doesn't appear to have an owner, a scouting party will disable the roaming automaton while a magnetic tube sucks it inside the sandcrawler for storage. Jawa sandcrawlers frequently visit moisture farms, where they offer up their goods at impromptu auctions, though the merchandise for sale is usually of questionable quality. Sandcrawlers' thick armor is a reliable defense against sandstorms, but it can't stand up to sustained blaster fire from Imperial stormtroopers. The droids R2-D2 and C-3PO briefly spend time aboard a sandcrawler before the Jawas that seized the pair sell them to Owen Lars. When the Empire tracks the droids to that particular Jawa tribe, they reduce the sandcrawler to a smoking ruin, which is later discovered by Luke Skywalker and Obi-Wan Kenobi.

Sandcrawler on the horizon
For most Tatooine settlers, sandcrawlers are the only way they can resupply their equipment. Jawas sometimes sell rare goods and will travel to even the farthest homesteads.

OG-9 HOMING SPIDER DROID

APPEARANCES II, III **MANUFACTURER** Baktoid Armor Workshop
TYPE OG-9 homing spider droid **AFFILIATION** Separatists

The OG-9 homing spider droid is a gigantic walker used by the Separatists throughout the Clone Wars. The homing spider droid moves slowly on four mechanical legs, with a powerful reactor situated in the heart of its spherical body. The top-mounted laser emplacement releases sustained-fire shots that quickly wear down a target's shields, while a bottom-mounted laser cannon keeps infantry at bay. Homing spider droids see action during the Battle of Geonosis, blasting away at Republic AT-TEs and formations of clone troopers.

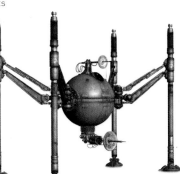

Armored hull plating

Command bridge

Warship
The *Acclamator* became the Republic's premier battleship at the start of the Clone Wars.

REPUBLIC ASSAULT SHIP (*ACCLAMATOR*-CLASS)

APPEARANCES II, CW **MANUFACTURER** Rothana Heavy Engineering **MODEL** *Acclamator*-class assault ship
TYPE Assault ship

The Republic assault ship is also known as the *Acclamator*. More than 700 meters (2,296.5 feet) long, it becomes the Republic's primary troop carrier at the start of the Clone Wars and also fills an offensive role against the Separatist navy. Each assault ship is armed with laser cannons, turbolaser turrets, concussion missiles, and heavy torpedoes, and carries ground vehicles such as AT-TE walkers. The *Acclamator* is capable of both ground and water landings.

Atmospheric escort
The LAAT/i gunship fills a crucial role for the Republic military, serving as both a troop carrier and an escort for ground and aerial forces. When hovering, the LAAT/i is an elevated gun platform.

Providing cover
Not only is the LAAT/i heavily armed with anti-personnel and anti-vehicle lasers, but the clone troopers who ride in it can also fire at targets using their blaster rifles.

REPUBLIC LAAT/i REPULSOR GUNSHIP

APPEARANCES II, CW, III **MANUFACTURER** Rothana Heavy Engineering
MODEL Low Altitude Assault Transport/infantry **TYPE** Repulsorlift gunship

The Republic gunship is also known as the LAAT/i, for Low Altitude Assault Transport/infantry. First deployed during the Battle of Geonosis, the gunship becomes one of the most familiar Republic military vehicles during the Clone Wars. A standard gunship can carry up to 30 clone troopers and is operated by a pilot and forward gunner. Two additional clone troopers operate the bubble turrets that swing out from the troop cabin. Two more turrets are located on each wing, while three smaller laser cannons are used to scatter enemy infantry. The gunship is excellent at destroying enemy vehicles such as hailfire droids with the missiles released from the underside of each wing. A gunship can reach speeds of up to 620 kilometers (385 miles) per hour. Clone troopers grow fond of their gunships during the Clone Wars and sometimes customize them with colorful nose art.

Lonely quest
Anakin Skywalker uses a speeder bike to travel
across the sands of Tatooine while searching for
his mother. A Jawa leaves the safety of his
sandcrawler to answer Anakin's questions

THE SEARCH FOR SHMI

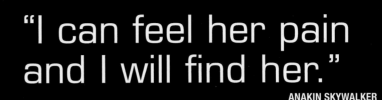

"I can feel her pain and I will find her."

ANAKIN SKYWALKER

When Anakin Skywalker learns his mother is a prisoner of the savage Tusken Raiders, he sets off across the sands of Tatooine to find her.

Just before the Clone Wars, Anakin Skywalker returns to Tatooine for the first time since abandoning the desert world a decade earlier to join the Jedi Order. Arriving with Padmé Amidala in her gleaming silver starship, he begins his exploration in the city of Mos Espa. Anakin and Padmé are ferried through the streets by a rickshaw-pulling droid until they arrive at Watto's workshop. The aging Toydarian tells Anakin that he sold Shmi Skywalker—Anakin's mother—to a local farmer who later married her. Anakin follows the trail to the Lars moisture farm, meeting his new stepfather Cliegg Lars, Cliegg's son Owen, and Owen's girlfriend Beru. But Shmi is nowhere to be found. Cliegg, now using a hover-chair after losing his leg to a Tusken Raider trap, breaks the news that Shmi is a Tusken captive and that all attempts to locate her have failed.

TOO LATE THE HERO

Anakin is determined to find his mother and takes a speeder bike into the Tatooine wastes to look for clues. A Jawa sandcrawler helps point him in the right direction. When he finally discovers the location of Shmi's captors, Anakin discovers that she has been so badly mistreated by the Tuskens that she is close to death. He has arrived too late to save her and, in despair, watches her die. Consumed with vengeance, Anakin forgets his Jedi training and slaughters every single one of the Tusken Raiders in the camp, before loading his mother's body on the back of the speeder bike and racing back to Lars' farm.

Royal landing
Padmé's sleek starship is an unusual sight on dusty Tatooine. Padmé parks the vessel below ground in a secure docking bay to hide the silvery ship from potential thieves.

Rapid deployment
The AT-TE carrier drops off its cargo and gets itself to safety as quickly as possible.

Thrust
Twin engines can reach maximum speeds of 620 kilometers (385 miles) per hour.

Flying solo
A single clone trooper pilots the carrier into enemy territory.

Personalized paint job
Clone troopers often decorate carriers with colorful nose artwork.

Firepower
Swiveling laser cannons are operated from the cockpit.

Clone Wars service
LAAT/c carriers participated in the Battle of Geonosis and returned to the planet later in the war to destroy a droid factory.

"...make sure you get yourself to that landing zone in one piece."
ANAKIN SKYWALKER

AT-TE CARRIER

APPEARANCES II, CW **MANUFACTURER** Rothana Heavy Engineering **MODEL** Low Altitude Assault Transport Carrier **TYPE** Repulsorlift gunship

The LAAT/c, for Low Altitude Assault Transport carrier, is a specialty variant of the LAAT gunship used to transport AT-TEs into battle. After latching onto an AT-TE with powerful magnetic clamps, the vessel's pilot ferries the heavy cargo to a designated drop zone and releases the vehicle. Two laser cannons mounted on the nose provide defense during vulnerable drop-offs.

Main cannon
The AT-TE's primary weapon has its own dedicated gunner who sits above the vehicle's hull.

Command center
The command cabin houses the pilot and spotter.

Firepower
Forward guns are effective against battle droids.

All terrain
Footpads can be magnetized for scaling metal walls.

Tanks advance
Manufactured in great numbers during the Clone Wars, AT-TEs are the backbone of Republic ground operations from the Core to the Outer Rim.

AT-TE (ALL TERRAIN TACTICAL ENFORCER)

APPEARANCES II, CW, III **MANUFACTURER** Rothana Heavy Engineering
MODEL All Terrain Tactical Enforcer **TYPE** Walker

The All Terrain Tactical Enforcer is an early example of walker technology used to great effect on the battlefield. The six-legged tanks are both assault vehicles and transports and can carry up to 20 clone troopers. Each AT-TE is operated by a crew of seven, made up of a pilot, a spotter, four gunners, and one cannon operator. The top-mounted mass-driver cannon has a slow rate of fire, but six smaller laser cannons mounted on the AT-TE's hull provide defense against enemy infantry.

Providing support
The AT-TE is excellent when used in conjunction with infantry, since it can lay down covering fire from an elevated angle.

HAILFIRE DROID

APPEARANCES II **MANUFACTURER** Haor Chall
Engineering **MODEL** IG-227 *Hailfire*-class droid
tank **TYPE** Tank

The IG-227 *Hailfire*-class droid tank is easily
identified by its treaded, hoop-like drive
wheels. The InterGalactic Banking Clan
commissioned the construction of the hailfire
prior to the Clone Wars, and the units saw
their first combat against Republic troops
during the Battle of Geonosis. A hailfire is
an armored missile platform best used to
destroy enemy vehicles. Each of the two
launchers mounted on a hailfire can hold
up to 15 guided missiles.

Rolling into battle
The hailfire is also called the wheel droid due to its
maneuverable and speedy drive system *(below)*.
Each missile from the droid leaves behind a trail of
black exhaust that darkens the sky *(right)*.

SPHA-T

APPEARANCES II **MANUFACTURER** Rothana
Heavy Engineering **MODEL** Self-Propelled
Heavy Artillery Turbolaser
TYPE Heavy Artillery

The 12-legged SPHA-T is one of the
biggest ground guns in the Republic's

imposing arsenal. Each SPHA-T is
operated by a crew of 30 clone troopers
and only uses its legs when maneuvering
between firing positions. When attacking
an enemy target, the SPHA-T remains
motionless to give the gunners added
precision for aiming the extraordinarily
heavy turbolaser beam.

GEONOSIAN STARFIGHTER

APPEARANCES II, CW **MANUFACTURER** Huppla
Pasa Tisc Shipwrights Collective
MODEL *Nantex*-class territorial defense starfighter
TYPE Starfighter

The needle-shaped *Nantex*-class starfighter
is the primary defensive craft of the insectoid
inhabitants of Geonosis. A single laser cannon
is mounted between the upper and lower
prongs that make up the starfighter's nose,
and 100 tiny tractor beam projectors aid in
precision aiming and grappling with enemy
vessels at close range.

Holding the line
Republic attack cruisers,
the primary defense against
the Separatists, become
commonly known as Jedi
cruisers during the war.

SOLAR SAILER

APPEARANCES II, CW **MANUFACTURER**
Huppla Pasa Tisc Shipwrights Collective
MODEL *Punworcca·116*-class interstellar sloop
TYPE Star yacht

Count Dooku's unique craft relies on a
retractable sail to collect stray interstellar
energies, which are directed to the ship's
engines to provide a near-limitless source
of fuel. The main body of the ship is a

luxurious sloop with a design that
closely resembles that of the Geonosian
starfighter—no surprise, as Dooku had
the foresight to commission the vessel
from his allies on Geonosis prior to the
outbreak of the Clone Wars. Dooku
uses an FA-4 pilot droid to handle
takeoffs and landings. Within the sailer,
a secure holonet transceiver allows the
Count to communicate with his Master,
Darth Sidious.

REPUBLIC ATTACK CRUISER

APPEARANCES CW, III **MANUFACTURER**
Kuat Drive Yards **MODEL** *Venator*-class Star
Destroyer **TYPE** Star Destroyer

The Republic attack cruiser is also known
as the *Venator*-class Star Destroyer and is
one of the first examples of the triangular
warships that would become a terrifying
symbol of Imperial power. First deployed
during the Clone Wars, Republic attack
cruisers quickly become the most
powerful capital ships in the Republic
navy. Each vessel serves double duty as
both a battleship and a starfighter carrier,

with armaments including heavy turbolasers,
laser cannons, proton torpedo launchers,
and tractor beam projectors. The vessel's
flight deck is built directly into the prow,
providing a 0.5-kilometer- (0.3-mile-)
long runway that allows starfighters to
scramble into space the instant the bow
doors are opened. An attack cruiser carries
more than 420 starfighters, 40 gunships,
and 24 AT-TEs, and operates with a crew
of more than 7,400 personnel. Throughout
the Clone Wars, Republic attack cruisers
remain on the frontlines, keeping the space
lanes free of Separatist interference and
providing cover for landing parties of Jedi
and clone troopers.

BANKING CLAN COMMUNICATIONS FRIGATE

APPEARANCES CW, III **MANUFACTURER**
Hoersch-Kessel Drive **MODEL** *Munificent*-class
star frigate **TYPE** Frigate

The InterGalactic Banking Clan operates
the *Munificent*-class frigate as both
a warship and a communications
vessel. It is equipped for secure
ship-to-ship transmissions
and the jamming of
enemy signals. Each
frigate is operated
by 200 crewers

**Hangar bays for
starfighters**

**Elongated wings
support defensive
weaponry**

but can carry up to 150,000 battle droids and
often skimps on life-support systems due to
the small size of its crew. Laser cannons, twin
turbolasers, and ion cannons allow the frigate
to put up a fight against enemy capital ships.

STEALTH SHIP

APPEARANCES CW **MANUFACTURER** Sienar Design Systems
MODEL Prototype stealth model **TYPE** Corvette

An experimental vessel developed by the Republic during the
Clone Wars, the prototype stealth ship incorporates a cloaking
device that renders it invisible. The stealth ship is outfitted with
communications antennas and defensive gun turrets, and
features an array of countermeasures to escape detection or
shake homing missiles. During the blockade of Christophsis by
the Separatists, the Republic deploys the stealth ship to allow a
crew to reach the surface undetected and assist in Senator Bail
Organa's relief mission. Anakin Skywalker decides to engage the
leader of the Separatist blockade, Admiral Trench, using the
ship's cloak to hide from Trench's sensors.

HYENA BOMBER

APPEARANCES CW **MANUFACTURER** Baktoid Armor
Workshop **MODEL** *Hyena*-class bomber **TYPE** Bomber

Separatists use the *Hyena* bomber to attack
warships and surface installations with high-yield
explosive warheads. *Hyena* bombers are rarely
seen during the Clone Wars, but do participate
in the Battles of Christophsis and Ryloth. Like
the Separatist *Vulture*-class starfighter, the *Hyena*
bomber is controlled by a droid intelligence and
is capable of splitting its wings and entering
a "walking mode." The *Hyena* bomber carries
armaments such as proton bombs, proton
torpedoes, and concussion missiles, all stored
in a ventral bomb bay.

Walking mode
The *Hyena* bomber uses its wings as limbs
when taxiing from one surface location to another.

ALL TERRAIN RECON TRANSPORT (AT-RT)

APPEARANCES CW, III **MANUFACTURER**
Kuat Drive Yards **MODEL** All Terrain Recon
Transport **TYPE** Scout walker

The AT-RT, or All Terrain Recon
Transport, is a bipedal walker built
for a single operator. The open
cockpit offers little protection to its
clone trooper driver, but the AT-RT
is speedy and sure-footed as a
reconnaissance vehicle. Its
chin-mounted laser cannon is
useful against battle droids, but too
weak to damage heavy vehicles.
Communications antennas allow
the AT-RT to transmit battlefield
intelligence. The Republic
uses AT-RTs throughout
the Clone Wars, including
at the Battle of Ryloth and during the
hunt for Master Yoda on Kashyyyk
following Order 66.

Ease of use
Simple controls are
similar to those of
speeder bikes.

Two-legged mobility
AT-RTs are able to handle many
types of planetary surfaces, ideal
for Republic troopers during the
galaxy-spanning Clone Wars.

Stability
A gyroscopic
system allows
the AT-RT to keep
its balance.

BARC SPEEDER

APPEARANCES CW, III **MANUFACTURER**
Aratech Repulsor Company **MODEL** Biker
Advanced Recon Commando speeder
TYPE Speeder bike

A swift reconnaissance vehicle, the
BARC speeder is named for the
specialized clone drivers who operate it.
Most BARC speeders are painted in the
traditional red and white colors of the
Republic Army, though some bear brown
or green camouflage markings. Each is
equipped with a forward-facing blaster
cannon and a repulsorlift engine capable
of reaching speeds up to 520 kilometers

In formation
Clone troopers use BARC speeders when scouting
unfamiliar terrain *(top)* and patrol in groups in
case of trouble *(above)*.

(323 miles) per hour. On Saleucami, Jedi
General Stass Allie pilots a BARC speeder
when her escorts suddenly receive
Order 66. The pursuing clone troopers
blast her BARC speeder, killing her.

TRIDENT DRILL ASSAULT CRAFT

APPEARANCES CW **MANUFACTURER** Colicoid Creation Nest **MODEL** *Trident*-class assault ship **TYPE** Gunship

The Trident drill assault craft is a Separatist gunship built for underwater operation, capable of drilling through the hulls of enemy vessels and installations. In the Battles of Kamino and Mon Calamari during the Clone Wars, Tridents attack with their drills and laser cannons while releasing squads of aqua droids from their holds.

Armored tentacles equipped with magnetic grapples

KHETANNA

APPEARANCES CW, VI **MANUFACTURER** Ubrikkian Industries **MODEL** Customized luxury sail barge **TYPE** Sail barge

Jabba's luxury sail barge, the *Khetanna*, is used by the Hutt crime lord whenever he leaves his palace to visit other parts of Tatooine. The vessel is driven by a repulsorlift engine in conjunction with two huge sails on the upper deck. Jabba never suffers the slightest discomfort inside the sail barge's vast interior, which is always packed with musicians, dancers, and staff serving refreshments. The *Khetanna* is protected by a huge blaster cannon and several smaller blasters mounted on the side railings.

Service vehicle
From his sail barge, Jabba the Hutt watches the executions of prisoners in shaded comfort *(above)*. Jabba's sail barge has been in use since the Clone Wars and is always accompanied by armed guards on desert skiffs *(left)*.

DESERT SKIFF

APPEARANCES CW, VI **MANUFACTURER** Ubrikkian Industries **MODEL** Bantha-II cargo skiff **TYPE** Repulsorlift skiff

Skiffs are common modes of transportation that operate using anti-gravity repulsorlifts. Most are used for moving cargo, but they can easily carry passengers. Jabba the Hutt uses a number of rugged skiffs equipped to survive the heat and sandstorms of the Tatooine deserts. The Bantha-II cargo skiffs have an elongated deck with a safety railing designed to protect passengers or cargo. The skiffs are piloted from a rear control station, and at their maximum speed, they can exceed 250 kilometers (155.3 miles) per hour.

Smooth flying
Controls in the rear of the skiff are designed to be operated by a single pilot.

Reinforced bow
The armored nose is built to withstand head-on collisions.

Botched execution
At the Great Pit of Carkoon, Jabba's skiff guards make a big mistake when they try to force Luke to walk the plank.

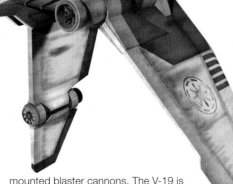

Deployed
During flight, the V-19 makes a three-pointed silhouette *(right)*. Clone troopers receive orders from Anakin Skywalker, with their V-19s waiting on the hangar deck *(bottom)*.

V-19 TORRENT STARFIGHTER

APPEARANCES CW **MANUFACTURER** Slayn & Korpil **MODEL** V-19 Torrent starfighter **TYPE** Starfighter

The V-19 Torrent is one of the fastest and most maneuverable starfighters used by the Republic during the Clone Wars. Its folding S-foils provide stability and a wider area of fire for its two wing-mounted blaster cannons. The V-19 is also outfitted with concussion missile launchers that can home in on targets. Though primarily flown by Republic clone pilots, V-19s are also used by Jedi commanders. During the Battle of Ryloth, Ahsoka Tano leads a squadron against the Separatists.

CORPORATE ALLIANCE NR-N99 PERSUADER TANK DROID

APPEARANCES CW, III **MANUFACTURER** Techno Union **MODEL** NR-N99 *Persuader*-class droid enforcer **TYPE** Droid tank

The NR-N99 *Persuader*-class tank droid is a Separatist war vehicle primarily used by the Corporate Alliance. It is driven by a huge central tread and supported on either side by forward-mounted outriggers. The tank can reach speeds of up to 60 kilometers (37.3 miles) per hour, useful for ramming barricades. Controlled by a built-in droid intelligence, it is armed with ion cannons, heavy repeating blasters, and missile launchers. NR-N99s lead the assault against a Wookiee city during the Battle of Kashyyyk.

TWILIGHT

APPEARANCES CW **MANUFACTURER**
Corellian Engineering Corporation
MODEL G9 Rigger freighter
TYPE Space freighter

The *Twilight* serves Anakin Skywalker and other Republic heroes as a faithful transport ship throughout the Clone Wars. Originally owned by Ziro the Hutt, the G9 Rigger space freighter is found by Anakin and his Padawan Ahsoka Tano on the planet Teth. The two Jedi steal the vessel and use it to ferry Jabba the Hutt's young son, Rotta, to Tatooine. When MagnaGuards attack, Anakin is forced to crash-land the *Twilight* into the desert sands. He later retrieves it, and the *Twilight* sees action in the Battle of the Kaliida Nebula and the raid on Skytop Station. The *Twilight* meets its final fate on Mandalore, when Obi-Wan Kenobi uses the vessel to try to escape a group of Death Watch soldiers. After the ship suffers critical hits from missile strikes, Obi-Wan and Duchess Satine evacuate the *Twilight* and it crashes into the surface below.

The *Twilight* is well-armed for a freighter, featuring three heavy blaster cannons mounted on the wings and a rotating laser cannon operated from a periscope sight. Additionally, a concussion missile launcher provides explosive punch against large warships. The *Twilight*'s most distinctive feature is its long outrigger wing, which extends from the starboard side of the main cabin and contains two secondary engines. A lower wing can be folded up during landing and extended during flight. The ship is designed to haul cargo and consequently features a tow cable and a rear-opening cargo hatch. The hold is roomy enough to accommodate a Jedi starfighter.

Escape hatch
The rear cargo door can open while in flight to dump sensitive cargo.

Defensive fire
Forward-mounted blaster cannons keep pirates at a distance.

Aerodynamic
Large outrigger wing provides flight stability.

"Grease bucket, you're my favorite ship ever!" AHSOKA TANO

Old but fully armed
The *Twilight*'s engines don't always perform well in planetary atmospheres *(above right)*. With multiple cannons, the *Twilight* is able to hold its own in a fight against those who would raid its holds *(right)*.

TANTIVE IV

APPEARANCES CW, R, IV **MANUFACTURER**
Corellian Engineering Corporation
MODEL CR90 corvette **TYPE** Corvette

The *Tantive IV* is an Alderaan cruiser of Corellian manufacture operated by the Royal House of Alderaan. Ships similar to the *Tantive IV* are sometimes called blockade runners due to their powerful engine banks and ability to race past slow-moving customs vessels. Like other corvettes of its type, the *Tantive IV* sports double turbolaser cannons on the top and bottom of the ship. The antenna dishes of the communications and sensor array are located just ahead of the drive system. Eleven ion turbine engines stacked on top of each other provide impressive sublight thrust. Within the confines of the *Tantive IV* are living quarters for the crew, dining rooms for hosting state dinners, and conference centers for sensitive negotiations with interstellar dignitaries. Escape pods give the passengers a chance to flee if the ship comes under attack.

The *Tantive IV* sees action during the Clone Wars and continues to serve Senator Bail Organa of Alderaan for nearly two decades. When Senator Organa's daughter Leia follows him into politics, the *Tantive IV* becomes her ship. Princess Leia becomes famous for her "mercy missions" to help populations in need, but the Empire suspects she is using the ship to carry out assignments on behalf of the Rebel Alliance. After the *Tantive IV* intercepts a rebel transmission containing the plans for the Death Star, Darth Vader chases the vessel and disables it above Tatooine. The *Tantive IV* is drawn into a Star Destroyer's docking bay and its passengers, including Princess Leia, are captured.

Firefight
The narrow hallways of the *Tantive IV* allow its crew to set up an ambush for a stormtrooper boarding party.

Bridge
The captain of the *Tantive IV* commands the vessel from this reinforced bridge section.

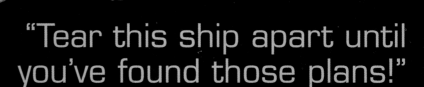

"Tear this ship apart until you've found those plans!"
DARTH VADER

Armed to the teeth
The superstructure is fitted with turbolasers for ship-to-ship defense.

Destructive capacity
The primary ion weapon is powered by the ship's reactor.

MALEVOLENCE

APPEARANCES CW
MANUFACTURER Free Dac Volunteers Engineering Corps
MODEL *Subjugator*-class heavy cruiser
TYPE Heavy cruiser

The *Malevolence* is the flagship of General Grievous. Massive ion cannons give the ship an unprecedented destructive capacity with the release of expanding waves of energy, which disable any ships caught in their path, leaving them vulnerable to the *Malevolence*'s 500 turbolasers. When the *Malevolence* destroys Plo Koon's fleet, Anakin tampers with the ship's navigation and the sabotaged vehicle crashes into a moon.

Superweapon
When fired, the *Malevolence*'s ion cannon releases a wave that interferes with electrical systems and leaves ships drifting in space.

SOULLESS ONE

APPEARANCES CW, III **MANUFACTURER** Feethan Ottraw Scalable Assemblies **MODEL** Belbullab-22 starfighter **TYPE** Starfighter

The personal starfighter of General Grievous, the *Soulless One* is a customized Belbullab-22 starfighter designed for speed and agility when dogfighting. It is armed with two sets of triple rapid-fire laser cannons and features a state-of-the-art hyperdrive allowing it to reach any location in the galaxy. Near the end of the Clone Wars, General Grievous brings the *Soulless One* to Utapau. After Obi-Wan Kenobi kills him, he uses the late general's starfighter to escape Utapau and rendezvous with Yoda and Bail Organa.

Sleek profile
The *Soulless One* is streamlined for maximum maneuverability in atmosphere.

CLONE TURBO TANK

APPEARANCES CW, III **MANUFACTURER** Kuat Drive Yards **MODEL** HAVw A6 Juggernaut **TYPE** Tank

The HAVw A6 Juggernaut, known as the clone turbo tank, is a heavily armed and armored Republic military transport. A single Juggernaut can carry up to 300 clone troopers and is operated by a crew of 12. The tank's superconducting armor absorbs and disperses enemy fire, and the tank retaliates with a heavy laser turret, anti-personnel cannons, a repeating laser, and projectile launchers. A clone spotter occupies a pod above the vehicle's back.

Leading the charge
Juggernauts are some of the Republic's strongest ground-assault weapons.

ARC-170 STARFIGHTER

APPEARANCES CW, III **MANUFACTURER** Incom Corporation
MODEL ARC-170 Aggressive Reconnaissance starfighter
TYPE Starfighter

The ARC-170 functions equally well as a fighter and a bomber. Its gigantic laser cannons are capable of punching holes in capital ship armor, while twin blaster cannons operated by a tail gunner cover the rear fire arc. Explosive ordnance comes in the form of proton torpedoes. Panels on the upper and lower surfaces of the wings can open during combat to bleed off excess heat. An ARC-170 is typically operated by a crew of three plus an astromech droid.

On patrol
ARC-170s are equipped to deal with any threat they encounter.

JEDI LIGHT CRUISER

APPEARANCES CW **MANUFACTURER** Kuat Drive Yards **MODEL** *Arquitens*-class light cruiser **TYPE** Light cruiser

This light warship is used by the Republic during the Clone Wars. Though not as large as other Republic ships, the vessel is armed with four quad laser turrets and four double-barreled turbolaser batteries, as well as concussion missile launchers. Obi-Wan and other Jedi generals often take command of these ships, which results in their common name.

Easily identifiable
Colored stripes identify the vessel's allegiance.

Tough combatant
The armored hull is protected by additional layers of energy shielding, making the Jedi light cruiser capable of taking a surprising amount of damage.

Protected
Turbolasers are evenly spaced to cover firing arcs.

TRANDOSHAN FLYING HUNTING LODGE

APPEARANCES CW **MANUFACTURER** Ubrikkian Industries **MODEL** Ubrikkian Floating Fortress **TYPE** Armed hover platform

Trandoshan hunters use this platform as a mobile base when hunting live prey on the moon of Wasskah. It features a trophy room, living quarters, and landing deck for airspeeders. In the Clone Wars, Ahsoka Tano and a few Wookiees attack the hunting lodge and the Trandoshans.

Underwater attack
Jedi Master Kit Fisto uses the Devilfish to rapidly travel between aquatic battlegrounds.

OMS DEVILFISH

APPEARANCES CW **MANUFACTURER** Kuat Drive Yards **MODEL** One Man Submersible Devilfish **TYPE** Submersible

The Devilfish is a Republic military craft designed for underwater use. It lacks armored protection, but features speedy propulsion jets and is armed with a forward-facing dual blaster cannon. During the Battle of Mon Calamari, Republic troops use a swarm of Devilfish craft to fight off Separatist aqua droids.

UMBARAN STARFIGHTER

APPEARANCES CW
MANUFACTURER Umbaran Militia
MODEL Umbaran starfighter **TYPE** Starfighter

The Umbaran starfighter is operated by a single pilot, who sits in a command chair surrounded by a spherical energy shield and flies the ship using holographic controls. The command chair plugs in to a spaceframe with loop-shaped wings. An Umbaran starfighter can defend itself with a single rapid-fire laser cannon and two electromagnetic pulse missile launchers.

HOUND'S TOOTH

APPEARANCES CW **MANUFACTURER** Corellian Engineering Corporation **MODEL** YV-666 light freighter **TYPE** Space freighter

The *Hound's Tooth* is the personal starship of the bounty hunter Bossk. This highly modified Corellian freighter contains holding cells for captured prisoners and an armory for stocking up on weapons. Many sensors allow Bossk to keep an eye on the integrity of the cages. The *Hound's Tooth* is armed with a quad-laser turret, an ion cannon, and a concussion missile launcher.

ANAKIN'S ETA-2 JEDI STARFIGHTER

APPEARANCES CW, III **MANUFACTURER** Kuat Systems Engineering **MODEL** Eta-2 *Actis*-class light interceptor **TYPE** Starfighter

Anakin Skywalker replaces his Delta-7B Jedi starfighter with a new Eta-2 interceptor model during the Clone Wars. This smaller, more maneuverable ship is armed with twin laser cannons and twin ion cannons. Its forward windshield bubble features an octagonal shape that is later carried over into the Empire's TIE fighters. On the tip of each wing, S-foils can swing up and lock into a vertical position and are used during combat to safely bleed off excess heat. The ship's dual ion engines and narrow profile allow it to make tight turns while dogfighting, but it lacks sufficient engine space for a hyperdrive. Instead, the Eta-2 relies on an external hyperspace docking ring when traveling across the galaxy. A plug-in socket inside the port wing can accommodate an astromech droid for onboard repairs, and soon Anakin and R2-D2 are flying together on vital missions against the Separatists.

Late in the Clone Wars, Anakin uses his starfighter to defend Cato Neimoidia from a Separatist attack. When a missile explodes near his ship, it releases a swarm of buzz droids, which cause extensive damage to the Eta-2. However, the ship is repaired in time for

HMP DROID GUNSHIP

APPEARANCES CW, III **MANUFACTURER** Baktoid Fleet Ordnance **MODEL** Heavy Missile Platform droid gunship **TYPE** Gunship

The HMP droid gunship, a heavily armed repulsorlift airspeeder, is the Separatist counterpart to the Republic's LAAT/i. Operated by an advanced droid brain, the HMP's frame accommodates numerous weapons, which can easily be interchanged for different missions. A droid gunship boasts a chin-mounted cannon, two laser turrets, and two light laser cannons on the wingtips, but the ship's real power is its payload of 14 high-explosive missiles. During the Clone Wars, droid gunships are modified to serve as troop carriers for battle droids.

Showdown
Three droid gunships fly in a tight formation *(far left)*, while laser cannons assault ground troops *(left)*.

Droid swarm
Dozens of buzz droids latch on to the hull of Anakin's starfighter.

the Battle of Coruscant. Accompanied by Obi-Wan Kenobi in a similar interceptor, Anakin fights his way through the Separatist navy and disables the hangar

shields on General Grievous's flagship *Invisible Hand*. As soon as the Eta-2 is parked inside, Anakin and R2-D2 leave the craft behind to cause trouble for Grievous.

Racing colors
Anakin painted his starfighter in a custom design inspired by his podracing past.

INVISIBLE HAND

APPEARANCES III **MANUFACTURER** Free Dac
Volunteers Engineering Corps
MODEL *Providence*-class carrier/destroyer
TYPE Capital ship

The Separatists employ a number of gargantuan warships during the Clone Wars, many of them falling under the command of the cyborg General Grievous. After Grievous loses the *Malevolence* in battle with the Republic, he claims the *Invisible Hand* as his flagship. This *Providence*-class vessel is 1 kilometer (0.6 miles) in length and is classified as both a destroyer and a carrier, a dual role that makes the Separatist dreadnought equipped for total planetary domination. It holds 20 squadrons of droid starfighters and more than 400 ground assault vehicles for use during invasions, while its numerous turbolaser turrets are capable of unleashing a surface bombardment from the safety of orbit. If threatened by Republic capital ships, the *Invisible Hand* can pummel the enemy with more than 100 proton torpedo launchers. An observation platform occupies a sensor pod high above the hull and allows commanders to get an

unobstructed view of battle. The side of the ship bears the Separatist emblem of the Confederacy of Independent Systems.

General Grievous uses the *Invisible Hand* during later Clone War skirmishes and soon receives orders to make a bold strike at the Republic's capital world of Coruscant. Accompanied by several Separatist warships, the *Invisible Hand* drops out of hyperspace and is soon embroiled in a space battle more intense than any conducted in the war to date. While the Republic responds to the naval threat, Grievous slips to the surface of Coruscant and kidnaps Supreme Chancellor Palpatine, bringing his captive back to the *Invisible Hand*. Anakin and Obi-Wan board the ship on a rescue mission. With the battle taking a terrible toll on his ship, Grievous blasts to safety in an escape pod. As the *Invisible Hand* breaks

up around him, Anakin successfully pilots the forward section of the ship into a fiery crash landing on Coruscant.

"Get to the command ship! Get the chancellor!" OBI-WAN KENOBI

Crash landing
As Anakin steers the wreckage of the *Invisible Hand* down to the surface, fire ships struggle to contain the damage.

Escape pods
The pods are lined up in rows along the *Invisible Hand*'s hull. They are intended to carry living occupants, not battle droids *(left)*. When General Grievous realizes the battle is lost, he activates the ship's escape pods and flees inside one of them *(below)*.

Firepower

The *Invisible Hand* has 14 quad turbolaser cannons, 34 dual laser cannons, 12 point-defense ion cannons, and 2 heavy ion cannons. It uses all its firepower during the Battle of Coruscant. In the end, the mighty warship is overwhelmed by the scale of the Republic's counterattack.

Battle of Coruscant
The fierce space battle that rages above the Republic capital proves to be the end of the *Invisible Hand*.

THE BATTLE OF CORUSCANT

"We're on your tail, General Kenobi. Set S-foils in attack position."
ODD BALL

The space above the Republic capital world is filled with flashing lasers and swooping starfighters. This is the Battle of Coruscant— the Clone Wars' most spectacular conflict.

A massive Separatist armada drops out of hyperspace above Coruscant, and the Republic fleet scrambles to intercept. The attacking warships are led by the *Invisible Hand*, a kilometer-long carrier/destroyer commanded by General Grievous. The cyborg general kidnaps the Republic's Supreme Chancellor from the planet's surface and returns to the *Invisible Hand* with his hostage. It's up to Obi-Wan Kenobi and Anakin Skywalker to rescue Chancellor Palpatine before the Separatists make their escape.

ATTACKED FROM ALL SIDES
The two Jedi take to the skies in their Eta-2 Jedi interceptors, accompanied by astromech droids in plug-in sockets. Providing cover are clone pilots in ARC-170 starfighters under the leadership of a veteran clone codenamed Odd Ball. Surrounded by heavy-hitting Republic Star Destroyers on one side and Trade Federation battleships and Banking Clan frigates on the other, the starfighter squadron weaves through the fray amid turbolaser blasts and superheated shrapnel. Separatist missiles, fired from vulture fighters, disgorge a horde of buzz droids that threaten Obi-Wan and Anakin's starfighters. R2-D2 fights them off, but Obi-Wan's astromech isn't as lucky and loses its head to the saboteurs.

The Jedi pilots board the *Invisible Hand* and rescue Palpatine, but by now the Separatist flagship is so damaged it begins to break up. General Grievous flees and releases all of the escape pods, leaving Anakin with no choice but to land the disintegrating ship on Coruscant. Fireships spray the flaming wreck as Anakin steers the ship to a bumpy landing.

All or nothing
The Republic scrambles every available vessel to meet the Separatist onslaught, including Eta-2 Jedi interceptors and ARC-170 attack craft.

Danger on every side
The Battle of Coruscant is a three-dimensional conflict, with enemies positioned above, below, ahead, and behind. With warships so tightly packed, the risk of being hit by friendly fire is high.

"She may not look like much, but she's got it where it counts."

HAN SOLO

MILLENNIUM FALCON

Agile and swift, the *Millennium Falcon* can easily slip from a Star Destroyer's grasp or fly into the bowels of the Death Star to destroy it.

APPEARANCES III, IV, V, VI, VII **MANUFACTURER** Corellian Engineering Corporation **MODEL** YT-1300 **TYPE** Light freighter (heavily modified)

A mind of her own
Heavily modified to suit the smuggling lifestyle, the *Millennium Falcon* can be quirky. The three droid brains communicate in a dialect even experienced translator droid C-3PO deems confusing, though astromech droid R2-D2 has less trouble discerning the status of its systems. Despite malfunctions during critical moments, Han insists the ship will come through when it counts.

PASSAGES
When Obi-Wan Kenobi and Luke Skywalker need swift, discreet passage to Alderaan, they choose the *Millennium Falcon*, the ship whose captain, Han Solo, brags made the Kessel Run in less than 12 parsecs. Optimized for smuggling, the *Falcon* has a few tricks up her sleeve when the Death Star seizes her. Time and again, the freighter proves elusive to her Imperial foes. As Darth Vader's forces invade Echo Base on Hoth, the *Falcon* whisks Princess Leia to safety. With a fleet of Star Destroyers on their tail, Han boldly takes cover in an asteroid field.

Risky business
Aboard the *Millennium Falcon*, Luke practices with his lightsaber *(top)*. Leia and Han investigate a mysterious landing site *(above)*.

PRINCESS'S RESCUE SHIP
Being a rebel princess is dangerous. When Leia Organa is captured by Darth Vader, the *Millennium Falcon* is the ideal getaway vessel to secure her freedom. With Obi-Wan sabotaging the Death Star's tractor beam, Han, Chewbacca, and Luke mount a prison break. Reunited at the *Falcon*, Obi-Wan duels Vader to distract him while the others escape. TIE fighters give chase, but the ship's powerful lasers in the upper and lower turrets dispatch them. Princess Leia, though, is convinced that the Empire let them get away.

Smuggler's ship
Hidden compartments under the deck plating *(above)* and laser cannons accessed by dorsal and ventral turrets *(right)* help the smugglers get out of tight spots.

Looks are deceiving
The *Millennium Falcon* may not look like much, but special modifications give her exceptional speed, intelligence, and agility, making her ideal for a smuggler like Han.

Death Star
The second Death Star is blown up in spectacular fashion by Lando Calrissian and his co-pilot Nien Nunb.

DEATH STAR NEMESIS

At the Battle of Yavin, the *Millennium Falcon*'s cannons save Luke from certain destruction as he attempts to destroy the Death Star. The torpedoes from Luke's X-wing set off a chain reaction that blows up the Death Star, cementing the reputations of Han, Chewbacca, and Luke as heroes of the rebellion.

Faced with a new Death Star, Han offers his ship to mission leader Lando Calrissian. This time, it is the *Millennium Falcon* that delivers the destructive shot to the Empire's newest superweapon.

Coward's retreat
General Grievous attempts to flee from Obi-Wan Kenobi, but is caught in a fatal duel.

GENERAL GRIEVOUS'S WHEEL BIKE

APPEARANCES III **MANUFACTURER** Z-Gomot Ternbuell Guppat Corporation
MODEL TSMEU-6 **TYPE** Personal wheel bike

General Grievous drives a TSMEU-6 on Utapau during the Clone Wars. This line of vehicles is also popular in mining areas, where long-distance travel underground is necessary on a variety of terrains. The TSMEU-6 is designed for a single passenger seated beside a large central wheel. The wheel bike has a maximum speed of 330 kilometers (205 miles) per hour rolling and 10 kilometers (6 miles) per hour running on its four retractable legs, and it carries enough fuel for approximately 500 kilometers (311 miles) of travel. With a wheel diameter of 2.5 meters (8 ft 2 in) and a length of 3.5 meters (11½ ft), the TSMEU-6 also boasts a powerful double laser cannon.

Blaster trigger

Shelter tarp

Guidance system

Speeder chase
Luke Skywalker and Leia Organa race to stop a biker scout from reporting their presence to the Imperials.

74-Z SPEEDER BIKE

APPEARANCES III, VI **MANUFACTURER** Aratech Repulsor Company **MODEL** 74-Z **TYPE** Scout speeder bike

The 74-Z is first used by the Republic during the Clone Wars, particularly on the planet of Saleucami. The speeder is used again by the Empire to patrol forests surrounding their shield generator on Endor. The speeder bike is ideally suited for patrols and scout missions over long distances in a variety of terrains, thanks to its exceptional maneuverability and self-charging battery system. Designed to carry one or two passengers, the 74-Z is controlled by four steering vanes, contains sensor and communications equipment between the handlebars, and includes a BlasTech Ax-20 blaster cannon for offensive strikes. The speeder measures approximately 3.2 meters (10½ ft) and can theoretically reach a maximum, but inadvisable, speed of 500 kilometers (311 miles) per hour.

V-WING STARFIGHTER (ALPHA-3 NIMBUS)

APPEARANCES III **MANUFACTURER** Kuat Systems Engineering
MODEL Alpha-3 Nimbus **TYPE** Starfighter

In use during the last days of the Galactic Republic, V-wings are compact support ships ideal in battle against large numbers of enemy fighters. V-wings are piloted by a single clone trooper backed by an astromech droid. The ship closely resembles various Jedi starfighter models (it is made by the same manufacturer) and, like those ships, lacks a hyperdrive. The most distinguishing feature of this craft is a pair of folding wings on either side of the hull, which extend above and below the ship. Dual rapid-fire laser cannons are situated on each of the two wing struts. The V-wing can also attain an impressive top speed of 52,000 kilometers (32,312 miles) per hour.

No mercy mission
A trio of V-wing starfighters escorts Emperor Palpatine back to Coruscant with a critically wounded Darth Vader.

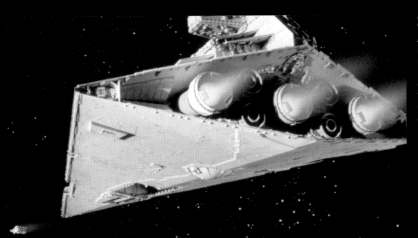

STAR DESTROYER

APPEARANCES R, IV, V, VI
MANUFACTURER Kuat Drive Yards
MODEL *Imperial I*–class **TYPE** Star Destroyer

Star Destroyers are the chief warships of the Imperial Navy and symbols of Imperial might. They enforce the Emperor's will by eliminating hindrances to commerce on Imperial worlds and bolstering their Imperial-backed governments. Admirals, Grand Moffs, ISB agents, and other senior Imperial commanders use Star Destroyers as their personal mobile headquarters. The ship's commanding officer can be just as intimidating as the approaching ship itself—and its shadow alone can bring results.

During the Clone Wars, *Venator*-class Star Destroyers (often called "Jedi cruisers" because they serve as flagships for Jedi generals) are utilized by the Republic. From this line of ships, the Empire develops the *Imperial I*–class Star Destroyers to wage war and maintain order across the galaxy. At first, Star Destroyers are deployed to subjugate worlds caught in turmoil during the Clone Wars and crush any signs of sedition. During the Galactic Civil War, the battleships hunt down high-priority targets and attack centers of rebel operations, playing key roles in the battles of Hoth and Endor.

During the Battle of Hoth, the Empire's fleet of Star Destroyers deploys a contingent of Imperial walkers that wages a successful ground war on the planet's surface. However, the Star Destroyers themselves exit hyperspace too close to Hoth and cost the Empire any advantage of surprise. During the rebel retreat, the Destroyers are too easily disabled, which allows rebel forces to escape. In the Battle of Endor, Star Destroyers deploy wings of 72 TIE starfighters, benefiting the war effort, but rebel fighters nonetheless exploit vulnerabilities in the Destroyers' shield generators and exposed bridges. *Imperial I*–class Star Destroyers prove far less effective against fleets of skilled rebel pilots than their *Venator*-class predecessors were against droid starfighters.

Imperial I–class Star Destroyers measure 1,600 meters (5,249.3 feet) in length, nearly 460 meters (1,509 feet) longer than the *Venator*-class. They are propelled by Cygnus Spaceworks Gemnon-4 ion engines and a class 2 hyperdrive. Armaments include 60 Taim & Bak XX-9 heavy turbolaser batteries and 60 Borstel NK-7 ion cannons. Tractor beams pull captured vessels into the main hangar bay, where squadrons of armed stormtroopers wait to board. In addition to a contingent of 9,700 stormtroopers, Destroyers carry a crew of 9,235 officers and 27,850 enlisted soldiers. Star Destroyers are fully equipped to engage in protracted combat on planet surfaces. A maximum contingent of auxiliary vehicles includes 8 *Lambda*-class Imperial Shuttles, 20 AT-AT walkers, 30 AT-STs or AT-DPs, and 15 Imperial Troop Transports.

Overpowering the enemy
Darth Vader's Star Destroyer, *Devastator*, chases the rebel ship *Tantive IV*, which is in possession of the stolen Death Star plans. Vader orders a tractor beam to draw his quarry into *Devastator*'s docking bay, where it is boarded by stormtroopers.

Mobile bases of operations
Imperial officers monitor space on the command bridge of the Super Star Destroyer *Executor* during the Galactic Civil War *(above)*. Agent Kallus's star destroyer orbits the planet Lothal hunting for the crew of the *Ghost* *(below)*.

"Imperials have locked down the ports and put Destroyers in orbit." OLD JHO

Operational space
Crew barracks, meeting rooms, training areas, and cell blocks are located on these levels.

"This Corellian ship matches the description of the rebel craft we've been looking for."

IMPERIAL SCANNING TECHNICIAN

GHOST

Piloted by Hera Syndulla, the *Ghost* is named for her ability to evade Imperial sensors. The *Ghost* is not only a starfighter, but also a freighter and home to her misfit crew. A smaller auxiliary fighter, the *Phantom*, makes the *Ghost* particularly adaptable.

APPEARANCES R **MANUFACTURER** Corellian Engineering Corporation
MODEL Modified VCX-100 light freighter **TYPE** Freighter

Team effort
Hera can manage a lot from the cockpit, but needs assistance from the crew to operate the lasers in the *Phantom* and dorsal turret.

HERA'S SHIP

Hera is the owner of the *Ghost*, so she is naturally protective of her. When things get out of hand, or if other crew members—namely Ezra, Zeb, and Chopper—become too rambunctious, she sends them on novelty errands (like shopping for meiloorun fruit) to get them away from the ship. The *Ghost* is an old vessel with a few battle scars from Imperial freighters and TIE fighter dogfights, but she still performs reliably. Nonetheless, Chopper makes a lot

of unusual modifications himself, to the extent that he might be the only one who knows how to fully repair her. Although Hera owns the *Ghost*, and her co-pilot Kanan also knows his way around the ship, in an emergency, sometimes Chopper seems to have better control of the situation.

Docking port
There are ports on each side of the ship.

Nose turret gunner station
Two forward laser cannons are located underneath the gunner station.

Curious cargo
The *Ghost* carries some interesting items in addition to her diverse crew. At times the cargo includes T-7 disruptors and E-11 stormtrooper blasters, Kanan's Joben T-85 speeder bike, a puffer-pig, and droids.

MISSION-READY

While the *Ghost* doesn't have a cloaking device, her countermeasure systems, such as jamming signals and transmitting false information, easily elude Imperial scanners. The *Ghost* is also a fast ship—she outruns Imperial starships, and not just local *Gozanti*-class cruisers. Her hyperdrive helps the crew escape Imperial entanglements on more than one occasion. Though most of the crew's missions are on Lothal, the *Ghost* takes members to far-flung worlds like Ryloth, Gorse, Garel, Kessel, and Stygeon Prime. The ship, however, is not beyond the Empire's reach and has to remain one step ahead of Imperial forces to evade capture.

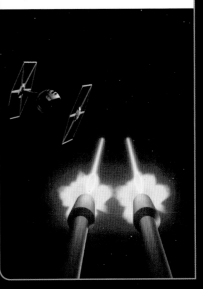

A BATTLESHIP

The *Ghost* has an advanced targeting system. The forward laser cannons can be controlled by Hera when a gunner is not available to manage the laser turrets below. The *Ghost* engages with Star Destroyers, but TIE fighters are no match for the ship's 360-degree dorsal laser cannon turret, the most important weapon station on the *Ghost*.

Kessel mission
The *Ghost* arrives at Kessel to rescue Wookiee prisoners from the Empire's spice mines. Working in the mines is a virtual death sentence for Wookiees, who are accustomed to living in open forests on Kashyyyk.

HoloNet News
The crew of the *Ghost* watches a holonet message in their common room, broadcast by the exiled senator, Gall Trayvis.

A SECRET REBEL BASE

The *Ghost* provides a mobile home base for its crew. They often land in Lothal's deserted wilderness and at other times visit more welcoming venues closer to town, like Old Jho's Pit Stop. The ship has an assortment of living areas, including four private rooms, a common area, and a kitchen, as well as cargo bays and connecting corridors. The common area is the social hub of the *Ghost*, where the crew plans future missions, watches the HoloNet News, or plays a game of dejarik (holographic chess). Typical of a Jedi, Kanan's living quarters are the most austere, while Sabine decorates hers with graffiti and posters.

PHANTOM

APPEARANCES R **MANUFACTURER** Corellian Engineering Corporation **MODEL** Modified VCX-series auxiliary starfighter **TYPE** Short-range Corellian shuttle fighter

The *Phantom* docks in the aft section of the *Ghost*, where it acts as the ship's third laser turret (when facing outward). A single-pilot cockpit is located at the front, with a small cargo section and fold-down seats situated in the rear. The *Phantom* is an ideal shuttle for making short-range supply runs.
However, when Zeb and Ezra forget to refuel the ship, Hera and Sabine find themselves shipwrecked on an asteroid and must bring the *Ghost* in for a rescue.

Main cargo hold
Four holds are located on each corner of the ship.

Stealth fighter
As a small ship, the *Phantom* can quietly maneuver through Imperial territory yet is capable of taking on TIEs and other small fighters in dogfights.

Wraparound brace and cargo compartments

Forward laser cannons

"Get your hands off my craft! This fighter is property of the Empire!" **BARON VALEN RUDOR (REBELS)**

TIE FIGHTER

TIE fighters are the signature starfighter of the Imperial Navy. Their versatility and precision are a symbol of prestige for the Empire and a bane of the Rebel Alliance.

APPEARANCES R, IV, V, VI **MANUFACTURER** Sienar Fleet Systems **MODEL** TIE/LN starfighter **TYPE** Twin ion engine starfighter

PRECISION AND SIMPLICITY

A TIE's twin ion engines provide thrust and minute boosters are capable of quickly adjusting the ship's direction. To minimize power drain and maximize maneuverability, TIE fighters lack key systems such as deflector shields and hyperdrives. A TIE fighter's central cockpit is tightly fitted, incorporating flight controls, viewscreens, targeting systems, tracking equipment, and room for a pilot, all in the central pod. The flight controls are so intuitive and easy to learn that rebel novices have been able to figure them out on the fly after stealing TIE fighters from Imperial landing fields.

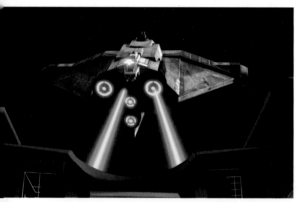

Dogfights
High above Lothal, a TIE fighter fires on the rebel ship *Ghost*.

Starfighters
A trio of TIE fighters returns to the Death Star after flying reconnaissance. Without a hyperdrive, TIEs are unable to travel far from base *(above)*. A TIE fighter pursues Luke's X-wing and is ambushed by Wedge's fighter *(right)*.

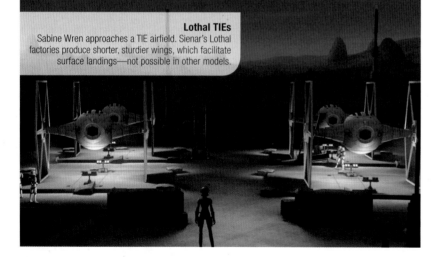

Lothal TIEs
Sabine Wren approaches a TIE airfield. Sienar's Lothal factories produce shorter, sturdier wings, which facilitate surface landings—not possible in other models.

STRENGTH IN NUMBERS

During the Galactic Civil War, the Imperial Navy subjugates numerous planets and orchestrates large battles. TIE fighters are the primary Imperial starfighter at the Battles of Yavin and Endor. TIE fighter pilots are instructed that their own well-being is secondary to their mission's objectives. Since the fighters are so fragile and the pilots expendable, TIEs achieve best results attacking in large groups. So many features are sacrificed to facilitate rapid mass production by Sienar Fleet Systems factories that TIE fighters can be continuously refreshed as they are lost in conflict.

EVOLUTION OF THE TIE FIGHTER

TIE fighters display certain similarities with other, outmoded starfighter models from the old Republic era. While TIEs employ vertical wings similar in appearance to earlier V-wing starfighters, the old Jedi Interceptors are even more familiar, with a central cockpit pod, twin ion engines, common weapons technology, and vertical wings like a TIE. In their TIE fighter designs, Sienar Fleet Systems borrowed heavily from the designs of Kuat Systems Engineering ships, thanks to acquiring key assets and engineers employed by their competitor.

A variety of other models have arisen from the TIE line, including TIE interceptors and TIE bombers. Sienar factories experiment with localized improvements, producing advanced models suited to local flying conditions and incorporating secret technological breakthroughs. The Inquisitor uses a TIE Advanced x1 prototype, heavily based on Sienar's own *Scimitar* (Sith Infiltrator), while Darth Vader himself flies a TIE Advanced x1 model.

Solar power
A pair of TIE fighters engages the *Ghost* above Lothal. A TIE fighter's black wings contain an array of solar energy collectors that pool power and direct it to twin ion engines and two low-temperature lasers.

THE BATTLE OF YAVIN

"We'll have to destroy them ship to ship." DARTH VADER

Darth Vader's TIE fighters annihilate most of the rebel X-wings and Y-wings, but the *Millennium Falcon* intervenes to help Luke Skywalker destroy the Death Star.

After careful analysis, the stolen Death Star plans reveal the seemingly impregnable station's vulnerable spot. Located at the terminus of a trench along the surface of the Death Star is an exhaust port. If a proton torpedo could be fired precisely into the port, it would cause a chain reaction within the reactor core, destroying the battle station. With the Death Star now approaching their base on Yavin 4, the Rebel Alliance must act immediately or be obliterated. As Luke Skywalker and the rebel pilots launch an attack, Han Solo leaves to escape the battle.

THE FALCON RETURNS
Once the rebels reach the Death Star, TIE fighters and X-wings dogfight above as Y-wings enter the trench. Darth Vader enters the battle, flying a TIE Advanced x1, and destroys the Y-wings before they can reach the exhaust port. Garven Dreis attempts a shot, but his X-wing is also destroyed. The rebels are now down to their last three X-wings. Vader destroys Biggs Darklighter's fighter and damages Wedge Antilles's, forcing him to retreat. At the crucial moment, Han Solo returns in the *Millennium Falcon*, destroying the pursuing TIE fighters, and sending Vader's ship spiralling into space. Luke then uses the Force to hit the target, causing the Death Star to explode.

Nowhere to hide
The Death Star's ray-shielded exhaust port blocks laser fire. It can only be hit by proton torpedoes fired at close range within the trench, where rebel fighters have no room to evade TIEs.

A ragtag fleet
The rebel fleet leaves Yavin 4, passing the planet Yavin, on its way to the Death Star. Red Squadron is composed of T-65 X-wing starfighters and led by Garven Dreis. Gold Squadron is composed of Y-wings and led by Dutch Vander.

LAMBDA-CLASS IMPERIAL SHUTTLE

APPEARANCES V, VI **MANUFACTURER** Sienar
Fleet Systems **MODEL** *Lambda*-class T-4a
shuttle **TYPE** Personnel shuttle

The *Lambda*-class Imperial shuttle transports
high-ranking officers and dignitaries, from
Captain Rae Sloane and Count Vidian to
Darth Vader and Governor Tarkin. It can also
be configured for sizable cargo shipments
and troop deployments. The ship works well
in both the vacuum of space and planetary
atmospheres. Its heavy shielding and
reinforced hull make it safe for important
officials, and its cockpit can be jettisoned
as a lifeboat and travel at sub-light speed
for short distances. The cockpit lacks room
for the shuttle's full quota of 20 passengers,
so priority is given to the highest ranks.

In the last days of the Empire, Emperor
Palpatine travels to the second Death Star
aboard his *Lambda*-class shuttle. The heavily
modified ship also carries his Royal Guards
and advisers such as Sim Aloo and Janus
Greejatus. At about the same time, Leia
and a team of Rebels, including Nien Nunb,
find themselves aboard a Star Destroyer
called the *Shieldmaiden*. One of the team
members sacrifices themselves and Nunb's
ship, the *Mellcrawler*, creating a path for
Leia and her team to escape in a stolen
Imperial shuttle which is revealed to be
the *Tydirium*. Using a stolen access code,
General Solo leads a strike team in this
shuttle past an Imperial blockade and on
to the moon of Endor, where they destroy
the Death Star's shield generator.

The Emperor arrives
Darth Vader arrives on the Death
Star to oversee its final construction
and is greeted by Moff Jerjerrod.

Shuttle *Tydirium*
Han Solo and Chewbacca sit in the cockpit of their
stolen Imperial shuttle, on their way to Endor.

At the end of the Battle of Endor, Luke
Skywalker evacuates the Death Star on board
Darth Vader's own Imperial shuttle. All three
ships play vital roles in the final moments of
the Galactic Civil War.

Imperial shuttles are 20 meters (65½ ft) long
and can carry a maximum cargo of 80 metric
tons (176,370 lbs). They are equipped with two
sub-light ion engines and a hyperdrive engine
for long-distance travel. Forward armaments
include two double blaster cannons and two
double laser cannons. In the aft, there is also
a retractable double laser cannon. Military
shuttles boast additional weaponry.

*"An Imperial troop transport has been
reported stolen from the
Lower City."* **AGENT KALLUS**

**Forward
transparisteel
viewport**

**One of six
troop/prisoner
compartments**

IMPERIAL TROOP TRANSPORT

APPEARANCES R **MANUFACTURER** Ubrikkian
Industries **MODEL** K79-S80
TYPE Armored troop transport

Imperial Troop Transports (ITTs) are some of
the army's most dependable vehicles. Their
sturdy construction and heavy armaments

make them an ideal mobile stronghold
for soldiers in minor conflicts. As ITTs
are designed to move stormtroopers
between important locations, citizens of
the Empire steer clear when they hear the
transport's loudspeakers approaching their
neighborhood. It always means one of two
things: either stormtroopers are moving in
or Imperials are moving locals out. Despite

Putting on a show
Pilots and commanding officers
sit in the front, while stormtroopers
or prisoners are seated in the rear
hold. On each side are three stalls to put
prisoners on display, as a warning to others.

not being specifically designed for
combat, the ITTs have protective laser
guns. When the Empire seizes land
from uncooperative farmers on Lothal,
it uses ITTs to forcibly relocate them.
When Ezra Bridger and Zeb Orrelios try
to rescue Morad Sumar and other settlers
with a stolen TIE fighter, they learn how
tough ITTs are.

TIE BOMBER

APPEARANCES V, VI **MANUFACTURER** Sienar
Fleet Systems **MODEL** Twin Ion Engine
bomber **TYPE** Bomber

TIE bombers are robust Imperial crafts
for planetary and ship bombardment.
As in TIE fighters, solar panels supplement
fuel tanks to power twin ion engines, but
the ship lacks a hyperdrive, which limits its
flight range. However, bombers are
deployed for longer use than fighters, so
they carry a two-day supply of air and
rations. Bombers not only have a
complete life-support system, but also
cockpit ejector seats. Armaments include
a pair of laser cannons and payloads of
concussion missiles, orbital mines,
and proton bombs.

Ordnance pod
A TIE bomber's secondary pod carries an assortment
of mines, missiles, and bombs.

Surplus

Model 614-AvA speeders are used by Imperials. Older models are sold to civilians. Ezra has an orange-and-green speeder.

Load haulers

Ezra Bridger watches from above as officers prepare to deliver a shipment of E-11 blasters on their Imperial speeder bikes.

Air intake cooling vents

Brake pedal

Altitude adjustment vane

Blaster cannon

Steering vane

LOTHAL IMPERIAL SPEEDER BIKE

APPEARANCES R **MANUFACTURER** Aratech Repulsor Company **MODEL** 614-AvA speeder bike **TYPE** Speeder bike

The 614-AvA speeder bike is a popular Imperial model on Lothal. Fitted with twin BlasTech JB-37 blaster cannons, Imperial speeder bikes are indispensable to the military. Working in tandem with AT-DPs and TIE fighters, the bikes form a surgical strike team to take on rebel forces. They are more maneuverable than landspeeders, allowing stormtroopers to cover diverse terrain. Their ease of use for pilots and minimal fuel consumption make speeders the ideal vehicle for distant reconnaissance missions and patrolling large areas. Pilots steer their speeders using handlebars and foot pedals that control three steering vanes attached at the front of the bike.

The rebels on Lothal are often chased by Imperial speeders, but occasionally manage to steal one of the bikes. Novices like Ezra may require lessons, but Zeb and Kanan Jarrus find the 614-AvA easy to drive.

Cargo ship

Imperial freighters carry crucial supplies to Imperial bases throughout the Outer Rim. They are protected by a complement of TIE fighters and laser cannons, lest they are attacked along hyperspace routes like the Kessel Run.

Shield projector

IMPERIAL FREIGHTER

APPEARANCES R **MANUFACTURER** Corellian Engineering Corporation **MODEL** Imperial *Gozanti*-class cruiser **TYPE** Armored freighter

Gozanti-class cruisers are heavily armored to deter pirates and rebels (particularly the crew of the *Ghost*). The freighters have been used by a variety of factions, but the Imperial model employs heavier shielding, faster engines, and superior weaponry. Imperial freighters are used to carry important payloads, such as weapons and prisoners, or to transport AT-DPs. These transports carry their own TIE fighter escorts and a rotating crew of stormtroopers to defend their cargo. The ships are fitted with large brigs containing multiple cell blocks to transport their prisoners to Imperial prisons and labor camps, such as the spice mines of Kessel or the Spire on Stygeon Prime.

Heavy laser cannon
The weapon easily destroys speeders.

Terrain-sensing stabilizer pad
The walker's "feet" bear half of the AT-DP's 11,200-kg (24,692-lbs) weight.

ALL TERRAIN DEFENSE POD (AT-DP)

APPEARANCES R **MANUFACTURER** Kuat Drive Yards **MODEL** AT-DP **TYPE** Imperial walker

One of several walker models used by the Empire, AT-DPs are an improvement over the AT-RTs used by the Republic during the Clone Wars. AT-DPs are essentially high-speed tanks on legs that carry two officers: a pilot seated in front and a gunner behind, who controls the Kyuzo Maad-38 heavy laser cannon. The Lothal garrison finds them very effective when clearing out squatting farmers from land appropriated for mines and factories. AT-DPs patrolling the streets of Lothal are an intimidating sight, meant to discourage rebel uprisings, and they are also ideal for patrols and short scouting missions. Like speeders, they allow a limited number of troopers to patrol large areas. While AT-DPs can chase suspicious vehicles, they lack the firepower of AT-STs required for substantial combat, and as such are often relegated to defensive roles, like sentry duty or policing.

C-ROC CARRIER SHIP

APPEARANCES R **MANUFACTURER** Corellian Engineering Corporation
MODEL Modified *Gozanti*-class cruiser **TYPE** Cruiser

The ore mined on Lothal is so valuable to the Empire that an Imperial Star Destroyer is permanently stationed above the planet. The ore is equally valuable to smugglers, who try to outrun the Imperial blockade. Modified from a *Gozanti* freighter frame, the C-ROC carrier ship has expanded open-bed cargo capacity to maximize the number of secured ore containers it can convey in one flight. The ship's five engine pods provide enough power to propel the C-ROC to high speeds quickly and evade the Imperial Navy's forces.

Engine pods

Ore containers

Blockade runner
The C-ROC's cargo capacity is modified to haul as much valuable Lothal ore as possible.

IMPERIAL LANDING CRAFT

APPEARANCES R, IV **MANUFACTURER** Sienar Fleet Systems
MODEL *Sentinel*-class landing craft **TYPE** Shuttle

The primary function of the Imperial landing craft is to shuttle the Empire's military forces from a Star Destroyer in orbit to planetside operations. When Darth Vader dispatches sandtroopers to track down the missing escape pod discharged by Princess Leia Organa's *Tantive IV* during its capture over Tatooine, these landing craft ferry them down to the planet's surface. These heavily armored landing craft come equipped with laser cannons and concussion missiles and can undertake missions such as short-range scouting, transporting cargo, and providing air support for ground troops.

Folded S-foil wing
Wings fold for storage in tight quarters.

Wing extension servomotor

Cockpit canopy

Blasting rebels
The prototype TIE Advanced has two powerful laser cannons for eliminating traitorous ships.

Latest tech
The Inquisitor has access to the Empire's very best technological developments, including prototype starfighters like the TIE Advanced.

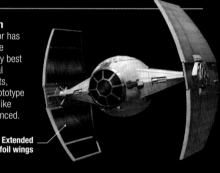

Extended S-foil wings

TIE ADVANCED PROTOTYPE

APPEARANCES R **MANUFACTURER** Sienar Fleet Systems
MODEL TIE Advanced (prototype) **TYPE** Starfighter

Compared to a standard TIE fighter, the prototype TIE Advanced used by the Inquisitor has faster engines, stronger laser cannons, and a projectile launcher, which he uses to fire tracking devices at ships. The foldable S-foils have solar panels for keeping the starfighter fully charged in most field conditions. Even the swift freighter *Ghost* has difficulty evading the TIE Advanced prototype.

LUKE SKYWALKER'S X-34 LANDSPEEDER

APPEARANCES IV **MANUFACTURER** SoroSuub Corporation **MODEL** X-34 **TYPE** Landspeeder

A civilian vehicle of mundane design, the X-34 landspeeder has neither weapon mounts nor armor, nor any other combat capability. Levitating no higher than 1 meter (3.2 feet) above the ground on its repulsorlifts, and propelled by three turbine engines, a landspeeder can travel smoothly over even the roughest terrain. With either an open-air or sealed cockpit to choose from, the landspeeder is perfect for Tatooine's harsh desert climate. In the years before he leaves his homeworld and joins the rebellion, Luke puts his landspeeder to extensive use.

Low trade-in value
After discovering his aunt and uncle murdered *(above right)*, Luke brings Obi-Wan Kenobi, C-3PO, and R2-D2 to Mos Eisley *(right)*. He sells his landspeeder to help fund the cost of passage to Alderaan.

Fond memories
Holding a T-16 model, Luke remembers his many adventures in his Skyhopper.

T-16 SKYHOPPER

APPEARANCES II, IV **MANUFACTURER** Incom Corporation
MODEL T-16 **TYPE** Airspeeder

Recognizable by its distinctive tri-wing design, the T-16 skyhopper high-performance airspeeder is a popular civilian vehicle throughout the galaxy, providing stable and reliable transportation on almost any world. Reaching speeds of up to 1,200 kilometers (745 miles) per hour from its ion drive and altitudes of 300 meters (984 feet) from its repulsors, the T-16 provides many youngsters with their first flight training opportunity. On Tatooine, Luke flies his T-16 through the dangerous twists of Beggar's Canyon, taking potshots at womp rats with the craft's pneumatic cannon. When he joins the Rebel Alliance, Luke benefits from the similarities between the controls of the T-16 and the X-wing starfighter, also manufactured by Incom.

Y-WING STARFIGHTER

APPEARANCES CW, IV, V, VI
MANUFACTURER Koensayr Manufacturing
MODEL Y-wing **TYPE** Starfighter

Perhaps less memorable in appearance than other starfighters, the Y-wing has the dubious distinction of remaining in service long enough to fly under the command of Anakin Skywalker and to be shot down by Darth Vader. During the Clone Wars, Anakin leads Shadow Squadron's Y-wings in an attack that disables the *Malevolence*, a heavy cruiser commanded by General Grievous and armed with a massive ion cannon. Decades later, at the Battle of Yavin, eight Y-wings from the Rebel Alliance's Gold Squadron take part in the assault on the Death Star. Darth Vader leads a trio of TIE fighters to confront them, personally shooting down Gold Leader and his wingmates; only one of the eight survives. Y-wings from Gray Squadron join the attack on the second Death Star at Endor.

The Y-wing is a single-pilot starfighter, although additional support for the pilot is provided by the astromech droid positioned aft of the cockpit. Equipped with a hyperdrive for making lightspeed jumps, the ship has a pair of ion jet engines for primary propulsion. This makes the Y-wing slower and less maneuverable than other starfighters, such as the X-wing and A-wing, flying in the Rebel Alliance fleet. For defense, the pilot must count on the energy shields and the heavy armor plating around the cockpit. When dogfighting is unavoidable, the Y-wing relies on two fixed, front-mounted laser cannons and a rotating turret with anti-starfighter ion cannons. More commonly, the Y-wing operates as a bomber against capital ships in fleet battles or for ground targets in planetside action, making multiple bombing runs to deliver proton torpedoes and proton bombs from its arsenal.

Fleet workhorse

For decades, various models of the Y-wing starfighter see combat in military conflicts. From the Galactic Republic's fleet during the Clone Wars to the Rebel Alliance's attacks on both Death Stars, Y-wings may not be the newest or flashiest starfighters, but their power and reliability are renowned.

Hyperdrive

Ion jet engines

Ion cannon turret

Squadron logo

Sensor array covering

Laser cannon

> "Stay on target." **GOLD FIVE**

Fatal run

On the moon Yavin 4, a Y-wing is prepped for the upcoming battle with the Death Star *(below)*. Gold Leader leads a pair of Y-wings through the Death Star's narrow trench *(right)*.

"This is Red Five; I'm going in."

LUKE SKYWALKER

RED FIVE

Red Five is Luke Skywalker's pilot designation when he destroys the first Death Star. The name becomes synonymous with the actual X-wing fighter he flies.

APPEARANCES IV, V, VI **MANUFACTURER** Incom Corporation **MODEL** T-65B **TYPE** X-wing starfighter

Faithful co-pilot
Even though Luke is a starfighter rookie at the Battle of Yavin, seasoned astromech R2-D2 is ready to back him up. During the attack run on the Death Star, R2-D2 keeps Red Five functional by making on-the-fly repairs until he is disabled by Darth Vader's laser blast. Rebel technicians are able to repair the droid, and he continues his legendary partnership with Luke.

Fusial thrust engines
These powerful and efficient engines provide top-notch speed and acceleration.

Attack position
The X-wing's S-foils remain closed for swifter flight, then spread open for combat.

Cockpit
Luke flies his single-pilot starfighter with assistance from R2-D2.

Blaster cannon
When firing synchronized blasts, the X-wing's guns easily vaporize TIE fighters.

Perfect shot
Red Five careens down the Death Star trench, heading for the exhaust port *(below)*. As he closes on the target, Luke shuts off his targeting computer *(left)*.

BATTLE OF YAVIN
Luke's experience in Tatooine flying T-16 skyhoppers, made by the same manufacturer as the X-wing, gives him enough familiarity with Incom flight controls to be assigned pilot duties in Red Squadron as the Death Star approaches the Rebel Alliance base on Yavin 4. Red Leader Garven Dreis assigns Luke the position of Red Five, with more experienced pilots Wedge Antilles and Biggs Darklighter rounding out the trio as Red Two and Red Three, respectively. During their run down the trench, Luke hears the ethereal voice of Obi-Wan Kenobi telling him to "use the Force." He turns off Red Five's targeting computer and fires his torpedoes into the Death Star's exhaust port, sealing the Rebel Alliance victory.

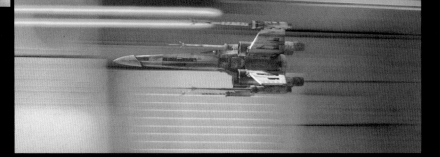

JOURNEY TO DAGOBAH

When a dangerous patrol around Echo Base on the ice planet Hoth puts Luke near death, a ghostly apparition of Obi-Wan appears and directs the rebel hero to seek out Yoda on the planet Dagobah. After a timely rescue by Han Solo, Luke joins Rogue Squadron to defend the base from an Imperial invasion. With the Rebel Alliance forced into a retreat from the doomed base, Luke hops in his X-wing and makes his escape. Although R2-D2 is ready to take over piloting duties on the way to the rendezvous point, Luke insists upon a detour to further his Jedi training. Despite Luke's formidable skills as a pilot, Dagobah's atmosphere proves sufficiently challenging that he crashes his X-wing into a boggy swamp.

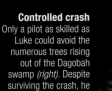

Controlled crash
Only a pilot as skilled as Luke could avoid the numerous trees rising out of the Dagobah swamp *(right)*. Despite surviving the crash, he is still wary of the many unseen perils waiting for him *(far right)*.

Proving a point
For Jedi apprentice Luke, Yoda's chief admonishment, "do or do not, there is no try," can be a difficult concept to grasp. After Luke gives up on levitating his crashed X-wing, Jedi Master Yoda proves to Luke it is possible.

SIZE MATTERS NOT

Faced with the task of shooting an impossibly small mark without a targeting computer during the attack on the Death Star, Luke confidently believes he can make that feat a reality. Yet, when it comes time for an important lesson in using the Force during his training with Yoda—levitating his X-wing from the bog into which it crashed—Luke's inexperience with the mystical Force creates a seemingly insurmountable obstacle. Yoda tackles this inhibition by revealing the amazing power within all Jedi. With a furrowed brow and a slight swipe of his tiny hand, Yoda frees Luke's starfighter. Ironically, this gesture enables Luke to leave Dagobah after he has visions of his friends in danger, even though Yoda pleads with him to stay and complete his training.

TIE ADVANCED FIGHTER X1

APPEARANCES IV **MANUFACTURER** Sienar Fleet Systems
MODEL Twin Ion Engine Advanced x1 **TYPE** Starfighter

Darth Vader only flies the best; his starfighter is a modified early prototype of the TIE Advanced x1 line. Unlike most TIE models, the Advanced x1 has a hyperdrive and deflector shield generator. Vader's fighter is even faster and more heavily armed, featuring fixed-mounted twin blaster cannons and cluster missiles. The custom cockpit matches Vader's exacting specifications and accommodates the unique features of his suit. After Vader thwarts several rebel runs on the Death Star's trench, cannon fire from the *Millennium Falcon* forces one of Vader's wingmen to collide with Vader's starfighter, spinning it out into the vastness of open space.

Rebel pursuit
In the meridian trench, Darth Vader chases rebel fighters intent on destroying the Death Star *(above)*.

Star power
High performance solar cells.

REBEL SNOWSPEEDER

APPEARANCES V **MANUFACTURER** Incom
Corporation **MODEL** T-47
TYPE Airspeeder (modified)

While on Hoth, the extreme cold creates a unique set of operational issues that threaten to permanently ground the Rebel Alliance's force of airspeeders. Ingenuity overcomes the bitter Hoth elements: the rebels modify their T-47 airspeeders to become snowspeeders. The craft is a wedge-shaped, two-man vessel armed with two forward laser cannons and a rear harpoon gun. It is designed to be flown by a single pilot, backed up by a rear-facing tail gunner.

The Imperial assault force that lands on Hoth is led by AT-AT walkers, which are tasked with destroying Echo Base's main power generator. Spearheading the defense of the generator is the elite Rogue Squadron, piloting the newly operational snowspeeders. As Rogue Squadron does not possess the necessary firepower to bring down the walkers, its commander, Luke Skywalker, suggests an alternative tactic: trip up the walkers with the tow cables mounted to the rear harpoon gun. Luke's gunner Dak Ralter is killed before he can take a shot, and their snowspeeder crashes into the snow.

Luke is nearly crushed by an AT-AT foot as he tries to retrieve his lightsaber from the cockpit. Wedge Antilles and Wes Janson have better luck, harpooning a walker and tripping it up with the snowspeeder's tow cable. Precision firing from Antilles finishes the job, as he hits the downed AT-AT's vulnerable neck. Nonetheless, despite Rogue Squadron, the power generator is destroyed, leaving the base vulnerable to invasion.

Rebel ingenuity
Former farm boy Luke Skywalker devises a way to take down the massive AT-ATs by using tow cables to lasso their legs.

Rogue pilot
A snowspeeder from Rogue Squadron barely evades enemy fire as it rapidly closes in on the invading Imperial AT-AT walkers.

EXECUTOR (SUPER STAR DESTROYER)

APPEARANCES V, VI
MANUFACTURER Kuat Drive Yards
MODEL *Executor*-class Star Dreadnought
TYPE Super Star Destroyer

The Super Star Destroyer is one of the largest, most powerful Imperial vessels in the galaxy and signifies the might of the Empire. Viewed from above, it presents an arrowhead-shaped profile, and boasts more than 1,000 weapons, including turbolasers, ion cannons, and concussion missile tubes. The main hangar bay is situated ventrally and forward and houses a mix of TIE fighters, TIE bombers, and TIE interceptors. The gargantuan craft is propelled through space by 13 colossal engine thrusters. The command tower rises from the aft of the central habitable island and is capped with two geodesic communication and deflection domes.

The Super Star Destroyer *Executor* is Darth Vader's personal flagship.

The *Executor* is specifically designed to accommodate the Sith's needs, including a meditation chamber where Vader can remove the helmet that protects his scarred and badly burned head to better commune with the Force. Under Vader's command, the *Executor* leads the Death Squadron and oversees the Imperial assault on the Rebel Alliance's Echo Base on Hoth. During the attack, Vader is displeased when Admiral Ozzel brings the fleet out of hyperspace near Hoth rather than stealthily using a wider approach from the system's outskirts. The tactical blunder buys the Alliance time to raise their base's energy shield. Having tired of Ozzel's incompetence, Vader telekinetically executes the admiral, but cannot prevent much of the rebel fleet from escaping. Serving as the Imperial command ship during the Battle of Endor, the *Executor* is finally destroyed when a rebel A-wing starfighter crashes into its command bridge, causing it to lose control and smash into the Death Star II.

REBEL TRANSPORT

APPEARANCES V, VI
MANUFACTURER Gallofree Yards, Inc.
MODEL GR-75 **TYPE** Medium transport

The GR-75 is a sister design to the civilian GR-45, which is used by shipping firms to haul cargo. The transport's outer hull is a thick shell with the interior entirely open for cargo pods. To maximize space, the GR-75 is minimally armed with four twin laser cannons and a deflector shield. Inexpensive to produce, the GR-75 is known for keeping maintenance personnel on their toes. Some of these transports are used as shuttles for high-ranking rebel personnel when the Alliance flees its base on Hoth.

Fleeing Hoth
GR-75 transports play a crucial role in the Rebel Alliance *(above)*. The last transport, *Bright Hope*, leaves Echo Base during the Battle of Hoth with the help of starfighter pilots Wedge, Hobbie, and Janson *(right)*.

ALL TERRAIN ARMORED TRANSPORT (AT-AT)

APPEARANCES V, VI
MANUFACTURER Kuat Drive Yards
MODEL All Terrain Armored Transport
TYPE Assault walker

The All Terrain Armored Transport, commonly known as the AT-AT, is a four-legged combat vehicle used by Imperial ground forces. The cockpit is located in the "head," while dual fire-linked, medium-repeating blasters protrude from the "temples," and two heavier Taim & Bak MS-1 fire-linked laser cannons are mounted under the "chin." The armor plating is impervious to blaster bolts, rendering the AT-AT nearly unstoppable.

At over 22 meters (72 feet), the AT-AT's size gives it a powerful psychological advantage, creating fear in its opponents as it marches forward like an armored behemoth. However, the AT-AT is not without its weaknesses. Its neck, especially, is vulnerable to blaster barrages. Unstable legs and the AT-AT's high center of gravity also make it susceptible to tripping. This tactic is employed by Rogue Squadron snowspeeders defending Echo Base on Hoth as key personnel flee the planet. When pilot Wedge Antilles makes a close pass on an AT-AT, his gunner Wes Janson fires an ace shot, harpooning the AT-AT with the tow cable. Antilles loops the speeder around the walker's legs until it tumbles to the snow. With the machine's neck better exposed, Antilles's next shot destroys the fallen AT-AT.

The walker also lacks armor covering on its underbelly, leaving the area open to mounted guns or portable missile launchers. For this reason, AT-STs are usually stationed around the flanks of the walker to protect the AT-AT's weak underside. The Empire never anticipates an attack as bold as Luke's—he uses an ascension gun to reach an AT-AT's underbelly and then drops a grenade through the walker's floor.

Target eliminated
On Hoth, the AT-AT succeeds in destroying the shield generator, allowing Imperial forces to attack Echo Base.

Sneak attack
After his snowspeeder is downed by an Imperial AT-AT and his gunner Dak Ralter is killed, Luke attempts to disable the walker another way. He ascends to the belly section, where he leaves behind a concussion grenade, destroying the walker's interior.

Walking death
Rebel ground troops on Hoth do not stand a chance against the Imperial invasion forces led by AT-ATs under the command of General Maximilian Veers. The walkers advance on the shield generator, decimating rebel troops in their trenches.

ALL TERRAIN SCOUT TRANSPORT (AT-ST/ SCOUT WALKER)

APPEARANCES V, VI
MANUFACTURER Kuat Drive Yards
MODEL All Terrain Scout Transport
TYPE Walker

A quick-strike companion to the larger and more formidable AT-AT walker, the AT-ST's lightweight bipedal design enables swift movement across most types of terrain. Its speed and agility make the AT-ST well suited for patrol and reconnaissance duties supporting Imperial ground operations, and lead to its moniker "scout walker." Despite the vastly different environments, the Empire deploys AT-STs against the Rebel Alliance in the ground battles at both Hoth and Endor's sanctuary moon. While the scout walkers rout the rebel forces at Hoth, they are soundly defeated at Endor.

For all its advantages in speed and size over the AT-AT, the AT-ST's offensive and defensive power is significantly compromised. The pair of chin-mounted medium blaster cannons offer a range of just 2 kilometers (1.2 miles), while the concussion grenade launcher and light blaster cannon fitted on either side of the head are effective only at close range

against infantry. Similarly, its much lighter armor can repel attacks from blasters and other small arms, but cannot withstand laser cannons, missiles, or other heavy weapons. The AT-ST is also vulnerable to a variety of other short-range attacks, exploited to great effect by the Ewoks in the Battle of Endor. Thick ropes slung across its lower legs like a tripwire can topple the walker, while rocks or other debris dropped from hang gliders can destabilize its footing. The Ewoks also discover that ramming logs that are suspended from trees into the sides of the walker's head will strike with enough force to smash through the light armor, destroying the cockpit.

Perhaps the scout walker's greatest weakness, though, is its susceptibility to hijacking. After swinging on a rope to land on top of an AT-ST, Chewbacca uses his mighty arms to rip open the roof hatch, reach inside to grab the pilots, and hurl them out of the cockpit. The Wookiee then uses the commandeered walker's cannons to destroy other AT-STs in the battle, as well as wreak havoc on the unsuspecting stormtrooper infantry.

Clean-up duty

Scout walkers are often deployed alongside the larger assault walkers for major ground operations. While the bigger cannons on the AT-AT devastate the opposing force's emplacements and vehicles, the AT-ST moves quickly to eliminate any infantry or other smaller threats that manage to evade the barrage. When Imperial ground troops invade the Rebel Alliance hideout on Hoth, the AT-ATs must trudge slowly across the snow-fields toward Echo Base, making them open to aerial attacks by the rebels' snowspeeders. The nimbler AT-STs, by contrast, are able to advance much faster across the frozen terrain to launch attacks against the trenches and laser cannons defending the base.

Forest failure
The Imperial AT-STs *(left)* struggle against Ewok ingenuity during the Battle of Endor. Chewbacca uses his commandeered AT-ST to turn the tide in favor of the Rebel Alliance at the shield generator complex *(above)*.

TWIN-POD CLOUD CAR

APPEARANCES V, VI **MANUFACTURER** Bespin Motors
MODEL Storm IV Twin-Pod **TYPE** Atmospheric repulsorcraft

A familiar sight over the skies of Cloud City, the bright orange twin-pod cloud car polices the airspace around Bespin. Specifically designed for patrol purposes, the pod is powered by an ion engine and a repulsorlift drive. The port-side pod houses the pilot, while the gunner in the starboard pod controls a pair of blaster cannons. When the *Millennium Falcon* seeks refuge in Cloud City for repairs, Han Solo nearly provokes a confrontation with a cloud car before receiving landing clearance from his old friend Lando Calrissian.

Primary communications array

REBEL CRUISER (NEBULON-B FRIGATE)

APPEARANCES V, VI **MANUFACTURER** Kuat Drive Yards
MODEL EF76 Nebulon-B **TYPE** Escort frigate

The Rebel Alliance deploys Nebulon-B frigates, with their highly versatile design platform, in several different capacities across its fleet. Equipped with heavy armament and powerful tractor beams, they escort convoys to protect transport ships against Imperial attacks and pirate raids. While some frigates are modified for deployment on long-range scouting missions or search-and-rescue operations, Nebulon-Bs become most famous for their use by the Rebel Alliance as medical frigates. These ships are equipped with bacta tanks to promote healing, medical droids, and full-service hospital facilities. When Luke Skywalker's hand is amputated in a lightsaber duel with Darth Vader, a surgical droid attaches the cybernetic replacement in a Nebulon-B medical frigate.

Warship escort
When fully armed, the Nebulon-B frigate can blast opponents with 12 turbolasers and an equal number of laser cannons, as well as capture adversaries in its dual tractor beams.

Main turbolaser

Main laser cannon

TIE INTERCEPTOR

APPEARANCES VI **MANUFACTURER** Sienar Fleet Systems
MODEL Twin Ion Engine Interceptor **TYPE** Starfighter

Easily recognized by its sharply pointed solar panels, the TIE
interceptor is a far deadlier opponent than a standard TIE fighter.
Although it also lacks shields and a hyperdrive, the interceptor
has four laser cannons mounted on its wingtips, as well as
upgraded engines providing considerably improved
maneuverability and speed. The Empire places its elite pilots
in interceptor cockpits to maximize the craft's effectiveness.
With these advantages, interceptors are ideally suited for their
main function: chasing down and eliminating rebel starfighters.

MON CALAMARI MC80 STAR CRUISER

APPEARANCES VI **MANUFACTURER** Mon Calamari Shipyards
MODEL MC80 **TYPE** Star cruiser

The MC80 star cruisers in the Rebel Alliance fleet operate as
command ships or battleships capable of direct engagement
with an Imperial Star Destroyer. Each MC80 has a unique
design, though common features include a tapered bow,
bulbous hulls, hangar bays, heavy armor and shielding, and
10 sublight thrusters. With over 5,000 crew at full strength,
it can deploy as many as 10 squadrons of starfighters into
a space battle. The MC80's own powerful weapons include
dozens of turbolasers and ion cannons.

HOME ONE (HEADQUARTERS FRIGATE)

APPEARANCES VI **MANUFACTURER** Mon Calamari
Shipyards **MODEL** MC80 **TYPE** Star cruiser

Sometimes called the Headquarters Frigate
because it houses the command and control
center for Admiral Ackbar at the Battle of Endor,
Home One is the most celebrated of the MC80
star cruisers in the Rebel Alliance fleet. Originally
a civilian Mon Calamari vessel intended for long
missions exploring deep space, *Home One* is retrofitted
for military service and can function as a flagship, battleship,
or carrier. With heavy hull plating and triple-strength shields,
the ship carries extensive offensive weaponry and boasts 20
hangars for bearing other warships or starfighter squadrons.

Admiral's flagship
The largest, most advanced capital ship in the
fleet, *Home One* brings pride to the Rebel Alliance
when she joins in battle *(top)*. From the bridge,
Admiral Ackbar leads the Rebel Alliance fleet at
the Battle of Endor *(above)*.

Spy craft
Using its full suite of sensor, tracking, and imaging systems,
the A-wing exploits its speed and maneuverability on
highly effective intelligence-gathering missions.

A-WING STARFIGHTER

APPEARANCES R, VI **MANUFACTURER** Kuat
Systems Engineering **MODEL** RZ-1 A-wing
interceptor **TYPE** Starfighter

The A-wing is one of the fastest starfighter
models in the galaxy. Essentially a cockpit
attached to two large engines, it requires
precision manipulation of the dorsal and
ventral stabilizers without assistance from
an astromech. As a result, only the best
pilots can fly an A-wing without losing
control. The A-wing possesses superior
speed, defensive shields, and a hyperdrive,
and is armed with two laser cannons and
12 concussion missiles. During the Battle
of Endor, an A-wing crashes into and
demolishes the bridge of the Imperial
flagship *Executor*.

Quick strikes
Powered by an ionization reactor that fuels four
high-performance engines *(above)*, the B-wing
races swiftly across the battlefield to engage
enemy capital ships *(right)*.

B-WING STARFIGHTER

APPEARANCES VI
MANUFACTURER Slayn & Korpil
MODEL A/SF-01 B-wing starfighter
TYPE Starfighter

With its unusual top-heavy design, the
B-wing is among the most heavily armed
assault starfighters in the Rebel Alliance
fleet. The cockpit's gyroscopic mounting,
with full 360-degree rotation, ensures the
pilot remains sitting upright regardless of
the fighter's orientation. The center of the
primary airfoil houses the engines, while the
fighter's far end holds the heavy weapons
pod, which includes ion cannons and proton
torpedoes. When extended, the smaller
S-foils broaden the firing arc of the B-wing's
twin laser cannons. Specializing in attacking
Imperial capital ships, squadrons of B-wings
play a major role in the Battle of Endor.

THE BATTLE OF ENDOR

"It's a trap!" ADMIRAL ACKBAR

Hoping to destroy the Empire's cruel grip on the galaxy, the Rebel Alliance risks everything in its attempt to ambush the second Death Star in the Endor system.

Many Bothan spies die to deliver word that the Emperor is personally overseeing the construction of a second Death Star. The opportunity to strike at the heart of the Empire cannot be missed. Han Solo agrees to lead a strike team to the Endor moon to destroy the shield generator. This will allow an assault force, led by Lando Calrissian in the *Millennium Falcon*, to attack the superweapon before it becomes operational. Accompanied by Princess Leia, Luke Skywalker, and Chewbacca, Solo pilots a stolen Imperial shuttle down to the moon. Unfortunately, the mission to reach the shield generator is fraught with obstacles that slow down the team, and when the Rebel Alliance fleet drops out of hyperspace, Admiral Ackbar realizes they have flown into a trap.

SHOCKED TO THE CORE
The Rebel Alliance has committed every vessel and starfighter available, from A-wings to Y-wings, to the battle. Yet all seems to have gone according to the Emperor's plan when his squadrons of TIE fighters, TIE interceptors, and Star Destroyers harry the rebel fleet. Not only is the Death Star well protected, it is also fully operational and begins picking off the larger rebel ships. Lando convinces Ackbar to give Han's team more time to destroy the Death Star's shield. The gamble pays off. The shield falls and the *Millennium Falcon* races toward the Death Star's core, with Wedge Antilles' X-wing and an A-wing providing cover. The A-wing splits off to draw away some of the TIE pursuers. Reaching the core, the *Millennium Falcon* and the X-wing deliver torpedoes that utterly destroy the second Death Star.

Stolen shuttle
A shuttle appropriated from the Empire enables the rebel strike team to reach the moon's surface. General Han Solo and Chewbacca pilot the shuttle out of the Rebel Alliance flagship *Home One*.

Timing is everything
The Rebel Alliance's plan is contingent on a strike force, led by General Han Solo, sabotaging the Death Star's shield generator on the moon of Endor. The fleet arrives before the mission is accomplished, forcing a fierce space battle.

BEHIND THE SCENES

"I've always been fascinated by speed, because of my interest in cars... because of that it has always been an element in the films." George Lucas

It is an overused term, but *Star Wars* vehicles truly are iconic. The *Millennium Falcon*, X-wing, and AT-AT are universal symbols not just of *Star Wars*, but also of the wider genre. When the saga's vehicles were designed, they were made to look real and lived in—as though they could exist and work in the way they are shown on screen. *Star Wars* is ultimately about characters, but the extraordinary diversity of its vehicles gives the series a richness that remains unparalleled in movie history.

1

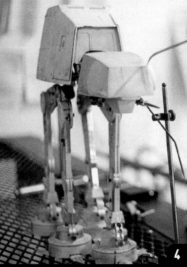

2

George Lucas gave these sketches of a TIE fighter, X-wing, and Death Star to concept artist Ralph McQuarrie when he started work on *Star Wars* **(1)** (he gave similar sketches to concept model maker Colin Cantwell). McQuarrie's concept artwork titled "Battle for the Death Star (fighters dive on sphere)" shows a preliminary concept for a Y-wing based on Colin Cantwell's design **(2)**.

3

4

This life-sized T-65 X-wing starfighter from Star Wars: Episode IV *A New Hope* is being lifted by a cable hooked to a crane outside "H" stage at Shepperton Studios, UK, so that it can be filmed from below to simulate takeoff **(3)**. The AT-AT walkers were based on Joe Johnston's vehicle designs. Models of various sizes were made and filmed using stop-motion and other techniques at ILM **(4)**.

5

6

The *Millennium Falcon* under construction at Elstree Studios, UK, for *Star Wars:* Episode V *The Empire Strikes Back* **(5)**. An AT-ST chicken walker model is painstakingly moved on a miniature Endor forest set by ILM model makers Paul Huston and Larry Tan for *Star Wars:* Episode VI *Return of the Jedi* **(6)**.

The digital animatic stage of Gasgano's podracer by David Dozoretz, one of the many spectacular vehicles to feature in the Boonta Eve Classic in *Star Wars: Episode I The Phantom Menace* **(7)**. Anakin Skywalker (Hayden Christensen) leaps aboard a swoop bike to rescue his mother in *Star Wars: Episode II Attack of the Clones*. The bluescreen will later be replaced by the arid landscape of Tatooine **(8)**.

7

8

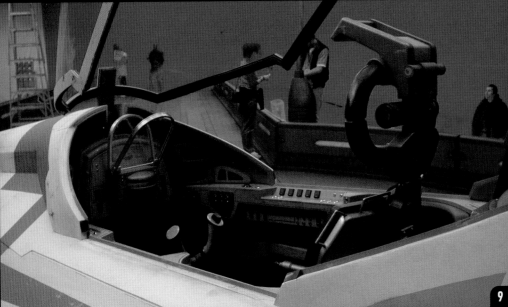

9

10

JEDI FIGHTER V.5
RYAN CHURCH
17 JUN 02
SW 3

11

The cockpit set for Obi-Wan Kenobi's Delta-7 starfighter from *Star Wars: Episode II Attack of the Clones* **(9).** An early digital stage of the high-speed duel between General Grievous, aboard his wheel bike (an initial CGI rendering), and Obi-Wan Kenobi, riding a varactyl named Boga **(10)**. Many concept artworks are created before a design is finally chosen— this art of Jedi starfighters for *Star Wars: Episode III Revenge of the Sith* is by concept design supervisor Ryan Church **(11)**.

INDEX

Penguin
Random
House

For Cameron + Company
Managing Editor Jan Hughes
Copy Editor Michelle Dotter
Proofreader Katie Moore
Senior Designer Suzi Hutsell
Designers Amy Wheless, Dagmar Trojanek, Jillian Lungaro
Publisher Chris Gruener
Creative Director Iain R. Morris

For Dorling Kindersley
Senior Editors Alastair Dougall, Cefn Ridout
Editor David Fentiman
Senior Designers Anna Formanek, Clive Savage, Anne Sharples
Designer Chris Gould
Senior Pre-Production Producer Jennifer Murray
Senior Producer Alex Bell
Managing Editor Sadie Smith
Managing Art Editor Ron Stobbart
Art Director Lisa Lanzarini
Publisher Julie Ferris
Publishing Director Simon Beecroft

For Lucasfilm
Executive Editor Jonathan W. Rinzler
Art Director Troy Alders
Story Group Pablo Hidalgo, Leland Chee, Rayne Roberts

Dorling Kindersley would like to thank:
Maxine Pedliham for initial design concept; Steve Hill (stormtrooper)
and Gary Hailes (handler); Matt Jones for tireless and invaluable
research; Toby Truphet for design assistance; Lauren Nesworthy for
editorial assistance; Helen Peters for the index.

First American Edition, 2015
Published in the United States by DK Publishing
345 Hudson Street, New York, New York 10014
15 16 17 18 19 10 9 8 7 6 5 4 3
010-273386-May/15

© & TM 2015 LUCASFILM LTD.

Page design copyright © 2015 Dorling Kindersley Limited

A catalog record for this book is available
from the Library of Congress.
ISBN: 978-1-4654-3601-6

DK books are available at special discounts when purchased in bulk for sales
promotions, premiums, fund-raising, or educational use. For details, contact:
DK Publishing Special Markets, 345 Hudson Street, New York, New York 10014
SpecialSales@dk.com

Printed and bound in China

A WORLD OF IDEAS:
SEE ALL THERE IS TO KNOW
www.dk.com

www.starwars.com